From *Paesani* to White Ethnics

SUNY series in Italian/American Culture
Fred L. Gardaphe, editor

From *Paesani* to White Ethnics

The Italian Experience in Philadelphia

Stefano Luconi

State University of New York Press

Published by
State University of New York Press, Albany

© 2001 State University of New York

All rights reserved

Printed in the United States of America

No part of this book may be used or reproduced in any manner whatsoever without written permission. No part of this book may be stored in a retrieval system or transmitted in any form or by any means including electronic, electrostatic, magnetic tape, mechanical, photocopying, recording, or otherwise without the prior permission in writing of the publisher.

For information, address State University of New York Press,
90 State Street, Suite 700, Albany, NY, 12207

Production by Kelli Williams
Marketing by Michael Campochiaro

Library of Congress Cataloging-in-Publication Data

Luconi, Stefano
  From paesani to white ethnics : the Italian experience in Philadelphia / Stefano Luconi.
    p. cm.—(SUNY series in Italian/American Culture)
  Includes bibliographical references and index.
  ISBN 0-7914-4857-6 (hc : alk. paper) — ISBN 0-7914-4858-4 (pb : alk. paper)
    1. Italian Americans—Pennsylvania—Philadelphia—Ethnic identity.
2. Italian Americans—Pennsylvania—Philadelphia—History—20th century. 3. Italian Americans—Pennsylvania—Philadelphia—Social conditions—20th century. 4. Philadelphia (Pa.)—Ethnic relations.
5. Philadelphia (Pa.)—History—20th century. 6. Philadelphia (Pa.)—Social conditions—20th century. I. Title.

F158.9.I8 L83 2001
974.8'1100451—dc21
                                                                          00-057330
                                                                          CIP

10 9 8 7 6 5 4 3 2 1

Contents

Acknowledgments	vii
Abbreviations	ix
Chapter 1 Introduction: Ethnicity as a Social Construction and the Case of Italian Americans	1
Chapter 2 The Transposition of Subnational Identities	17
Chapter 3 The Development of a National Identity	39
Chapter 4 Italianness in the Depression Years	57
Chapter 5 The Impact of World War II and Its Aftermath	95
Chapter 6 From Italian Americans to White Ethnics	119
Chapter 7 Conclusion	149
Notes	159
Bibliography	211
Index	255

Acknowledgments

Research for this volume has been made possible in part by grants from the Franklin and Eleanor Roosevelt Institute (Hyde Park NY), the Balch Institute for Ethnic Studies (Philadelphia PA), the Herbert Hoover Presidential Library Association (West Branch IA), the Harry S. Truman Library Institute (Independence MO), and the Gerald R. Ford Foundation (Grand Rapids MI). Some sections of this volume re-elaborate and develop part of the contents of the following previous essays: "Bringing Out the Italian-American Vote in Philadelphia," *Pennsylvania Magazine of History and Biography* 117, no. 4 (October 1993): 251–85, published by the Historical Society of Pennsylvania; "The Political Dimension of Multicultural Society: Italian-Americans and Ethnically Balanced Tickets in Philadelphia during the New Deal," in *Italian Americans in a Multicultural Society*, ed. Jerome Krase and Judith N. DeSena (Stony Brook NY: Forum Italicum, 1994), pp. 184–99; "The New Deal Realignment and the Italian-American Community of Philadelphia," *Journal of American Studies* 28, no. 3 (December 1994): 403–22, published by Cambridge University Press; "Machine Politics and the Consolidation of the Roosevelt Majority: The Case of Italian Americans in Pittsburgh and Philadelphia," *Journal of American Ethnic History* 15, no. 2 (Winter 1996): 32–59, published by the Immigration History Society; "The Changing Meaning of Ethnic Identity among Italian Americans in Philadelphia during the Inter-war Years," *Pennsylvania History* 63, no. 4 (Autumn 1996): 561–78, published by the Pennsylvania Historical Association; "The Influence of the Italo-Ethiopian War and the Second World War on Italian-American Voters: The Case of Philadelphia," *Immigrants & Minorities* 16, no. 3 (November 1997): 1–18, published by Frank Cass Publishers.

Abbreviations

ACS	=	Archivio Centrale dello Stato, Rome, Italy
ACWA	=	American Clothing Workers of America
ADA	=	Americans for Democratic Action
AFL	=	American Federation of Labor
BIES	=	Balch Institute for Ethnic Studies, Philadelphia
CBEP	=	County Board of Elections of Philadelphia, tabulation sheets of the election returns, Philadelphia City Archives
CPC	=	Ministero dell'Interno, Direzione Generale di Pubblica Sicurezza, Casellario Politico Centrale, ACS
DS-RG59	=	Department of State, Record Group 59, National Archives II, College Park MD
FDRL	=	Franklin D. Roosevelt Library, Hyde Park NY
HSP	=	Historical Society of Pennsylvania, Philadelphia
HSTL	=	Harry S. Truman Library, Independence MO
IDCC	=	Independent Democratic Campaign Committee
IHRC	=	Immigration History Research Center, University of Minnesota, St. Paul MN
MCP	=	Papers of the Ministero della Cultura Popolare, ACS
OSIA	=	Order Sons of Italy in America
PCA	=	Philadelphia City Archives, Philadelphia
PRTEU	=	Philadelphia Rapid Transit Employees Union
PTC	=	Philadelphia Transportation Company
RCA	=	Radio Corporation of America
SPD-DSG	=	Segreteria Particolare del Duce, Carteggio Ordinario 1922–1943, box 289, folder 15318 "Di Silvestro, Giovanni," ACS

TUUA	= Temple University Urban Archives, Paley Library, Philadelphia
TWU	= Transport Workers Union
UNRRA	= United Nations Relief and Rehabilitation Administration
WPA	= Works Progress Administration
WPA-ES	= Records of the WPA Historical Survey, Ethnic Survey, Job no. 66, "Italians in Pennsylvania," BIES

Chapter 1

Introduction: Ethnicity as a Social Construction and the Case of Italian Americans

A series of three arsons in less than three months almost completely destroyed Palumbo's Cafe-Restaurant in Philadelphia between late June and mid-September 1994. The damaged remains of the complex had to be demolished for safety reasons after the fires. Francesco Palumbo set up the original part of Palumbo's as a boarding house catering to recent immigrants from the Italian region of Abruzzi in 1884. The facility expanded over the years. It eventually turned into an entertainment mecca that featured such Italian American celebrities as Frank Sinatra and Jimmy Durante. It also came to occupy the whole city block bounded by Eighth, Ninth, Darien, and Catherine Streets in the South Philadelphia district, which formed the heart of the local Italian American community. For the members of this nationality group, however, Palumbo's was much more than a place where they could eat ethnic food and enjoy good entertainment. It was primarily a landmark institution that played a major role in the social and political experience of the city's Italian Americans. Ethnic associations held their banquets and honored Italian American personalities at Palumbo's. Politicians of Italian descent kicked off their election campaigns there and candidates from other national backgrounds came to Palumbo's to court Italian American voters. As a leader of the Italian American community—Democratic Councilman Joseph Vignola—pointed out in a letter to the *Philadelphia Inquirer* a few days after the first fire broke out, "Palumbo's was no mere restaurant. We gathered there for those sacred rites of passage that changed our lives. We met friends knowing we could carry a fresh loaf of bread home. The photos of bygone days that hung on the walls drew our attention time after time. It was a rare thread that wove its way through all our families."[1]

For that reason, in the words of an anonymous Italian American interviewee, the burning down of Palumbo's marked "the end of an era." He referred to decades during which a strong sense of commonly shared national ancestry forged a cohesive ethnic community out of individuals of Italian descent who could still speak Italian as their main language. As author Albert Di Bartolomeo remarked in his commentary on the demise of Palumbo's for the *Philadelphia Inquirer*, "[W]hat went up in flames, then, as well as the building, was identity."[2]

However, just as it was symbolically incinerated in the Palumbo's arsons, the Italian identity at which Di Bartolomeo hinted had never been static. Indeed, the self-image of the people of Italian extraction in Philadelphia was the product of a continuous process of redefinition that was under way even in the heyday of their local ethnic landmark, when—to quote Di Bartolomeo again—"it was not uncommon . . . to walk an entire block near Palumbo's and not hear a word of English. You heard Italian, of course, and all you saw were Italians."[3]

This study is an analysis of how the Italian immigrants and their offspring in Philadelphia elaborated and transformed their ethnic identity over the century that witnessed the establishment, the growth, and the destruction of their own metaphoric communal institution—Palumbo's. As such, this work is not a history of Italian Americans in Philadelphia in the more than a hundred years during which Palumbo's stood at Ninth and Catherine Streets. Nor is it concerned with the demographic profile, the social stratification, the economic structure, or the political experience and voting behavior of the community in that period. Yet, this essay deals with such topics whenever they yield insights into the focus of this research: a case study of how Philadelphians of Italian ancestry constructed and renegotiated their ethnic identity between the late nineteenth century and the mid-1990s. Moreover, this work pinpoints some spheres of the expression of group identity, not only because these have left traces in historical records but also because, as in the case of politics, they have played a key role in the formation and redefinition of the self-perceptions of minorities in U.S. society.[4]

Ethnicity is rather an elusive notion encompassing a great number of aspects that contribute to make up the identity of a community or a people. Scholarship concerned with the formation of group identities has increasingly stressed that, rather than a primordial category, ethnicity is a situational and instrumental concept whose distinguishing features are extremely flexible and in constant evolution. In this view, the perception of ethnic affiliation is a social construction through which some cohorts of the population of any country assert their own commonly shared sense of peoplehood by classifying other members of the same society as aliens according to a criterion of inclusion and exclusion based on allegedly inherited biological or cultural differences. Ethnic identities arise in conjunction with some available primordial peculiarities that include the descent from common ancestors. But members of an ethnic group can modify and reinterpret these characteristics, and ethnicity becomes one of the resources that people use in a variety of social situations in order to accommodate their lives within a given society. External forces also engage in the elaboration and reshaping of ethnic identities. Actually, the self-image of an ethnic minority is as much a matter of individual choice as a constraint that other groups and the broader society as a whole impose on the members of that specific minority. The ongoing construction of ethnic identities occurs within a dialectic situation. Both interaction with others and labelling from the outside contribute to the subjective and voluntary process of self-identification on behalf of the group. For this very reason, ethnicity is usually created and invented in specific situations of competition, confrontation, or conflict among the diverse components of any given society. In this context, ethnicity is a symbolic means by which boundaries are built and groups define themselves against others. It may even occur that peoples remake the reality of their own heterogeneity into the fiction of a common culture which, in turn, over time becomes fact. Thus, they create the background for the setting up of a group. Therefore, ethnicity is instrumental in eliciting mutual participation and commitment. In the case of minorities, it is often a purposeful invention that results from resistance and assertiveness among individuals who may initially lack any feeling of solidarity. It provides effective stimuli for the mobilization of groups struggling for power and status. It also offers resources to negotiate social standing and power relationships, to challenge existing forms of dominion, and to establish new ones. Consequently, ethnicity pertains not only the realms of culture and anthropology but also the field of politics in its broadest sense.[5]

The interpretation of ethnicity as a social construction has specifically come to dominate the debate over the meaning of ethnic identities in the United States since the late 1960s and 1970s. The ethnic revival and the ensuing legitimization of diversity in American society have led to the demise of acculturation and Americanization as the issues central to the analysis of the immigration experience of the various minorities and nationality groups. In this pluralistic perspective, the identity of members of the single ethnic groups—be it imposed, voluntary, or a combination of both—hardly draws on inherited biological differences or on the immutable ancestral values that the earliest immigrants carried from their native land to the society of their adoption and handed down to their offspring without remarkable changes. Rather, ethnic identity is the result of a dynamic process of redefinition and renegotiations through which a mutual sense of peoplehood develops from historical circumstances and shared structural conditions such as occupation, residence, and institutional affiliation. In this view, ethnic groups can also act as interest groups. The persistence of their distinctiveness in the course of time depends less on the symbolic legacy of the past than on the salience of economic matters and political conflicts. Furthermore, the concept of the invention of ethnicity has come to be interpreted as a successful attempt on the part of national minorities in the United States to preserve their cultural values and to curb the levelling action of the forces of Americanization. This was achieved by continuously refurbishing their own sense of peoplehood and by negotiating their own identity over the years with both mainstream society and the other immigrant groups in a dialectical integration. Such an interpretation reflects the increasing emphasis on the agency of the foreign-born newcomers and their native offspring in recent scholarship.[6]

Richard Polenberg has contended that the United States was still a country fundamentally divided along the fault lines of class, race, and ethnicity in the late 1970s. By the term ethnicity, he has referred primarily to the sense of national identity resulting from the ancestral country of the offspring of single immigration groups. Polenberg has also conceived the racial structure of American society mainly in terms of a white-versus-black polarization.[7]

Nonetheless, it has been suggested that a so-called "ethno-racial pentagon" has replaced the more conventional white-colored dichotomy as a more suitable means of aggregation along racial lines in the contemporary United States. In this perspective, people nowadays elaborate their own identity within the articulations of a "quintuple melting pot" of European Americans, African Americans, Asian Americans, Hispanic Americans, and Native Americans. Moreover, in the face of the growing conceptualization of ethnicity as one among many criteria for the formation of a reference group, research has shown that the sources of identity of a number of minorities tend over time to move beyond native national boundaries. The descendants of the African slaves can choose their native land within a range of more than thirty nations. But they think of themselves as members of a single African American ethnic group. Similarly, present-day mainstream society has contributed to impose a mutual pan-Asian American identity on the Chinese, Korean, and Vietnamese newcomers who have settled in United States in the last few decades, regardless of their different cultures and countries of origin. The Hispanic population has built a common ethnic self-image in upstate New York during the recent deindustrialization of this region. An analogous process of economic decline has stimulated the articulations of a white racial identity among Detroiters of European ancestry. Likewise, common suburban residence, middle-class status, and fears of the growing African American militancy have turned the offspring of eastern- and southern-European immigrants into white ethnics at least since the early postwar decades.[8]

Of course, there have been countertrends to this process of identity formation, too. For example, Mary Patrice Erdmans has demonstrated that such a major nationality group as the Polish Americans still lacked ethnic cohesion in the late 1980s. Focusing on the Polish community in Chicago, she has shown that it divided along immigrant and generational lines. In this specific case study, fractures resulted from the fact that the so-called Solidarity-era newcomers, who had come to the United States after the imposition of martial law in their native country in 1981, distanced themselves from American-born Poles and longtime residents of Polish origin in part on the account of political radicalism and a different class consciousness.[9]

Some studies have also questioned the thesis that the development of a mutual "whiteness" among European newcomers and their offspring was hardly under way prior to World War II and occurred primarily after the end of the conflict. Conventional scholarly wisdom has long had it that the descendants of the European immigrants elaborated a common white self-image in the mid and late 1960s, when they joined forces to react against ghetto rebellions and black power and to oppose the potential threats of the African American civil rights movement to their own middle-class achievements. Yet, recent works have placed the racialization of U.S. society within a much broader perspective that encompasses the whole course of American history and extends as far as the working-class cohorts of the population of European descent. Against this backdrop, Barbara Jeanne Fields has held that the concept of race has no biological foundation in the United States but is a social construction that white people elaborated to support an economic system based on slavery. Similarly, it has been argued that the ruling class had devised the concept of a white race as a long-term solution to the problem of the social control of the foreign-born proletariat almost since colonial times. Thus, for instance, Irish immigrants redefined themselves as whites in order to secure their position in their adoptive country as soon as the salience of race became pivotal as a line of social stratification in antebellum United States. In this view, the Irish and other newcomers of European origin lacked a white identity upon arrival in America and did not develop it until they realized that it served to consolidate their own status within U.S. society. It has been also suggested that the appearance of a trans-ethnic American working class of non-Anglo-Saxon descent in the 1930s hardly included black laborers. Rather, it was essentially confined to the white proletariat of European descent that found a common ground in opposing the claims of African American co-workers for racial equality on the shop floor during World War II.[10]

However, regardless of different interpretations about the timing and the mechanics of the racialization of European minorities, current research has tended to emphasize that politics and culture have had more to do than nature in the process by which members of immigrant minorities from the Old World have merged into one Caucasian ethnic group in the United States. This approach has come to affect legal studies as well. For instance, Ian F. Harney Lopez has recently examined the key role of precedent-setting cases in the construction of race and whiteness.[11]

Scholars also disagree as to what extent individuals of Italian extraction in the United States have redescribed their own ethnic identity over the generations. Many historians have corroborated the sociological analysis of the Italian immigrants as "urban villagers." In this view, even after they had settled in their adoptive land, newcomers from Italy were rather late in perceiving themselves as members of a common nationality group. Instead, they retained their linkages to their native towns at least into the early decades of the twentieth century. For instance, they established communities and social institutions that long tended to include only fellow villagers and to exclude all the other Italian immigrants.[12]

Several case studies, however, have suggested different and conflicting interpretations. Humbert S. Nelli, for instance, has acknowledged that northern Italians in Chicago initially did not consider fellow countrymen from the south of Italy as members of their own ethnic group and moved from their first neighborhoods in the city out of dislike for the new dwellers from southern Italian background. Yet, he has also claimed that Italian immigrants soon lost their regional identities and thought of themselves as "Italians" a very short time after their arrival in the country of their adoption. Likewise, John W. Briggs has pointed to an early demise of a localistic sense of loyalty among Italian newcomers to Utica, Rochester, and Kansas City. Conversely, contrary to the thesis of an early disappearance of the subnational affiliations of the people of Italian extraction in the United States, anthropological fieldwork by Carla Bianco has shown that, as late as the mid 1960s, third-generation Italian Americans in Roseto, Pennsylvania, still identified themselves as *Pugliesi* (namely, people from a southern Italian region by the name of Puglia) and regarded northern Italians from the Veneto region in nearby Bangor and Pen Argyl as belonging to a different "race" of Waspish, tall, blue-eyed, and fair-haired people. Nonetheless, many Italian Americans in California hardly identified themselves with the region of their descent in Italy and played an active role in the inner division of U.S. society along racial lines in the late 1970s.[13]

Within the broader perspective of the participation of Italian Americans in the making of white America, a few scholars have maintained that third- and later-generation Italian Americans, too, had entered the "twilight of ethnicity" and merged into the larger white "European American" ethnic group by the 1980s. In this view, such process of assimilation resulted from a number of factors that include an increase in intermarriage and suburban residence, the acceptance of mainstream culture, the progressive disappearance of discrimination based on national descent, and the achievement of national averages for other white Americans in income and educational attainments. A recent decline in the social activities and institutions that Italian Americans previously shaped on their own ancestral roots seems to confirm the selection of the 1980s as the terminus ad quem for the entry of the grandchildren and great-grandchildren of the turn-of-the-century Italian immigrants into the ranks of white ethnics. Specifically, according to sociologist Herbert J. Gans, Italian Americans have become almost indistinguishable from other European American minorities and nowadays retain only a symbolic self-consciousness of their national ancestry. In Gans's opinion, this current form of Italian ethnicity is generally confined to leisure time activities such as eating spaghetti, purchasing ancestral collectibles, attending traditional religious festivals, or visiting the native country of one's grandparents.[14]

This interpretation also seems to suggest that the ethnic revival of the late 1960s and the 1970s was a "myth" in the case not only of other European minorities but of Italian Americans as well. According to this argument, which Stephen Steinberg has best exemplified, the resurgence of ethnicity in those years was short lived since it was little more than a white working-class response, disguised as ethnic consciousness, to the political and social gains of African Americans in those years.[15]

It has been held that the Italian American radicalism of the early decades of the twentieth century drew in part on the pre-emigration experience of the newcomers and on the ethnic heritage of their offspring. For instance, a case study has highlighted the transposition of a radical political culture from Sambuca, a small town in Sicily, to a number of Italian American settlements in the United States. Further research has revealed the trans-Atlantic connections of the values and identity of the Leftist militants of Italian descent in America. On the other hand, it has been maintained that reaction against the pressures toward Americanization contributed to the widespread pro-Fascist feelings of Italian Americans in the interwar years. In this perspective, Mussolini's regime provided first- and second-generation immigrants with an ideology of compensation that could help them preserve an Italian self-image in the face of the dominant assimilationist paradigm in U.S. society.[16]

Both these interpretations, albeit from the opposite fringes of the political spectrum, have stressed that ethnic identity allegedly served the purpose of challenging different forms of dominion in the past by defending the cultural values of Italian Americans and by advancing their claims to status. Consequently, the present-day reduction of ethnic awareness to a mere symbolic dimension implies that the current sense of ethnicity is nothing more than a social pacifier for Italian Americans as well as for other nationality groups. In this view, it is also easily arguable that symbolic ethnicity provides the establishment with a means to prevent members of minorities from rising to power. Mainstream society can offer ethnic identity as a pacifying surrogate for political and labor militancy that obscures class struggle and preserves social inequalities. The establishment can also exploit ethnic consciousness in order to fan the flames of ethnic animosities, to split up the potentially common front of out-of-power minorities, and to preserve the status quo.[17]

Contrary to this latter thesis, however, the academic father of the white ethnic movement—Michael Novak—has held that the construction of a white self-perception by minorities of European ancestry enables ethnicity to retain a role as an essential instrument for the negotiation of power, in contemporary America as well. With reference to New York City on the eve of the ethnic revival of the late 1960s, sociologists Nathan Glazer and Daniel Patrick Moynihan have pointed to Italian Americans as an ethnic group that behaved mainly as a political interest group like other minorities such as the Irish, African Americans, Puerto Ricans, and Jews. Similarly, moving to a nationwide level, political scientist Theodore H. White has contended that Italian Americans were "the most important among the rising ethnic groups" and "the newest dynamic political force" in the United States in the 1960s and 1970s. Novak has further developed and extended the conception of Italian Americans as an interest group. In particular, he has emphasized the political implications of the Italian American identification with other European Americans. Actually, he has placed Italian Americans' construction of this sense of affiliation within a common effort by the members of the ethnic minorities of eastern- and southern-European descent to compete for power with both African Americans and Protestants of Anglo-Saxon extraction in the 1960s and early 1970s. In Novak's opinion, Italian Americans bulked large among the "PIGS." By this term, he has referred to the lower-middle-class and working-class individuals of Polish, Italian, Greek, and Slav descent who forged a mutual white identity in their common fight against the claims of both the increasingly politicized inner-city blacks and the "limousine liberals," namely the Wasp suburban sympathizers of African Americans.[18]

Focusing on Harlem's community, Robert Orsi has even antedated the beginning of Italian Americans' acquisition of whiteness and has contended that it occurred in the years before World War II. According to Orsi, Italian Americans held the middle ground between whites and blacks for a long time because of their olive complexion. They eventually took sides with the former in defining their own self-image as soon as the Depression and Italy's invasion of Ethiopia intensified their conflicts with black New Yorkers in the 1930s. As Orsi's argument goes, Puerto Rican immigration into East Harlem in the immediate prewar years further consolidated the self-perception of local Italian Americans as whites.[19]

Nevertheless, scholars such as Lawrence H. Fuchs have tended to regard the political dimension of the post-1960s dynamics of re-ethnicization as a prerogative of non-European minorities such as African Americans, Native Americans, or Mexican Americans. They have, therefore, excluded Italian Americans from that process of redescription of group identities. In addition, prominent theorists of the white ethnic movement other than Novak have denied that most Italian Americans joined it under the pressure of antipathies toward blacks and other nonwhite minorities. In particular, Geno Baroni even envisioned a transracial alliance between working-class whites and blacks resulting from a shared consciousness of common oppression. Baroni was a central figure in the 1960s African American civil rights movement. He marched with Martin Luther King Jr. in Selma and was pastor of St. Agustine's Church, the oldest black Catholic parish in Washington, D.C., before serving as undersecretary of the Department of Housing and Urban Development in the Carter Administration. Baroni was convinced that not only African Americans but also white minorities of southern- and eastern-European descent, including Italian Americans, were victims of economic and social discrimination in the United States. Consequently, in his opinion, all these groups had to join forces both to improve their conditions and to obtain a more positive image in the eyes of mainstream America.[20]

Baroni's vision of a new and broader civil rights coalition uniting blacks and white ethnic groups of working-class extraction was less an interpretation of current and past events than a speculative blueprint for the near future. Indeed, the backlash at African Americans is still the most credited mechanics to account for the creation of white ethnics in the United States. For this very reason, the hypothesis that also Italian Americans have eventually developed a white self-perception seems to imply that they, too, have come to share the racist attitudes of mainstream America or, at least, that they have absorbed such feelings as a side effect of their acculturation. Furthermore, in the face of the increasing polarization of U.S. society along racial lines, it can easily be suggested that a white identity tends to pigeonhole Italian

Americans—along, of course, with other minorities of eastern- and southern-European ancestry—in the same category as the WASP Mayflower descendants. In this perspective, Italian Americans become part of the dominant racial group in U.S. history. Yet, this view does not account for decades of anti-Italian intolerance and bigotry on the very grounds of the national ancestry of the Italian immigrants to the United States. Nor can this interpretation explain, for instance, mass lynchings of Italian immigrants in the South at the turn of the century, the rage of Klansmen against them, or the discriminatory failure of the Dillingham Immigration Commission of Congress (1907–1911) to include Italians in the white race owing to the olive skin of many southern newcomers. Early biased references to Italian newcomers as the "Chinese of Europe" further points to the initial vagueness of their racial identification and insulation from the white establishment of Anglo-Saxon descent.[21]

It is hardly surprising, therefore, that a few authors of Italian descent have emphatically made the case for the present-day vitality of the Italian ethnic identity among the descendants of the turn-of-the-century newcomers from Italy. In their works, academic insights have often interwoven with anguished autobiographical tones, and ethnicity has been a personal preoccupation as well as a scholarly problem. Rudolph J. Vecoli, Raymond A. Belliotti, and Richard Gambino have mainly cited lingering anti-Italian biases and prejudices in American society along with the allegedly significant number of the 1980 and 1990 U.S. Census respondents who claimed an Italian ancestry instead of identifying themselves as mere "whites." Consequently, they have argued that, even if the Italian sense of ethnicity has recently intermingled with mainstream patterns, it still retains some significance. In their opinion, Italian ethnicity today is not only a residual of the initial immigration experience. It has also acquired new, though rather vague, contents and supposedly remains central to the characterization of people of Italian descent as a nationality group in its own right.[22]

In particular, Vecoli has acknowledged that the rise of black power in the 1960s stimulated a revitalization of the ethnic self-consciousness of the European immigration minorities. Yet, he has also maintained that each nationality group rediscovered an identity of its own. In addition, he has argued that African American militancy provided above all a model for the activism of the single European American minorities against ethnic defamation and discrimination. In his view, therefore, the resurgence of ethnicity among whites in the 1960s cannot be interpreted as a mere reaction against the black power movement. Specifically, Fred Barbaro has pointed out that a surge in affiliation with Italian American organizations occurred in the wake of the enactment of Civil Rights legislation. As a result, in his opinion, the years of affirmative action witnessed a revival of the Italian identity of Italian Americans rather than their absorption in the broader ranks of white ethnics. Likewise, according to a number of other scholars and authors such as Alfred Aversa, Nicholas Pileggi, and Humbert S. Nelli, the racial conflicts that tore apart U.S. society in the 1960s and 1970s, pitting blacks against whites, did not halt the emergence of the "ethnic Italian." Rather, they saw the climax of the rediscovery and reaffirmation of Italianness on the part of the offspring of turn-of-the-century immigrants.[23]

To Robert Viscusi, however, a multicultural self-perception is the final outcome of the reshaping of Italian Americans' identity over time. In his view, people of Italian ancestry have long faced prejudicial scapegoat images, such as their notorious characterization as criminals, that have tended to relegate them to the margins of U.S. society. As a response, a few Italian American writers have come to emphasize their ethnic ties to other minorities. This approach has meant, for instance, stressing the middle-ground racial position of Italian Americans between white and black Americans.[24]

Viscusi's thesis sounds politically correct in the age of multiculturalism. It also counteracts those interpretations that have pointed to Italian Americans' confrontational attitude toward African Americans. Yet, such a multicultural Italian ethnic identity is the elaboration of a handful of Italian American intellectuals like Viscusi himself and can hardly reflect the self-perception of the great bulk of the U.S. population of Italian descent.

In the heyday of the polarization of American society along racial lines, the United States witnessed the formation of a number of Italian American organizations that planned to advance the ethnic claims of their members and to influence the federal and local governments about a wide array of concerns that ranged from fair treatment for people of Italian descent to ending anti-Italian Mafia-related stereotypes. The National Italian American Foundation, the Commission for Social Justice of the Order Sons of Italy in America, the National Italian American Women's Organization, and the Italian American Congressional Delegation were among the leading Italian American associations that had been established by the mid-1970s. Scholars have mentioned this new outburst of ethnic organizational life and its survival into the 1990s as a further proof of the persistence of a sense of Italianness among Americans of Italian ancestry.[25]

Most of those associations have been in the forefront in fighting anti-Italian stereotyping and discrimination in present-day United States. But the resurgence of an Italian sense of identity among Americans of Italian origin since the late 1960s has not resulted from ethnic defensiveness only. It has also been associated with "positive" values. In this view, for instance, the successful marketing of a wide range of Italian-style consumer goods from food to clothing has contributed to make Italy fashionable in the eyes of the broader American society and has encouraged people of Italian descent to rediscover their ancestral roots.[26]

Nonetheless, scholars have usually regarded defensiveness as a main factor in the ethnicization of Italian Americans. For example, according to a recent study by David A. J. Richards, the ethnic identity of Italian Americans was elaborated under the circumstances of social injustice based on American racism. In Richards's opinion, while members of this minority did not contest racial discrimination in general, they, too, were victims of those discriminatory attitudes to such an extent that they became a nonvisibly black cohort of American society. As a result, the whitening of European immigrant groups hardly challenged the peculiarity of Italian Americans' self-perception. In the face of American racism, Italian newcomers and their offspring withdrew from public discourse and developed a privatized sense of ethnic identity that they continue to maintain even today.[27]

It has also been suggested that the family is the dimension in which third- and fourth-generation Italian Americans nowadays still retain a sense of their Italian ethnicity. This self-perception is more than symbolic, and is firmly grounded in an actual web of social relations. In this view, however, such an identity reflects less the consciousness of a national affiliation than the echo of localistic loyalties that result from the network of kinsfolk and fellow villagers as well as from the recollection of dialectal expressions. In other words, the present-day vitality of ethnicity of Italian Americans draws especially upon a rediscovery of their subnational roots.[28]

In the face of these disputes over both the meaning of the Italian American self-perception and the redefinition of Italian Americans' sense of ethnicity over time, this essay provides a case study of how Italian immigrants to the United States and their descendants elaborated and reshaped their ethnic identity over generations in a specific city. In particular, this work focuses on Italian Americans in Philadelphia and outlines the process by which individuals from different places of origin in Italy who had shied away from one another upon arrival in the United States at the turn of the century came together to form one ethnic group on the basis of their common national descent during the interwar decades. This research also details how Italian Americans further broadened their self-referential ethnic boundaries in the postwar years and eventually came to think of themselves as white Americans by the 1970s.

As such, this volume also purposes to fill a void in the scholarly literature on Italian American history in the United States. Actually, there is no comprehensive work on the intertwinement of the immigration experience, community development, and ethnic identity formation in any specific "Little Italy."[29]

The only research available in this field does not extend beyond 1940. It, therefore, fails to document the fuller impact of World War II on the ethnic self-perception of Italian Americans and is also unable to address the controversial issues concerning the alleged emergence and consolidation of a white self-image among people of Italian ancestry in the postwar decades. Moreover, it relies too much on the recollections of its author's interviewees so that it turns out to be less an analysis of the renegotiations of ethnic identity by Italian Americans than an attempt to reconstruct the re-elaboration of ethnicity in Italian American popular memory.[30]

Likewise, in a recent analysis of the formation of the Italian American settlements in Philadelphia before the 1880s, sociologist Richard N. Juliani has overemphasized the allegedly early emergence of a sense of Italianness among newcomers from Italy. He has quoted Italian American leader Lorenzo L. Nardi as stating to an audience of immigrants in the 1880s: "You are Italians, and not Neapolitans, Genoese, or Tuscans." On the very basis of such flimsy evidence, Juliani has concluded that "Nardi accurately anticipated what was already taking place. His observation provided a succinct summary of the transcending of regionalism and the development of a more nationalistic ethnicity that was making *paesani* into Italian Americans and Philadelphians simultaneously." Yet, Nardi's words were less an insight than wishful thinking. As chapter 2 will show, rank and file members of Philadelphia's Italian American community were hardly responsive to their leaders' exhortations to think of themselves as Italians rather than *paesani*. Moreover, as an immigrant from Tuscany, a region in central Italy, Nardi was not representative of the southerners who would pour into Philadelphia en masse after his death in 1892. Unfortunately, Juliani's coverage of the Italian presence in Philadelphia ends before the decades of mass immigration and, therefore, cannot make any significant contribution to the debate on the transformations of Italian Americans' ethnic self-perception in the last one hundred years.[31]

However, Philadelphia offers a valuable setting for an examination of the changing contents of ethnic identity among Italian Americans over the decades. This city included a patchwork of people from disparate Italian regions. In addition, it became home to the second largest Italian settlement in the United States as early as 1890 and has contained one of the most populous Italian American communities in the nation from then on.[32]

Specifically, chapter 2 examines how a localistic, provincial, or regional sense of allegiance and community shaped the ethnic identity of the Italian immigrants who arrived in Philadelphia at the turn of the century. Chapter 3 reconstructs the emergence of a self-image based on national origin in the wake of World War I and as a consequence of the resurgence of anti-Italian intolerance and discrimination in the late 1910s and early 1920s. Chapter 4 analyzes the persistence of such a recently acquired Italian self-perception during the economic crisis of the 1930s. Chapter 5 focuses on the failure of World War II and its aftermath to undermine the national self-representation of Italian Americans and to fully Americanize them. Chapter 6 outlines the renegotiation of the ethnic identity of the Philadelphians of Italian descent within the white ethnic movement in the postwar decades.

Chapter 2

The Transposition of Subnational Identities

The first Italians arrived in Philadelphia early in the second half of the eighteenth century. They included not only such travellers as Luigi Castiglioni, Paolo Andreani, and Giambattista Scandella or artists like sculptor Giuseppe Ceracchi, who visited the city as part of their American tour or lived temporarily there. Italian newcomers also comprised a handful of merchants and musicians such as Giovanni Gualdo who came to reside permanently in Philadelphia. One James Latta graduated from what is now the University of Pennsylvania in 1757 and one Joseph Batacchi, a surgeon from Tuscany, practiced in the city in the 1760s. The 1791 *Directory of Philadelphia* listed only nine Italians. It was a very small number which, however, may have overlooked the newcomers from Italy who had Americanized their last names after moving to the United States. In any case, these individuals usually married people who were not of Italian origin, and soon assimilated into the larger host society.[1]

Their fellow countrymen who settled in Philadelphia in the first half of the nineteenth century laid the institutional foundations for the development of an Italian American community. They secured the creation of the city's first Italian parish, St. Mary Magdalen de Pazzi, in 1852 and established the first Italian American mutual-aid and beneficial association, the Società di Unione e Fratellanza Italiana, in

1867. Yet, the size of the population of Italian extraction was negligible in Philadelphia until the 1880s.[2]

At the outset of that decade, Philadelphia was home to as few as 1,656 Italians. They made up less than 0.2 percent of the total population and dwelt primarily in the South Philadelphia district within a relatively small area that was bordered by Christian, Seventh, Carpenter, and Ninth Streets. By 1890, however, Italian immigrants and their offspring had increased to 10,023, which meant almost 1.0 percent of the city's inhabitants at that time. This number soared to 46,648 in 1900 and to 76,734 in 1910, respectively 3.6 percent and nearly 5.0 percent of the total population in those years. In the meantime, the original Italian colony spread north to Bainbridge Street as well as southwest along Passyunk Avenue to Federal Street. New, though smaller, settlements also emerged in other districts of Philadelphia such as Manayunk, Roxborough, West Philadelphia, North Philadelphia, Frankfort, Overbrook, Chestnut Hill, Mount Airy, Nicetown, Mayfair, and Germantown.[3]

Philadelphia had become the intended destination for the third largest group of Italian immigrants to the United States by the late nineteenth century. Nonetheless, this city was never a major port of entry for Italians. Actually, the annual number of Italians who landed at Philadelphia failed to reach eight hundred individuals from 1880 through 1894, the last year for which a nationality breakdown is available for disembarkations at single U.S. ports. Specifically, Italian arrivals in Philadelphia fell from a peak of 784 in 1880 to forty-four in 1894, with a low of thirty-six in 1884. No regular direct service for passenger ships existed between the Mediterranean Sea and Philadelphia before 1909. Even after this year, however, the great bulk of Italian immigrants to Philadelphia reached it via New York.[4]

From their very beginning, the Italian colonies in Philadelphia produced a leadership of their own, the so-called *prominenti*. They included primarily contractors and professionals who provided services almost exclusively for their fellow ethnics. But there also were a couple of early entrepreneurs. They were Agostino Lagomarsino and his nephew Frank Cuneo, who established a macaroni factory in 1865.[5]

Most of these leaders rose to social standing from the ranks of the working class. Charles C. A. Baldi Sr., an immigrant from Castelnuovo Cilento in the province of Salerno, started out as a lemon hawker after settling in Philadelphia in 1877 at the age of fifteen. He subsequently worked as an interpreter for the Italian consulate, became a paymaster for the Schuylkill Valley Railroad, secured a mining contract, opened a bank as well as a steamship agency, and extended his business activities to real estate, which earned him the title of "slumlord." By 1914, Baldi's holdings had come to include several stores and funeral establishments, a hotel, a factory, a warehouse as well as other properties and buildings for an overall value of $149,150. Similarly, Italian-born Robert Lombardi got his first job as a water boy on the railroad constructions. He arrived in Philadelphia from Fornelli, in the province of Campobasso, in 1890, when he was sixteen. He subsequently made his way to heavy construction contractor in sewerage and subways. Lombardi's firm became one of the largest in the city and employed about 1,500 people in the late 1920s.[6]

Other Italian leaders in turn-of-the-century Philadelphia had experienced a lower-middle-class background in Italy. This status had been rather precarious in Italy herself and could hardly grant them an analogous social standing in the United States. Consequently, these *prominenti*, too, were indeed self-made men. For instance, Giovanni Di Silvestro—born in Pizzoli, in the province of L'Aquila, in 1879—was an elementary school teacher in Italy before leaving for the United States in 1903. Once in Philadelphia, Di Silvestro made ends meet as a journalist. So did his brother Arpino Giuseppe—a native of Bussi, in the province of L'Aquila, where he had been born in 1874—who had settled in town five years earlier. While writing for Italian-language newspapers, however, Giovanni Di Silvestro took a masters degree in political science, graduated from law school, and established a law practice that secured him a prominent position in the Italian community.[7]

According to an inquiry into Italian businessmen and entrepreneurs that the local Italian consulate conducted throughout Pennsylvania, in 1909 Philadelphia numbered ten lawyers, sixteen physicians, thirty-one contractors as well as forty-one bankers and steamship agents. As in the case of Baldi, one could hardly distinguish these latter two professional figures. Actually, in its survey of the immigrant banks in the United States, the Dillingham Commission pointed out that there were few incorporated banks. Conversely, newcomers operated "privately owned steamship agencies, labor agencies, and real estate offices which masquerade under the name of bank, but which are not legally authorized as such."[8]

Although an Italian American middle class had appeared in Philadelphia by the turn of the century, working-class individuals made up the great bulk of the Italian newcomers. In 1900, for instance, common laborers accounted for 34.8 percent of the city's work force, industrial workers for 32.6 percent, and professionals and businessmen of relatively high occupational status for 10.5 percent.[9]

Actually, the mass influx of Italian immigrants coincided with the creation of an increasing number of jobs following the growing industrialization of Philadelphia. After the end of the Civil War, Philadelphia underwent a steady process of economic transformation from a banking and commercial center into a manufacturing city. However, contrary to other major industrial centers of the United States, differentiation was Philadelphia's trademark. Moreover, the economy of the city did not depend on heavy industries but relied on a wide range of finished products and consumer goods.[10]

Textile and clothing industries had become the leading sector by the eve of the U.S. intervention in World War I. In 1915, they employed nearly one third of the city's work force, which amounted to about 250,000 individuals overall. They also accounted for more than 30 percent of the total value of the industrial output in Philadelphia. Claiming 480 women's clothing firms in 1919, Philadelphia was second only to New York in women's apparel production and was the fourth major menswear center after New York, Chicago, and Rochester. With 54,000 laborers in 1915, metal products were the second largest manufacturing sector in Philadelphia, followed by leather goods and the building trades, which employed 15,000 people each, and by the printing business, which numbered 12,000 workers.[11]

The Philadelphia and Reading Railroad Company as well as the Pennsylvania Railroad Company were the major providers of jobs for Italian immigrants in the 1880s and 1890s. The railroad companies lured many Italian workers into coming to Philadelphia. These newcomers settled permanently there but later moved on from the railyards of Germantown and South Philadelphia to better paying jobs in the building trades. Yet, railroad construction remained among the leading sources of employment of the city's Italians until World War I. The development of war industries and the ensuing physical growth of Philadelphia opened up new jobs for Italian immigrants in the shipyards as well as in the construction of the Broad Street and Market Street subways. In the same years, a few Italian Americans managed to establish their own contracting firms in the building trades and made business almost exclusively with the city and county administrations.[12]

Construction jobs—which also included street grading and housing construction—had the greatest concentration of Italian unskilled workers. In the decades of mass immigration to the United States, most Italian newcomers to Philadelphia belonged to this category. Other common laborers of Italian origin served as ragpickers, peddlers, sidewalk sweepers, garbage collectors, and longshoremen or worked in street, subway, and railroad maintenance.[13]

The clothing industry was another major area of employment for Italians and a sector that flourished during World War I. Since the turn of the century, the South Philadelphia district had been notorious for its high concentration of sweatshops. Italian and Jewish laborers made up the great bulk of the work force. Unlike Italian Americans, however, a disproportionate number of Jews held positions as foremen and supervisors. In particular, the garment trades attracted Italian women. Such operations as hand-finishing on button holes, linings, collars, and cuffs could easily be performed at home. Consequently, the wives and daughters of the Italian newcomers could find jobs as home workers and, thereby, combine daily household duties with economically productive activities that helped their own families to make ends meet. For this reason, Italians had constituted about one third of the men's ready-to-wear clothing female labor force by 1910. Home work throve among them until the passing of the 1933 National Industrial Recovery Act. The manufacturing of hats was an additional garment-related important source of occupation for Italian immigrants. Several newcomers had been hatters before leaving their mother country and easily obtained jobs in local hat-making firms such as the John B. Stetson Company, which was the largest in the world before the Depression of the 1930s. In the slow summer season, when temporary layoffs occurred in the clothing industry, many families of the Italian garment workers joined fellow-ethnic unskilled laborers and moved to the farms of contiguous southern New Jersey in order to supplement their own earnings by picking cranberries, strawberries, blackberries, blueberries, and other fruit.[14]

In addition, the clothing industry provided Italians with opportunities for entrepreneurship. The traditionally small size of Philadelphia's textile and apparel mills made it relatively easy even for prospective businessmen of Italian ancestry to establish and manage their own firms because they did not need large sums of money to finance their plants, equipment, and inventories. In 1894, before the full impact of the mid-1890s economic crisis hit Philadelphia, Italian entrepreneurs owned 110 contract clothing workshops out of a total of six hundred citywide. Although the number of these manufacturers had fallen to sixty-one by

1902, the interwar years witnessed the rise to prominence of a few contractors of Italian descent in the garment trades such as Nicholas Ranieri, Anthony Massimiano, Charles Miserendino, and John Palladino. They usually manufactured on behalf of larger firms that did not belong to their fellow ethnics, specialized in only one type of garment such as coats or pants, and concentrated primarily in the field of men's clothing. Ranieri and Massimiano, for instance, were pants contractor for J. H. Cohen and employed 105 and ninety-eight workers, respectively, throughout the 1930s. During the same decade, the work force of other Italian firms was even smaller. For example, Miserendino's employed sixty-two laborers and Palladino's as few as forty-seven.[15]

A few Italians also worked as barbers and almost monopolized this trade citywide. Other Philadelphians of Italian descent operated as shopkeepers, grocers, bakers, saloon keepers, butchers, and shoemakers. They were 235, 232, 151, 81, 58, 73 and 43, respectively, according to the 1909 survey mentioned earlier. Their number was to further increase in the subsequent years following the expansion of the population of the Italian colonies.[16]

The development of the radio industry in the interwar decades made new job opportunities available to Italians in the three leading companies of the Philadelphia area in that field: Philco Corporation, Atwater Kent, and Radio Corporation of America (RCA) in nearby Camden, New Jersey. Thanks to their pre-emigration experience as cabinetmakers, Italians had become the largest group of foreign-born workers in radio manufacturing in Philadelphia by the late 1920s. During this decade, the radio industry replaced metal products as the second most important employer of the city's labor force.[17]

The beginning of the era of mass emigration from Italy to Philadelphia and a significant change in the regional origin of the newcomers from Italian background occurred simultaneously. These transformations reflected a broader trend in the history of the Italian immigration to the United States. Before the 1880s, the largest number of immigrants nationwide came from northern and central Italy. Conversely, the South contributed about 70 percent of Italian emigration to the United States after 1880, when the collapse of the economy in southern Italy stimulated mass emigration from this area, too.[18]

Likewise, the great bulk of the early immigrants to Philadelphia arrived from northern Italy, while individuals from other places such as Naples and Sicily were only a scattering within the local Italian population. By the mid-1860s, most Philadelphians of Italian origin had come from Liguria and Piedmont, specifically from the areas around Genoa, Chiavari, Bobbio, and Tortona. In the last quarter of the nineteenth century, however, northern Italians were progressively joined by fellow countrypeople from such southern regions as Abruzzi, Basilicata, Calabria, and—though to a lesser extent—Sicily and Puglia. These latter outnumbered northerners by the turn of the century and dominated the Italian immigration in the following decades. Abruzzi and Campania were the regions that provided the greatest inflow of Italian newcomers before the outbreak of World War I.[19]

With 136,793 first- and second-generation individuals, Italian Americans were the second largest nationality group in Philadelphia in 1920. They retained that position ten years later, when their nationality group totalled 182,368 members. During that period, the Italian-American share of the city's total population also grew from 7.5 percent in 1920 to 9.3 percent in 1930.[20]

Yet, the idea of a common Italian ancestry was a much more viable concept for the U.S. Census enumerators than for the great bulk of the rank and file members of the Italian settlements in Philadelphia. Except for a handful of emigrés, newcomers from an Italian background usually failed to think of themselves as Italians.

Most political refugees from northern and central Italy, who went to the United States on exile before the late nineteenth century, settled in New York City or made their way to Boston. Some, however, like Giacomo Sega came to Philadelphia. Even Piero Maroncelli, the well-known companion of Silvio Pellico in the Spielberg prison, spent some time there in 1834.[21]

These *fuorusciti* had fought to free Italy from foreign rulers and to make her a unified country under a single government. The concept of the existence of an Italian nation had inspired their struggles in their motherland before the exile. Their sense of group membership differed remarkably from the perception of the ethnic community of the Italian peasants and agricultural laborers who arrived in Philadelphia from the rural South to pursue economic opportunities after the 1870s. Of course, there were also exceptions. Nationalism and the *Risorgimento* politics, for instance, shaped the world view of Frank S. Spiziri, a shoemaker from southern Italy who settled in Philadelphia at the turn of the century. Yet, most of Spiziri's fellow Southerners usually failed to think of themselves as Italians.[22]

The Kingdom of Italy was established out of preexisting regional states as late as 1861 and its territorial acquisitions continued until the end of World War I. The belated achievement of national unification in Italy caused the Italian people to retain a parochial sense of regional, provincial, and even localistic allegiance. Italians spoke such different dialects that a Sicilian could not understand a Calabrian. The concept of affinity and community of the Italian people did not extend beyond the boundaries of their native villages. This attitude characterized especially the southern regions, where the sense of the state had been negligible for centuries. In particular, the perception of the new Italian state as a hostile entity that confined itself to collecting taxes and drafting young men into the army also contributed to preventing the spread of a strong consciousness of the common nationhood among ordinary Italians.[23]

The strong municipal spirit of the Italian population in the post-unification years did not escape American observers such as novelist William Dean Howells, who served as U.S. Consul in Venice during the Lincoln administration. As he remarked about an Italian fellow traveler from Rovigo, whom he met while leaving Venice in 1864, "[O]ur honest man of Rovigo was a *foreigner* at Padua, twenty-five miles north, and a foreigner at Ferrara, twenty-five miles south; and throughout Italy the native of one city is an alien in another."[24]

Regardless of the city of destination in the New World, the experience of emigration from their native land failed to create the consciousness of a common nationality among Italians from different geographical backgrounds. A persisting localistic spirit fanned the flames of mutual antagonism and suspicion among the immigrants who had not come from the same region or province. For instance, according to Rosa Cassettari, who arrived in the United States from Lombardy in 1884, compatriots from Sicily were not Italians but Sicilians. In her opinion, people from Tuscany made up another ethnic group of their own.[25]

The newcomers who settled in both the United States and Canada continued to identify themselves more with their own native towns than with the country of their origin at the outset of their stay in America in the late nineteenth and early twentieth centuries. Fellow villagers and people from the same province or region grouped in specific neighborhoods and established such subnational colonies as a "Little Avigliano" in East Harlem, a "Little Cinisi" in Manhattan, a "Little Calabria" on Mulberry Street in New York City, a "Little Lapio" in Boston's North End, a "Little Frosolone" on Providence's Federal Hill, or a "Little Laurenzana" and a "Little Rende" in Toronto. Similarly, immigrants from a number of small towns in Abruzzi and Sicily organized their own distinct communities around parochial loyalties in Cleveland. As Antonio Mangano remarked about New York City's "Little Italy" in 1904, "the Italian colony is divided into almost as many groups as there are sections of Italy represented." Likewise, a few years later, Amy Bernardy argued that any Italian American settlement was nothing more than a series of as many separate nuclei as the sum of the Italian villages from which their dwellers had come. William Foote Whyte has even reported that "one can mark out sections of Corneville [the "Little Italy" in Boston's North End] according to the town of origin of the immigrants" as late as the early 1940s.[26]

Groups of newcomers from different areas in their native land shied away from each other not only in large cities such as Boston and New York but also in mid- and small-size towns. For instance, in Norristown—a borough in Pennsylvania with fewer than 30,000 residents in the early twentieth century—people from Marche settled in an enclave of their own on East Main Street. They thought of themselves as "central" Italians, as opposed to the southern immigrants who made up the bulk of the Italian presence there. Likewise, Sicilians from the village of Sciacca established their own "Little Sciacca" in Norristown because all the other Italians shunned them on the grounds of their alleged "African roots." Similarly, Italian newcomers from the same town or region grouped together in Cortland, New York, a small city that had a population of about 11,500 inhabitants at the turn of the century, when immigration from Italy started.[27]

Philadelphia provides an insightful example of the subnational sense of affiliation of Italians in early-twentieth-century America. By that time, as in almost all the other destinations of Italian newcomers throughout the United States, the arrival of Italians in Philadelphia was primarily a matter of chain migration based on family and village connections. Social networks were the main channel of Italian immigration to the Americas in the decade preceding World War I. For instance, 61 percent of the Italians who settled in the United States in 1910 had made their way across the Atlantic to join relatives or friends. The letters that previous immigrants had sent home, whose circulation did not usually extend beyond a relatively narrow circle of kinsfolk and fellow villagers, were a major factor that encouraged new tides of arrivals. Even the Italians who immigrated through recruiters of laborers, however, retained some homogeneity regarding their place of origin. For example, 10,321 individuals out of the 17,338 Italians who arrived in Philadelphia through the help of the Di Bernardino Firm between 1900 and 1919 came from the Abruzzi region and, specifically, from the provinces of Teramo and Chieti. The owner of the firm himself, Frank Di Bernardino, was born in the village of Torricella Peligna in the province of Chieti.[28]

Italian immigrants were generally unaware of the specific opportunities available in Philadelphia except for a vague idea that they could somehow make money there. They, therefore, headed for places where a relative, a friend, or a *paesano* (literally, someone from the same *paese*, or village, but broadly speaking also someone from the same province or region) lived. Kinsfolk, acquaintances, and fellow villagers supplied the newcomers with lodging and helped them to find a job. Actually, according to a survey by the Works Progress Administration, 49 percent of the Italians in the city's work force got their first job through family or *paesani* connections as late as 1936. When the newcomers could eventually afford to rent a room, an apartment, or a house, they settled in the immediate vicinity of their previous caretakers. For instance, Sicilian-born Josephine Reale recalls that, as soon as her mother managed to save enough money for a place of her own, she moved just one block from her fellow-villager mother-in-law's house, where she had spent about one year after arriving in Philadelphia. In turn, once these recent immigrants found an accommodation of their own, they were ready to put up other *paesani*, who were to make their way to Philadelphia in the following months or years.[29]

As a result, Italian immigrants to Philadelphia tended to cluster together along regional, provincial, or even village lines in separate but overcrowded neighborhoods within the broader Italian settlements. According to a 1904 survey of thirty families of Italian origin in South Philadelphia, 123 persons lived in as few as thirty-four rooms. Individuals who shared the same room included a number of adults who were not relatives. Lack of space involved using even cellars for living purposes. Sanitary conditions were miserable, too. In a block where primarily Italian immigrants resided, the average was one bath for twenty-two families and one tub for 102 individuals. The investigator also found that eleven families had one court hydrant as their sole water supply. Housing conditions did not improve in the following years. For instance, in 1914, almost three fourths of housing violations in Philadelphia were concentrated in the major areas of the Italian settlements.[30]

Donna R. Gabaccia has remarked that the Italian men and children living in New York City's Lower East Side at the turn of the century escaped overcrowding by spending most of their spare time outside their tenement houses and meeting other residents of their own blocks on street corners and in backyards.[31] In Philadelphia, however, that kind of outdoor socialization could hardly cross subnational borders because of the heavy concentration of neighborhood dwellers along localistic lines.

In an early study of the city's Italians published at the end of World War II, M. Agnes Gertrude observed that "it was a familiar phenomenon to anyone with some acquaintance of Italians to find one side or end of the city block populated by those from one small district in Italy, while on the opposite side or end dwelled those from another locality." Actually, the local Italian American community did not develop as a cohesive "Little Italy." Most Italians and their offspring resided in a district called South Philadelphia. This area, however, was divided into a series of single subnational colonies. For instance, immigrants from the province of Catanzaro, in the Calabria region, lived along Ellsworth Street, while the territory around Eight and Fitzwater Streets was home primarily to people from Abruzzi. In turn, however, this latter settlement was split into a number of smaller subregional enclaves made up of newcomers from specific villages in Abruzzi. The natives of Tollo clustered at Eight and Fitzwater Streets, while a colony of Italians from Torricella Peligna was located at the intersection of Fitzwater and Delhi Streets. This latter settlement further extended to an area between South, Ninth, and Tenth Streets. People from Vasto lived west of Ninth Street and south of Bainbridge Street. Similarly, Sicilians from different towns in their native region lived in separated neighborhoods. Immigrants from Casa di Siracusa dwelt on South Sixth Street. Newcomers from Caccamo resided between Sixth and Carpenter Streets. Those from Giarre settled at Eleventh and Catherine Streets.[32]

The most striking example of that self-segregated pattern of residence along subnational lines was an Italian American enclave in Montrose Street established by Albanian-speaking people who could not understand any Italian idiom. These immigrants came from a single village in the province of Cosenza, in Calabria, by the name of Spezzano Albanese. There were, however, other localistic clusterings of Italian newcomers outside South Philadelphia. For instance, most individuals from Friuli, who worked primarily as stonemasons, settled next to the quarries on Chestnut Hill.[33]

Each colony's people spoke their own dialect. They also patronized their own neighborhood shops and stores that *paesani* ran. There, Italian Americans could find traditional food that was either produced in the United States to meet their Old World tastes or imported from their area of origin in Italy. This latter, for instance, was the case of the La Fara macaroni and the Abruzzese punch and olive oil. The Angelucci family, wineshop Criscuolo, and Frank Di Bernardino's import firm brought these products into Philadelphia "directly from Abruzzi," as their ads read, for the immigrants coming from this specific region. Similarly, Mascagni Restaurant on 8th Street did not offer Italian-style dishes but "Neapolitan cuisine." Only a few blocks away, Andrea D'Alonzo's saloon featured *Abruzzesi* delicatessen on Saturday evenings. Even when Italian Americans needed a lawyer, an undertaker, or a physician, they went to a fellow ethnic in their neighborhood. For this reason, Doctor Raffaele Melocchi made a point of stressing that he was a "physician from Abruzzi" in the ads that he placed in the local Italian-language press in 1907. Remarkably enough, a few years later, Joseph Talese—an immigrant from Maida in the province of Catanzaro—decided not to enter the hospital of the University of Pennsylvania for an operation as soon as he learned from a cousin of his that a doctor from his own native town practiced in South Philadelphia. Likewise, people from Abruzzi addressed themselves to an *Abruzzese* pharmacy, and an Italian Albanian pharmacy operated for newcomers from Spezzano Albanese. Italian Americans also relied upon *paesani* savings banks to deposit their money or to send it to relatives in their home villages. For instance, at the turn of the century, an immigrant from L'Aquila, Thomas D. Yannessa, owned the Banca dell'Aquila. Its patrons were almost exclusively newcomers from the province of L'Aquila. The denominations of other early Italian American banks also suggest the subnational concentration of their clients. The Banca Torino, rechartered in 1890, was named after the capital of Piedmont; the Banca Napoli, founded in 1901, after the capital of Campania; the Banca Calabrese, established in 1902, after the Calabria region.[34]

Of course, it was much easier to talk business in one's own dialect. Moreover, distrust in anyone who did not belong to one's family or, at least, to the narrow circle of the *paesani* was a side effect of the localistic loyalties of the Italian immigrants, a feeling which is better known as *campanilismo*. As *Mastro Paolo*—a short-lived Italian-language weekly published in Philadelphia—pointed out in 1915, the city's immigrants of Italian origin hardly ever went into a business partnership with someone who had not come from the same village. Political organizations were fully aware of such an attitude. In order to reach out to the Italian American electorate in Philadelphia, they usually resorted to party workers who matched not only the national ancestry but also the regional descent of their constituents of Italian background.[35]

Subnational divisions also extended to religious life. Philadelphia was home to a few Protestants of Italian origin. Teofilo D. Malan established the Italian Evangelical Church on Catherine Street in 1899. The First Italian Presbyterian Church opened three years later and the Second Italian Presbyterian Church, later renamed the Presbyterian Church of Saint Andrew and Saint Paul, was organized with fifty charter members at Simpson and Callohill Streets on 5 April 1910. The Italian evangelical community was large enough for an Italian-language Baptist weekly, *L'Aurora*, to start publication in 1903.[36]

Yet, the great bulk of the Italian immigrants and their offspring in Philadelphia were Catholic, at least nominally. The increasing Italian presence in the city in the mid nineteenth century persuaded bishop John N. Neumann to establish St. Mary Magdalen de Pazzi's as an Italian national parish, the first one throughout the United States, as early as 1852. It is hardly surprising that most of the initial parishioners of this church came almost exclusively from Liguria and Piedmont because these two areas were the native regions of the great bulk of the earliest Italian settlers in Philadelphia. However, St. Mary Magdalen de Pazzi's maintained a disproportionate number of northern Italian members even after the city had become the destination of mass immigration tides from the south of Italy. Italian descent, regardless of the place of origin in the mother country, was the only requirement for admission to the parish. But, in general, the clergy did not encourage Sicilians and other southern newcomers to join St. Mary Magdalen de Pazzi's. It referred these immigrants to Our Lady of Good Council, which was founded as Philadelphia's second Italian national parish in 1898 in order to provide for the southern Italians who were rejected by St. Mary Magdalen de Pazzi's. Father Antonio Isoleri took a particularly active part in the effort to keep southern Italians away from St. Mary Magdalen's. A native of Villanova in Liguria, he served as pastor of this church from 1870 to his retirement in 1926.[37]

Concentration of members along subnational lines characterized other Italian parishes. For instance, immigrants from Genoa and their own offspring attended the church of St. Michael of the Saints. Conversely, newcomers from Calabria and their children went to the church of Our Lady of Pompei. Besides reproducing the regional and provincial distribution of Italians in Philadelphia's neighborhoods, this separation also reflected subnational diversities in religious rites. Residual paganism and a remarkable absence of formal observance distinguished the practices of southern Italians from the more orthodox rites of the northerners. For example, unlike these latter, peasants in southern Italy venerated an array of saints rather than God. They offered them gifts and sacrifices to propitiate them and neutralize malevolent spirits. Each southern village had a patron saint and the climax of the local religious life was his feast day—not official Catholic holidays such as Christmas or Easter—when the residents paraded his statue to invoke his protection.[38]

Regional antagonism was not confined to Catholics of Italian descent in Philadelphia alone in the early decades of the century. Father Marcellino Moroni, for instance, remarked that his parishioners of northern Italian origin in New York City refused to mix with fellow Italians from Napoli, while Buffalo's Sicilians denounced the anti-southern feelings of their own pastor, don Martinelli. Similarly, Sicilians on St. Louis' Hill backed away from the church of St. Ambrose out of resentment for the Lombards who allegedly controlled the parish. Rifts between northern and southern Italians characterized Catholic congregations in Providence, too. In particular, Italian immigrants from the South repeatedly petitioned their bishop and asked for the removal of the northerner priests of their parishes between the turn of the century and the early 1920s.[39]

Not only space as well as different dialects and customs but also regional and provincial antipathies divided Italians in Philadelphia. The members of each subnational group usually considered countrymen of other local backgrounds as inferior types and made them the target of ethnic slurs and stereotypes. In particular, like their fellow immigrants throughout the United States, Philadelphians from northern Italy transplanted their contemptuous disposition toward southern Italians, which was notorious in their native land, to the country of their adoption. Prejudicial attitudes, however, also distanced members of one regional group from people of another among southerners themselves. For instance, the *Abruzzesi* regarded the Sicilians as dishonest and revengeful. Conversely, these latter considered the *Calabresi* as stubborn.[40]

Although Italians shared a remarkable tradition of associational activities both in their mother country and abroad, localistic affiliations characterized the early social life of Italian American communities in the United States. Membership in beneficial and fraternal organizations was not open to all Italian newcomers but was usually restricted to immigrants from a specific region, province, and even town or village. These requirements were enforced not only in such large cities as, for instance, St. Louis and San Francisco but also in small towns like, for example, Kenosha, Wisconsin.[41]

Philadelphia was no exception. In the attempt to provide a nationalistic concept of ethnic identity and curb the *campanilismo* prevailing among the Italian immigrants, the local lodges of the Order Sons of Italy in America (OSIA) recruited their members among Italians and their offspring regardless of their place of origin or descent in their mother country. The OSIA was a nationwide organization with lodges scattered throughout the United States and Canada. But the great bulk of Italian American benevolent and fraternal associations had a local basis. In addition, contrary to the OSIA, their membership was confined only to those immigrants who had come from a specific Italian region, province, or village, and excluded all the remaining people of Italian ancestry.[42]

Lorenzo L. Nardi and other *prominenti* established the first Italian American mutual-aid society in Philadelphia—the Società di Unione e Fratellanza Italiana—in 1867 and incorporated it the following year. Nardi was from Lucca, but most of the other officials were from Liguria. Treasurer Agostino Lagomarsino, for instance, was born in San Colombano Certenoli, a village near Chiavari. Founding members Bartolomeo Alfredo Cavagnaro, Paul Cavagnaro, Frank Cuneo, and Stefano Cuneo also had roots in Liguria. In particular, the Cuneos were from San Colombano. Actually, despite its own name, the Società di Unione e Fratellanza Italiana grouped individuals who had come almost exclusively from the cities of Chiavari and Genoa in Liguria or from the surrounding areas.[43]

The bylaws of the Società di Unione e Fratellanza Italiana let any individual of Italian descent join its ranks. That, however, was not the case of many other Italian American associations in Philadelphia. For instance, admittance to the Società Italiana Unione Abruzzese in Philadelphia—familiarly known as Unione Abruzzese—was limited to newcomers from Abruzzi and their kinsfolk. Likewise, the Christopher Columbus Mutual Aid Society accepted individuals from Genoa alone, while only people from the village of Castrogiovanni and the province of Caltanisetta in Sicily were allowed to join the Società di Mutuo Soccorso fra Castrogiovannesi e Provinciali. Similarly, the Società Fraterna Cosenza was for people from the city of Cosenza and its vicinity.[44]

The events leading to the foundation of the Società Sulmonese give further evidence of the pervasiveness of the municipal spirit of the Philadelphians of Italian origin in the early twentieth century. On 29 April 1906, a meeting was called in order to establish a new mutual-aid society. Its purpose was to "put an end to internal animosities" within the community in Philadelphia and to "promote harmony and the common good" among the city's Italians. Ironically enough, however, the organizers of the event were a group of immigrants from Sulmona and invited only people from Sulmona to attend the gathering that was to create an association with no other name than Società Sulmonese.[45]

As John W. Briggs has remarked, boarding houses and saloons were the first cores of Italian American communities. Similarly, Gary Ross Mormino has observed that, before the implementation of the Eighteenth Amendment, the tavern was a key social center for poor working-class Italian immigrants and their male offspring who could not afford to meet anywhere else. Both boarding houses and saloons, however, took shape along subnational lines in Philadelphia. For instance, Corona di Ferro, a boarding house in South Tenth Street, provided accommodation for newcomers from Pescara. Similarly, Roma Cafe was a center for Sicilians from Giarre, while Palumbo's initially served immigrants from Abruzzi as a whole. An old story even goes that individuals from Abruzzi arrived in Philadelphia with pieces of paper reading "Palumbo" pinned on their suits so that they could more easily move to their final destination in the city.[46]

Subnational divisions also affected the beginnings of the Italian American periodical press in Philadelphia. With the exception of *La Gazzetta Italiana*, which briefly came out in 1853, the city's first Italian-language newspapers did not address the whole community but targeted immigrant readers from single regions or provinces. They published local news from the specific native towns or villages of their prospective readers. For instance, *Il Vesuvio*, a short-lived weekly paper that started publication in 1882, reflected its localistic approach even in its own heading, as it was named after the volcano in the bay of Naples. The very purpose of this earliest kind of journalism was to keep immigrants in touch with the place of their origin in Italy, to which most of them hoped they would later go back. Actually, a sojourner mentality initially prevailed among Italian newcomers. Most were temporary or even seasonal immigrants who went back and forth across the Atlantic in order to make a living. The fact that *La Gazzetta Italiana*, the first newspaper for all the city's Italians regardless of their geographical backgrounds, ceased publication after a few issues further demonstrates the lack of a cohesive community in the initial stages of the Italian immigration to Philadelphia.[47]

The desire to write history from the bottom up underlying the ethnic revival in migration studies has made many scholars wary of the social elite of the U.S. national minorities. Obviously, leaders could not and did not create ethnic groups on their own. Nonetheless, some authors have acknowledged that they did contribute to shaping the ethnic consciousness and sense of identity of the rank and file members of their communities.[48]

In Philadelphia, the *prominenti* were among the few individuals who encouraged their own fellow ethnics to think of themselves as Italians and to supersede their parochial loyalties and identification. On the one hand, these notables created institutions that aimed to bring together the population of Italian ancestry across localistic, provincial, and regional boundaries. On the other hand, they presented themselves as the defenders of the immigrants and their children in situations that threatened their community as a collectivity beyond any subnational division. Therefore, the *prominenti* helped the Italian newcomers to realize that they had a common national origin regardless of the place of birth of the single members of the city's "Little Italies."

The first function included the publication of Italian-language newspapers for the immigrant community as a whole and the foundation of associations that did not discriminate against prospective members of Italian descent on the grounds of their local extraction. Charles C. A. Baldi Sr. and the Di Silvestro brothers stood out in both fields. Baldi initiated *L'Opinione* in 1906. This newspaper became the city's main Italian-language daily and remained the only one after 1916. It served the community for nearly thirty years, until 1935. Similarly, Arpino Giuseppe Di Silvestro established *Il Popolo*, a weekly, in 1899. Seven years later, on 1 May 1906, he and his brother Giovanni consolidated *Il Popolo* with another Italian-language periodical, *La Voce della Colonia*, and originated *La Voce del Popolo*, a daily. The Di Silvestros discontinued the publication of this latter newspaper in 1916. In less than one year, however, they replaced *La Voce del Popolo* with a new weekly, *La Libera Parola*, which became the organ of the Pennsylvania Grand Lodge of the Order Sons of Italy in America. Actually, it was Arpino Giuseppe Di Silvestro who introduced the OSIA to Pennsylvania. He was among the founders of the Pennsylvania Grand Lodge in 1913 and served as its first Grand Venerable, a colorful title for state leader, until 1923. His brother Giovanni was elected Supreme Venerable, namely, national president, of the same organization in 1922. Baldi, too, was active in fraternal associations and was president of the Circolo Italiano, a club that was open to any Philadelphia professional of Italian descent.[49]

The publication of newspapers and involvement in the community's social life were part of a long struggle between Baldi and the Di Silvestros. Both parties aimed to build up their personal power among the people of Italian descent in Philadelphia and, possibly, to increase it at the expense of their own rivals. Giuseppe Di Silvestro, for instance, outspokenly acknowledged that he had conceived *La Voce del Popolo* as his mouthpiece to curb Baldi's growing influence in the Italian colonies after the latter had established *L'Opinione*. Once Baldi had begun to publish a daily newspaper, Di Silvestro, too, needed his own daily in order to counter his rival's organ effectively. Two other Italian-language weeklies that came out in 1917 but were short-lived, *La Rassegna* and *La Ragione*, were also created as weapons in the conflict that pitted Baldi against the Di Silvestro brothers. The editor of the former, Silvio Liberatore, sided with Baldi and the editor of the latter, F. Silvagni, made his newspaper a resonance box for the views of the Di Silvestros. Yet, *La Ragione* also proclaimed that it intended to be an "organ in defense of Italianness."[50]

Actually, besides fighting one another, Philadelphia's *prominenti* aimed at extending the group consciousness of Italian immigrants beyond the narrow boundaries of their respective native villages because any leader could hardly exist as such without a relatively broad community. For this reason, Baldi and the Di Silvestros endeavored to exploit the opportunities that let them act as representatives of their fellow ethnics to the host society. Indeed, the role of broker or spokesperson enhanced the status of a leader in the eyes of both the members of the "Little Italies" in Philadelphia and the city's establishment. The publication of Italian-language newspapers as well as the involvement in the self-help societies and recreational clubs of the local Italian colonies helped the *prominenti* to legitimize their position as representatives of Italian immigrants and their children. However, the function of mediator between mainstream America and the Italian community also required establishing a high profile during significant crises in the relations between their fellow ethnics and the larger U.S. society.

One of these confrontations occurred in 1906, when Congress began discussing a literacy test provision that would restrict immigration to the United States by excluding prospective newcomers who could not read and write in their native language. On this occasion, Baldi led a delegation of the representatives of Philadelphia's major Italian associations to Washington in order to lobby House Speaker Joseph G. Cannon and President Theodore Roosevelt against the passing of that measure. The literacy test would have heavily penalized Italian immigrants because their educational level was generally very low. Actually, 64 percent of the Italians who arrived in the United States at the turn of the century were illiterate. The United States would not enact a literacy test until 1917, although Baldi's efforts actually played a negligible role in the postponement of the implementation of that measure. Yet, the apparently successful outcome of Baldi's mission to Washington increased his reputation for effective leadership in the eyes of his fellow ethnics. Besides making a remarkable contribution to the recognition of Baldi's elite status, his lobbying endeavors also marked an initial step toward the unification of the Italian colonies in Philadelphia across subnational boundaries. *L'Opinione* gave the city's Italians some sense of their common ancestry. It stressed that the literacy test was a menace to "Italians" as a whole, regardless of their native regions. The newspaper also urged its readers to protest against that measure as a single group. Furthermore, the making of the delegation to Washington was an early effort to induce Italians in Philadelphia to close the ranks across their localistic divisions in the pursuit of a common goal.[51]

The Italian notables took other initiatives that, though instrumental in consolidating the personal power of the individual leaders, also promoted the initial stages of the development of a national identity among the local population of Italian ancestry. While Italian-sponsored Christopher Columbus festivities in Philadelphia dated back to 1869, in 1892 the fourth centennial of the discovery of America by the Italian navigator was a major opportunity to celebrate the Italian legacy in the United States. This occasion witnessed the first attempt to bring together all the city's Italian associations, even if the scope of such an effort was limited to the planning and coordination of the ceremonies in honor of Columbus by a short-lived umbrella organization named United Italian Societies of Philadelphia. Remarkably, this syndicate included both southerners like Baldi and northerners such as Emanuel V. H. Nardi, the son of Lorenzo L. Nardi, among its officials. Similarly, on 7 July 1907, the first centennial of the birth of Giuseppe Garibaldi—the reputed hero of the unification of Italy—a one-issue newspaper published with the Di Silvestro brothers' money, *Giuseppe Garibaldi*, called on Philadelphians of Italian descent to strengthen the "awareness of their Italianness." Appeals to Italian pride and community-wide ethnic solidarity also characterized the 1909 dedication of a monument to Italian composer Giuseppe Verdi and the establishment of the "Italian Hospital" in Philadelphia. Baldi offered most of the funds to pay for the monument to Verdi and donated a three-story building for the "Italian Hospital." He exploited even the death of Italian poet Giosuè Carducci in the attempt to stir up some sense of their common national origin among Italian immigrants in Philadelphia. A lengthy obituary published on the front page of *L'Opinione* made a point of reminding its readers of their Italianness.[52]

The natural calamities that hit Italy in the early twentieth century supplied the Italian leaders with additional potential opportunities to enhance the sense of the national identity of their own fellow ethnics. On these occasions, the *prominenti* launched appeals to the whole community and asked its members for their help to relieve the hardships of Italians in the mother country regardless of their place of residence. "We are all brothers," proclaimed—for instance—the Di Silvestro brothers' *Il Popolo* when it asked its readers to collect money for both the earthquake-stricken Calabrians in 1905 and the homeless Campanians who had suffered from the 1906 eruption of Vesuvio.[53]

Still, the endeavors of Philadelphia's *prominenti* to forge a more unified Italian community out of subnational colonies were of little avail until the outbreak of World War I operated as the powerful catalyst of a heightened awareness of common national peoplehood among the Italian newcomers and their offspring. Baldi did not succeed in carrying out his plan to consolidate all the city's fraternal and mutual-aid localistic organizations into a single Italian association. He managed to hold influential positions in a great number of subnational clubs such as the Società di Mutuo Soccorso Maria Santissima delle Grazie di Acquavilla-Cilento or the Società di Mutuo Soccorso Santa Barbara. Yet, he eventually failed to have their members renounce their parochial allegiance and let their societies merge into any broader association. In 1910, Philadelphia numbered eighty-three Italian societies. They were named primarily after the patron saint of a native village or after some regional, provincial, or local connection of their own members. Only three of these societies, however, agreed to merge into the Italian Federation of Philadelphia, which was established in 1912 in the fruitless effort to unite all the Italian American organizations in the city. By contrast, membership in the Società di Mutuo Soccorso Roma e Provincia, chartered in 1912, was restricted to newcomers from Rome and its province. Similarly, after arriving in Philadelphia in 1913, Ottaviano Capponi founded the Società Beniamino Gigli fra' Marchegiani, which admitted immigrants from the Marche region only.[54]

Even the Circolo Italiano eventually split into two factions, the one backing Baldi and the other supporting the Di Silvestros. The official cause of this conflict was the accusation that Baldi had tried to monopolize a banquet for an Italian diplomatic mission to Philadelphia. Such a pretext reflected the growing tendency of Philadelphia's *prominenti* to show off their Italy-oriented patriotism in their search for status and respect in the community. The inner motivation of the discord, however, was the heightening tension between the Di Silvestros and Baldi in their fight for power within Philadelphia's community.[55]

The 1906 campaign on behalf of the victims of the eruption of Vesuvio, too, pitted Baldi against the Di Silvestro brothers. This time, they struggled over the issue of who was entitled to represent Philadelphia's community in the collection of funds and could, hopefully, enjoy the rewards of that charitable action in the eyes of its rank and file members. Similarly, a delay in the dedication of Verdi's monument paved the way for innuendoes that Baldi had embezzled the money of the other donors.[56]

Chapter 3

The Development of a National Identity

It was World War I that offered Italians and Italian Americans who retained localistic self-perceptions a chance to construct some sense of their common Italian national identity. Enthusiasm and jubilance welcomed the news of Italy's declaration of war against the Austrian-Hungarian empire at the state convention of the OSIA in May 1915. The Pennsylvania Grand Lodge also sent a telegram to Italian Prime Minister Antonio Salandra to congratulate him on Italy's intervention in the war and collected $12,479.76 to support her military machine. Moreover, while their ethnic leaders and the Italian-language press organized parades and raised money with bombastic rhetoric in order to back Italy's war effort, the rank and file members of Philadelphia's Italian American community realized that they had something to share despite their different places of origin in the mother country. Not only did they contribute to fund raising for Italy but a few unnaturalized immigrants even went back to their native land and joined the Italian army.[1]

In addition, after the United States had entered the war at the side of Italy, Great Britain, and France against the German and Austrian-Hungarian empires, Italian immigrants and their offspring became conscious that their national origin was no longer a stigma. Italians had been the victims of ethnic stereotyping and other forms of discrimination because of their ancestry since the beginning of mass immigration. Other Philadelphians were unable to make subnational distinctions among the generally short and dark-skinned Italians who often spoke only a little broken English. To both other foreign-born minorities such as the Irish and native white Anglo-Saxon Protestants, "wops" and "dagoes" (both derogatory terms that were commonly used to designate Italians and Italian Americans) were "wops" and "dagoes" whatever their place of origin in Italy. Irish policemen had harassed all Italian Americans alike and Irish politicians had prevented their rise in politics since the turn of the century. Employers generally relegated laborers of Italian origin to low-paying unskilled and semi-skilled jobs. Fellow workers of other national ancestries distrusted Italians for their supposedly little interest in labor militancy and their reputation as strikebreakers. In particular, the Jewish members of the Amalgamated Clothing Workers of America (ACWA) often discriminated against their co-laborers of Italian descent and contributed to rumors that these latter were glad to work for less than the wage standards their own union had set. Philadelphians of Italian origin usually had to sit together with African Americans in segregated sections of theaters located outside their own neighborhoods. A number of the city's districts were even closed to them. Gangs of local residents often attacked those Italians who dared to walk alone in Polish or Irish areas.[2]

Even the Irish hierarchy in the Catholic Church tended to regard Italian worshipers from different regional backgrounds as a single group that had to be controlled, in order to curb the allegedly unorthodox, superstition-prone, and sometimes pagan religious practices that they had supposedly carried from their mother country. The Irish-dominated archdiocese established the Madonna House and the Assunta House in South Philadelphia in early 1916 in order to take care of the spiritual and material lives of local Italian Americans. These agencies aimed specifically at eradicating any legacy of Italian Catholics' pre-emigration religious and ethnic culture by offering them Irish-oriented programs such as songs and plays related to Ireland for entertainment purposes. Efforts to turn newcomers from Italy into full-fledged Irish Catholics came hand in hand with overt anti-Italian discrimination. Philadelphia's diocesan newspaper, the *Catholic Standard and Times*, did not refrain from publishing derogatory pieces and ethnic slurs about Italian immigrants in the early 1910s. One of them, for instance, entitled "McAroni Ballads," mocked Italian Americans' well-known taste for pasta.[3]

Moreover, the Irish pastor who served the church of St. Paul during the first two decades of the century was notorious for his anti-Italian feelings and usually barred prospective worshipers of Italian descent from his parish. As a second-generation Italian American woman has recalled, when her immigrant parents tried to have their daughter baptized in their own neighborhood parish, the Irish priest dismissed them. He told them to "go to an Italian church," although St. Paul's was supposed to accept any Catholic living within its parish boundaries.[4]

At St. Paul's, however, not only the Irish pastor but also fellow parishioners of Irish ancestry did not welcome the Italian members of the church. Actually, anti-Italian bigotry and discrimination on the part of the Irish were so widespread in the parish that ethnic prejudices induced a few Italians to become Protestants.[5]

Nonetheless, conflicts between the Irish and Italian Americans in religious life were not specific to Philadelphia. In East Harlem, New York, for instance, congregations of Italian descent were confined to the basements of churches for Italian-language services in Irish-dominated parishes.[6]

According to Luigi Villari, the Italian vice consul in charge of immigration matters in Philadelphia in the early twentieth century, Italian newcomers continued to be despised even after becoming American citizens. Nonetheless, while the United States and Italy were allies in World War I, fellow Philadelphians no longer viewed Italian immigrants and their offspring with hostility and contempt. Rather, they accepted Italian Americans as partners in the fight for democracy that was being waged in Europe. For instance, local personalities from other ethnic backgrounds usually invited representatives of the Italian community to share the stump with them at rallies in support of the allied powers. Another form of recognition for Italian Americans came from the *Public Ledger*, the most authoritative local daily. On the occasion of the third recurrence of Italy's entry into the war, to the great satisfaction of Philadelphia's Italians, the *Public Ledger* remarked that "this anniversary should be Italy-America day. There are men of Italian birth fighting under the American flag. There are Italian soldiers in France where our own are." *Il Momento*, a local Italian-language weekly published by Costantino Costantini, joyfully reprinted this editorial and pointed to it as an example of the new "unity of spirit" that had come to characterize the relations between Italians and Americans not only overseas but also in the United States.[7]

Further similar tokens characterized the celebration for the victory of the Allies over Austria-Hungary on 4 November 1918. William Potter, Pennsylvania's state fuel administrator and a former U.S. minister to Italy, made an address in which he publicly saluted "the brave liberty-loving Italian people." Likewise, the mayor of Philadelphia, Thomas B. Smith, issued a proclamation calling on the city's residents to display the Italian flag along with the Stars and Stripes from homes and places of business. He also granted Italian American leaders the use of Independence Square for a mass rally to hail the triumph of their native country in the war.[8]

On Italy's victory day, work was virtually suspended in South Philadelphia, while jubilant Italians and Italian Americans paraded through the principal streets of this district carrying Italian flags. They later converged toward Independence Square, where they joined the official delegations of the city's Italian American societies. There, Italian Consul Gaetano Poccardi, the Di Silvestro brothers, and other *prominenti* spoke to the crowd. Enthusiastic shouts of *"viva l'Italia"* (hurrah for Italy) often interrupted their addresses.[9]

Of course, support for Italy's intervention in World War I was not unanimous among Philadelphians of Italian descent. The staunchest advocates of the Italian neutrality were radical groups such as the anarchist club Circolo Francisco Ferrer, which published the Italian-language monthly *La Comune*. Giuseppe Bruno, a well-known Italian freemason and the publisher-editor of the Italian-language weekly *Mastro Paolo* was against the war as well. However, opponents of Italy's entry into the war were a minority. Boycott by its readers forced *Mastro Paolo* to discontinue publication, while other Italian American newspapers such as *L'Opinione* and *La Voce del Popolo* disavowed their initial neutralist stand in order to pander to the growing nationalistic feelings of their readership. Even a few anarchists defected to the interventionist camp. They included Filippo Bocchini, a leader of the Circolo Francisco Ferrer and an editorialist for *La Comune*, who had emphatically stigmatized Italy's imperialism just few years earlier at the time of the Italo-Turkish War in 1912.[10]

Rudolph J. Vecoli has argued that "the First World War, while stimulating the competing ideologies of Italian and American nationalisms, was a transitory phenomenon which did not basically alter the apolitical character of the immigrants." Yet, Philadelphia's Italians remained sensitive to nationalistic appeals even after the end of the war. For instance, they held mass rallies to support Italy's claims to the Adriatic port of Fiume, the region of Dalmatia, and other territories that both their mother country and Yugoslavia wanted to annex in 1919. When flamboyant Italian poet Gabriele D'Annunzio led a band of adventurers to occupy Fiume in late September 1919 and proclaimed the annexation of the city to the kingdom of Italy in defiance of the ongoing international talks, Unione Abruzzese hurried to raise funds among Philadelphia's Italians for the "poet-soldier," who was a native of Abruzzi himself. The local community also collected money to symbolically help Italy pay off the war debts she had incurred, and gave General Armando Diaz, the chief of staff of the Italian army in the last year of World War I, a triumphal welcome when he visited Philadelphia in November 1921.[11]

Politics itself provides further evidence that Italian Americans retained both nationalistic feelings and a sense of identification with their motherland after the war. While hailing the contribution of the Italian immigrants and their offspring to the war efforts of the United States, *La Libera Parola* contended that they were "so inflamed with patriotic sentiment and resolutions [that they] show by every act and conduct their love for American institutions and ideals." In order to persuade its own readers to purchase U.S. war bonds, however, this same newspaper had to point out that by aiding the United States financially "we indirectly aid Italy also, because Italy and America fight the same battle and have the same objectives."[12]

Concerns for their native country continued to be paramount among Philadelphians of Italian descent even after the end of hostilities in Europe. A significant number of Italian American voters bolted the Democratic Party throughout the United States to protest against President Woodrow Wilson's neglect of the interests of Italy at the Paris Peace Conference. Many Italian Americans lashed back at the Democratic Party in the 1920 presidential elections in Philadelphia, too. *La Libera Parola* itself, which had an estimated circulation of ten thousand copies at that time, called on its readers to go over to the Republican Party in revenge for President Wilson's opposition to Italy's territorial ambitions. The appeal of the Italian-language weekly to the Italian American electorate was unambiguous: "Your duty is clear, to reject Wilson and support Warren Harding." As a result, the Democratic vote fell by nearly 10 percent in some Italian American neighborhoods in Philadelphia between 1916, the year of the previous presidential contest, and 1920.[13]

In the following years, candidates for local offices appealed to the most trivial aspects of the emergent nationalism of Italian Americans in order to secure their votes. Former mayor of Philadelphia J. Hampton

Moore offered a case in point. When he ran for a second term in 1927, in the attempt to secure the support of Italian American voters, Moore made a point of reminding them that "he had the honor, as mayor of the city, to receive and entertain General Diaz.... All Italians will remember the wonderful reception given to General Diaz at City Hall."[14]

The aftershocks of World War I also helped to bring together Italian Americans from disparate local backgrounds because they realized that subnational divisions did not pay in coping with the country of their adoption. *Il Momento* called "depraved and perverse" those members of the community who argued that U.S. citizens of Italian ancestry had to be faithful only to their adoptive country during World War I. It also warned the naturalized Italian-born immigrants who had volunteered to serve in the U.S. Army not to forget their motherland. The enthusiasm of the various immigration groups for the war efforts of their respective native countries raised doubts about the loyalty of the different ethnic minorities to the United States and stimulated the movements for "One Hundred Percent Americanism" and for the restriction of immigration. Committees for the Americanization of immigrants, such as that promoted by the local Chamber of Commerce, mushroomed in Philadelphia in the postwar years. Moreover, after the brief honeymoon of 1917 and 1918, the "Red Scare" of the early postwar years contributed to the portrayal of Italian Americans as outcasts in the United States for their alleged radicalism and threat to American democracy. This campaign culminated in the controversial execution of Italian-born anarchists Nicola Sacco and Bartolomeo Vanzetti in 1927. However, it also had repercussions in Philadelphia. Erasmo Abate—the former editor of *La Comune*, which had ceased publication in December 1915—and other local radicals with such Italian-sounding names as Luigi Bruni and G. Baldassare were among the leftist militants who were arrested in police raids on the Industrial Workers of the World in 1920.[15]

The 1921 and 1924 Quota Acts further pushed Italians and Italian Americans farther toward the margin of U.S. society regardless of their region of origin in their mother country. The 1921 Emergency Quota Act limited the annual number of immigrants of each nationality to 3 percent of the number of the foreign-born persons of that nationality who resided in the United States according to the 1910 federal Census. The 1924 Johnson-Reed Act cut the previous quota to 2 percent and used the 1890 Census as the basis to calculate it. Both provisions were ethnically biased in order to keep the national homogeneity of the population of the United States as it was at the turn of the century. Actually, these measures were formulated in order to welcome northern Europeans, whose ancestors were still a majority of the American people at that time, and to limit the arrivals of people from southern and eastern Europe, whose assimilation into mainstream society was regarded as being difficult to carry out. In particular, the restrictive immigration laws of the 1920s discriminated against the Italians. More than 400,000 Italian citizens applied for passports for the United States in 1922. The previous year, the number of requests was 7,277 in Abruzzi alone. As mentioned in the previous chapter, this region had by then become the area that provided the greatest inflow of Italian immigrants to Philadelphia. Nonetheless, Italy was granted a quota of as few as 42,075 visas per year under the 1921 Quota Act. Her number of entries was further reduced to 5,802 immigrants under the national origins provision of the Johnson-Reed Act.[16]

The fact that anti-Italian bias underlay the Quota Acts emerged clearly in Philadelphia from a series of articles about the new legislation that James J. Davis, the secretary of the Department of Labor, published in a local daily newspaper, the *Evening Bulletin*, between 19 May and 21 June 1924. In his opinion, immigration restriction would be profitable to the growth of the labor movement and would prevent the United States from turning into the "dumping ground" of criminals from eastern and southern Europe. Specifically, Davis compared figures about the spread of crime among the different nationality groups in the United States, and argued that Italian immigrants had the third highest crime rate after the Turks and people from the Balkan regions. This meant, according to Davis's own figures, as much as five times the rate of British Americans and six times that of German Americans. Philadelphia's Italian Americans were fully aware of such discriminatory attitudes. It is unsurprising that *L'Opinione* placed Davis among "the promoters of a prejudicial and fanatic policy which created the principle of the superiority of one race on all the others in America."[17]

In the early postwar years, anti-Italian nativist feelings characterized primarily the Ku Klux Klan, the white supremacist organization that was revived in 1915. The new Klan was less concerned with African Americans than its model in the Reconstruction years had been, and devoted itself to the preservation of its own concept of the American way of life from the alleged corrupting influence of Catholics, Jews, and immigrants in general. Furthermore, the activities of the postwar Klan were no longer confined to the South, but went national and spread to Pennsylvania, too. This state became the most important "realm" in the Klan's so-called "Domain of the Northeast." The Ku Klux Klan opened its headquarters in Philadelphia in 1921 and came to number about 225,000 to 300,000 members statewide in the mid 1920s. When the Klan staged a 40,000-person parade down Pennsylvania Avenue in Washington, D.C., on 25 August 1925, the Philadelphia delegation included more than one thousand individuals. In addition, the third largest number of initiations into the Klan in a single city in the interwar years (about 35,000) reportedly occurred in Philadelphia.[18]

As Catholics, foreign-born, and former or current subjects of such a totalitarian regime as Fascism, Italian immigrants were among the main targets of the Klan in Pennsylvania. Indeed, in the mid 1920s, a Philadelphian "klavern" published a flyer that read: "[W]e should register and fingerprint all aliens. Stop immigration for ten years. Deport all aliens and undesirables. Banish from our country every foreign 'ism,' Nazism, Communism, Fascism." Prewar advocates of nativism such as U.S. Senator Henry Cabot Lodge still drew a distinction between "Teutonic Italians," whom they welcomed, and southern Italians, whom they despised and wished to keep out of the United States. Yet, as *La Libera Parola* denounced, "the Ku Klux Klan lumps together all the people from Italy and wants to throw them overboard."[19]

Klansmen's anti-Italian attitude was not only verbal. A few Italian immigrants were injured on the occasions of demonstrations staged by the Ku Klux Klan in western Pennsylvania. As a result, delegations of Philadelphia's lodges of the OSIA made their way across the state in order to participate in local protest rallies. OSIA Supreme Venerable Giovanni Di Silvestro himself attended the gatherings. *La Libera Parola* also attacked the two major parties for their appeasing approach to the Klan in the peak years of its influence in the mid-1920s.[20]

When Italian Ambassador Vittorio Rolandi Ricci came to Philadelphia in May 1921, the *Evening Bulletin* contended that "the Italians have been tested and found of the metal that quickly emerges from the 'melting pot' into the moulds of good citizenship, and Ambassador Ricci's visit directs attention to the distinction of the local leaders who were his hosts, and the patriotic quality of their Americanized countrymen." Such remarks were made on the occasion of Memorial Day and echoed the commendation of the patriotism of the Philadelphians of Italian ancestry during the war months. Yet, they no longer represented the prevailing characterization of the population of Italian descent in the postwar years. Actually, a cartoon published in the *Evening Ledger* in March of the following year, which derogatorily depicted Italians as shoeshines and mobsters, well epitomized the reemergence of prejudices against the members of this minority group during the early 1920s. Significantly enough, while the degree of ethnically based residential segregation of Italian immigrants and Italian Americans underwent a decline in Philadelphia between 1910 and 1920, it rose again to the prewar level in the subsequent decade.[21]

As the views of Labor Secretary Davis themselves in part reveal, much of Philadelphians' hostility toward fellow residents of Italian descent resulted from these latter's supposed involvement in organized crime. A grand jury investigation into the city's racketeers conducted in 1928 demonstrated that local gangsters were primarily of Jewish background. Nonetheless, Philadelphia's newspapers had tended to stress the leading role of Italian Americans in criminal organizations since the early days of Prohibition. At that time, the Lanzetti brothers, born of a family of Italian origin, began their rise to power in South Philadelphia's underworld. By the mid-1920s, Pius, Ignatius, Lucien, Teo, Leo, and Willie Lanzetti had come to control the dope ring as well as prostitution, bootlegging, and numbers writing in South Philadelphia's "Little Italy." Their ruthless rule was a godsend to the local press because newspapers relied primarily on racket-associated news to broaden a readership fascinated with violence and criminality.[22]

The repeal of the Eighteenth Amendment in 1933 did not deprive Philadelphia's English-language newspapers of crime stories featuring Italian or Italian American racketeers. A bloody war for control of the numbers game broke out between the Lanzetti brothers and John Avena, another Mafia chieftain with an Italian-sounding last name. At least twenty-five murders were related to that struggle, including the killings of Avena and Pius, Leo, and Willie Lanzetti.[23]

It seems that such pieces resulted mainly from the attempt to increase the circulation of newspapers by pandering to the taste of their readers for violence and the macabre. When Willie Lanzetti was killed in 1939, for instance, a detailed account in the *Evening Bulletin* described how his corpse was found beheaded with the head sewed up in a burlap bag and a bullet in the brain. Nonetheless, these articles also played upon ethnic prejudice and thereby contributed to perpetuating anti-Italian stereotypes that associated Italian Americans with organized crime. In particular, as Italian Vice Consul Luigi Villari had already complained as early as 1908, the overemphasis on offenders of

Italian descent in newspaper reports about violent acts fostered negative attitudes toward Italian American defendants in the courts of the city. Specifically, although Mafia activities were then confined to few regions in southern Italy, the English-language press in Philadelphia tended to convey the idea that dishonesty as well as bloodthirstiness were national traits of the Italian people. The local press also implied that immigrants had imported these characteristics and that almost all the Philadelphians of Italian ancestry were at least potential criminals. As Giovanni Di Silvestro still complained in the late 1930s, "[T]he American press takes the opportunity of any felony to lay the blame on the Italians and makes a point of stressing the Italian origin of the offenders in banner headlines." For example, in a two-page-long article that appeared in its widely read Sunday edition on 20 May 1934, the *Philadelphia Daily News* portrayed South Philadelphia's "Little Italy" as the domain of the "kings of the underworld" and the "gangdom" of "triggermen." In this district, according to the newspaper, extortions, banditry, robberies, and murders were "typical of everyday life among Premier Benito Mussolini's former countrymen."[24]

Historian Mark H. Haller has stressed the persistence of the close links of Philadelphia's racketeers to some politicians, law enforcement agents, and members of the ethnic communities into the 1930s. This intertwinement, however, seemed to have a specific Italian flavor in the reports of the city's English-language newspapers. The local press was even eager to dwell upon the alleged offenses of a few local Italian American elective judiciary officials. The *Evening Bulletin* exposed the connections of Italian American police magistrate Joseph Perri to well-known gamblers and revealed that he had extorted money from prisoners to release them. Likewise, although it was a pro-Democratic daily, the *Philadelphia Record* could not refrain from publishing stories about the supposed corruption, misdemeanors in office, and felonies of Italian American Democratic magistrates Charles Amodei and Angelo M. Panetta. The English-language newspapers also covered events that emphasized violence within the Italian American settlements. In late January 1933, for instance, both the *Public Ledger* and the *Philadelphia Inquirer* carried front-page reports of a bomb attack that blew up the house of Giovanni Di Silvestro and killed his wife. They linked this episode to a series of previous acts of terrorism that Di Silvestro's fellow-ethnic political opponents had presumably committed.[25]

The common experience of anti-Italian sentiments that Italian Americans shared again in Philadelphia after World War I helped them overcome their localistic divisions and consolidate the sense of Italianness which had begun to emerge during the war. Remarkably, the campaign against the restriction of immigration witnessed the participation of the representatives of all the different subnational components of Philadelphia's community. Italians and Italian Americans eventually found some mutual ground, resulting from the awareness that they were discriminated against because of their common national ancestry. They, therefore, established an American Committee Against Racial Discrimination to lobby the city's congressmen against the passing of the national origin system. In addition, despite the declining influence of radical groups in Philadelphia in the aftermath of the "Red Scare," parades for the release of Sacco and Vanzetti, fund raisers for their defense, and demonstrations of public protest against their electrocution provided opportunities to unite Italian Americans in a common effort. This sense of purpose superseded regional and provincial animosities as well as political cleavages and social difference. Thus, a pro-Fascist *prominente* from Abruzzi such as Giovanni Di Silvestro, who had agreed to serve as vice president of a Comitato pro Sacco-Vanzetti, could find himself by the side of a Socialist common laborer from Calabria such as Antonio Margariti.[26]

The implementation of the national origins provision of the 1924 Quota Act also contributed to undermine the parochial identities of Italian Americans in Philadelphia. The volume of Italian immigration nationwide never fell below 29,000 people per year in the early 1920s after a peak of 349,042 in 1920. Therefore, by restricting the number of Italian immigrants to the United States to only 5,802 individuals per year, the new legislation put an end to the inflow of *paesani* who had formerly strengthened the ties of Philadelphia's Italian Americans to their native villages, provinces, or regions. Actually, 12,136 Italian immigrants arrived in Philadelphia between 1911 and 1914. Their number fell to 4,525 in the following five years, since the outbreak of World War I virtually halted emigration from Italy until 1919, and rose again to 9,421 from 1920 through 1924. Nonetheless, as few as 3,109 Italians came to Philadelphia between 1925 and 1930.[27]

The restrictionist legislation of the 1920s also closed the era of the "birds of passage," temporary or even seasonal newcomers who travelled back and forth across the Atlantic between their home town in Italy and Philadelphia. Indeed, according to historian Caroline Golab, repatriates were one of the "two categories which accounted for a majority" of the Italian immigrants to Philadelphia until the 1920s.

Giovanni Di Silvestro argued in 1908 that newcomers from Italy just wanted to work, make money, and go back to their native country. Likewise, in the view of Michele Renzulli, a professor of Italian literature at Temple University and a contemporary eyewitness, the final goal of a large number of the Italians who arrived in Philadelphia before World War I and in the early postwar years was to return to their birthplaces and enjoy their American savings there. The proceedings of the First Congress of Italians in the United States, which convened in Philadelphia in 1911, cast further light on both the sojourner mentality of Italians and the persistence of their ties to their native land. Actually, appeals to immigrants to naturalize went hand in hand with petitions to the Italian government to smooth procedures for the repatriates who wished to regain their Italian citizenship. Yet, the restrictive legislation of the 1920s put an end to temporary and seasonal immigration from Italy and cut another channel that had previously contributed to keeping subnational loyalties alive in Philadelphia's community.[28]

Statistics on Italian "birds of passage" include no breakdown for single cities. Yet, even nationwide data can provide a clear picture of the disruptive impact of immigration restriction on the flow of Italian temporary newcomers. The total number of Italian returnees from the United States was 1,058,000 from 1902 to 1910 and ranged between 100,000 and 150,000 yearly from 1911 to 1914. After migration between the two countries came to a temporary end during World War I, 76,910 Italians made their way back to their mother country in 1919 in the wake of the enactment of the 1917 Literacy Test that excluded people who could not read and write in their native language. Following the passing of the Quota Acts, the annual average number of Italian repatriates further fell to 44,277 between 1921 and 1924, to 40,893 between 1925 and 1927, and to as few as 12,846 between 1928 and 1940. Moreover, while an estimated 63.2 percent of all Italian immigrants to the United States returned to Italy during the second decade of the century, this percentage dropped to 25.6 percent in the 1920s and to 8.5 percent in the 1930s.[29]

The Italians who decided to remain in Philadelphia after the enforcement of the Quota Acts were aware that their immigration had become permanent. Thus, they realized that localistic divisions hindered them in coping with their adopted society. By the mid-1930s, the local Italian American organizations had undergone a phase of consolidation along national lines. The OSIA incorporated a number of village-based societies as new lodges and spearheaded a reorientation of community life toward a fuller sense of national identity that characterized the Order in other cities such as Cleveland, Providence, San Francisco, and Utica. Additional clubs established along subnational lines merged together in Philadelphia, and thereby overcame their initial parochial nature, in order to survive in the aftermath of the economic crisis.[30]

Many associations, including the previously mentioned Unione Abruzzese, also began to accept individuals of Italian descent regardless of their geographical background in their native land. The end of mass immigration from Italy to the United States, as well as the emergence of an American-born and English-speaking second generation of Italian Americans, made previous membership requirements anachronistic. Indeed, the children of the immigrants, who grew up in a city located thousands of miles from their ancestral villages, could hardly share the localistic sense of allegiance of their parents. Furthermore, as an editorial in *L'Opinione* pointed out in 1933, it was absurd that a Russian Jew could join the Unione Abruzzese because he had married a woman from Abruzzi, while a full-blooded Italian was barred from the same association because he or his parents had been born in another region.[31]

This article in *L'Opinione* not only called for building bridges across subnational divisions within the Italian American community. It also reflected the increasing conflict between Philadelphians of Italian descent and other ethnic minorities such as the Irish and the Jews. Before gaining momentum in the 1930s in the wake of the persistence of the Depression, ethnic antagonism originated in part because Italian American workers initially met the Irish and the Jews above all at the workplace. The proprietors, supervisors, and foremen of the Italian American laborers in the construction industry were mostly Irish. Similarly, families of eastern European Jewish descent owned such clothing firms as Pincus, Middishade, and Makransky in which Italian American tailors made up the great bulk of the work force. In addition, since Irish, Polish, and Italian workers competed to secure the same unskilled positions available in the city, shrinking job opportunities exacerbated ethnic animosities during the decade of the economic crisis. So did the struggle for cheap housing following the territorial expansion of Philadelphia's "Little Italies." This conflict gained momentum as the children of the immigrants came of age, got married, and moved out of their parents' homes in the late 1920s and 1930s.[32]

The incorporation of the Graduate Club, which occurred in 1931 after a number of unofficial meetings in the late 1920s, provides an illuminating example of the new fashion of social networking among Italian Americans in Philadelphia. This association was open to any college graduate of Italian ancestry and its membership chiefly comprised physicians and lawyers. The Graduate Club had two main purposes. On the one hand, it planned to promote the business activities of white-collar professionals. On the other, it sought to offer a counterpoint to the traditional stereotyped images of Italian Americans either as illiterate and unskilled laborers or as bloodthirsty and ruthless gangsters.[33]

Of course, there were also countertrends to the consolidation of Italian American societies along national lines during the interwar years. In 1934, for instance, Antonio Valeo and Giuseppe Cianfalone founded the Circolo Maidese in Philadelphia. The purpose of this localistic association was "to get all the people from Maida living in Philadelphia together as if they were a single family." Yet, even if the Italian American community never achieved a comprehensive social unification under any single organization, the efforts to preserve the existence of subnational associations were now confined primarily to Italian immigrants such as Valeo or Cianfalone themselves. Conversely, such endeavors hardly affected the second-generation Italian Americans who had been brought up far from the localistic rivalries that usually split residents of even adjoining villages in Italy.[34]

The merger of Italian American organizations across subnational divisions occurred in other communities. For instance, in Kenosha, Wisconsin, immigrants from northern Italy usually looked down upon newcomers from Calabria. By 1935, however, their American-born children had established a single society that welcomed any individual of Italian descent. Similarly, the emergence of a spirit of national unity also shaped the reorientation of associational life among Italian Americans in Providence in the 1930s. The establishment of the Aurora Club of Rhode Island in this city in 1932 replicated the foundation of the Graduate Club in Philadelphia in terms of both membership and goals.[35]

The American-raised offspring of the Italian immigrants was more tolerant of regional diversities and more inclined to join forces with fellow Italians than their parents had been. However, defensiveness against anti-Italian prejudice and discrimination continued to be the main force that bound together Italian Americans from disparate regional backgrounds. The idea that the children and the grandchildren of the Italian newcomers had to close ranks regardless of the place where their ancestors had been born in order to stand up for their rights and to compete successfully with other nationalities usually characterized the calls for unity within the Philadelphia community. As Francesco Saracco, a member of the Società di Mutuo Soccorso e Beneficienza Unione Calabrese, pointed out with reference to the factionalism that separated his fellow ethnics along subnational lines, "[S]ingle flowers do not make up a wreath and isolated soldiers cannot win a battle. Only by getting together... can soldiers be strong, fight, and protect themselves." Similarly, elaborating on the reason why Philadelphians of Italian ancestry should stand together, L'Opinione maintained that "it is necessary we strike back effectively at a long tradition according to which Italian Americans can be denied everything just because they are of an ancestry of their own." This newspaper also urged Italian Americans to follow the example of the city's Germans and Irish. In the views of L'Opinione, these two groups reacted against the ethnic discrimination that had previously prevented their election to public office in Philadelphia by establishing two cohesive political organizations that allegedly swept away subnational divisions. According to the Italian-language daily, Italian Americans should do the same.[36]

Indeed, politics provides an illuminating example of the shift of Philadelphia's Italian Americans from regional or provincial loyalties to one national identity. Politics also highlights the reasons that induced many members of the community to overcome localistic rivalries.

When Eugene V. Alessandroni, an Italian immigrant from the Abruzzi region, ran for the Court of the Common Pleas in 1927, the recurring theme of the campaign that the Unione Abruzzese orchestrated on his behalf was the call for the election not of Philadelphia's first judge of Italian origin but of the city's first judge from Abruzzi. Such regionally oriented political campaigns, however, had died out by the beginning of the following decade. Representatives from a number of Italian American associations named after disparate places throughout Italy established a confederation called Società Unite in 1931. The purpose of this organization was to unite the votes of the Italian American electorate in Philadelphia and deliver that bloc to the Republican candidate for mayor, J. Hampton Moore. In return, since jobholders of Italian descent were still underrepresented in clerical occupations at City Hall as opposed to employees of Anglo-Saxon stock, the leadership of the Società Unite expected to obtain a larger share of the municipal patronage for the Italian American community as a whole from the incoming city administration. By the same token, protesting against anti-Italian discrimination in judicial appointments, even the Unione Abruzzese joined the drive to lobby Governor Gifford Pinchot to appoint any Italian American lawyer, regardless of the place of his descent, to fill a vacancy in the Court of Common Pleas in 1933. Italian Americans were still little conscious of their national ancestry in 1921. In contempt for the chauvinistic appeals of *La Libera Parola*, they failed to prevent African American Amos Scott from carrying the 2nd ward—the heart of South Philadelphia's "Little Italy"—against their fellow-Italian Henry Di Bernardino in the 1921 Republican primaries for police magistrate. Conversely, in 1934, a movement was launched to consolidate the still scattered subnational Italian American political clubs into a single association. The purpose of this organization was to support candidates of the "Italian race," as the promoters called it, against the members of other nationality groups in the forthcoming congressional and state elections.[37]

Religious life, too, offers evidence that ethnic defensiveness stimulated the cohesion of the city's population of Italian descent after decades of conflicts and divisions that had split up their community along subnational lines. Dennis Cardinal Dougherty, the Irish American archbishop of Philadelphia, closed a few Italian national parishes in the early 1930s in order to foster the religious acculturation of the local Italian American Catholics. St. Rita's, which had served an Italian-language congregation in South Philadelphia since its establishment in 1907, was turned into a territorial parish in 1930. Three years later, Cardinal Dougherty also interdicted the church of Our Lady of Good Counsel and required its parishioners to join the integrated territorial church of the neighborhood of their residence instead of attending another separate Italian national parish. While the conversion of the character of St. Rita's had met with negligible resistance, the closing of Our Lady of Good Counsel set up an actual revolt that cut across any subnational sense of affiliation. Significantly enough, the backlash at the archbishop's decisions was not confined to the southern Italians and their offspring who made up the great bulk of the congregation of Our Lady of Good Counsel. It also involved the Italian American community in Philadelphia as a whole. The parishioners of Our Lady of Good Counsel occupied their own church and took a priest, Father Simplicio Gatt, as a hostage. In addition, more than twenty thousand people representing the major Italian American religious associations in the city paraded to the seat of the archdiocese to the sound of the Italian national anthem in the fruitless effort to persuade Cardinal Dougherty to change his mind. While the march itself was taking place, Italian American shopkeepers put up the shutters throughout South Philadelphia as a token of sympathy with the protesters.[38]

Such manifestations of ethnic militancy in religious life, however, were not confined to Philadelphia alone. The Italian consul general in Chicago, for instance, reported that the population of Italian descent of Rockford, Illinois, joined forces and overcame previous regional antipathies in 1935 to rebel against the decision of their bishop to impose a Polish priest on their parish.[39]

Subnational aggregation in church attendance also came to an end in Philadelphia in the interwar years. For instance, after Father Isoleri's retirement in 1926, an increasing number of southern Italians began to join the parish of St. Mary Magdalen de Pazzi. In 1937, a native of Valenzano (a southern Italian village in the province of Bari), Father Vito C. Mazzone, was even named as pastor of St. Mary Magdalen de Pazzi's church. Italian Americans from Sicily, Calabria, Campania, and Abruzzi became the largest cohorts of parishioners during his tenure.[40]

Chapter 4

Italianness in the Depression Years

Scholars have suggested that the 1930s saw the creation of a more homogeneous American working class out of previously divided nationality groups. In this view, the corporate welfare system and ethnic institutions such as mutual-aid as well as savings and loan associations generally provided for first- and second-generation immigrant workers during the 1920s. Nonetheless, these traditional sources of support collapsed and went bankrupt in the wake of the Depression. As a result, the Democratic Party and the movement for industrial unionism, which eventually originated the Congress of Industrial Organizations (CIO), replaced them as vehicles to promote and protect the welfare of ordinary people of foreign ancestry. As this argument has it, ethnically oriented beneficial organizations and savings banks contributed to preserve the foreign heritage of their patrons. Conversely, the Democratic Party and the CIO operated primarily as cross-ethnic institutions through which laborers of different nationality groups found a common ground to defend their own class interests and to acquire an American identity. As Gary Gerstle has pointed out, although the Democratic Party worked feverishly to secure the vote of the hyphenated electorate, the Roosevelt administration did not pass any specific measures for ethnic groups. Yet, nationality minorities profited by the New Deal because their members bulked large among the destitute and the industrial workers whose concerns were addressed by the federal relief programs and labor legislation of the 1930s.[1]

The economic crisis deeply affected Philadelphia's Italian Americans. The South Philadelphia district, where most Italian Americans lived, had the highest unemployment rates citywide in 1929 and the early 1930s. The percentages of the residents out of work in these areas, which broadly corresponded to school districts 3 and 6, were 18.9 percent and 14.8 percent in 1929, 19.7 percent and 15.0 percent in 1930, and 35.7 percent and 29.1 percent in 1931. Furthermore, about one third of the family heads who applied to the city's settlement houses for relief in the early 1930s were of Italian origin. Relief, however, hardly helped Italian Americans make ends meet. As the daughter of an Italian-born laid-off worker of the Philadelphia and Reading Railroad Company wrote President-elect Franklin D. Roosevelt after the 1932 elections, "[W]e can't go out because we haven't any shoes, clothing, or coats. We stay in the house all the time.... The house is almost empty. Only four chairs and beds are in the house. The welfare is only giving us $ 4,50 a week and a quart of milk every day."[2]

As mentioned earlier, the radio industry and clothing manufactures were the leading employers of Italian Americans in Philadelphia in the pre-Depression years. RCA began to lay off its own work force at the very outset of the economic crisis. In addition, for laborers who managed to keep their jobs, wages fell from a minimum of twenty-eight dollars per week in 1927 to an average of fifty dollars per month in the mid-1930s. Unemployment took even a heavier toll of the garment sector, which had already undergone the beginning of a steady decline by the mid-1920s. In the wake of the Depression, many clothing companies shut down and relocated to farm areas of New Jersey or as far away as Cuba in search of cheaper workers who could keep their operation profitable despite the collapse of sales. The building trades, another major source of occupation for Italian Americans, were heavily struck, too. For example, the number of Italian American contracting companies fell from sixty-nine in 1927 to fifty-six in 1930.[3]

The economic crisis also swept away welfare capitalism. Philadelphia was notorious as "the national sweatshop nest" in the 1920s. At that time, clothing companies such as the A. B. Kirschbaum Co. resorted not only to the open shop, scabs, police repression, and courts' injunctions but even to gangsters in order to fight against unionization drives and to break strikes. Employers had managed to reduce the number of unionized workers in Philadelphia to a mere 10 percent of the city's labor force by the end of the 1920s. They achieved this aim not only by the heavy-handed methods described above, but also through various schemes to provide welfare benefits for their own workers. For instance, the programs of the John B. Stetson Hat Company—a manufacturer that provided many Italian Americans with jobs, as noted earlier—were well known nationwide. They ranged from life insurance and profit-sharing plans to turkey giveaways on major holidays. They also included access to a building loan association, a cooperative store, and a savings bank as well as a great number of recreational activities. All these programs were discontinued during the Depression. As a result, Stetson's employees walked out of the company union and joined the United Hatters, Cap, and Millinery Workers International.[4]

Nevertheless, the impact of the economic crisis on the ethnic structures of the Italian American community in Philadelphia was not as devastating as one might expect. For instance, a random sampling of the ads that the local Italian-language press carried through 1942 offers evidence that the collapse of the stock exchange in 1929 did not cause the demise of the sizable core of the city's leading Italian American financial institutions. Indeed, throughout the subsequent decade, they continued to offer Italian American clients an opportunity to retain their ethnic identity.[5] The Banca d'Italia & Trust Co., the Banca Commerciale Italiana & Trust Co., the Banca M. Berardini, and the Sons of Italy Bank were among the local Italian American savings banks that survived the Depression and still advertised in Italian-American newspapers after the outbreak of World War II. So did a number of Italian American insurance and real estate companies. However, the disappearance of smaller banks with subnational denominations such as the Banca Napoli, which Philadelphia's city directories last listed in 1930, demonstrates that not only the social organizations but also the financial institutions of the community had superseded localistic orientations by the late 1930s. In addition, a number of Italian American fraternal and mutual-aid associations merged across subnational boundaries in March 1933 in order to join forces for the specific purposes of preventing bankruptcy and providing benefits to their members despite the hardship of the economic crisis.[6]

Several key Italian American ethnic institutions outlived the Depression. Therefore, the premise of the thesis about the alleged role of the economic crisis in Americanizing the U.S. nationality groups can hardly be applied to the case of Italian Americans in Philadelphia. Similarly, the ensuing hypothesis that regards the Democratic Party and the CIO as vehicles for Americanization does not fully reflect what happened in this city's Italian American community in the 1930s. In fact, few Italian Americans considered the Democratic Party to be a cross-ethnic institution that could protect their class interests regardless of their national ancestry. Most Philadelphians of Italian ancestry looked to it in order to assert their own political rise as a national minority in their adoptive country. The Democratic Party itself pandered to the emerging Italian identity of the Italian American electorate to gain its votes. In addition, although Italian American workers entered labor unions in a mass in the mid-1930s, they sometimes pursued an ethnic-style unionism.

A majority of Italian Americans and the great bulk of the members of almost all the late-nineteenth-century-tide immigration groups joined the Democratic Party throughout the United States during the early 1930s in response to the failure to cope with the Depression that characterized the Republican presidency of Herbert Hoover.[7] The voting behavior of the Italian American electorate in Philadelphia mirrored a similar trend in the wake of the economic crisis. The emergence of the pro-Democratic inclination of the community, however, was delayed until the mid-1930s.

The Italian American wards in Philadelphia were a stronghold of the Republican Party before Roosevelt took office in 1933. The local political organization of boss William S. Vare secured the support of Italian Americans by means of the traditional methods of machine politics. Through the brokerage of Charles C. A. Baldi Sr., the almost-unchallenged political leader of his fellow ethnics until his death in 1930, Vare's organization supplied the unemployed with jobs in the city and county administrations, provided the destitute with free clothing and baskets of food on major holidays, and helped people in trouble with the law. In particular, the Republican machine had given Philadelphians of Italian descent a virtual monopoly on street cleaning positions since the late nineteenth century. In 1914, for instance, Philadelphia had nearly 1,600 street sweepers. They were almost exclusively of Calabrian and Sicilian ancestry. The GOP was also instrumental in granting Italian Americans jobs in the U.S. Navy yard. Vare himself was a contractor and his own company, the Vare Bros. Construction Co., was a major provider of employment for workers of Italian origin in the building trades. The Italian American electorate reciprocated these favors by casting ballots for Vare's candidates. As a result, voters from Italian background made a leading contribution to the Republican hold over local politics before the emergence of the New Deal.[8]

When Vare himself ran for the U.S. Senate in 1926, he swept the Italian American community by an astounding 97.4 percent landslide. Although New York State's Democratic Governor Alfred Smith received 56.9 percent of the Italian American vote in his unsuccessful 1928 bid for the White House, this was an exception, and the bulk of the Italian American electorate went back to the Republican fold in the following years. In fact, the GOP candidates for U.S. senator and mayor won 79.3 percent and 96.1 percent among Italian Americans in 1930 and 1931, respectively. Even President Hoover managed to obtain a 52.5 percent majority in the Italian American districts in 1932. It was only in 1934 that the Democratic Party succeeded in carrying Philadelphia's community. Its candidate for governor, George H. Earle, received 52.3 percent of the Italian American vote. Two years later, President Roosevelt increased the political following of the Democratic party within the city's Italian American electorate to 65.1 percent.[9]

Italian immigrants—along with Greeks, Portuguese, and Spanish, whose presence was however negligible throughout Pennsylvania—were the largest cohort of the foreign-born population that received aid from the federal government through the Works Progress Administration (WPA). In particular, Italian Americans profited extensively from the New Deal relief in Philadelphia. For instance, while the WPA created about forty thousand jobs to relieve unemployment in this city in June 1936, about one third of the foremen employed in WPA projects for the 1936 Democratic convention were of Italian ancestry. Moreover, 30 percent of the family heads in South Philadelphia in the area below Bainbridge Street, where 40 percent of the population was of Italian descent, were on federal relief in 1936. A number of Italian American clothing workers who had been laid off by the early 1930s also managed to obtain new jobs manufacturing uniforms for the Civilian Conservation Corps, the postal service, and federal hospitals. In addition, the Home Owners' Loan Corporation, the federal agency that authorized extensive refinancing of house mortgages at low interest rates, helped a large number of Italian American families that had been forced to mortgage their homes in the early years of the Depression. According to a 1933 report, "[I]n South Philadelphia . . . thousands have lost their property for non-payment of interests and taxes. They've been having sheriff's sales at the rate of 1,300 a month." Specifically,

52 percent of the houses of the 2nd ward, the heart of South Philadelphia's "Little Italy," were mortgaged.[10]

Ordinary Italian Americans pledged to support Roosevelt in 1936 in appreciation of the New Deal programs. As a Democratic committeeperson remarked about the president's sweep in Philadelphia's Italian American community, "[N]o amount of talking by me or by anybody else swung the Italians . . . bread in the stomach was the issue. Roosevelt gave them that." Even a Republican worker acknowledged that "most in our division regarded their vote for Roosevelt as a sacred thing. . . . I suppose the reason is, as Al Smith once said, 'no one shoots Santa Claus.' They believed they were protecting their relief and WPA jobs." The New Deal benefits, however, did not account by themselves for the pro-Democratic leanings of a majority of the Italian American electorate in the mid and late 1930s. Ethnic motivations had caused the short-lived Italian American bolt to the Democratic party in 1928. They continued to retain an influential role among the determinants of the electoral behavior of the voters of Italian ancestry in Philadelphia during the following decade.[11]

The defeat of the GOP among Philadelphia's Italian American voters in 1928 mirrored in part the national shift of the political affiliation of the minority groups of southern and eastern European origin from the Republican to the Democratic Party following the presidential bid of New York State Governor Alfred Smith on the Democratic ticket. Smith was a Catholic of Irish descent and the first politician to run for the White House as the candidate of either major party who did not belong to the WASP establishment. As such, he became the champion of the unpedigreed ethnic groups and pulled them into the Democratic fold. His stand against Prohibition also pleased the national minorities that abhorred the puritanical restraints the Eighteenth Amendment had imposed. As a result, Smith won the support of the additional ethnic voters who bolted the GOP owing to the dry pledge in the 1928 Republican platform.[12]

Smith's wet stand gratified the campaign that Italian Americans had waged against Prohibition in Philadelphia since the ratification of the Eighteenth Amendment. Actually, according to the local English-language press, the "tremendous wet sentiment" of the residents of South Philadelphia easily accounted for the surprising defeat of the Republican Party in this district. As the correspondent for the *Indiana Democrat* reported about the political feelings in South Philadelphia's "Little Italy" on the eve of the presidential election,

I drove this afternoon through miles of streets in the solid wards controlled by Bill Vare, . . . through election districts in which ordinarily not a single Democratic vote is ever cast or ever counted if cast. I saw the windows of every shop and almost every dwelling of these Italian . . . quarters displaying Al Smith election lithographs. Not one Hoover picture was to be seen. I was informed that a stone through the window is the risk that a dweller in these parts of the city takes by displaying a Hoover poster.[13]

A majority of the Italian American electorate in Philadelphia also lashed back at the GOP for the presence of incumbent U.S. Senator David A. Reed on the Republican slate in Pennsylvania. Reed was not only the co-sponsor of the 1924 Quota Act but even called it "America's second Declaration of Independence." He also allegedly advocated theories concerning the inferiority of the Italian people. Consequently, Reed became the political archenemy of Philadelphia's Italian Americans. The city's Italian-language newspapers threatened political retaliation against Reed for his role in the passing of the new immigration legislation and asked the GOP to drop him from its 1928 ticket. After Reed obtained the Republican nomination for another term, immigration restriction and its discriminatory anti-Italian motivation became major issues in the election campaign in Italian American neighborhoods. In order to profit from his congressional record to win the votes of the population of Anglo-Saxon descent, Reed maintained that the 1928 elections were a referendum on U.S. immigration legislation and that he deserved another term in the Senate because he had saved the standard of living of native workers "from the competition of hordes of aliens who were willing to work for the scantiest of existence."[14]

Of course, that campaign strategy was most counterproductive among Italian American voters. As the *Philadelphia Record* pointed out in explaining the unprecedented Democratic success in the city's largest "Little Italy" in 1928, "[S]peakers went up and down the district daily declaring that Senator Reed had said the Italians were an inferior people and worse. The whole Smith movement in South Philadelphia crystallized around that one issue." After all, the fact that Vare had specifically voted against the Quota Acts and opposed immigration restriction in general had made a significant contribution to his 1926 landslide victory in the local Italian American community. His stand for free immigration secured Vare the ballots of the great bulk of the independent electorate of Italian descent, which the Republican machine could not control through the allotment of patronage and other political services. Similarly, the chairperson of the Philadelphia Campaign Committee of incumbent US Senator George W. Pepper, the candidate that Vare defeated in the 1926 Republican primaries, acknowledged that it was impossible to stir up support for Pepper among the local Italian American voters because, unlike Vare, Pepper had endorsed the Johnson-Reed Act in 1924.[15]

Ethnic motivations influenced the electoral behavior of Italian Americans in Philadelphia even in the peak years of the Democratic vote in their community. As shown earlier, the New Deal clearly aided Philadelphians of Italian descent in terms of social security and welfare benefits. In the Depression years, the Democratic Party also resorted to traditional machine methods in order to capture Italian American voters. For example, its committeemen usually distributed food baskets among the destitute at Christmas time.[16] Nonetheless, it was the Democratic Party itself that played on ethnic politics to enhance and consolidate its own electoral following among Italian Americans in Philadelphia. Indeed, the Democratic Party managed, first, to increase significantly its electoral following and, then, to receive a relatively stable majority among Italian American voters only when its ticket acquired some ethnic appeal through the inclusion of a few local Italian American leaders as candidates for major offices.

A seat in the Pennsylvania House of Representatives was as much as an Italian American Republican politician could aim at in the early Depression years and during the previous decades. Although the city's Italian Americans had a long tradition of Republican identification, Vare hardly ever rewarded their allegiance to the GOP by granting their community some kind of political recognition. Italian Americans were still underrepresented in elective positions in Philadelphia in the 1920s. They succeeded in obtaining a couple of lesser judiciary offices through Vare's help. Joseph M. Perri was elected police magistrate in 1921 and John De Nero replaced him six years later. In addition, thanks to Vare's sponsorship, Eugene V. Alessandroni became a judge of the Court of Common Pleas in 1927. Yet, neither major party had ever slated an Italian American for Congress or the State Senate. Only five members of the community had served on the City Council before World War I—Paul Cavagnaro (1902–1904), Robert Lombardi (1910–1912), Frederick Cuneo (1912–1915), Charles C. A. Baldi Jr. (1914–1916), and Ferruccio A. Giannini (1915)—and none afterward. Moreover, in the postwar years, only two Italian Americans, Republicans Nicholas

Di Lemmo and Charles C. A. Baldi Jr., managed to win election to the Pennsylvania House of Representatives. However, while Baldi retained his seat from 1917 through 1936, Di Lemmo served only a single term between 1919 and 1920. The fact that Baldi's father was the leading Republican organizer and ethnic political broker among the local Italian Americans on behalf of the GOP machine easily accounts for the long career of Charles C. A. Baldi Jr. Vare did appease Charles C. A. Baldi Sr. with a seat in the State Lower House for his son. But as long as Vare could rely upon his own patronage and other political favors to carry Philadelphia's community for the Republican party, he did not have to place other Italian Americans on the ticket of the GOP in order to secure the votes of their fellow ethnics.[17]

After all, going over to the Democratic Party because Vare neglected their community in the allotment of political recognition would have been useless for Italian Americans because Philadelphia was virtually a one-party city. Vare's hold over local politics was so pervasive and unchallenged that the chairperson of the Democratic City Committee, John O' Donnell, was on the Republican payroll. The GOP even paid the rent of the Democratic headquarters in Philadelphia. Significantly enough, when Charles Pellegrino—a Democratic precinct captain—asked the Democratic City Committee to pay the poll tax on behalf of a number of eligible unemployed Italian American voters of his own district as late as 1932, O'Donnell told him to advise his constituents to register Republican and charge the registration fee to Vare's organization.[18]

In 1928, however, the Democratic Party—which enjoyed more freedom from Vare's control on the occasion of presidential elections than in local contests—slated Italian-born former Republican activist Biagio Catania for the Pennsylvania House of Representatives in South Philadelphia. Democratic officials hoped that a vote-for-a-fellow-ethnic campaign could bring additional support to Alfred Smith's candidacy in the local "Little Italy." Placing Catania onto the Democratic ticket turned out to be a wise decision. Not only did Smith carry the Italian American community, but Catania himself became the first Democratic representative of Italian origin to serve on the General Assembly of Pennsylvania. Similarly, in 1932, two other Italian American Democratic candidates for the Pennsylvania House of Representatives—Anna M. Brancato and Charles Melchiorre—managed to get elected in South Philadelphia, although President Hoover received a majority of the votes of their fellow ethnics.[19]

The response of Italian Americans to the presence of Catania, Brancato, and Melchiorre on the Democratic slate proved that ethnic politics could become a pivotal tool to counter the GOP among nationality groups. The Democratic Party lacked patronage to win votes among the destitute who still depended on Republican workers to make ends meet in the early Depression years. Yet, it could cash in on the allotment of places on its own ticket to lure voters of foreign descent in Philadelphia. This was the strategy of a group of independent Democrats who thought that, with the weakening of the GOP nationwide in the wake of the economic crisis, it was high time to get rid of Vare's hold over their own party and to challenge the Republican hegemony in Philadelphia's politics as well. In 1933, the anti-Vare Democrats established the Independent Democratic Campaign Committee (IDCC). Under the leadership of John B. Kelly, a millionaire brick contractor of Irish ancestry and a well-known former rowing Olympic champion, the IDCC aimed to defeat O'Donnell's slate in the 1933 Democratic primaries for county and city offices and to move on to win the general elections. Of course, the New Deal was the paramount campaign issue for independent Democrats. They argued that a vote for the candidates of the IDCC was a vote for Roosevelt and his relief programs. But the IDCC also made a point of being competitive in Vare's ethnic strongholds because Kelly and his allies regarded the local 1933 contests in Philadelphia as a dress rehearsal for the 1934 gubernatorial election. In 1933, they endeavored to lay the foundation of a coalition of voters that could ensure a Democratic victory in 1934. In this view, without the support of ethnic minorities in urban areas, it would be almost impossible to outweigh the traditional Republican hold over rural counties and capture the governorship. Previous experience with Philadelphia's Italian Americans suggested that an ethnically balanced ticket could help the Democratic Party make inroads into immigrants' constituencies. For this very reason, the 1933 slate of the IDCC accommodated representatives of Philadelphia's two largest nationality groups as well as a member of the black community. Among the candidates of the independent Democrats there were two Irish Americans (Thomas J. Minnick for coroner and Harry V. Dougherty for register of wills), one African American (Edward W. Henry for police magistrate), and as many as four Italian Americans (Joseph Tumolillo for judge of the Municipal Court along with Angelo M. Panetta, Vincent Girard, and Joseph Amodei for police magistrates).[20]

The slate of the IDCC not only defeated O'Donnell's regulars in the Democratic primaries but also won the general elections. Nonetheless, the GOP carried the Italian American community. Vare granted Italian Americans eleventh-hour political recognition. He slated John De Nero for police magistrate and Joseph De Vito for the Municipal Court. Moreover, in hard times for the community because of the Depression, Italian Americans heavily depended on the local patronage of the Republican machine. Vare's organization established welfare committees that handed out food, coal, and clothes, besides paying gas and electricity bills for the destitute. Actually, in 1931, 26.6 percent of the city's neighborhood relief organizations were political. Even the New Deal programs ended up contributing to strengthening the Republican hold over the Italian American electorate. Since federal agencies operated through state and county officials at the local level, the Republican control over these administrations in both Pennsylvania and Philadelphia enabled Vare to exploit the distribution of relief to the benefit of his own party.[21]

However, with 42.0 percent of the Italian American vote in 1933, the Democratic Party received its largest share of electoral support among Philadelphia's Italian Americans in any local contest since the turn of the century. Kelly replaced O'Donnell as chairperson of the Democratic City Committee in 1934. The awareness that the allotment of candidacies to Italian American leaders had helped the Democratic party make inroads among the rank and file members of their community persuaded him to continue to accommodate Italian American politicians within the Democratic ticket in the mid-1930s. Specifically, Joseph Marinelli obtained the Democratic nomination for the U.S. House of Representatives in 1934. Two years later, the Democratic City Committee endorsed Anthony Di Silvestro for the Pennsylvania Senate. Marinelli was a prominent South Philadelphia attorney. Di Silvestro operated a pharmacy in the heart of South Philadelphia's "Little Italy" and had become the editor and publisher of *La Libera Parola* after the death of his father Arpino Giuseppe. U.S. representative and state senator were the highest offices for which either major party had ever slated an Italian American from Philadelphia. Significantly enough, Di Silvestro did not enter the 1936 senatorial primaries. Kelly co-opted him as a replacement for the winner of the Democratic nomination, William A. Hagan, after the City Committee had induced this latter politician to withdraw to the benefit of a candidate who could more effectively secure the Italian American vote.[22]

The 1934 campaign offers an insightful example of the influence of the sense of Italianness on the Democratic vote among Italian Americans in Philadelphia. It also highlights how ethnic defensiveness strengthened the impact of this specific determinant of voting behavior.

Marinelli secured the Democratic nomination for Congress thanks to the endorsement of both Kelly and other leading officials of the party in a very divisive primary election that split the Italian American community into five factions, each one supporting a different contender of Italian descent. Unhealed post-primary scars might have been likely to jeopardize Marinelli's election to Congress in November. Yet, the article about the spread of crime in South Philadelphia's "Little Italy," published by the *Philadelphia Daily News* on 20 May 1934 and mentioned earlier in this study, provided an opportunity to unite the Italian American electorate beyond Marinelli's candidacy. It also helped downplay rumors that Marinelli was not the true representative of the Philadelphians of Italian descent but Irish Kelly's handpicked stooge. Referring to that reportage, *L'Opinione* argued that a campaign to defame Italian Americans was under way in Philadelphia. In the view of this newspaper, the purpose of the article was to brand members of the Italian American community as mobsters in order to encourage voters of other nationality groups to cast their ballots for Marinelli's Republican opponent, incumbent Congressman Harry C. Ransley, in the fall elections. Since the GOP endeavored to exploit ethnic bigotry to prevent an Italian American politician from sitting in the U.S. House of Representatives, according to *L'Opinione*, the duty of all Italian Americans who were eligible to vote was to refute anti-Italian prejudice by creating a landslide for Marinelli. Although Ransley eventually defeated Marinelli, *L'Opinione*'s appeal to ethnic solidarity was nevertheless fruitful. Even Marinelli's leading Italian American challenger in the Democratic primaries, Michael A. Spatola, endorsed him and campaigned for him in the fall.[23]

The outcome of the 1936 elections, too, stresses the role of ethnic identity in shaping the electoral behavior of Italian Americans in Philadelphia in the 1930s. Di Silvestro won 69.9 percent of the vote in the predominantly Italian American districts of his constituency in contrast to the 65.1 percent that Roosevelt obtained.[24] Therefore, Di Silvestro clearly did not ride the president's coattails among his own fellow ethnics in his successful bid for the State Senate. The fact that he received a larger share of the ballots cast in the Italian American community than Roosevelt provides further evidence that ethnic issues made a leading contribution to the creation of a Democratic majority among Italian Americans in Philadelphia. Di Silvestro's impressive showing in the Italian districts also suggests that his fellow ethnics still recognized their Italianness in the mid-1930s and that such awareness did not yield to class consciousness in determining their party choice and voting behavior during the New Deal.

Anthony Di Silvestro had endorsed President Hoover's re-election bid in 1932. In fact, in the attempt to lure the Italian American electorate in Philadelphia by appealing to their sense of ethnic identity, the Democratic Party capitalized on the defection of several influential Italian American leaders who had bolted the Republicans as soon as the surge toward the Democrats loomed up in Pennsylvania and the United States.[25]

Charles J. Margiotti was one of them, along with Di Silvestro. A nationally known criminal lawyer who had been born of Italian immigrants, Margiotti tried unsuccessfully to wrest the 1934 Republican gubernatorial nomination from incumbent State Attorney General William Schnader. Notwithstanding his own defeat, Margiotti enjoyed a relatively large following in Philadelphia's Italian American community. Despite the hostility of the GOP machine, he received 32.4 percent of the Italian American vote, as opposed to the 6.3 percent he obtained citywide. In the aftermath of the primary campaign, as WPA investigator Lorena Hickok reported to Work Progress Administrator Harry Hopkins, Democratic officials made a deal with Margiotti. They agreed to reimburse him for the one hundred thousand dollars that he had spent on his campaign and promised him a top position in the Earle administration in order to secure the almost fifty thousand Italian American votes that Margiotti allegedly controlled throughout Pennsylvania. The agreement was productive at least in the case of Philadelphia. Many Italian Americans who had defied the directions of the Republican machine in the primary followed Margiotti when he went over to the Democratic Party and endorsed Earle for governor. For instance, in the 34th ward, where Margiotti had received 89.5 percent of the Italian American vote in the Republican primaries, Earle obtained 60.1 percent of the ballots of the Italian American electorate in November.[26]

The Democratic Party made further inroads into Philadelphia's community through the allotment of patronage to Italian Americans. Earle's election to the governorship turned out to be a real bonanza in terms of political spoils. Margiotti's appointment as the first Italian

American attorney general in the history of Pennsylvania was an outstanding gesture of recognition toward his ethnic group and earned the Democratic Party a large political following among his fellow ethnics. In addition, Margiotti surrounded himself with officials and employees of Italian descent. Six Italian Americans became his deputies: Joseph A. Rossi, Joseph J. Cimino, Adrian Bonnelly, Michael Spatola, Joseph Marinelli, and Michael Goglia. The latter four were residents of Philadelphia. Moreover, more than 10 percent of the staff of the Pennsylvania Department of Justice was of Italian ancestry during Margiotti's tenure of office. Conversely, only two Italian Americans had been listed in the personnel directory of the Department of Justice under Attorney General Schnader during the previous Republican state administration of Governor Pinchot. Neither of them had held a high-ranking position.[27]

Marinelli was the first politician of Italian descent to capture the nomination for Congress of either major party in Philadelphia. State senator was the highest office an Italian American ever won in Pennsylvania. Margiotti's appointment further raised the expectations of the Italian American community in Philadelphia. For instance, billboards reading "Margiotti for Governor" began to appear in South Philadelphia as early as September 1937 and an Italian-American Citizens' Alliance was established in mid-December of the same year to spearhead Margiotti's candidacy among local Democratic officials.[28]

Yet, the Democratic Party did not meet Italian Americans' claims for greater political recognition after 1936. Any additional increase to the benefit of Italian Americans would have been detrimental to the other ethnic minorities that were also part of the Democratic coalition and, thereby, might have jeopardized the contribution of these groups to the electoral following of the Democratic Party. As a result, a few Italian American voters who had joined the Democratic camp in appreciation for Kelly's ethnically balanced tickets began to go back to the Republican column. This phenomenon, too, highlights the persistence of the Italian identity of Philadelphia's Italian Americans as a main source of their partisan allegiance throughout the 1930s.

The 1938 elections well exemplify both these trends. The business of choosing a candidate for governor split the Democratic Party in Pennsylvania. U.S. Senator Joseph F. Guffey slated incumbent Lieutenant Governor Thomas Kennedy. Conversely, Philadelphia's Democratic leader Kelly, outgoing Governor Earle, and Secretary of the Commonwealth David Lawrence supported the bid of Charles Alvin Jones, the county solicitor of Allegheny County in western Pennsylvania, for the Statehouse. In the hope of profiting by the ensuing infighting within the Democratic Party, Margiotti, too, entered the 1938 gubernatorial primary.[29]

Margiotti's opponents exerted a strong appeal in terms of the socioeconomic determinants of the vote. Kennedy easily embodied the New Deal because his main supporter, U.S. Senator Guffey, was Roosevelt's man in Pennsylvania as well as the provider of federal patronage in this state. Moreover, as secretary-treasurer of the CIO, Kennedy could potentially enjoy a massive following among the large Italian American membership of Philadelphia's locals of the CIO-affiliated Amalgamated Clothing Workers of America. Likewise, as the candidate of the Earle administration, Jones was associated with the social and pro-labor measures of the so-called "Little New Deal" of Pennsylvania, which reproduced a few pivotal measures of Roosevelt's social and labor legislation at the state level.[30]

Nevertheless, Margiotti managed to carry the Italian American community with 62.5 percent of the vote in the Democratic primaries. Since he won only 13.3 percent in Philadelphia as a whole, his success resulted primarily from the ethnic appeal of his candidacy based on of his Italian ancestry. After all, Margiotti's running mates in the primary elections—Slovak American State Senator John J. Haluska for lieutenant governor and Irish American Mayor of Johnstown Edward McCloskey for U.S. senator—won little support among Italian Americans. Haluska obtained only 33.3 percent of their votes, while McCloskey got only 5.3 percent.[31]

Margiotti was not only unsuccessful in securing the endorsement of Democratic officials in his bid for the nomination for governor. After he refused to withdraw from the primary contest, Earle also dismissed him from the position of attorney general. The governor did not replace Margiotti with any of his Italian American deputies but selected a lawyer who did not belong to Margiotti's nationality group as the new attorney general. The appointment of Margiotti to Earle's cabinet had flattered the ethnic pride of Italian Americans. Conversely, the failure of the Democratic party to endorse Margiotti for governor and his dismissal wounded their ethnic self-esteem. His supporters advised the Italian American electorate to vote a straight Republican ticket in November 1938 in order to avenge itself for the "mistreatment" of Margiotti by the Earle administration, since the governor himself was running for the U.S. Senate. As a result, the Italian American vote for the Democratic Party fell from 65.1 percent in the 1936 presidential election to 52.5 percent in the 1938 senatorial contest.[32]

The defection of a few Italian Americans to the GOP also resulted from the balanced-ticket strategy that the Republican Party, too, adopted to regain the support of the ethnic minorities in Philadelphia in the late 1930s. After Marinelli's defeat in 1934, Democratic officials decided that state senator was the highest office for which they could productively slate a politician of Italian descent. For this reason, in 1938, the city's Democratic Committee refused to endorse not only Margiotti for governor but also two other Italian Americans—attorney Louis A. Manfredi and incumbent Police Magistrate Vincent Girard—for Congress. Consequently, both of them waged an unsuccessful primary campaign against incumbent Congressman Leon Sacks for the Democratic nomination in South Philadelphia's first district of the U.S. House of Representatives. This was the same district where Marinelli had run in 1934. Instead, the GOP slated lawyer John Alessandroni, Eugene's brother, for Congress against Sacks in 1938 and Temple University law professor John Da Grossa for state senator against Anthony Di Silvestro in 1940. In both years, the Republican ticket also included candidates of Italian descent for the Pennsylvania House of Representatives in larger numbers than the total of their fellow ethnics on the Democratic slate. Thus, the ethnic appeal to the Italian identity of the electorate of Italian descent, which had aided the Democratic Party in 1934 and 1936, began to encourage Italian American voters to shift their allegiance back to the Republican Party in the following years. The Democratic Party carried the Italian American community in 1938 and 1940. But the percentages of split tickets that benefited Alessandroni and Da Grossa among their fellow ethnics show the progressive return of Italian Americans to the Republican fold. Alessandroni obtained 49.3 percent of the Italian American vote in 1938, as opposed to the 47.5 percent of Republican senatorial candidate James J. Davis. Likewise, Da Grossa ran 1.5 percent ahead of GOP presidential candidate Wendell L. Willkie in 1940.[33]

The Italian ethnic identity of many Italian American voters persisted notwithstanding the alleged role of both the Depression and the Democratic Party in Americanizing nationality groups in the United States. This ethnic consciousness also prevented some of them from building stable political ties with two minorities with whom they shared membership in the Democratic party in the mid and late 1930s. African Americans and Jews were two other solid pre-New Deal Republican constituencies in Philadelphia that went over to the Democratic camp along with Italian Americans after Roosevelt's election to the White House. Yet, the local echo of such international crises as Italy's imperialistic venture in Ethiopia in 1935-1936 and the passing of antisemitic decrees by Italian dictator Benito Mussolini in 1938, as well as the persecution of Jews by Nazism in Germany, tended to bring together African Americans and Jews and to pit them against Italian Americans. On the one hand, African Americans organized boycotts of merchants of Italian descent in the wake of Italy's attack on Ethiopia in early October 1935. Furthermore, racial discord often brought African Americans and Italian Americans to the verge of riots. On the other hand, antiblack attitudes and antisemitic feelings spread in the Italian community in the mid and late 1930s. For instance, the argument that African Americans opposed Italy's intervention in Ethiopia because they were too uneducated to realize that Mussolini planned to civilize that country characterized the pro-Fascist Italian-language press in Philadelphia even before the invasion started. Similarly, when the *Philadelphia Record* took a firm stand in favor of economic sanctions against Italy during the Italo-Ethiopian War, *La Libera Parola* accused that newspaper of being subservient to the "Judaic interests." After the American Federation of Labor (AFL) had urged the boycott of Italy for her attack on Ethiopia, *La Libera Parola* also accused the AFL of selling out to corrupt Jewish chieftains.[34]

The intensification of racial tensions with African Americans and Jews inspired by the policies of the Fascist regime affected Italian American communities in other cities. Scholars have documented this strife in the cases of Jersey City, New York, and Boston.[35] In Philadelphia, however, such ethnic animosities specifically influenced the electoral behavior of Italian Americans and contributed to the retreat of several voters of Italian descent to the Republican camp. In the aftermath of Italy's invasion of Ethiopia, most of them refused to cast their ballots for African American candidates. For instance, the vote for J. Austin Norris—a black politician who ran on the Democratic ticket for the City Council in 1935—had a –0.56 correlation index with the percentage of the residents of Italian stock in his district. The attitude of the Italian American electorate toward Jewish Democratic Congressman Leon Sacks provides another insightful case in point. Sacks was elected to the U.S. House of Representatives in 1936 as the candidate of a coalition of Italian American and Jewish voters in South Philadelphia. Two years later, the repercussions of the antisemitism of

Mussolini's regime shattered this alliance. The Italian American vote for Sacks fell from 67.6 percent in 1936 to 50.6 percent in 1938 following a racist campaign that urged voters of Italian descent not to cast their ballots for Sacks because Jews were regarded as being an "inferior race" in Fascist Italy.[36]

Fascist-stimulated antisemitism added to the Italian American rivalries with Jews over housing and at the workplace that have been examined in the previous chapter. Scholars have often associated the antiblack feelings of European immigration groups with the Americanization and acquisition of a white identity on the part of their members. Yet, strife with Jews and Irish in the wake of the Depression and in the aftermath of the Italo-Ethiopian War demonstrates that Philadelphians of Italian descent hardly came to think of themselves as white Americans in the 1930s despite their mounting conflicts with the local black population in these years. After all, in the mid-1930s, while ethnic animosities with African Americans were coming to a climax, the Italian American residents of the 2nd ward in South Philadelphia were among the staunchest opponents of a "whites only" housing project for urban renewal that, according to its advocates, would safeguard the racial stability of the dwellers of the neighborhood but would also encourage non-Italian people of European origin to move into this district.[37]

Indeed, the racist views of Philadelphia's Italian Americans resulted less from the elaboration of any white identity than from the appeal of Fascism to the members of the city's community. Worries about the alleged decline of the white race and assertions about the supposed inferiority of blacks echoed Fascist propaganda rather than the fact that white Europeans were closing ranks in the United States. According to *La Libera Parola*, for instance, the cruelty of the Ethiopian soldiers fighting against Mussolini's army was a proof of the barbarism of black people. Similarly, this newspaper contended that English support for Ethiopia in the war put the supremacy of the white race in danger. *La Libera Parola* also made a point of claiming the existence of an "Italian race" in its own right. Among the elements that distinguished Italian Americans from other white peoples in the United States, Di Silvestro's weekly cited the fact that the former, unlike the latter, did not engage in lynching African Americans.[38]

An Italian-oriented ethnic behavior characterized not only the political and social experience of Philadelphia's Italian Americans but also their labor militancy. They had begun to join forces with members of other minorities to pursue their class interests by the Depression years. Yet, as members of a self-conscious nationality group, they also continued to retain ethnic concerns that sometimes conflicted with an interethnic concept of transnational working-class solidarity.

The long pre–New Deal history of Italian American Republican allegiance might lead to the conclusion that a conservative attitude prevailed inside Philadelphia's community. However, some of its members had been active in unions since the late nineteenth century, although their initial forms of labor activism and struggle were confined to the Italian American community alone and hardly stimulated any attempt to join forces with members of other ethnic groups.

Indeed, the earliest unions that grouped Italian American workers in Philadelphia at the turn of the century were nothing more than temporary organizations established in order to protect their own members from the exploitation of their fellow-ethnic employers. Rudolph J. Vecoli has observed that the "most visible embodiment" of capitalism in the "Little Italies" was "the padrone-banker-labor agent." Indeed, the set purpose of *La Plebe*, an Italian-language radical weekly that briefly came out in Philadelphia from 24 August 1907 to 26 September 1908, was to defend laborers of Italian descent against the local *prominenti* and the Italian consular officials who allegedly preyed on their illiterate fellow countrymen. The editor of this newspaper was Carlo Tresca, an immigrant from Sulmona, in Abruzzi, who was to become a notable figure of Italian American radicalism in the United States. Tresca made a point of exposing Italian contractors and employment agents who extorted undue fees from prospective workers, bankers who took to the woods with their depositors' money, interpreters of courts who sold favors to people in trouble with the law, and officials of mutual-aid societies who only concerned themselves with getting rich at rank and file members' expense. He also uncovered the connivance of local Italian diplomats with these profiteers and charged them with selling unnaturalized immigrants exemptions from military duty in Italy. Conversely, *La Plebe* took little interest in promoting proletarian solidarity across national ethnic boundaries, although Tresca regarded his own fight against all those exploiters of the Italian immigrants as class warfare. He had already resorted to this strategy while editing *Il Proletario*, the then Philadelphia-based weekly organ of Italian Socialist Federation of North America, between 1905 and 1906. Even if Tresca considered himself "an internationalist by creed," he acknowledged that his concept of class struggle at that time hardly crossed the boundaries of the Italian American community. As he wrote in his autobiography a few decades later with reference to his years in Philadelphia, "I remained indifferent to the efforts made by the American comrades to bring nearer to its realization the millenium for which I myself was fighting. I was still living in Italy, both with my heart and mind. Though living in America, my thought, my talks, my habits of life and my enemies were all Italians."[39]

In subsequent years, however, Italian American laborers began to reach out to co-workers of other minorities. An Italian-language local of the Journeymen Tailor's International Union was formed in Philadelphia after the turn of the century. Italian American clothing workers also joined German and Jewish tailors in a walkout that paralyzed the city's garment industries in December 1909. In addition, Philadelphia's longshoremen of Italian origin made a relevant contribution to the strike that the Marine Transport Workers called in May 1913. This union had a large African American membership and was affiliated with the Industrial Workers of the World.[40]

After the repression of the "Red Scare" years, the Italian American workers of the A. B. Kirschbaum Co. took an active part in an unsuccessful wave of walkouts for the recognition of the Amalgamated Clothing Workers of America between 1919 and 1922. Their fellow-ethnic co-workers of the Bettain Brothers Co. also went on strike for a similar but fruitless purpose in 1923. Organizers with such unmistakably Italian-sounding last names as Albert Morriconi, Angelo Palermo, or Sam Nocella also spearheaded the unionization drives for the ACWA in Philadelphia in 1929.[41]

Moreover, the city's industrial workers of Italian ancestry, who were employed primarily in the garment and radio sectors, were glad to profit from the pro-labor legislation of the Roosevelt administration. In particular, they trooped into the ACWA as well as into the Radio and Metal Workers Industrial Union, following the implementation of section 7a of the 1933 National Industrial Recovery Act (NIRA), which granted workers the right to organize and to bargain collectively. For example, Local 156 of the ACWA acquired 389 Italian Americans out of its 392 new members in 1934, and 101 out of 105 enrollees in the following three years. Similarly, Local 56 of the same union gained 209 Italian Americans out of 305 of its new adherents between 1936 and 1937. Galvanized into action by the NIRA, Philadelphia's stonemasons, who were almost exclusively of Italian descent, repeatedly went on short strikes from 1933 through 1936. They eventually forced building companies to grant them increases in wages at the rate that their Industrial Workers of the World–affiliated union had previously set.[42]

However, most Italian American workers enrolled in locals that were Italian either by designation of the unions themselves, such as Local 139 of the ACWA ("Italian-speaking coatmakers"), or *de facto* because Italian Americans made up a large majority of their members. This latter, for example, was the case of Local 122 of the ACWA. Such an ethnic concentration may have reflected a disproportionate presence of Italian Americans in the work force of some specific shops. Nonetheless, the ACWA retained locals that were mainly Italian in membership into the 1950s.[43]

The fact that Italian American laborers were active above all in locals that were predominantly Italian in character prevented unionization from serving as an effective vehicle for Americanization. For instance, the Italian American radio workers of Philco Company organized a large rally to celebrate Italy's victory in Ethiopia and to show off their own "Italianness." Likewise, although the ACWA fiercely fought against antisemitism and had a long tradition of bringing together workers of Italian and Jewish origin, Congressman Sacks denounced the fact that several Italian American members of this union opposed his 1938 bid for reelection "making a racial issue of this campaign" in the aftermath of the passing of Italy's antisemitic legislation.[44]

Within a broader strategy that aimed at forging a more class-conscious labor movement out of divided nationality groups, the ACWA also organized naturalization drives and citizenship classes for Italian-born workers who wished to become U.S. citizens. Yet, the acquisition of American citizenship did not necessarily mean that the Italian immigrants developed an American identity and lost their Italian self-perception. The call for the Americanization by the ACWA was primarily instrumental and aimed to increase the cohort of the potential supporters of the Democratic Party with the set purpose of defending the labor legislation of the New Deal. Many Italians, however, entered the active electorate in the mid and late 1930s to support fellow-ethnic Democratic candidates such as Anthony Di Silvestro. Although such Italian American politicians as Di Silvestro were active in naturalization and registration drives, their fellow ethnics became U.S. citizens and went to the polls in response to stimuli based on the consciousness of their national ancestry. After all, the Italian-language press had been arguing since the late 1920s that naturalization and voter participation were powerful means by which Italian Americans could empower their own ethnic minority, protect their own community against the encroachments of other more active nationality groups, and further friendship between their native land and their adoptive country.[45]

Italian American electoral participation in Philadelphia doubled between 1926 and 1940. In this period, the number of voters of Italian descent who went to the polls rose by 100.7 percent. A breakdown of this growth by individual years clearly shows that each increase in turnout coincided with the enlargement of political recognition of Italian Americans on the tickets of the two major parties. When Catania ran for the Pennsylvania House of Representatives in 1928, the percentage of the Italian Americans who cast their ballots on Election Day grew by 23.7 percent over 1926. Conversely, a standstill in the allotment of candidacies to Italian American politicians in 1930 inspired a drop of 8.2 percent in voter participation among their fellow ethnics. Two years later, however, the presence of Brancato and Melchiorre on the Democratic slate caused a further rise in Italian American turnout. Even if Roosevelt could not exert an ethnic appeal as strong as Smith's in 1928, in 1932 Italian American voter participation increased by 16.8 percent over 1930 and by 7.3 percent over the previous presidential election. Significantly enough, in response to the candidacy of a young woman like Brancato, who described herself as "the best vote-getter that the [Democratic] party has among women," female participation even jumped by 22.9 between 1928 and 1932. The Italian American turnout continued to rise in 1934, when Marinelli made his bid for the U.S. House of Representatives. Although one might have expected a decline in participation between a presidential contest and a midterm election, in 1934 the number of Italian American voters expanded by 19.9 percent over 1932. Anthony Di Silvestro's 1936 candidacy for the Pennsylvania Senate further enlarged the cohort of the Italian American participating electorate. Turnout in the community increased by 19.1 percent between 1934 and 1936.[46]

The failure of Philadelphia's Democratic Party to pander to the call of local Italian Americans for greater political recognition in the late 1930s did not halt the upward trend of voter participation in their community. The Italian American turnout continued to rise as the Republican Party, too, began to slate Italian American politicians in order to secure the votes of their fellow ethnics. Indeed, John Da

Grossa's bid for the Pennsylvania Senate on the Republican ticket in 1940 marked a further increase of 2.0 percent in electoral participation between 1936 and 1940.⁴⁷

The appeals of the Italian-language newspapers for the mobilization of Italian American eligible voters suited the needs of Fascism. In fact, in the early 1930s, Mussolini's regime tried to persuade Italian immigrants in the United States to obtain U.S. citizenship and the franchise so that they would turn into a pressure group that could influence the foreign policy of the U.S. government and attune it to the needs of Fascism. In November 1931, Italian Foreign Minister Dino Grandi himself came to Philadelphia to talk immigrants into Americanizing and to dispel doubts about the meaning of their naturalization. He stressed that, far from being unbecoming for steadfast Italians, the acquisition of U.S. citizenship was a sort of confirmation of their love for Italy. Similarly, according to Giovanni Di Silvestro, U.S. citizenship was instrumental in empowering Italians to defend the interests of their native country in the United States and to attain important goals on behalf of the Fascist regime. It is hardly by chance that the Italian immigrants who became U.S. citizens in the interwar years included such staunch nationalists of working-class extraction and pro-Fascist bending as the previously mentioned former anarchist Filippo Bocchini.⁴⁸

Scholars have also maintained that the Depression of the 1930s and the spread of consumerism, contributed to Americanizing the U.S. nationality groups. In their view, these factors caused major changes in the field of popular culture that affected both ethnic communities and their host society as a whole. Immigrants' newspapers ceased publication because the economic crisis cut down their readership substantially. Neighborhood shops that offered ethnic products had to close down because, in hard times, they could no longer compete successfully with the emerging chain stores that sold national brands at lower prices. Local radio stations helped nationality groups keep in touch with native cultures by featuring foreign-language programs and ethnic music. Nonetheless, in order to survive in the Depression years, they joined national networks and discontinued many broadcasts for immigrant minorities. In the meantime, they also underwent a process of commercialization that purposed to turn ethnic audiences into American consumers of the major U.S. brands.⁴⁹

This is a fascinating and appealing hypothesis. Yet, the case of the Italian American community in Philadelphia suggests a more complex story, which points to the persistence of the Italian ethnic identity among its members in the interwar years.

L'Opinione and *La Libera Parola* were the two most widely read Italian-language newspapers published in Philadelphia on the eve of the stock market crash in 1929. The former had a daily circulation of 35,107 copies. The latter sold 32,190 copies per week.⁵⁰

Charles C. A. Baldi Jr. inherited *L'Opinione* after his father's death in 1930. Two years later, however, shrinking profits forced him to sell his daily to Generoso Pope, a New York–based businessman who controlled a chain of Italian American newspapers. In 1935, Pope consolidated *L'Opinione* with *Il Progresso Italo-Americano*, a New York City daily. The newspaper that resulted from the merger was briefly called *L'Opinione-Il Progresso Italo-Americano* before it dropped the name of its predecessor. It was nothing more than the national edition of *Il Progresso Italo-Americano* with one additional page of local news from Philadelphia. Indeed, *L'Opinione* actually ceased publication following its consolidation with *Il Progresso Italo-Americano*. Still, the Italian American community in Philadelphia soon managed to regain an Italian-language daily of its own. In early June 1935, a few weeks after the disappearance of *L'Opinione* as a newspaper in its own right, a group of its former employees established *Il Popolo Italiano*. In order to stress the continuity between *L'Opinione* and the new daily, the name of this latter newspaper was *L'Opinione Italiana* from 2 June through 7 June 1935. It was changed to *Il Popolo Italiano* starting with the issue of 8 June to prevent a lawsuit by Pope.⁵¹

Another Italian-language weekly added to *La Libera Parola* the following year. Although the OSIA was formally a nonpartisan organization, the leadership of the Pennsylvania Grand Lodge was strictly connected to the Republican Party. Giovanni Di Silvestro, the national head of the OSIA from 1922 through 1935, campaigned for President Calvin Coolidge in 1924, was a member of the Columbia Republican League in the early 1930s, served as alternate delegate at the 1932 Republican Convention in Chicago, and was appointed to the post of director of the Italian-American Division of the Foreign Language Bureau of the Republican National Committee in 1936. Eugene V. Alessandroni—the Grand Venerable of the Pennsylvania Grand Lodge since he replaced Arpino Giuseppe Di Silvestro in 1923—was a protege of Republican boss William S. Vare, who had sponsored Alessandroni's election to the Philadelphia Court of Common Pleas in 1927. Despite the defection of many Italian Americans to the Democratic Party in the

1930s, Alessandroni kept his Republican allegiance throughout this decade. After Anthony Di Silvestro had sided with the Democratic Party and run for the Pennsylvania Senate on its ticket in 1936, Alessandroni saw to it that the Pennsylvania Grand Lodge expelled Di Silvestro from the OSIA and discontinued the use of *La Libera Parola* as its own organ. Consequently, the Pennsylvania Grand Lodge needed a mouthpiece of its own and decided to bring out a new Italian-language weekly, *Ordine Nuovo*. This newspaper was designed to compete with *La Libera Parola* and to target primarily the Italian American readership in Philadelphia, where Anthony Di Silvestro had his own constituency.[52]

The same random sampling of the ads in the Italian-language press used earlier offers evidence that the impact of both the Depression and consumerism on Philadelphia's Italian American community did not impair the ethnic identification of its members in the purchase of commodities. National brands such as Planters Nut and Chocolate Co. or Pepsi-Cola began to spread into the Italian American market during the 1930s. But some, like Camel, long coexisted with small Italian American companies, such as De Nobili Cigarettes or Sole Mio Cigars, which were still on sale as late as the early 1940s. In addition, a few national companies targeted Italian Americans with tailor-made commodities that met their specific ethnic tastes. A leading example was California Fruit Products Co., which advertised its own "La Campagnola" (the Italian term for country-style) tomato sauce for spaghetti. This and similar marketing strategies based on the ancestral national identity of prospective buyers prove the persistence of Italian ethnic tastes among the consumers of Italian descent in Philadelphia.

American industries sometimes managed to replace their local Italian American competitors. General Electric and RCA flooded the South Philadelphia market with cheap radio sets and swept away a small company owned by Antonio Calvello, who last placed his ads in the local Italian American press in December 1927. Nonetheless, ethnic shops that belonged to *paesani* retailed these electronic products. South Philadelphia's Italian Americans bought Westinghouse refrigerators from Sorgi's, Norge washers from Louis P. Sanza's, and Zenith as well as RCA radio sets from Porreca's. This latter retailer was still in business in 1954. A directory of Italian Americans in Philadelphia for this year claimed that Norman Porreca's store was "one of the most exclusive" for the purchase of RCA products.[53]

Chain stores accounted for 48.5 percent of groceries in Philadelphia in 1935, as against a national average of 38.8 percent. The American

Stores Co. and the Great Atlantic & Pacific Tea Co. operated twelve and thirty-nine groceries, respectively, in Philadelphia in 1935. None, however, was located within any area with a large population of Italian descent.[54]

That numerous neighborhood grocers and clothes shops with Italian-sounding names continued to place advertisements in the city's Italian American press in the early 1940s further confirms that chain stores had failed to push small independent Italian American shops out of business by that time. Notably enough, Italian American stores were located not only along 9th Street, in the area of the so-called Italian market, but also throughout the Italian settlements in Philadelphia. Conversely, large retailers such as Woolworth were conspicuously missing from ads in the local Italian-language newspapers. According to an eyewitness, the absence of chain stores was a striking feature of the Italian American neighborhoods as late as 1947.[55]

Even the growth of consumer-oriented radio broadcasting did not jeopardize the community's ethnic identity. Philadelphia's stations underwent a consolidation trend in the interwar years. Nonetheless, this phenomenon, too, helped to strengthen the ethnic self-perceptions of local Italian Americans.

The history of WRAX provides a case in point. This station was established as an independent radio broadcaster in early 1930, but WPEN took it over at the end of the same year. WPEN intensified the commercial nature of its new affiliate. Yet, it reinforced the ethnic orientation of WRAX as well. Indeed, WPEN turned WRAX into a foreign-language radio station that broadcast primarily for the largest non-English-speaking nationality groups in Philadelphia. As a result, WRAX addressed itself primarily to Italians, Jews, Poles, and Germans. The Italian-language programs took the lion's share. WRAX was a daytime station and could broadcast only from sunrise to sunset. Notwithstanding this constraint, the time devoted to the Italian American audience increased over the years, from one hour per day in 1930 to as many as seven hours daily at the beginning of World War II. However, the outbreak of the hostilities between Italy and the United States not only prevented any further development of the Italian-language programs but scaled them down.[56]

WRAX was a commercial radio station that treated its audiences of foreign ancestry almost exclusively as prospective markets for its own advertisers' products. Yet, it hardly impaired the ethnic identity of its Italian American listeners. Seeking access to the pocketbooks of

Italian American consumers, WRAX turned to merchants and entrepreneurs who belonged to the same ethnic community and exploited the Old World tastes of their potential customers to sell their products. WRAX's leading advertisers for its Italian American audience were San Giorgio Macaroni and Simonni Oil, two companies that produced traditional Italian-style food.[57]

In order to lure Italian American listeners, WRAX also aired a series of programs that were of almost exclusively ethnic interest. Directed by Ralph (Raffaele) Borrelli, an immigrant from Naples who had become an American citizen in 1918, WRAX's Italian-language broadcasts included not only Italian pop and classical music but also news from Italy. WRAX even covered major events in the local Italian American community live, such as the funeral of Charles C. A. Baldi Sr. on 30 December 1930. In addition, WRAX often gave the *prominenti* opportunities to address their fellow ethnics and to discuss issues of communal interest. For instance, after his 1936 election to the Pennsylvania Senate, WRAX granted Anthony Di Silvestro a few minutes every Saturday to talk in Italian about his legislative activities in Harrisburg on behalf of his Italian American constituents.[58]

However, WRAX was not the only radio station in Philadelphia that carried programs for the local Italian American community during the 1930s. WDES, for example, featured an "Italian Hour" with news from Italy that was sponsored by Conte Luna Products Inc., a large company that produced macaroni and forty other varieties of traditional Italian-style pasta in nearby Norristown.[59]

These Italian-language broadcasts were central to the everyday life of Italian Americans in Philadelphia. They appealed to the ethnic identity of their audience and contributed to keeping it alive in terms of both culture and consumption. As Joseph Valinote remarked in a rather ungrammatical letter that asked the management of WRAX for further development of the broadcasts in Italian in 1935, "Mr. Raffaele Borrelli should be very much praised for giving the Italian programs—receiving the Italian news—music and other clear Italian talents—also informations where we can purchase something you cannot get anywhere else." Other ordinary Italian American listeners such as Donato Iverso and Amato Prudente thanked Borrelli in writing because his Italian-language programs revived their own sense of Italianness.[60]

Despite increasing pressures toward the Americanization of immigrants and their offspring in the interwar years, the rise of Fascism in Italy played a significant role in the consolidation of the emerging

Italian identity of the members of Philadelphia's Italian American community. Actually, Mussolini's regime fostered strong pride in their Italian ancestry. Although he scaled down his official protests after coming to power, Mussolini favored the cause of Sacco and Vanzetti in order to portray himself as the protector of Italians abroad. Furthermore, his government initially endeavored to make the United States lift restrictions on Italian immigration and grant Italy a quota of one hundred thousand entries per year before passing its own anti-emigration measures in the late 1920s. At the very beginning of its own rule, therefore, Fascism ended up supporting the two major campaigns that united Italian Americans in Philadelphia in the early postwar years.[61]

Because the Fascist regime apparently stood by Italian immigrants and their offspring in the United States, perhaps for the first time Italian Americans did not think that their ancestral land neglected them. They also overcame their mental images of the Italian state as a hostile entity that confined itself to collecting taxes and drafting youngsters into the army. It was this very concept of the Italian state that had initially prevented the immigrants' identification with Italy and helped the persistence of localistic senses of allegiance among Italian Americans after the unification of their mother country.[62]

After all, the growing nationalistic feelings of Italian Americans were chiefly responsible for their adherence to Fascism. Nationalism was so strong among Philadelphia's Fascists that the city's *fascio* (Fascist club) initially admitted only Italian immigrants and barred their American-born children from membership.[63]

In addition, many Fascist leaders had previously been staunch nationalists. Giuseppe Del Russo, the founder of Philadelphia's *fascio*, was an Italian veteran of World War I. So was Umberto Menicucci, a Philadelphia tailor who was also a member of the executive council of New York's *fascio*. A similar case was that of Agostino De Biasi, who had contributed to establish *L'Opinione* in 1906 and served as its first editor before moving to New York. De Biasi was an outspoken advocate of Italy's entry into World War I and supported her claims to Fiume and Dalmatia at the end of the conflict. He also became the first prominent Italian American pro-Fascist leader in the United States, although he later fell into disgrace with Mussolini.[64]

Giovanni Di Silvestro, who pledged the loyalty of the roughly three hundred thousand members of the OSIA to Fascism in his capacity as Supreme Venerable of the Order in 1922, had been a pro-war propaganda agent among Philadelphia's Italian Americans on behalf of the Italian and U.S. governments during World War I. In addition, on 25 September 1922, one month prior to Mussolini's seizure of power, Di Silvestro had signed a covenant for mutual representation between the OSIA and the nationalist Lega Italiana per la Difesa degli Interessi Nazionali (Italian League for the Safeguard of National Interests), which was to merge with the Fascist party one year later. Di Silvestro's identification with his own mother country was so strong that he did not refrain from criticizing Mussolini himself in 1928. The target of Di Silvestro's objection was a Fascist ruling about immigrants' role in politics in their adoptive lands. The Italian dictator originally forbade, at least formally, the members of the Fascist clubs abroad to get involved in the domestic affairs of their host countries in order to prevent them from being a cause of embarrassment for the Italian government. Contrary to Mussolini's initial orders, in Di Silvestro's opinion, Italian immigrants should have been encouraged to naturalize and to participate in U.S. politics so that they could lobby Congress and the White House to the benefit of Italy and protect her interests on the international scene. As shown earlier in this chapter, Mussolini's regime itself was to adopt this policy for Italians in the United States in the early 1930s.[65]

Of course, not all the members of the Philadelphia community were Fascist sympathizers. Italian Americans staged anti-Fascist demonstrations and the local Italian Consulate was the target of an anarchist bomb attempt in November 1923. Italian Americans organized a local branch of the Anti-Fascist Alliance of North America in the same year and another anti-Fascist association, the Italian Workingmen's Progressive Institute, was established in the late 1920s. Letters to the local English-language newspapers protested against a statement made by Giovanni Di Silvestro that his own fellow ethnics were 'heart and soul' with Mussolini at the time of Italy's invasion of Ethiopia in 1935. In addition, Paul Fragale, the Grand Secretary of the Pennsylvania Grand Lodge of the OSIA, and other representatives of local anti-Fascist Italian American organizations mobilized successfully to persuade Mayor S. Davis Wilson to deny permission for a pro-Fascist parade in celebration of the Italian victory at the end of the Italo-Ethiopian War in May 1936.[66]

Giovanni Di Silvestro pressured the Italian authorities into replacing the non-Aryan personnel of the consular service in the United States after the passing of the Fascist antisemitic legislation. Yet, many members of Philadelphia's community distanced themselves from Mussolini's antisemitic decrees. Frank Palumbo, the then owner of Palumbo's and the grandson of its founder, successfully organized a movement among several Italian American associations to protest against the spread of racial intolerance in Italy. After all, some Italian Americans in Philadelphia were Jews themselves and their number increased after the arrival of a few refugees who left Italy after the enforcement of the antisemitic legislation.[67]

Opposition to Fascism and rejection of the antisemitism of the Italian regime also galvanized Italian American radical groups into action in the late 1930s. Representatives of a few local labor unions published the Italian-language monthly *La Voce Indipendente* between 1938 and 1942. Likewise, an anarchist Italian American biweekly, *Intesa Libertaria*, briefly came out in 1939.[68]

Yet, the great bulk of Philadelphia's Italian Americans revealed a prevailing pro-Fascist bent. For instance, in 1927, the local branch of the Anti-Fascist Alliance of North America itself complained that it lacked enough strength and following to disrupt a pro-Fascist demonstration on the occasion of a reception for Italian aviator Francesco De Pinedo.[69]

The first *fascio* in Philadelphia was established in 1921, one year before Mussolini himself rose to power in Italy. Italian American Fascists in the United States also held their first convention in Philadelphia. In addition, not only Di Silvestro but a number of other local Italian American leaders such as Judge Alessandroni were outspoken admirers of Mussolini. All the main Italian-language newspapers— *L'Opinione*, *La Libera Parola*, *Il Popolo Italiano*, and *Ordine Nuovo*—backed *Il Duce's* dictatorship until Italy declared war on the United States in December 1941. A number of short-lived Italian American newspapers even came out to counteract the anti-Fascist propaganda. This was, for instance, the case of *Il Maglio*. Luigi Borgo, a little-known lawyer, briefly published it in the aftermath of the kidnapping and murder of Giacomo Matteotti, a leading opponent of Mussolini and a socialist member of the Italian parliament. Pro-Fascist feelings were so widespread among Italian Americans in Philadelphia that, when Mussolini's Foreign Minister Grandi visited this city on 20 November 1931, the delegations of 168 Italian American associations and clubs welcomed him at the Baltimore and Ohio Railroad station, while a huge crowd greeted him outside.[70]

Many Italian Americans in Philadelphia became receptive to the nationalistic appeal of Fascism especially after the re-emergence of

Italy's expansionism in the mid 1930s. A Comitato Amici dell'Italia (Friends of Italy Committee) was established in Philadelphia in September 1935, even before Italy's invasion of Ethiopia on 3 October of the same year. Its purpose was "to support the Italian legitimate expansionistic policy in Ethiopia" and "to show off that the sons of Rome . . . retain spiritual ties to their mother country." Few local unnaturalized Italian reservists volunteered to serve in Mussolini's army in Africa. Nonetheless, while the League of Nations was discussing the imposition of economic sanctions on Italy, tens of thousands of Philadelphia's Italian Americans paraded along Broad street on 11 November 1935 to support Italy's bid for an empire. After the League of Nations passed its sanctions, the donation of wedding rings to provide financial aid to Mussolini's colonial campaign as well as fundraising drives for the Italian Red Cross—actually, a cover-up for war contribution to the Fascist regime—became quite popular in Philadelphia's community. The city's Italian Americans also shipped copper and cotton to their mother country in order to help her dodge the sanctions. The Philadelphia chapter of the Federation of Italian World War Veterans was very active in the solicitation of funds. This organization operated under the close supervision of the local Italian consul, Ludovico Censi, and included both Italian-born American citizens and unnaturalized Italian immigrants. The Comitato Amici dell'Italia collected $32,894.60 for the Italian Red Cross on its own and also protested against the decision of the Roosevelt administration to warn U.S. citizens against travelling on Italian vessels. The lodges of the OSIA in Philadelphia raised another $31,331.06 for the Italian Red Cross. Mussolini himself officially commended them for their allegiance to Fascism on the occasion of the Italo-Ethiopian War.[71]

In response to appeals by *La Libera Parola* and *Il Popolo Italiano*, a number of Italian Americans voters even joined a nationwide letter-writing campaign and successfully lobbied their congressmen against the passing of the Pittman-McReynolds Bill. This proposed piece of legislation aimed to embargo key U.S. exports to Mussolini's military in the Ethiopian venture such as oil, petroleum, lubricants, and trucks. In particular, when the controversy over the prospective U.S. sanctions against Italy came to a climax in January 1936, Judge Alessandroni led a delegation of Philadelphia's prominent Italian Americans to Washington DC. They went to Capitol Hill for the purpose of killing the Pittman-McReynolds Bill by abetting the fears of the American neutralists who wanted Congress to vote down any initiative that could drive the United States into a foreign war. On 15 January, before the House Committee on Foreign Affairs, Alessandroni testified that Mussolini would consider restrictions on American trade in oil as an act of hostility against Italy on the part of the United States. A few days later, Giovanni Di Silvestro and a group of other lawyers of Italian descent from Philadelphia met with Senator Key Pittman and other members of the Senate Committee for Foreign Relations in order to reaffirm what Alessandroni had previously declared.[72]

As soon as Mussolini announced that the Italian army had occupied Addis Ababa—the capital of Ethiopia—on 5 May 1936, thousands of Italian Americans took to the streets in Philadelphia to rejoice over the event. They also poured into the office of the Western Union in South Philadelphia to send Mussolini and King Victor Emmanuel III telegrams of congratulations. One week later, they celebrated the proclamation of the Italian empire and the Pennsylvania Grand Lodge of the OSIA organized a "pilgrimage" of its members to their mother country from 20 August to 23 September 1936 in order to mark such a supposed turning point in the history of their ancestral land. In addition, following Italy's victory in the war, many Italian Americans vainly pressured the U.S. government into recognizing Mussolini's conquest of Ethiopia. Moreover, on 18 November 1937, two years after the League of Nations had moved to impose economic sanctions on Italy and six months after Italy had annexed Ethiopia, Philadelphia's community gathered to celebrate the alleged triumph of their motherland over the combined efforts of the fifty-two countries that held membership in the League.[73]

In early 1934, Tresca's radical newspaper *Il Martello* warned that a pro-Fascist association, the "Khaki Shirts," was making inroads among Italian Americans in Philadelphia. Even the Italian ambassador in Washington thought that this organization was too extremist. However, with a few exceptions such as the case of the members of the "Khaki Shirts," the commitment of Italian Americans to Fascism was emotional rather than ideological. Actually, when anarchist turned nationalist Filippo Bocchini—at that time an editorialist for *L'Opinione*—founded the Fascist Party of Pennsylvania and ran on its ticket for the state House of Representatives in 1934, he received only thirty-one votes out of the 70,011 cast throughout South Philadelphia. Similarly, in the 1936 presidential election, William Lemke obtained as little as 0.7 percent of the Italian American vote on the ticket of the Union party, although the leader of this party and Lemke's kingmaker was

Father Charles E. Coughlin, a well-known admirer of Mussolini, advocate of the Fascist regime, and supporter of Italy's attack on Ethiopia.[74]

However, the nationalistic appeal of Fascism had a significant impact on the Italian American community in Philadelphia. After being denigrated for decades because of their ancestry, Italian Americans were glad to identify themselves with the country of their origin as soon as the aggressive foreign policy of the Fascist regime managed to accommodate Italy among the Great Powers and made their native land respected and feared in the United States, too. According to *Il Popolo Italiano*, Mussolini had made Italians abroad proud of themselves. Similarly, in a couple of editorials for *L'Opinione*, Di Silvestro argued that, for Italian Americans, being Fascist meant "eliminating the prejudices of race, religion and extraction" that had previously haunted them. He also held that the purpose of Fascism in the United States was to bring Italian Americans together and empower them to fight for their own rights. As a welcome message to Italian Ambassador Fulvio Suvich on the occasion of his visit to Philadelphia on 25 June 1938, he argued that Italian Americans drew strength and power to make their way in American society from the very achievements of their ancestral country under Fascism.[75]

The reasons given by the Italian-language press for urging its readers to support Mussolini's Ethiopian venture provide further evidence of the mutual involvement between pro-Fascist sympathies and ethnic assertiveness. For example, *Il Popolo Italiano* pointed out that if Italy became more powerful on the international scene, Italian Americans would command greater respect in the United States. In addition, according to this newspaper, by lobbying Congress against the Pittman-McReynolds Bill, Italian Americans demonstrated that they had "the same rights of the citizens of Jewish and other races as well as of the public officials of Irish, Scottish, and German descent, who regard themselves as the true sons and daughters of this nation because, by mere chance, their names do not end with a vowel." In the view of *Il Popolo Italiano*, the protection of the interests of Fascist Italy equalled the defense of the reputation of Italian Americans, while *La Libera Parola* contended that standing by Italy's invasion of Ethiopia was necessary "to strike back at those individuals who try to diminish our rights here." Likewise, the Philadelphia edition of *Il Progresso Italo-Americano*, hailed the defeat of the Pittman-McReynolds Bill as a significant step toward the fuller empowerment of Italian Americans in the United States.[76]

The intertwinement of nationalism and ethnic defensiveness as a source of pro-Fascist feelings was not confined to Mussolini's Italian American supporters in Philadelphia alone but generally characterized their fellow ethnics throughout the United States. Noticeably enough, not only the *prominenti* but also the rank and file working-class members of Italian American communities shared this attitude. Ethnic leaders could exploit their connections with Mussolini's regime in order to strengthen their own standing and power within the "Little Italies." Ordinary people got redress for the anti-Italian ethnic intolerance and discrimination that they had long suffered in their adoptive country. Historian Gaetano Salvemini, a prominent anti-Fascist émigré who spent several years in the United States after leaving Italy, highlighted this point. As he remarked, Italians "arrived in America illiterate, barefoot and carrying a knapsack . . . they were treated with contempt by everybody because they were Italians. And now even the Americans told them that Mussolini had turned Italy into a mighty country, that there was no unemployment, that there was a bathroom in every apartment, that trains arrived on time, and that Italy inspired awe worldwide." In the opinion of another well-known anti-Fascist, Massimo Salvadori, Italian Americans embraced Fascism because "in America they became Italian nationalist." Likewise, an anonymous anti-Fascist woman of Italian descent observed that "you've got to admit one thing: He [Mussolini] enabled four million Italians in America to hold up their heads, and that is something. If you had been branded as undesirable by a quota law you would understand how much that means."[77]

In Philadelphia, WRAX radio pandered to the emerging nationalistic feelings of many members of the local Italian American community. Thereby, it further helped its members to overcome localistic divisions and to merge into one ethnic group. WRAX provided live coverage of Grandi's visit to Philadelphia from his arrival at noon to his address at a banquet of the Order Sons of Italy in America in the evening. An unprecedented number of Italian Americans who could not attend the celebrations tuned in and made this broadcast the most successful radio program in the community for several years. In addition, Ralph Borrelli himself invited the consuls and other officials of the Italian government in Philadelphia to make speeches for Italian Americans on the radio. These broadcasts usually offered opportunities to extol the alleged achievements of the Fascist regime in Italy. Likewise, the Italian-language programs covered the annual celebrations for Fascist anniversaries such as the foundation of Rome, a public holiday that Mussolini introduced to glorify the greatness of the Roman empire and its revitalization under Fascism, and the "March on Rome," the event that marked Mussolini's seize of power on 28 October 1922. The "Italian hours" on local radio stations also contributed to raise money for the Italian Red Cross at the time of the Italo-Ethiopian conflict.[78]

The official propaganda of the Fascist regime spread through the local Italian consulate and the Italian-language programs that EIAR (Italy's state-owned radio broadcasting corporation) aired for Italians in the United States. Fascism also resorted to propagandistic movies such as *Il coraggio della gioventù mussoliniana* (The Bravery of Mussolini's Youth). Pro-Fascist groups promoted other activities that helped to strengthen the new self-perception of the members of Philadelphia's community as Italians. For instance, the OSIA organized annual journeys to Italy for its members. The main purpose of these "pilgrimages," as they were called, was to facilitate the ideological indoctrination of ordinary Italian Americans by lecturers and firsthand experience of how the Fascist regime had supposedly benefited Italy and her people. Such journeys, however, also resulted in a "baptism of *italianità* (Italianness)" for the participants. Traveling from Palermo to Rome and from Trieste to Turin, Italian Americans came to feel themselves part of a broader ancestral land than their native village or region, and extended their self-referential group from the narrow circle of the *paesani* to the community of their fellow countrymen.[79]

Moreover, the OSIA resorted to campaigns that evoked the common national extraction of Italian Americans through their compelling imageries, stimulated first- and second-generation immigrants from diverse geographical backgrounds to rally together as members of a unified group, and provided them with symbols to express their Italian ethnic identity. This was the case of a drive for the legalization of Columbus Day as a public holiday in the United States. "On behalf of the hundreds thousands [sic] readers of *L'Opinione* of Philadelphia," Generoso Pope, too, joined the Columbus Day campaign and stirred it up. The Italian American leaders in Philadelphia had long exploited Columbus Day to emphasize the unity of their fellow ethnics and to call for the legitimacy of their presence in U.S. society. On the occasion of the 1920 celebration, for instance, attorney Joseph Bartilucci—whom Mayor J. Hampton Moore had recently appointed as chief clerk of the Municipal Court—declared: "We Italians have contributed to the glory of the United States. Our Mayflower came long before the Pilgrims' Mayflower. We have done our part and shall continue to do so." Roosevelt's eventual recognition of Columbus Day as a legal holiday in 1934, as Joseph Salituro has observed, was much rewarding for the ethnic pride of Italian Americans. It officially made them part of the nation's heritage because it acknowledged the role of their fellow-ethnic forerunner to the shores of the New World in the establishment of American civilization. In the words of *La Libera Parola*, for the Philadelphians of Italian descent, the celebration of Columbus Day was an opportunity both to stress the Italian contribution to American society and to show that they were proud of their Italian roots.[80]

Other organizations helped Philadelphia's Italian Americans to consolidate their Italian identity in the interwar years. The Centro Educativo (Educational Center) Arnaldo Mussolini, named after *Il Duce*'s deceased brother, on the pretext of stimulating Italian American schoolboys and schoolgirls to learn Italian, freely distributed Italian-language books that encouraged the children of the Italian newcomers to keep their allegiance to the land of their descent regardless of their U.S. citizenship. A Biblioteca Circolante del Littorio (Lictor Lending Library), which was attached to the Italian consulate in Philadelphia, served similar purposes.[81]

Indeed, although the interwar years witnessed numerous attempts to exploit public schooling in order to Americanize both the Italian immigrants and their offspring, education turned out to be a major tool that was used to reinforce the national ethnic self-image of Italian Americans. Italian classes offered people of different ancestral regions an opportunity to supersede local dialects and, thereby, an additional chance of perceiving themselves as individuals sharing a common culture. Furthermore, a few Italian schoolteachers in Philadelphia participated in the efforts of the Fascist regime to enhance the identification of Italian Americans with Italy. A recrudescence of such indoctrinating activities marked the mid 1930s in a number of other cities in the United States. Specifically, Italian Consul Leone Sircana and teachers attached to the local Italian consulate such as Marcello Zerqueni carried out these propaganda efforts in Philadelphia. Unlike other Catholic minorities, Italian Americans preferred public to parochial schools. In addition, working-class parents usually underestimated the importance of extended education and had their children leave school relatively early to find jobs so that they could contribute additional money to the budgets of their own families. Thus, low public school attendance, especially at the high school level, further helped to counteract the role of public education as a building block of American consciousness among Italian Americans in Philadelphia.[82]

Conversely, the American-born students of Italian descent attending Catholic parochial schools were exposed to an intense work of propaganda to galvanize their own Italianness. As the U.S. authorities themselves acknowledged, "[I]n the Italian parochial schools where the children are compelled to take their daily lessons in Italian from an instructor fresh from the Italy of today and aided by a textbook where everything Italian is lauded and the virtues of Mussolini and the Fascist state are extolled, there is doubtless created in the minds of the children a feeling of distinct friendliness to Italy." For instance, to make the case for the expansionist policy of the Fascist regime, an Italian-language textbook included Dalmatia and Albania within Italy's boundaries and contended that this had been "Dante's dream of Italy." Similarly, another volume implied that Corsica and Malta belonged to Italy.[83]

Fascism also relied on Italian priests to promote ethnic nationalism among Italian Americans in the United States. As a result, in Philadelphia, the influence of Mussolini's regime on the church life of the local community contributed to curb Cardinal Dougherty's attempt to Americanize the Italian immigrants and their children through Catholicism in the interwar years. This was a long-term project that the archbishop also pursued by such measures as the suppression of a few Italian national parishes such as Our Lady of Good Counsel or St. Rita's. Cardinal Dougherty's efforts, however, were of little avail. Indeed, in the archdiocese of Philadelphia, the number of the Italian parishes increased from twenty-seven in 1920 to thirty-seven in 1940. Likewise, the number of Italian parochial schools grew from six in 1920 to fifteen in 1940, after reaching a peak of seventeen in 1930.[84]

On 11 November 1929, Mussolini and Pope Pius XI's secretary of state signed the Lateran Treaties. This agreement recognized the Vatican City as a papal sovereignty and made Catholicism Italy's state religion. The 1929 concordat between the Italian government and the Catholic Church put an end to almost six decades of conflict between Italian nationalism and Catholicism that had originated from the refusal of the Catholic Church to recognize the kingdom of Italy following Italy's annexation of the papal state in 1870.[85]

Furthermore, the 1929 compact marked the beginning of years of cooperation between Fascism and the Catholic Church that conditioned the stand of the Catholic clergy of Italian origin in the United States. There were, of course, a few exceptions to this pattern. For instance, Monsignor Joseph Ciarrocchi, pastor of the Church of Santa Maria, was a forceful anti-Fascist leader in Detroit. Still, though to different degrees, the Italian Catholic priests usually operated as vehicles for Fascist propaganda among their fellow ethnics in cities such as Chicago, Cleveland, or San Francisco. Significantly, Mussolini conferred a medal on Father Fiorenzo Lupo, the pastor of St. Ambrose in St. Louis's "Little Italy," in appreciation of his services to the Fascist regime.[86]

Prominent Catholic priests of Italian descent in Philadelphia, too, became Fascist sympathizers and exploited their sacerdotal influence to talk their Italian American congregations into strengthening their sense of allegiance to their ancestral country. Fathers Vito C. Mazzone, Bruno Guasco, and Salvatore La Cavera, for instance, were active members of the Comitato Amici dell'Italia and did not refrain from supporting its campaign against the Pittman-McReynolds Act. Guasco also participated in the annual celebrations for the anniversary of the "March on Rome" and made speeches to glorify the achievements of Italy under the Fascist regime. Mazzone even used the example of Reginaldo Giuliani, an Italian army chaplain killed during the Italian invasion of Ethiopia, in order to extol the civilizing mission of Fascism in Africa and to encourage Italian Americans to rally to support Italy. Similarly, the pastor of St. Rita's did not refrain from praising Mussolini for "doing more than any other individual to stimulate respect for Italy." The Italian parishes in Philadelphia also became major centers to collect funds for the Italian Red Cross during the Italo-Ethiopian War.[87]

Chapter 5

The Impact of World War II and Its Aftermath

Italian Americans had become fully aware and proud of their Italian identity by the outbreak of World War II. Their reaction to Italy's entry into the conflict and to the repercussions in the United States of the end of the Italian neutrality exemplify the full development of this feature of their ethnic consciousness.

On 10 June 1940, the very day the Fascist regime joined Nazi Germany in the war against France and Great Britain, Franklin D. Roosevelt condemned Mussolini's decision in an address at Charlottesville. Specifically, he stigmatized Italy's eleventh-hour attack on France by the metaphor "the hand that held the dagger has struck it into the back of its neighbor." Many Italian Americans perceived the president's words as an anti-Italian ethnic slur and broke with the Democratic Party. Indeed, Roosevelt drew on derogatory stereotypes, namely the alleged fondness of the Italian people for the stiletto and their conventional representation as sanguinary wielders of knives. Resentment for the "stab-in-the-back" speech caused a significant slump in support for the Democratic Party in Italian American communities throughout the United States. Specifically, Roosevelt barely won a 54 percent majority in New Haven's Italian American neighborhoods in 1940 after having carried them by a 73 percent landslide in 1936. In addition, between 1936 and 1940, the Democratic vote among Italian Americans declined from 85 percent to 72 percent in Hartford and from 85 percent to 63 percent in Boston. The Republican vote also increased from 9 percent to 42 percent in San Francisco. Roosevelt's electoral following reached a low of 42.2 percent in New York's "Little Italy" in 1940, after the community had gone Democratic by 78.7 percent four years earlier. Democratic activists even needed police escort to avoid harassment while campaigning in Italian American wards in New York City.[1]

The "stab-in-the-back" address received extensive coverage in Philadelphia's press. In late June, *Observer*, a local weekly, predicted that Roosevelt's words would hurt the Democratic ticket among Italian Americans in November. As election day drew closer, *Il Popolo Italiano* reminded its readers of the president's speech and called upon them not to support Roosevelt because he had allegedly besmirched their motherland at Charlottesville. Indeed, a sizeable cohort of the electorate of Italian ancestry followed the anti-Democratic appeal of *Il Popolo Italiano* and the Italian American vote for Roosevelt in Philadelphia fell from 65.1 percent in 1936 to 53.5 percent in 1940.[2]

Undaunted by the growing anti-Fascist feelings in Philadelphia, *Il Popolo Italiano* also made a point of celebrating the initial victories of the Italian army in France. It even reprinted the editorials that Virginio Gayda, the spokesperson for Mussolini's Ministry of Foreign Affairs, wrote for the Rome-based *Giornale d'Italia* and several articles that came out in other Fascist mouthpieces in Italy. Furthermore, in February 1941, *Il Popolo Italiano* raised $2,520.90 among its readers for the Ente Opere Assistenziali. This association was officially an Italian welfare agency but in practice a political organization of the Fascist Party. Similarly, with the assistance of Ludovico Censi, the Italian consul in Philadelphia, and Annibale Di Febo, an employee of the local consulate, the Federation of Italian World War Veterans initiated a new fund-raising campaign for the ancestral country of its own members. It collected about nine thousand dollars for the Italian Red Cross among Philadelphians of Italian descent between 10 May and 28 June 1941.[3]

Several Italian American leaders such as Eugene V. Alessandroni also refused to return the numerous decorations that the Italian government had previously conferred on them. At that time, Alessandroni was still a judge of the Court of Common Pleas and the Grand Venerable of the Pennsylvania Grand Lodge of the OSIA. Despite the criticism of anti-Fascist groups, however, the rank and file members of Italian American associations did not remove Mussolini's fellow travellers such as Alessandroni from the offices they held in ethnic organizations. In February 1941, Ernest L. Biagi, the Grand Secretary of the Pennsylvania Grand Lodge, still took issue with anti-Fascists. A few months prior to the Pearl Harbor raid and Italy's ensuing declaration of war on the United States, Giovanni Di Silvestro even argued that Mussolini was a peacemaker who had been drawn into the war against his will because an anti-Fascist derogatory campaign by the common enemies of both Italy and the United States had undermined *Il Duce*'s plans for a peaceful settlement of the European crisis.[4]

After all, Italian Americans continued to celebrate the anniversary of the establishment of the Fascist empire in Philadelphia as late as 1940. In late November of the following year, only a few days before the Pearl Harbor raid, local lodges of the OSIA named after Fascist leaders, such as the Italo Balbo Lodge, still operated in this city.[5]

The vehemence of Roosevelt's 1940 "stab-in-the-back" speech demonstrated that, though still formally neutral, the United States had actually taken sides with France and Great Britain against Italy and Germany in the war that was being waged in Europe. As a result, several Italian American eligible voters in Philadelphia hurried to sign the electoral petitions of the communist candidates. The Communist Party had never pursued any ethnic politics strategy to secure the support of nationality groups in Philadelphia. In the opinion of the Italian American signers, however, a Communist victory in the forthcoming 1940 elections could contribute to preventing the United States from entering World War II against Italy because of the staunch neutralist stand of the Communist Party at that time.[6]

Philip Gleason has contended that World War II witnessed the climax of a period in which ethnic factors receded from prominence in discussions of national identity in the United States. He has also argued that this military conflict made the need for national unity more compelling and eventually helped to Americanize ethnic minorities. Specifically, Max Ascoli, a prominent anti-Fascist, remarked in 1942 that "the war has given the final blow to the segregation of the Italian communities in America." Likewise, historian John P. Diggins has maintained that World War II "was the fuel of the melting pot" for Italian Americans. In Lawrence Di Stasi's opinion, too, the war was a "watershed" for members of this minority group. In this view, even though the conflict did not mark the demise of Italian Americans' ethnic self-perception, it caused its "silencing" until the revival of the late 1960s.[7]

Yet, even the outbreak of hostilities between Italy and the United States failed to weaken the Italian identity of many members of Philadelphia's community. Unnaturalized Italians living in the United States were designated as "enemy aliens." This classification required them to obtain permits to travel. It also forbade them to possess certain articles such as firearms, ammunition, cameras, and short-wave radios. As a result, local leaders such as Alessandroni petitioned President Roosevelt and urged him to adopt the Eliot Bill. Such a proposed piece of legislation would have provided for the automatic naturalization of almost all the American residents of foreign citizenship who had not been involved in subversive activities. Instead of reflecting any yearning for Americanization, however, Alessandroni's request resulted from the desire of Italian Americans to prevent discrimination against their unnaturalized fellow ethnics on the grounds of their national origin. As the petition itself read, the purpose of the Eliot Bill was "to take out of the hate [sic], undeserved 'Enemy Alien' status those who have close relatives in the service, or are over 50 and have been here many years, or are awaiting naturalization, or can show their loyalty to a government board."[8]

Rather than the New Deal, it was World War II that marked the demise of the Depression in Philadelphia's Italian American community. According to U.S. Census data, as late as 1940, the average unemployment rate in the largest Italian American districts was 14.6 percent, with a high of 25.7 percent in census tract 3A and a low of 8.7 percent in tract 34M. But the U.S. intervention in the war made possible the achievement of full employment in Philadelphia following the development of the local defense plants. The end of the economic crisis benefited not only heavy industry but also other sectors in which Italian American workers made up the bulk of the labor force. In mid-January 1942, for instance, ACWA business agent Thomas Di Lauro, an Italian American himself, reported that "[clothing] shops are working in full capacity" for the production of uniforms for the armed forces. Indeed, it was only during World War II that the textile industry reached a level of forty thousand laborers in Philadelphia for the first time after the losses it had suffered in the Depression years.[9]

Nonetheless, after the beginning of World War II, ethnic intolerance became again a major concern for Italian Americans. Following Italy's attack on France, *Fortune* warned against the presence of a pro-fascist "fifth column" in America that was allegedly made up of individuals who were ready to take the field as "enemy soldiers within our borders" in case of the outbreak of a war between Italy and the United States. This magazine also pointed to Philadelphia's Italian-language weekly *L'Osservatore* as an example of Mussolini's mouthpieces in the country. In addition, *Collier's* stressed the spread of growing hostility against Italian Americans and discrimination in employment. This attitude affected the hiring not only of unnaturalized Italians but also of American-born laborers who were identifiable as of Italian ancestry. Ethnic discrimination was not restricted to the defense sector. In April 1941, Harold B. Hoskins, a State Department investigator reported "increasing restrictions, even in non-defense industries, on the employment of foreign born citizens by virtue of their foreign-born names." He also highlighted "a smoldering suspicion on the part of American-born citizens against all citizens with foreign-born names, particularly those of German, Italian, or Slavic origin."[10]

Anti-Italian prejudice was overt in Philadelphia. Adrian Bonnelly, a judge of Italian descent sitting on the city's Municipal Court, complained that his fellow ethnics were denied naval commissions because of their national ancestry on the pretext of their failure to qualify for medical examinations. After the United States entered the war, Philadelphia's WPEN radio station even dismissed Ralph Borrelli, who was still a very popular figure among the local Italian Americans, almost overnight from his position as director of its Italian programs on the grounds that he was a Fascist sympathizer. Furthermore, Philadelphia witnessed massive layoffs of unnaturalized Italians employed as longshoremen, dock warehousemen, as well as ship repairers and builders. Rear Admiral Emory S. Land, the chairperson of the U.S. Marine Commission, warned President Roosevelt that these dismissals "might have serious and immediate effects" on local marine work. The Office of War Information also reported the persistence of anti-Italian hostility among the workers of Philadelphia's shipyard and the beatings of Italian Americans as late as 1944. At that time, the United States and Italy were no longer at war.[11]

Italian Americans in Philadelphia were very sensitive to the risk of becoming victims of ethnic bigotry owing to their own national origin. Indeed, as early as 1939, State Senator Anthony Di Silvestro and all the city's representatives of Italian origin in the Lower House of the Pennsylvania General Assembly, regardless of their party affiliation, denounced this menace. They harshly criticized a state law that, reflecting the federal Alien Registration Act, mandated the registration of the unnaturalized foreign-born residents of the state. According to the

Italian American legislators, this measure would make all members of nationality groups look like subversives. In their opinion, that piece of legislation would also encourage discrimination against immigrant minorities on a prejudicial basis other than individual behavior and loyalty to the adoptive country.[12]

A local branch of the nationwide Comitato Italiano per la Difesa degli Immigrati (Italian Committee for the Defense of Immigrants) was established in Philadelphia in 1939 to protect Italians against discrimination. After the outbreak of hostilities between Italy and the United States, Italian American State Representatives from Philadelphia Paul D'Ortona and Charles Melchiorre also introduced a resolution asking that Italian citizens living in the United States be termed not "enemy aliens," as federal regulations required, but "unnaturalized residents."[13]

Racial and ethnic tolerance had grown nationwide during the Depression years, especially as a reaction against the antisemitism of the German Nazi regime and its contempt for eastern European peoples. But World War II witnessed a significant resurgence of nativism in Pennsylvania. Bills pending in the General Assembly in 1941 would bar aliens from any position in any branch of the state administration and exclude them from benefits such as relief, old age assistance, and unemployment compensation. The targets of this proposed legislation were, of course, the unnaturalized citizens of the Axis Powers.[14]

A new tide of anti-Italian intolerance seemed to loom on the horizon. Therefore, Italian Americans in Philadelphia hurried to distance themselves from Fascism and to show off their patriotism toward the land of their adoption as soon as Japan raided Pearl Harbor on 7 December 1941 and Italy declared war on the United States on 11 December. The city's leading Italian-language newspapers disavowed their previous pro-Fascist sympathies and stated that the American citizens of Italian descent were "one hundred percent" for the United States. As *Il Popolo Italiano* maintained, for instance, "[I]t is our duty as Americans to give our loyal, unquestioning and absolute support to the president of the United States to achieve complete and absolute victory for the armed forces of the United States." Similarly, *Ordine Nuovo* declared that "our only thought is for America. Standing at attention, we await the command of our president, our governor, and the other authorities of our Commonwealth." On behalf of the Pennsylvania Grand Lodge of the OSIA, Grand Venerable Alessandroni also sent telegrams to FBI Director J. Edgar Hoover on 12 December and to President Roosevelt on 15 December, and pledged the full support of the members of his own organization to the United States. That the telegram to Hoover was sent three days before the telegram to Roosevelt clearly highlights the fears of an anti-Italian crusade that underlay the display of allegiance to their adoptive country on the part of Italian Americans. As late as 1943, Carlo Manerba, a reporter for *Il Popolo Italiano*, called the overemphasis on patriotic sentiments toward the United States "rhetoric...necessary...in order to be in harmony with the times."[15]

Alessandroni had been so faithful to the Fascist regime that Mussolini's ambassador to Washington, Augusto Rosso, relied on him as a broker in the fruitless effort to obtain favorable coverage of Italy's situation in the *Saturday Evening Post* at the time of the war against Ethiopia in January 1936. Almost six years later, however, Alessandroni led Italian Americans to repudiate Fascism and to proclaim their unconditional love for democracy and the United States.[16]

Deportation of unnaturalized immigrants after their motherland had declared war on the United States affected Italians primarily in California. Only 233 individuals were interned and 265 people paroled nationwide out of the 695,363 unnaturalized Italian citizens who lived in the United States. Yet, several factors further cemented the consciousness of a common ancestral nationhood among Italian Americans in Philadelphia. They included the risk of becoming victims of social intolerance owing to their national origin, the fears of discrimination in hiring and layoffs as a result of their ethnic allegiance, and rumors that Italian immigrants had been excluded from relief programs because their loyalty to the United States was questioned. Thus, the Office of War Information reported in December 1942 that local Italian ethnic associations were joining forces in social and other activities during these hard times for their minority group."[17]

The remnants of localistic self-images faded away during World War II because the members of the community shared the same gloomy future regardless of the region of origin of their parents in Italy. Still, Italian Americans retained the awareness of their ethnic descent. In 1941, for instance, both *Ordine Nuovo* and a few speakers at the convention of the Pennsylvania Grand Lodge of the OSIA pointed out that a military conflict between Italy and the United States would be a fratricidal fight for Italian Americans.[18]

Moreover, despite the menace of the resurgence of anti-Italian intolerance, many Italian Americans continued to cherish their Italian ancestry. They were glad to support the war effort of the United States by joining the army or buying war bonds not as mere Americans but as American citizens of Italian descent. As Gene Rea proudly stressed in *La Libera Parola* in late July 1942, "Four hundred thousand young American men of Italian extraction are now wearing the uniforms of Uncle Sam in every branch of the service . . . and are enough in themselves to start any major offensive against the Axis powers." It is hardly by chance that the major drives to encourage the members of Philadelphia's community to purchase war bonds were launched on Columbus Day—the leading Italian American holiday—and in response to events involving Italy and Italians. These incidents included Italy's declaration of war on the United States in December 1941, the exclusion of unnaturalized Italian immigrants from the classification of "enemy aliens" in October 1942, and the armistice between the United States and Italy in September 1943. Furthermore, ethnic associations such as the Pennsylvania Grand Lodge of the OSIA initiated such drives. This latter organization pledged to buy war bonds totalling at least two million dollars. It actually reached a total of $3,333,681.33 in July 1944 after the end of its last purchase drive. Ralph Borrelli's "Italian Hour" on WTEL radio station, which he joined after an FBI investigation had cleared him, and the Italian-language Local 122 of the Amalgamated Clothing Workers of America also played a major role in stimulating the purchase of war bonds. The Italian-American members of the ACWA locals in Philadelphia, for instance, had already bought bonds in the amount of about $25,000 worth by early February 1942.[19]

Although patriotic pledges and unending lists of war bond subscribers concealed the inmost feelings of Philadelphia's Italian Americans, the persistence of a strong sense of identification with their ancestral country caused many members of the community to resent Roosevelt for the state of war between the United States and Italy. Significantly, for instance, Democratic candidates made a point of denying any responsibility on the part of the president for the conflict with Italy when they campaigned in Italian American neighborhoods in 1942. In particular, incumbent U.S. Representative Leon Sacks usually stressed that it was Italy that had declared war on the United States, in compliance with the Fascist alliance with Japan and Germany, while Roosevelt had not included Italy in the U.S. declaration of war on Japan because Mussolini's government had played no part in the Pearl Harbor raid. In response to the outbreak of hostilities between the United States and Italy, however, a majority of the Italian American electorate in Philadelphia left the Roosevelt coalition for good in 1942. In that year, the Republican Party won 64.6 percent of the Italian American vote and carried the community for the first time in a federal or state election since 1932.[20]

At the time of the campaign for the 1942 midterm elections, President Roosevelt urged the American people to vote for those candidates "who have a record of backing up the Government." The campaign strategy of the Democratic officials, however, further damaged the political following of their party among Italian Americans. F. Clair Ross, the Democratic candidate for governor of Pennsylvania, implied that his victory would be a vote of confidence in Roosevelt's foreign policy. Likewise, at a Democratic rally in Philadelphia, Pennsylvania's U.S. Senator Joseph F. Guffey stressed that the 1942 "election is an important and necessary part of the war effort," and added that "in this campaign we have a real issue: win the war."[21]

In addition, several Philadelphians of Italian descent were disappointed at the results of the 1943 Casablanca Conference. President Roosevelt's and British Prime Minister Winston Churchill's announcement that the war would end only with the "unconditional surrender" of the Axis Powers clashed with their hopes of finding a lenient solution to ease Italy's way out of the conflict.[22]

Even the president's personal prestige failed to bring a majority of Philadelphia's Italian American electorate back to the Democratic camp. Roosevelt managed to win only 41.2 percent of the vote in the community when he ran for a fourth term in 1944.[23]

The Italian ambassador to Washington, Prince Ascanio Colonna, observed in early July 1940 that especially working-class and elderly Italian Americans revealed "some sympathy" with Italy's declaration of war on France. Yet, notwithstanding mass consent for Fascism in the prewar years, the ties of Italian Americans to their ancestral land were primarily sentimental. Popular demonstrations in Philadelphia's "Little Italies" celebrated the end of Mussolini's regime after King Victor Emmanuel III replaced *Il Duce* with Marshal Pietro Badoglio, following a palace coup, on 25 July 1943. Even the national commander of the Federation of Italian World War Veterans, Damiàno Sassi, rejoiced over the fall of Mussolini, in spite of the pro-Fascist tilt of his own organization before Pearl Harbor. Similarly, feelings of relief spread in South Philadelphia as soon as news of Italy's surrender to the United States began to circulate on 9 September 1943. As an anonymous interviewee of Italian descent declared to the *Philadelphia Record*, for instance, "[N]ow our boys in the American army won't have to kill their own kind." These very words, however, provide additional evidence that Italian Americans in Philadelphia retained their Italian self-image during World War II.[24]

The negligible participation of Philadelphians of Italian ancestry in the so-called "hate strikes" of the war years further points to the fact that Italian Americans had still retained the perception of their Italianness and had not yet acquired a full-fledged American identity by the mid-1940s. Scholars usually regard the strike of white workers opposing the hiring and promotion of African American laborers during the war as a sort of rite of passage in the creation of a white American working class out of immigrant groups of European origins that had previously been divided along ethnic lines. While these "hate" walkouts occurred in the major U.S. industrial centers, the longest and most bitter took place in Philadelphia itself.[25]

On 1 August 1944, at four o'clock in the morning, approximately six thousand white employees of the Philadelphia Transportation Company (PTC) went on strike to protest against the upgrading of African American fellow workers from maintenance to platform jobs such as motormen, conductors, trainmen, and bus drivers. Black laborers had previously been excluded from all these positions. Most strikers were members of the Philadelphia Rapid Transit Employees Union (PRTEU), the company union that had lost the collective bargaining election to the CIO-affiliated Transport Workers Union (TWU) in February 1944. TWU officials contended that the strike was little more than an attempt by the PRTEU to unseat the TWU as the collective bargaining agent for the PTC employees. Still, it cannot be denied that the walkout was racially motivated. Not only had the race controversy been critical during the February election because the TWU opposed the PRTEU with a nondiscrimination platform. The leader of the protesters himself, James McMenamin, did not hesitate to declare that the strike was about "a strictly black and white issue."[26]

The walkout paralyzed almost all trolley, bus, and subway service in Philadelphia. It lasted five days until the army took over the operation of the system, issued an ultimatum for the resumption of work, and arrested the leaders of the strike for interference with war production because the PTC provided workers with transportation to defense plants. The 185 strikers who had not reported to work by the deadline were also fired. They included, however, only one Italian American, a

Pat Inverso. In addition, neither Inverso himself nor any other of his fellow-ethnic employees of the Philadelphia Transportation Co. was involved in the strike executive committee. Indeed, no individual of Italian descent was among the thirty defendants charged with violation of the War Labor Dispute Smith-Connally Act on 4 October 1944 for "unlawfully instigating, coercing, inducing, and encouraging" the walkout of the previous August. Moreover, while covering the strike and its aftermath, *Il Popolo Italiano* stressed primarily the troubles for the population. Remarkably enough, despite its own taste for black-bashing since the time of the Italo-Ethiopian War, this newspaper did not stand by the strikers and even neglected to mention the case of Inverso.[27]

Many Italian Americans were, however, afraid of revealing their ancestry during the war for fear of discrimination. They felt free to come out of the closet only after the hostilities between Italy and the United States ended with the signing of an armistice between the two countries in September 1943. As American-born Joseph Mangione told a reporter of the *Philadelphia Inquirer* during a mass celebration for Italy's capitulation, "[O]f course I still have Italian in me."[28]

Galvanized by the demise of Fascism and undaunted by Italy's subsequent defeat in World War II, many Italian Americans continued to identify themselves with their mother country and to pursue her interests. After Italy signed the armistice with the United States and the Badoglio government declared war on Nazi Germany in October 1943, Italian Americans lobbied the Roosevelt administration for the recognition of Italy as an ally of the United States. Representatives of eleven Philadelphia-based ethnic organizations and Italian-language labor union locals attended the hearings of the House Committee on Foreign Affairs on this matter. Philadelphians of Italian descent also hurried to raise funds for the population of war-torn Italy. According to Cornelia Bryce Pinchot, the wife of former Governor of Pennsylvania Gifford Pinchot, the sense of identification of Italian Americans in Philadelphia with their ancestral land was still remarkably strong as late as the mid-1940s. In her opinion, Roosevelt had only one chance of carrying their community in 1944. As she put it to the president's secretary, Roosevelt should "express sympathy for the Italians in the agonies that Italy has gone through, sympathy for their troubles of today, placing the blame squarely on Mussolini and saying that he and all Americans look forward to the day when Italy will once again take her place as a power in the world."[29]

Roosevelt himself was fully aware that the Italian identity of the Italian American voters was still a key determinant of their voting behavior throughout the United States. In 1942, the president endeavored to exploit the removal of unnaturalized Italians from the category of enemy aliens in order to profit from the gratitude of their fellow-ethnic U.S. citizens at the polls. As Francis Biddle—who officially lifted the enemy alien status in his capacity as U.S. attorney general—remarked, the announcement of this ruling a few weeks before the 1942 midterm elections, on the occasion of Columbus Day, was not only "a masterly stroke of international statesmanship" but also "good politics."[30]

That change in regulations was in line with the resolution that Melchiorre and D'Ortona had already introduced to the General Assembly of Pennsylvania. Philadelphians of Italian descent hailed it with jubilation. After a crowd of nearly four thousand members of the community, who had gathered at the Academy of Music to celebrate Columbus Day, heard the news that the Italian citizens living in the country would no longer be regarded as enemy aliens, they pledged to buy more than four million dollars worth of war bonds. They had previously set a quota of one million dollars as the goal for the citywide purchase drive launched that very day, but they decided to raise it in appreciation of the decision made by the U.S. government. Similarly, in an open letter to Francis Biddle published in the *Philadelphia Record*, Damiano Sassi expressed the "gratitude . . . of the Italian Americans for your act of patriotism and justice in removing the label of enemy alien from Italians—our people, who have proved by deeds . . . that the minds and hearts of all America's Italians are in fact 100 percent Americanized."[31]

The renewed proclamation of Italian Americans' allegiance to the United States, however, did not overshadow their persisting concerns about their native country. For instance, in a telegram to thank the attorney general for his ruling about unnaturalized Italians, the representatives of a few Italian American societies in Philadelphia pledged their own organizations to support not only "the war effort for American victory" but also "Italian liberation." Similarly, besides stressing that Biddle's decision was a "historical tribute to the faithfulness and sense of responsibility" of Italian Americans, an editorial in *Ordine Nuovo* remarked that "we have won a great battle for America, for ourselves, and for Italy, our mother country." This article also emphasized once again that "American Victory and Italian Liberation" were the twin goals of Italian Americans.[32]

In 1942, the United States and Italy were still at war and Republican workers had resumed their strategy to play on the resentment of the Italian American electorate for the fight of their adoptive country against their motherland, beginning with the primary campaign in May. Freeing the Italians from the enemy alien stigma was not enough to let the Democratic Party win a majority of the Italian American vote in Philadelphia. Indeed, as shown earlier, the GOP carried the Italian American community in the 1942 gubernatorial election. *Il Popolo Italiano* stigmatized Biddle's ruling as a cosmetic act and belated amends for an unjust, prejudicial, and ethnically biased measure that the Democratic Party itself had supported despite the opposition of Republican Secretary of War Henry L. Stimson.[33]

Roosevelt made another major bid for the support of the Italian American electorate nationwide in 1944, this time by the means of economic and humanitarian assistance for Italy. In particular, the so-called "Hyde Park Declaration," which the president and British Prime Minister Winston Churchill issued on 26 September 1944, committed the United States to the recovery of Italy, granted her economic aid under a United Nations Relief and Rehabilitation Administration (UNRRA) program, provided for more power for the Italian government as well as for its diplomatic representation in Washington and London, and made a few concessions to rebuild trade between Italy and the United States. The Roosevelt administration also eased the procedures for the shipment of relief goods and money from the United States to the Italian provinces that were under the control of the Allies.[34]

Still, the policy of the U.S. government toward Italy fell short of the expectations of many Italian Americans in Philadelphia. Acting Secretary of State Edward R. Stettinius Jr. contended that it was Congress, not the president, that was entitled to grant Italy the status of an ally. Therefore, contrary to the wishes of the Italian American community, he concluded that Italy would remain a cobelligerent of the United States because these two countries had not signed a peace treaty. *Il Popolo Italiano* stigmatized the "Hyde Park Declaration" as a series of empty promises that failed to include such a key provision to the Italian recovery as the extension of the lend and lease benefits to Italy. It also published several statements by Italian American leaders who criticized the failure of the U.S. government to cope with Italian economic problems. For instance, in the opinion of both Herman E. Carletti, the secretary of the Philadelphia-based Italo-American Republican League of Pennsylvania, and Americo V. Cortese, an assistant district attorney in Philadelphia county, the inefficiency of the Roosevelt administration caused the clothing that Italian American associations had collected for the Italian people to "rot in warehouses." According to a speech that Edward Corsi—New York State's commissioner of labor in the Republican administration of Governor Thomas E. Dewey—delivered in Philadelphia, the fifty-million-dollar UNRRA aids to Italy were "only a drop of water in the desert." Similarly, *Ordine Nuovo* calculated that since the state of New York had spent thirty million dollars per month to support one million and a half unemployed workers during the Depression, fifty million dollars were not enough for a population of twenty million destitute people in Italy. However, Republican members of the community were not alone in voicing criticism that the United States supposedly mishandled Italy. James Iannucci, for instance, blamed the delay in American aid to Italy for an alleged fifty percent increase in infant mortality among the Italian population after the armistice. Iannucci had been a Democratic candidate for Philadelphia's city council in 1943 and was the head of the Order of Brotherly Love, an ethnic organization that claimed to be the second-largest Italian American association in Philadelphia.[35]

Unlike Roosevelt, Republican presidential candidate Thomas E. Dewey appeared ready to satisfy the demands of Philadelphia's Italian Americans for their mother country. In a message he released on the occasion of Columbus Day, 12 October 1944, Dewey declared that "freed Italy is now a friend and an ally, not a mere cobelligerent." Later on, he also argued that "the Italian people deserve something better than the improvised, inefficient administration which personal New Deal government is giving them."[36]

The results of the 1944 presidential election in Philadelphia show that Cornelia Bryce Pinchot was right about the persistence of the Italian identity among voters of Italian ancestry notwithstanding the impact of World War II on their sense of ethnic allegiance. Indeed, as Dewey seemed more concerned about Italy than Roosevelt, the Italian American community delivered a 58.2 percent majority for the Republican candidate.[37]

Italian Americans in Philadelphia remained Italian-minded even after the end of the war. This time, however, instead of focusing on humanitarian and economic aid for their motherland, they rallied on the issue of the peace settlement. Specifically, they asked for a fair treaty for Italy, which meant preventing territorial mutilations to the benefit of France and Yugoslavia, requesting the payment of reasonable reparations in recognition of the Italian contribution to the war against Germany in the period of the cobelligerency with the United States, and allowing a revision of the peace treaty in five years. Prominent Philadelphians of Italian descent such as Furey Ellis, a leading insurance broker, also promoted a nationwide organization, the American-Italian Congress, which intended to persuade U.S. Secretary of State James F. Byrnes to let Italy retain her pre-Fascist colonies—Libya, Eritrea, and Somaliland—or, as an alternative, to have them administered by a committee of U.S. citizens of Italian ancestry.[38]

Notwithstanding the efforts of Italian Americans not only in Philadelphia but also in the United States as a whole, the Paris peace conference drafted a treaty that penalized Italy and disregarded the Italian American demands on her behalf. Most notably, the treaty deprived Italy of Istria, which was assigned to Yugoslavia, and Trieste, which was made a free territory. In addition, Italy had to pay burdensome reparations—which claimants could also obtain through confiscation of Italian properties abroad—not only to the Allies but even to Albania and Ethiopia. Conversely, Italy was not permitted to receive compensation from Germany, in spite of the Nazi occupation of the country since October 1943. The Italian armed forces were also strictly limited to a level sufficient solely to maintain internal public order and local defense of the frontiers. Italy only succeeded in retaining her pre war borders with Austria.[39]

Like their fellow ethnics throughout the nation, Italian Americans in Philadelphia resented the punitive peace that the Allies had imposed on their ancestral country at the Paris peace conference in 1946 and the De Gasperi government had to sign the following year. As a result, the community mobilized in the fruitless attempt to prevent Congress from ratifying the peace treaty. It also supported a proposal for entrusting Italy with the administration of her pre-Fascist colonies under the supervision of the United Nations. In August 1948, news that Dewey, who seemed the certain winner in the forthcoming presidential election, had endorsed the trusteeship plan caused an outburst on enthusiasm in Philadelphia's Italian American neighborhoods.[40]

Many Italian Americans elaborated a fuller sense of their Italianness in the interwar years. The military conflict between their native and adoptive lands potentially caused crisis of identity. Yet, the continuity of Italian American concerns for both the nation of their origin and her territorial ambitions demonstrated that the identification of most members of Philadelphia's community with their mother country survived

World War II. Contrary to Diggins's thesis, as if World War II and the fall of Fascism had not been a watershed in the history of Italian Americans in Philadelphia, their community selected the same representative to spearhead the claims of its members on behalf of Italy in both the 1930s and 1940s. The perseverance of this pro-Italian lobbying and the presence of the same spokesperson, too, offer evidence of the persistence of the national consciousness of the city's Italian Americans across World War II. After his testimony before the House Committee on Foreign Affairs at the time of the Italo-Ethiopian crisis in 1936, Fascist turned anti-Fascist Alessandroni returned to Capitol Hill in 1945 to make the case for the recognition of Italy as an ally before the same committee. The following year, he vainly flew to Paris in order to urge Secretary of State Byrnes to ease the most punitive clauses of the peace treaty with Italy. Finally, Alessandroni was the spokesperson for the stand of Philadelphia's community against the ratification of the peace treaty at the senatorial hearings in May 1947 and led the Italian American delegation that secured Dewey's endorsement of the proposal for entrusting Italy with the administration of her pre-Fascist colonies in August 1948. Less than one month later, on behalf of the OSIA, Alessandroni also attended a meeting with President Harry S. Truman to advocate the retention of Libya, Eritrea, and Somaliland on the part of Italy.[41]

The Italian American members of the Philadelphia locals of the Amalgamated Workers of America were another very active group in these campaigns. Their dedicated efforts on behalf of Italy further demonstrate that unionization was not necessarily a vehicle for the Americanization of workers of Italian ancestry in the interwar years. Philip De Luca, a member of the Philadelphia Joint Board of the ACWA and the national vice president of the Free Italy American Labor Council, joined forces with former Fascist leader Alessandroni in order to pressure the U.S. government into recognizing Italy as an ally after her declaration of war on Germany. Local 122 of the ACWA mobilized to send aid to the Italian regions occupied by the Allies in order to relieve the hardships of the population during the last two years of World War II. Union members brought in clothes they no longer used and collected food, and medicine, as well as other relief goods, to be shipped to Italy. In 1946, the executive board of Local 122 also recommended that all affiliates donate a day's pay to the Italian people in dire need. According to ACWA records, this proposal met with "excellent co-operation" from rank and file members who "made the Italian Relief Drive a distinctive success."[42]

Italian Americans in Philadelphia continued to be responsive to the appeals on behalf of their ancestral land in the late 1940s. This attitude offers further evidence that World War II did not halt the process of their ethnicization along national lines. The involvement of Italian Americans in the parliamentary elections held in Italy in April 1948 provides an additional case in point.

The Christian Democrats of Prime Minister Alcide De Gasperi and a coalition made up by the Communist and Socialist Parties were the leading contenders for success at the polls. Following the communist coup of February 1948 in Czechoslovakia, in blatant contempt of any principle of noninterference in the internal affairs of another country, the U.S. government intervened massively in the election campaign to help De Gasperi's party for fear that a victory of the Left would eventually push Italy, too, into the Soviet bloc.[43]

The many ingenious schemes to prevent the Communists and their allies from coming to power included appeals to Italian Americans in the United States to send letters to their relatives in Italy and warn them against voting for the communist and socialist candidates. Many Philadelphians of Italian descent participated enthusiastically in this propaganda effort. *Ordine Nuovo* and *Il Popolo Italiano* printed Italian-language anticommunist letters to be copied, signed, and mailed to voters in Italy. *Il Popolo Italiano* also echoed Cardinal Dougherty's appeal to his Italian American confession to contribute to spreading anticommunism in their ancestral land. Eugene V. Alessandroni issued a circular for the lodges of the OSIA. He advised their members to write kinsfolk and friends in Italy and to call on them to reject "atheistic and dictatorial Communism" when they cast their ballots. A group of Italian Americans recorded a message against the Communist Party and had it broadcast in Italy. Another paid for posters that portrayed the vote as a choice between Christ and Antichrist, and encouraged the Italian electorate to support the Christian Democrats. Vincenzo D'Auria, the Grand Curator of the Pennsylvania Grand Lodge of the OSIA, had his photograph taken and published in *Ordine Nuovo* while he was dropping several envelopes in a mail box. Furey Ellis promoted a committee that distributed about fifty thousand copies of a leaflet "appealing to Italian Americans to write letters to their friends and relatives in Italy."[44]

Of course, it is impossible to calculate how many letters the members of Philadelphia's community actually sent to Italy. The estimates of the local Italian American newspapers may sound hollow because the ethnic press usually tended to exaggerate when it came to providing quantitative data about the outcome of its own campaigns. Nonetheless, the outbreak of jubilation in South Philadelphia, as also the more reliable and objective English-language dailies reported, at the news of the defeat of the communist-socialist coalition and the duration of the celebrations for several days showed the persistence of the identification of Italian Americans with their ancestral country. The *Evening Bulletin* estimated that about 22,000 Philadelphians of Italian extraction signed a letter to Pope Pius XII to congratulate him on the victory of the Christian Democrats at the polls. On 25 April, on the third anniversary of Italy's liberation from Nazi occupation, all the local lodges of the OSIA held meetings to rejoice over the escape of their ancestral country from the threat of the establishment of a communist dictatorship. Four days later, Amerigo Palumbo—of the well-known family of restaurateurs—led a delegation to the Vatican in a sort of votive pilgrimage in gratitude for the defeat of the Communist Party. As late as 2 May, Italian Americans paraded in North Philadelphia to celebrate the consolidation of Italian democracy that resulted from the outcome of April's parliamentary elections.[45]

Italian Americans had long revealed their interest in the fate of their ancestral land. In particular, they had endeavored to influence the policy of the U.S. government toward their mother country at least since 1920, when they lashed back at President Wilson's postwar settlement in the presidential contest. Their interference in the 1948 parliamentary elections, however, marked a watershed in their efforts to shape the relations between the United States and Italy. Previous campaigns such as the lobbying against the passing of the Pittman-McReynolds Bill in 1936 and the attempt to prevent Congress from ratifying the peace treaty with Italy in 1947 placed Italian Americans in conflict with the position of the United States. Conversely, the 1948 anticommunist letter-writing campaign apparently pandered to the aims of the Truman administration.

Scholars have suggested that, in the postwar years, opposition to communism became a key component of the hyper-patriotism of many nationality groups whose members had developed status anxiety because of their foreign ancestry. According to Philip Jenkins's study of Cold War attitudes in Pennsylvania, Catholic immigrant minorities were among the staunchest anticommunist cohorts of the state's population. Specifically, Nathan Glazer and Daniel Patrick Moynihan have contended that Italian Americans embraced the dominating Cold War paradigm in the late 1940s and the 1950s to demonstrate that they had definitively become an undistinguishable part of their adoptive country. In their opinion, after being charged with disloyalty to the United States during World War II because of their previous pro-Fascist sentiments, Italian Americans overtly nurtured anticommunist feelings to make their own allegiance to the land of their acquisition indisputable.[46]

However, the adherence of Philadelphians of Italian descent to the Cold War strategy of the U.S. government in 1948 did not necessarily result from the demise of their identification with their ancestral country. Although they embraced the anticommunist strategy of the Truman administration in their motherland, many Italian Americans also planned to advance Italy's national interests even when her demands were in conflict with the policy of the United States. Indeed, while encouraging friends and kinsfolk in their ancestral country not to vote for the Communist-led coalition, Italian Americans lobbied the U.S. government on behalf of Italy. Against the backdrop of the Cold War, they fought communism to show off their patriotism and dispel potential charges of disloyalty toward the United States when they supported Italy's claims against the course of action of the Truman administration.

After the success of the Christian Democrats at the polls, *Il Popolo Italiano* linked the definitive defeat of communism in Italy to concessions to this country. For instance, in a commentary on the outcome of the parliamentary elections, it warned that "in the showdown the Communists were beaten but they did not lose any of their previous strength." After admonishing that destitution was "the lifeblood of Communism which breeds and grows in an atmosphere of hunger, discontent, and human misery," *Il Popolo Italiano* offered its own solution for the definitive demise of any Red menace in Italy. As the newspaper put it hinting at Italy's problem of overpopulation, "[A] move by the United States towards the restoration of colonial possessions in one form or another would serve a two-fold purpose. It would, over a span of years, help in alleviating the problem of too many people trying to live on too little land and it would take away from the powerful Communist element their argument that America is trying to dominate Italy by holding over her head the threat of withdrawing aid unless Italy does as we say."[47]

Likewise, on behalf of the OSIA, Judge Alessandroni contended that Italy's trusteeship over Eritrea, Libya, and Somaliland "would strengthen the position of the Italian government in its fight for democracy at home." As late as 1951, Samuel B. Regalbuto—a prominent politician from Philadelphia and the chairperson of the Italian Division of Pennsylvania's State Committee of the Democratic Party—maintained that "in order to seal a firmer bond between our country and the people of Italy in the fight against world Communism a more just and equitable peace treaty should be entered into."[48]

The election results for the 1948 race for the White House show that the U.S. policy toward Italy was still a paramount political issue for Italian Americans in Philadelphia. The idea that the United States had contributed to save Italy from communism by strengthening the De Gasperi government through the economic aid of the Marshall Plan helped President Truman in a few Italian American communities. There, a sizeable number of the voters who had bolted to the GOP following Roosevelt's 1940 "stab-in-the-back" speech went back to the Democratic Party in the 1948 presidential election in appreciation of the intervention of the United States to secure the political and economic stabilization of Italy in the late 1940s. Truman, for instance, won 85.7 percent of the Italian American vote in Boston, 80 percent in Hartford, and 60 percent in New Haven.[49]

This, however, was not the case of the Italian American electorate in Philadelphia, since Dewey obtained 58.7 percent of their votes as opposed to the 40.7 percent that Truman received. Yet, the outcome of the 1948 presidential election in this city, too, resulted from the deep concerns of local Italian Americans for the their ancestral land. Dewey carried Philadelphia's community because he seemed to be more sympathetic with Italy than President Truman was.[50]

Indeed, as mentioned earlier, Dewey endorsed the proposal for entrusting Italy with the administration of Eritrea, Libya, and Somaliland. Conversely, Truman retorted that such a matter was for the Allies or the United Nations to discuss and that the United States could make no decision on their own. Even the Philadelphia edition of *Il Progresso Italo-Americano*, which usually sided with the Democratic Party, admitted that Truman was uncommitted to vindicate Italy's rightful claim to rule her pre-Fascist colonies. Moreover, Truman's stance was an opportunity for the pro-Republican *Il Popolo Italiano* to stigmatize the Italian policy of all three Democratic presidents of the century: Wilson, who had deprived Italy of Fiume; Roosevelt, who had had the Neutrality Acts repealed to force the United States into World War II against Italy; and Truman, who wanted to sell off the Italian colonies to England or, even worse, to the Soviet Union.[51]

The issue of communism also turned into an asset to Dewey in Philadelphia. On the one hand, Pennsylvania's Republican Governor James F. Duff warned that the U.S. government was unprepared to face a Soviet aggression against Italy and GOP national chairperson Hugh Scott, whose congressional district was in Philadelphia, relied heavily on the Hiss case for attacking Truman. On the other, Republican charges that communists had infiltrated the federal administration found a strident echo in *Il Popolo Italiano*. Truman also paid for the indignation of Italian Americans for the peace treaty forced upon Italy. Even the local edition of *Il Progresso Italo-Americano* called it "a shameful turnabout of the Atlantic Charter" and "a scandalous mess, made by the Big Four," that "humiliates, debases, and disarms Italy."[52]

According to the U.S. government, the OSIA was the "principal instigator" of the 2,524 form letters and 1,074 communications urging the United States to let Italy retain her pre-Fascist colonies that the Department of State received between 16 August and 10 September 1948. However, Italian Americans' commitment to advance Italy's demands did not come to an end after 1948. In particular, despite Dewey's defeat, Philadelphians of Italian extraction continued to lobby for the return of Eritrea, Libya, and Somaliland to Italy. On 9 March 1949, for instance, Ernest L. Biagi, the Grand Secretary of the Pennsylvania Grand Lodge of the OSIA, wrote to President Truman to pressure the U.S. government into letting Italy retain her pre-Fascist colonies. The 1949 convention of the Pennsylvania Grand Lodge passed a resolution to the same effect. It also urged the Truman administration to appoint a commission to examine possible ways of improving the economic and social conditions in Italy. Pledges to anticommunist vigilance, loyalty to the United States, and "support of the principles on which our great country was founded" once again provided a broader framework for Italian Americans' claims on behalf of Italy.[53]

John Bodnar has suggested that middle-class ethnic leaders attempted to exploit patriotism as a means of increasing their power and status in American society. A memorandum prepared for President Truman reveals that Alessandroni, Biagi, and the other representatives of the OSIA who met with him to discuss the matter of the Italian colonies in September 1948 "realize that the President cannot make any commitments whatsoever to them." Yet, they wanted to meet Truman anyhow because "they hope the president will say something about the work the Sons of Italy did in pushing the Marshall Plan and Relief Bill. They hope to have a picture taken to be published in their monthly periodical." A photograph of OSIA leaders with President Truman eventually ended up on the front page of *Ordine Nuovo*.[54]

One could argue that prominent Italian Americans such as Alessandroni embraced anticommunism to enhance their social standing with little regard to the fate of democracy in Italy or to the role that such an issue could play in persuading the United States to follow a more lenient policy toward their ancestral country in the postwar years. In this view, allowing the leadership to speak for the rank and file members of the Italian American community might produce a misleading evaluation of the persistence of an Italian self-perception among ordinary Italian Americans. It is difficult to evaluate whether Alessandroni and the other leaders of the OSIA mobilized against communism out of expediency only or also because they did identify themselves with Italy. However, the enthusiasm of the average Philadelphians of Italian descent for the success of the Christian Democrats in the 1948 parliamentary elections and the outcome of the presidential contest of the same year in Philadelphia's community demonstrate that the official stand of the *prominenti* was nonetheless representative of the attitude of rank and file Italian Americans. Furthermore, if ordinary Italian Americans no longer identified themselves with their motherland, their leaders could hardly set themselves up as spokespersons of their community on Italy-related issues and hope to boost their prestige among their fellow ethnics by advocating the interests of their native country.

Local issues also contributed to the 1948 Republican plurality in Philadelphia's "Little Italy." However, these determinants of the vote, too, point to the persistence of an Italian identity among Italian Americans.

In 1948, the Democratic City Committee refused to endorse James Altieri, an Italian American war veteran, in Philadelphia's first congressional district and slated William Barrett, an Irish American politician who had already been defeated in his first bid for the U.S. House of Representatives two years earlier. Indeed, the Democratic City Committee had never again endorsed a politician of Italian extraction for Congress since Marinelli's defeat in 1934. Conversely, in 1948, the Republican organization dropped incumbent representative James Gallagher from its ticket and replaced him with one of its chieftains of Italian ancestry, John De Nero. Unlike Irish American Gallagher, De Nero was more likely to appeal to Italian American voters, who made up the bulk of the electorate in South Philadelphia and had long been claiming greater political recognition.[55]

Indeed, De Nero carried the Italian American community with 61.8 percent of the vote. Significantly, he did not run on Dewey's coattails but received a larger plurality than the Republican presidential candidate. That De Nero obtained 3.1 percent more than Dewey reveals the persistence of an Italian self-perception among Italian American voters. At least 6.1 percent of Truman's supporters of Italian descent split their tickets and went over to the Republican Party in the Congressional elections to cast their ballots for a fellow Italian American.[56]

Chapter 6

From Italian Americans to White Ethnics

Philadelphia's Italian Americans revealed the survival of an ethnic self-consciousness based on national ancestry in the 1950s and 1960s, too. The centennial of the unification of Italy, for instance, provided an opportunity for the celebration of the Italianness of the local population of Italian ancestry in 1961. Ethnic militancy also found expression in a campaign that aimed at having Passyunk Square renamed Columbus Square to celebrate the memory of the Italian navigator who discovered America. Philadelphians of Italian ancestry also rallied against the publication of the memoirs of gangster Joseph Valachi because his emphasis on the Italian presence within U.S. criminal organizations besmirched their reputation as a nationality group. In particular, with reference to the Valachi case, the local lodges of the OSIA publicly asked "for the kind of fairness from the public which does not accuse Italian Americans of exercising a monopoly in crime in this country." For a similar reason, in July 1967, two prominent attorneys of Italian descent—Joseph Girone and Donald C. Marino—established a local committee of the Italian-American Anti-Defamation League, a nationwide organization whose primary purpose was to teach people not to use such terms as Mafia and Cosa Nostra in connection with members of the Italian community in the United States.[1]

Other ethnic slurs continued to touch a sensitive nerve among Philadelphians of Italian extraction in the 1960s. For instance, when

William Miller—the national chairperson of the Republican Party—referred to Secretary of Health, Education and Welfare Anthony Celebrezze and other Italian Americans in the Kennedy Administration as "Sinatra types infesting 1600 Pennsylvania Avenue" at a 1963 dinner honoring former President Dwight D. Eisenhower, *Il Popolo Italiano* hurried to voice the resentment of Philadelphia's community.[2]

However, reflecting the declining appeal of Italian festivities to Italian Americans in the postwar decades, the celebration for the one hundredth anniversary of the unification of Italy was organized mainly under the auspices of local business people of Italian descent who wished to promote commercial relations with their ancestral country rather than strengthen the ethnic identity of the members of their community. In addition, not all Italian Americans in Philadelphia worried about the defamation of their own minority group on account of mob-related ethnic stereotypes. For example, novelist and university assistant professor Jerre Mangione assailed the need for the Italian-American Anti-Defamation League in a letter to the *New York Times*. He argued that it was a negative and superfluous organization because "the majority of Americans are bright enough to realize that criminal elements represent a tiny fraction of the Italian American population."[3]

Political developments in Italy continued to be of particular concern to Italian Americans in Philadelphia after 1948. Another anticommunist letter-writing campaign took shape on the occasion of the 1953 parliamentary elections in their ancestral country. Vito C. Mazzone, the pastor of St. Mary Magdalen de Pazzi's and a fierce foe of radicalism in politics, led a new drive to encourage the members of the community to contact their relatives and friends in Italy in support of De Gasperi's Christian Democracy. Samuel Regalbuto hurried to send funds for Sicilian orphanages before the election days in the hope that a good showing of American help could demonstrate U.S. friendship toward Italy in the eyes of this nation's electorate and make a contribution to the defeat of the Communist Party.[4]

This time, too, Italian Americans' anticommunism intertwined with their lobbying endeavors to advance the interests of their native land and her people. For example, *Il Popolo Italiano* implied that the actual return of Trieste to Italy would defuse the nationalistic resentment on which the Communist Party could play to win a majority at the polls. Likewise, the Philadelphia edition of *Il Progresso Italo-Americano* exploited the issue of the communist threat in a fruitless effort to have the United States reinstate Italy among the great powers of the Western world. When a summit among the United States, France, and Great Britain was scheduled for early June 1953, the newspaper argued in vain that an invitation to Italy's representatives to attend the meeting would enhance the prestige of the De Gasperi government and strike the Communist Party the final blow with regard to the forthcoming parliamentary elections.[5]

After the votes had been counted, *Il Popolo Italiano* maintained that De Gasperi had failed to win an absolute majority of the seats in the Chamber of Deputies because the U.S. government was unpopular in Italy. According to its argument, because the United States was the chief foreign ally of the Christian Democrats, the decision of the Eisenhower administration to maintain a very low quota for Italian immigrants to America had enraged Italian voters and pushed them into the arms of the parties of the extreme Left and Right in 1953.[6]

The issue of immigration was also central to the success of Democratic presidential candidate Adlai Stevenson among Philadelphia's Italian Americans in 1952. Stevenson carried the community with 57.6 percent of the vote in the race for the White House, as opposed to the 42.4 percent for the Republican standard bearer, General Dwight D. Eisenhower.[7]

Stevenson had headed a U.S. Economic Survey Mission to Italy in the Winter of 1943–44. Back in the United States, he had persuaded the Roosevelt administration that American aid to Italy should ensure not only the minimum of subsistence for the Italian people but also pave the way for the rehabilitation of civilian industry and agriculture.[8]

During the 1952 presidential campaign, Democratic activists stressed Stevenson's intervention on behalf of Italy in order to win Italian American votes. Yet, Stevenson cashed in primarily on President Truman's veto to the 1952 McCarran-Walter Act. This law reaffirmed the national origins system in the allotment of immigration visas and reduced the Italian quota to 5,654 individuals per year at a time when there were as many as 32,107 Italians who were waiting to emigrate to the United States.[9]

The passing of the new immigration measure over Truman's veto made Italian Americans in Philadelphia aware that anti-Italian prejudice and discrimination were still alive in the United States. As Judge Alessandroni remarked, the condition of equality and peaceful coexistence with other ethnic groups that his fellow ethnics seemed to have achieved in fact looked like an illusion and a waking dream. In addition, Italian Americans considered the McCarran-Walter Act as being insulting to the members of their own national minority. Its provisions implied that Italian newcomers were potentially harmful to American institutions, although U.S. citizens of Italian descent had fought loyally and died bravely for the United States in World War II. Therefore, even pro-Republican newspapers such as *Ordine Nuovo* and *Il Popolo Italiano* praised Truman's veto and the subsequent pledge of the platform of the 1952 Democratic convention to revise "our immigration and naturalization laws to do away with any unjust and unfair practice against national groups which have contributed some of our best citizens."[10]

Both Pat McCarran and Francis Walter were Democratic congressmen. Nonetheless, the backlash of Philadelphia's Italian Americans inspired by the postwar immigration-related resurgence of anti-Italian intolerance hit the Republican Party because the records of the leading candidates in the community in 1952 tended to identify the GOP with nativism. Pennsylvania's Republican Senator Edward Martin, who stood for reelection that very year, voted to override Truman's veto. So did Richard M. Nixon, Eisenhower's running mate. Conversely, Democratic Congressmen William Barrett and William T. Granaham—who represented the districts that included the largest Italian American settlements in Philadelphia—sustained the president's veto. Barrett even introduced a bill to grant Italy a temporary extension of her quota in order to let her people employ the allotment of immigration visas that they had been unable to utilize during the years of World War II.[11]

In 1952, the National Committee of the GOP issued a guidebook for Republican congressional candidates. It included suggestions for a campaign strategy that could appeal to the Italian American electorate. Specifically, this guidebook advised Republican candidates to declare that they advocated the revision of the quota system. Senator Martin's re-election campaign literature never mentioned his vote for the McCarran-Walter Act. Yet, the ethnic press continually reminded the Italian American electorate in Philadelphia of the pivotal contribution of the Republican candidates running in the Italian American districts to the new immigration regulations. Regardless of their partisan leanings, the local Italian-language newspapers printed over and again the lists of "our foes." This term referred to the congressmen who had overridden Truman's veto. The names of Republican Senators Martin and Nixon always stood out at the top of the lists.[12]

The Italian American vote for Martin was 3.9 percentage points lower than that for Republican presidential candidate Eisenhower, who had not voted on the McCarran-Walter Act because he was not a member of Congress. The percentage of the Italian Americans who split their ballots against Martin offers further evidence that, as the senator himself was to acknowledge some time later, his endorsement of the McCarran-Walter Act damaged his candidacy in the eyes of the Italian American electorate.[13]

Sensitivity to anti-Italian defamation remained central to the ethnic commitment of Italian Americans in Philadelphia in the following years. It also continued to influence their electoral behavior.

The Italian American vote for Stevenson fell from 57.6 percent in 1952 to 51.0 percent four years later. In 1956, incumbent Republican President Eisenhower, who ran for a second term against Stevenson, benefited from his own endorsement of the 1953 Refugee Relief Act. The measure did not increase Italy's immigration quota but let about 45,000 Italians from Trieste and the territories annexed by Yugoslavia at the end of World War II enter the United States as extra-quota immigrants.[14]

Furthermore, the candidacy of Senator Estes Kefauver of Tennessee for vice president on the Democratic ticket was a liability to Stevenson. As the chairperson of the Special Committee to Investigate Crime in Interstate Commerce in 1950 and 1951, Stevenson's running mate contributed to legitimizing the notorious Mafia stereotype that associated Italian Americans with organized crime. While the televised broadcasts of the hearings of the Kefauver Committee reached an estimated audience of twenty to thirty million people, the sensationalistic testimonies of their witnesses about the involvement of Italian Americans in illegal activities consolidated the public perception of a centralized Sicilian, or at least Italian, organization that controlled criminal syndicates around the United States.[15]

The Kefauver Committee held two days of hearings in Philadelphia, on 13 and 14 October 1950. Additional testimony concerning organized crime in the city was heard in Washington a few months later, on 19 and 20 February 1951. The investigation focused on the numbers game and, as usual, mentioned a series of alleged Philadelphian racketeers with such Italian-sounding names as Mike Caserta, Frank "Blinky" Palermo, and Louis J. Crusco. It also hinted at the possible involvement of Frank Palumbo, one of the most popular and respected leaders of the local Italian American community. His nightclub was mentioned as a meeting place for about fifty numbers banks.[16]

Against this backdrop, the activities of the Kefauver Committee touched a sensitive nerve among Italian Americans in Philadelphia. Indeed, the electorate of the community lashed back at Kefauver not only in 1956 but earlier in 1952, when Kefauver entered the Democratic primaries for the White House almost unopposed nationwide on his record as a Mafia exposer before losing the nomination to Stevenson at the national convention. In particular, Kefauver had no opponent in Pennsylvania. But less than 0.1 percent of the registered Democrats of Italian ancestry supported him in Philadelphia. All the others preferred to cast write-in votes for a wide range of unlikely candidates spanning from President Truman, who had already withdrawn from the nomination contest, to N. Warren Benedetto, the Italian American director of the Department of Public Property in the city's municipal administration, who obviously had no presidential ambitions.[17]

Ethnic defensiveness affected the voting behavior of the Italian American electorate in Philadelphia in the 1960s as well. The 1964 senatorial election offers a case in point. Michael A. Musmanno, an Italian American Associate Justice of the Pennsylvania Supreme Court from Pittsburgh, made an unsuccessful bid for the Democratic nomination for U.S. Senator. Although he was defeated statewide, Musmanno managed to carry the Italian American districts in Philadelphia by an 81.9 percent landslide after charging U.S. Senator Joseph S. Clark Jr., the most outspoken supporter of his opponent, with having anti-Italian prejudices. Clark implied that Musmanno was not a full-fledged Italian American because his last name had used to be Musmann in his youth. Such a casual remark was enough for Musmanno to cry out against Clark's supposed anti-Italian bigotry and for Italian American voters to rally in his support at the polls.[18]

Italian Americans' responsiveness to appeals to their ethnic identity as a nationality group in the 1950s and 1960s is hardly surprising. After all, in the early postwar decades, the strengthening of communal ties based on national ancestry was a typical phenomenon among Italian Americans throughout the United States. For instance, a strong sense of localistic allegiances and the ensuing perception of fellow Italians from other regions as different and even inferior people had long doomed any project for cooperation among Italian Americans in Chicago, but in 1945 the first community-wide Italian American organization—the Italian Welfare Council—was established in the Windy

City. Seven more years were to elapse before this social agency gave way to the Joint Civic Committee of Italian Americans. Such a new enterprise promised to protect Italian Americans from defamation, to preserve their cultural heritage, and to stimulate their participation in the civic affairs of the city, the county, and the state of Illinois.[19]

Chicago's Italian Americans also provided the backbone of the American Committee on Italian Migration. Starting in 1951, this organization fought against the immigration quota system, until the passing of the Hart-Celler Act of 1965 put a definitive end to the discriminatory allotment of visas on the basis of applicants' national origins and allowed the entry of the immediate relatives of U.S. residents without limit.[20]

In 1976, Americo V. Cortese—a prominent member of the OSIA in Philadelphia—was among the advocates of a meeting of leaders of major Italian American organizations from all over the country with President Gerald R. Ford. The agenda for discussion reflected the concern of many Italian Americans that their own minority risked growing marginalization in U.S. society, as opposed to the alleged achievements of African Americans who could benefit from the help of the federal government. Actually, the complaints included such issues as "lack of sensitivity on the part of federal officials to the needs of the less visible ethnic minorities," "ethnic neighborhood decline," and "affirmative action programs which do not consider Italian Americans who still face discrimination in American corporations and in educational institutions."[21]

Ethnic defense, however, was no longer the task of individual nationality groups in many fields in the postwar decades. Philadelphia's Italian Americans joined forces with members of other European American minorities to fight against common forms of ethnic defamation. In 1978, for example, local representatives of the OSIA, the Polish American Affairs Council, and the American Jewish Committee threatened a common boycott against Hallmark, unless that company recalled supposedly offensive greeting cards that played on anti-Italian, anti-Polish, and anti-Jewish ethnic stereotypes.[22]

Nonetheless, it was primarily antagonism against African Americans that induced working-class Italian Americans and Polish Americans, lower-middle-class Jews, as well as middle-class and working-class Irish to bridge what had once been considerable ethnic and class cleavages. World War II had barely induced Italian Americans to renegotiate their ethnic identity beyond ancestral national boundaries. Yet, the pressures of racial tensions caused Philadelphians of Italian descent to band together and to find some common ground with members of other European minorities in the late 1960s and in the 1970s.

The struggle of some Italian American residents against the destruction of their homes in Corona, a small district within New York City, in connection with a controversial public housing project intended for low-income blacks, revitalized Italian ethnic awareness in their community. Nonetheless, such confrontations seldom pitted only Italian Americans against local governments and therefore provided few opportunities to galvanize the sense of their national extraction among the protesters. Indeed, Italian Americans often found themselves side by side with other European members of the population and were able to broaden their group consciousness during the ensuing mutual efforts to protect their neighborhoods from allegedly disruptive social changes. For instance, Boston's Italian Americans joined forces with Irish Americans to oppose compulsory busing for racial balance in public schools. Similarly, Italian Americans and Jews developed a sense of communal purpose in Canarsie, Brooklyn, in the fight against residential integration with African Americans and the assignment of black students from another district to Junior High School 211 in the early 1970s. After their efforts failed, Canarsie's Italian Americans and Jews also led the white flight from school integration and contributed, for instance, to the dwindling of the white student body of Junior High School 211 to 8.35 percent by 1997.[23]

In an era of escalating racial upheavals and rioting, the backlash at the assertiveness of African Americans forced Italian Americans to reach out to other European groups in Philadelphia, too. The proportion of the African American population grew from about one tenth of the city's residents in 1930 to one third in 1970. Regardless of the country of birth of their ancestors, many white Philadelphians shared constant dread of the increasing number of African American newcomers who settled in the city in the wartime and postwar years. In particular, they progressively came to identify African Americans as well as indigenous and immigrant Puerto Ricans with the spread of crime and urban blight in Philadelphia.[24]

The issues of race and housing had intertwined in the minds of many working-class and lower-middle-class whites throughout the United States since the war years. For instance, community groups of white residents stood for racially homogeneous neighborhoods and fought residential integration in Detroit as early as the 1940s. Similarly, the settlement of the first African American family in Trumbull Park Homes, a public housing project in Chicago, in 1953 sparked off a campaign of violence and terror by the white homeowners of the surrounding South Deering district. In both cases, resistance to the influx of African Americans came from members of a variety of ethnic groups, who found a common ground in their own whiteness despite the heterogeneity of their national ancestry.[25]

The attempt to put an end to de facto residential segregation by means of public housing projects met the opposition of whites in Philadelphia, too. Racial conflicts ensuing from this issue dated back to the early 1950s. By the middle of that decade, they had escalated to such an extent that the first six months of 1955 alone witnessed 213 housing-related racial incidents.[26]

In particular, fears not only of a slump in real estate values but also of the alleged arrival of black drug addicts and street gangs forced South Philadelphia's Italian Americans to ally themselves with local dwellers from Irish, Polish, and Russian backgrounds. Their main aim from 1956 through 1980 was to oppose a project by the Philadelphia Housing Authority and the U.S. Department of Housing and Urban Development to build low-cost public housing in a southeastern section of South Philadelphia—known as Whitman Park—and to integrate this area racially. As thirty-eight residents stated in a letter opposing the project that the *Evening Bulletin* published on 27 April 1971, "[M]ost of us know people who live in neighborhoods near public housing and the problems they have. They are afraid to walk the streets after dark. Robberies, rapes, beatings, and murders are commonplace." In that year, the Whitman Park crisis came to a climax following groundbreaking for the project in December 1970. Angry residents first picketed the prospective public housing site in order to prevent construction from proceeding. Then they filed suit against the Philadelphia Housing Authority on charges that there had been inadequate citizen participation in the planning of the project. While the most disruptive protesters climbed on the bulldozing equipment, demonstrations were basically peaceful. Children usually played around the site and bingo tables were set up in the middle of the streets to block trucks. Opponents of the construction also organized block parties with pizzas and meatballs to raise money to pay the legal costs of the fight. Notwithstanding the Italian flavor in food, opposition to the Whitman Park project resulted from a multiethnic white coalition of ordinary people. They included not only such Italian American housewives as Marie Candilora and Jayne Cucetta, but also Polish American longshoremen such as William Romanowski and Russian American policemen such as Alexander Jablonski.[27]

Cooperation among white South Philadelphians of European ancestry in civic affairs, however, was not confined to the Whitman Park controversy. For instance, representatives of the various European nationality groups established the Federation of Community Councils and Neighborhood Associations in 1965. The purpose of this organization was "to present a united front in situations which could adversely affect the total area [of South Philadelphia]." In addition, tension between white and black residents in this district became so high in the next few years that the city's Commission on Human Relations decided to open a field office there in mid-1969. The purpose of this agency was to lessen racial antipathy by promoting understanding and cooperation between local people. The activities of this race relations office primarily targeted the gangs of white and black youths, who had transformed the borders along their own neighborhoods into a series of war zones.[28]

Schooling was another major area in which resistance to the claims of the black population brought together Italian Americans and other white minorities of European descent. Demands regarding the field of public education ranked high among the priorities of African Americans throughout the United States in the 1960s. Such claims could also easily be framed in ways to split up single cities into conflicting racial groups that cut across class divisions. In Philadelphia, the problems concerning the local public school system provided Italian Americans with a major opportunity to develop a white ethnic identity that they could share with other nationality groups of European ancestry while opposing the claims of African Americans.[29]

On the occasion of the 1961 primary elections, the Philadelphia Board of Public Education promoted a referendum to gain the voters' approval for an increase in its own borrowing capacity. The Board submitted a ten-million-dollar bond issue to the electorate. Despite widespread fears that the electorate would reject the proposal, voters approved the loan by a 76.9 percent landslide. Support for the bond issue was larger among Italian Americans than in the city as a whole. Indeed, 80.6 percent of the Italian American voters cast their ballots to authorize raising the debt limit of the Board of Public Education. Yet, the attitude of Italian Americans toward the appropriation of funds for public schools changed dramatically as soon as African American assertiveness began to affect the school system in Philadelphia, and that city, too, witnessed an outburst of racial tension and riots.[30]

In the summer of 1961, just a few week after the approval of the referendum, the local chapter of the National Association for the Advancement of Colored People denounced the Philadelphia Board of Public Education for discriminating against students on the grounds of race. It also suggested that the busing of African American students to schools in predominantly white residential areas such as Jenks School in Chestnut Hill, would be the only viable solution to cope with the overcrowding of public schools in African American neighborhoods.[31]

Italian Americans contributed to Democratic Richardson Dilworth's reelection as mayor of Philadelphia with 58.5 percent of their votes in 1959. Four years later, however, the Republican mayoral candidate— James T. McDermott—carried the Italian American community with 52.9 percent, although he was defeated by Democratic James H. J. Tate in the city as a whole by 54.7 percent of the vote. Tate secured the support of the *Il Popolo Italiano* in 1963. But its endorsement turned out to be of little avail among Italian Americans in the wake of growing African American claims and violence. In fact, the 1963 election took place in the aftermath of a black uprising. This tumult followed the fatal shooting of a twenty-four-year-old African American by a police officer and resulted in at least five hundred blacks looting stores and pelting the cars of white drivers with bricks on 27 and 28 October 1963.[32]

Unlike Tate, McDermott came out against busing.[33] The fact that many Italian Americans in Philadelphia perceived African Americans as a potential menace accounts for the stampede of a majority of the Italian American electorate to the Republican party in 1963.

Racial strife also affected labor relations. In May 1963, picketers who belonged to the Philadelphia Congress of Racial Equality and to the local chapter of the National Association for the Advancement of Colored People halted construction on the Municipal Service Building and on a school site at 31st and Dauphin Streets. Protesters called for equal employment opportunities for African American workers on city building projects. They also advocated the end of white union monopolies in the construction trades in Philadelphia. Turmoil resulted from the demonstrations. At least twenty-three people were injured as picketers clashed with members of labor unions who resented the shutdown of construction and accused African American protesters of causing the loss of their jobs. The Tate administration eventually struck a deal for the resumption of work on city projects but it had to overcome opposition from labor unions. Unlike what had happened in 1944, this time Italian Americans were active in the attempt to curb the claims of African American workers. Joseph B. Meranze and Henry Fornara, for instance, represented the Philadelphia Building Trades Council and the Electrical Workers Local 98, respectively, and voiced the claims of their white members in talks with the City Commission on Human Relations.[34]

In those years, African Americans were not welcome in Italian American neighborhoods and local residents strongly resisted their attempts to move into these areas. Such feelings and attitudes gained progressive footing in the Italian American community as the increasing spread of African American urban violence and riots, which had affected a number of cities since 1964, hit Philadelphia, too. By the end of the 1960s, *Il Popolo Italiano* maintained that black nationalism was the main threat to U.S. society.[35]

On 28 August 1964, the arrest of two African American motorists degenerated into a two-night uprising that caused two deaths, 339 wounded, and about three million dollars in property damages. In a comment on this incident, the *Sons of Italy Times* called for "law and order" against "thugs, thieves, and hoodlums." This newspaper was an English-language semi-weekly, published by the OSIA in Philadelphia, that had replaced *Ordine Nuovo* as the organ of the Order since 1959. It took a similar stand after the police disrupted a relatively peaceful demonstration that high school black activists held at the School Administration Building on 17 November 1967 to ask for more courses in African American history and culture as well as for permission to wear African-style clothes at school. The *Sons of Italy Times* hurried to "strongly commend the effective action of the uniformed police under the able command of Commissioner Frank Rizzo in bringing under control an unruly crowd of 3500 people [who] had become inflamed and threatening to the safety of innocent persons and property." According to civil-rights attorney Lois G. Forer, the policemen on duty "dragged" girls "along the street by their hair" and "a club was broken over a boy's back." Yet, Robert L. Sebastian, a prominent Italian American attorney and a member of the Philadelphia Board of Public Education, was ready to echo the scant tolerance of his fellow ethnics for African American public disturbance. He strongly and publicly disagreed with Board chairperson Richardson Dilworth, who had criticized the use of force by the police.[36]

Other Catholic minorities shared the anxiety of Italian Americans over the School Administration Building incident. Besides fearing escalating African American protests, such ethnic groups also worried about the increasing tax burden to pay for the city's public schools. These expenses failed to benefit most of their children because they attended primarily parochial schools. Many Italian American families had avoided the Catholic educational system for decades before World War II and then had begun to send their kids to parochial schools in the 1950s because they did not want their children to mix with African Americans in public schools. In addition, in the opinion of many working-class whites of Italian, Irish, or Polish ancestry, the local public school system was too lax with troublemakers and too concerned with African American grievances. A few days after the black demonstration at the School Administration Building, School Superintendent Mark R. Shedd received a sizable amount of letters from white parents of local students who asked for more security for their children. Suggestions included the adoption of such measures as "ridding the classrooms of all troublemakers," "police protection," "identification cards, with pictures, to keep non-students out of the schools," "strict punishment for pupils caught carrying concealed weapons," and "more protection for students' personal property." A Harvard-trained liberal, however, Shedd was not as responsive to white demands as he was willing to accommodate African American requests.[37]

In the 1969 primary elections, another referendum was held to authorize the city administration to issue bonds and borrow ninety million dollars, which were necessary to build a number of new public schools in Philadelphia. Italian American voters had overwhelmingly accepted the 1961 proposal to extend the debt limit. This time, however, the majority of Italian Americans rejected the request of the Board of Public Education.

Following the decline in white attendance at public schools in the face of the increasing presence of black students, the ninety-million-dollar loan could easily have appeared to be a measure that would be charged to white taxpayers but would benefit primarily African Americans. These were the conclusions of a post-election analysis for the Board of Public Education. Indeed, the leading African American organizations in Philadelphia came out for the 1969 proposal enthusiastically.

Conversely, Italian Americans seemed interested less in supporting public schools than in financing Catholic schools in the 1960s. Significantly, the Pennsylvania Grand Lodge of the OSIA endorsed a bill, introduced in the state legislature in 1968, that would establish a School Authority with powers and resources to fund non-public schools for elementary and secondary pupils. As OSIA Grand Trustee Armand Della Porta stated before the Pennsylvania House Committee on Education on 17 April 1968, "[A]t this critical moment when our non-public schools are facing their most serious educational crisis, our concern is directed toward their plight. We cannot and shall not stand idly by watching this great system of schools, which has educated so many of our members and is educating tens of thousands of our members' children, falter in its task." Philadelphia's Italian Americans also asked for the implementation of the Pennsylvania governor's pledge to make special state money "available for non-public school children in their quest for a quality education."[38]

The election results for the 1969 referendum revealed a remarkable polarization of voters along racial lines. The predominantly African American wards in the North Philadelphia and West Philadelphia districts were solidly in favor of the loan proposal. Conversely, a coalition of white voters from the Kensington, Richmond, Northeast Philadelphia, and South Philadelphia districts made the difference and soundly defeated the bond issue with a total of 56.6 percent of the vote.[39]

The Columbus Forum—an organization that grouped the employees of Italian origin of the Board of Public Education—supported the loan. Yet, Italian Americans made a remarkable contribution to the white opposition to the demands of the Board of Public Education and rejected the bond question by a 69.8 percent landslide. A similar proposal was placed on the ballot the following November. It requested authorization for a sixty-five-million-dollar loan for the construction and improvement of school buildings through the issue of municipal bonds. This time, the referendum won the approval of 63.8 percent of the Philadelphia electorate. Nonetheless, the bulk of Italian American voters joined the white opponents of the school bond issue on this latter occasion, too. Supporters of the loan secured the endorsement of prominent Italian American leaders such as Republican Councilman Thomas M. Foglietta. Anthony Cortigene, the sitting manager of the Philadelphia Joint Board of the Amalgamated Clothing Workers of America, even served as honorary co-chairperson of the campaign committee for the approval of the bond issue, along with Republican

U.S. Senator Hugh Scott. Nonetheless, a majority of the rank and file members of the Italian American community disregarded the pro-loan stand of their own leadership and 55.7 percent of the Italian American electorate voted against the bond issue in November.[40]

Politics was the main field that revealed the common efforts of Italian Americans and other minority groups of European extraction. In particular, as a Democratic committeeperson remarked in 1969, the "dislike of racial conflict" was the "one issue" that brought together white voters in Philadelphia.[41]

The 1971 mayoral contest offers a case study of such an attitude. This election campaign pitted Italian American Police Commissioner Frank L. Rizzo, the Democratic candidate, against Republican W. Thacher Longstreth. A coalition of Italian American, Polish American, Irish American, and Jewish voters elected Rizzo to City Hall. Longstreth was a former executive director of the Greater Philadelphia Chamber of Commerce and a member of the City Council. He usually denounced police brutality in confrontations with African Americans as opposed to Rizzo's pledge to crack down on disruptive blacks and to resort to warfare against the Black Panthers. Rizzo even refused to campaign in African American neighborhoods in order to emphasize that he stuck to the white cohort of the electorate and had hardly anything to do with colored people. Against this backdrop, while the election campaign polarized Philadelphia along racial lines, Longstreth had no chances of beating Rizzo among white voters. His patrician extraction and the endorsement of the Southeastern Pennsylvania chapter of Americans for Democratic Action (ADA) contributed to Longstreth's characterization as a "limousine liberal" and further made the white electorate distance itself from the Republican candidate.[42]

In particular, while Rizzo obtained 53.2 percent of the vote in Philadelphia at large, he carried the Italian American community by 86.1 percent. Of course, not all Italian Americans supported him against Longstreth. Novelist Jerre Mangione even came out for Rizzo's opponent in the Democratic primaries, William Green Jr., and established an Arts Committee for Green. Still, Rizzo obtained the endorsement of key segments of the Italian American electorate. For instance, Anthony Cortigene, the manager of Philadelphia's sixteen locals of the Amalgamated Clothing Workers of America, was a strong backer of Rizzo's bid for mayor.[43]

Rizzo was a latecomer to a group of populist mayoral candidates who had endeavored to capitalize on the ethnic backlash of the white electorate throughout the United States since the 1960s. They included Louise Day Hicks, who exploited her opposition to busing in order to wage two unsuccessful campaigns against Kevin White for mayor of Boston in 1967 and 1971; Charles Stenvig, a police officer who became mayor of Minneapolis in 1969 running on the pledge that he would enforce the law against black militants and would not impose racial integration on the city's neighborhoods; Alfreda Slominski, who made her own antagonism to racial balancing in the schools of Buffalo the leading issue in her fruitless bid to defeat incumbent Mayor Frank A. Sedita in 1969; as well as Mario Procaccino and John Marchi, whose mutual stand against crime and racial disorder split the votes of conservative New Yorkers and let incumbent mayor John Lindsay win reelection in the same year.[44]

A paramount plank in Rizzo's 1971 platform was his pledge to dismiss Mark R. Shedd. The school superintendent had been very controversial among white residents because of his alleged pro–African American bent since the 1967 incident at the School Administration Building. For example, as late as mid-October 1969, almost two years after the black demonstration, a second-generation Italian American and his wife still complained about "the irresponsibility of Dr. Shedd . . . in not being able to control a few thousand students" on that occasion. Rizzo's commitment, however, was only an election campaign stunt to secure the support of white voters. Actually, as ADA local chairperson Jon Blum pointed out, it was the Board of Public Education—not the mayor—that had the power to hire, and thereby also to fire, the school superintendent.[45]

In his pursuit of the votes of white Philadelphians, Rizzo could also profit by a nationwide reputation for his strong-arm methods against troublemakers in general and African American activists in particular. Not only did Rizzo lead his men against the demonstrators at the School Administration Building in 1967, he also ordered numerous raids on the hideouts of the Black Panthers and other extremist African American organizations such as the Revolutionary Action Movement. Rizzo kept confidential dossiers on their members and made himself a name for his notorious technique of "beating first and asking questions later" in police confrontations with African Americans and alleged criminals. A picture in the local newspapers of Black Panthers being stripped naked and searched by policemen in front of photographers at 2 A.M. after their headquarters had been stormed came to epitomize Rizzo's law-and-order stand in the eyes of his prospective electorate. Indeed, friendly coverage by conservative press mogul Walter Annenberg's *Philadelphia Inquirer* largely contributed to Rizzo's reputation and credit for "keeping the lid on" during the racial tensions of the 1960s. Rizzo himself stated after the School Building incident: "We are not going to back down in riots and insurrections. We are going to stop all this lawlessness. We are going to maintain law and order. Nobody is going to make a patsy out of the Police Department." In addition, he reportedly declared that, as mayor, "I will make Attila the Hun look like a faggot."[46]

Rizzo's election in the heyday of the postwar ethnic revival was a timely opportunity for Italian Americans in Philadelphia to galvanize consciousness of their national ancestry. To say the least, it compensated decades of Italian American marginality in local politics at the hands of Irish Americans. The very fact that Mayor James H. J. Tate himself, the nominal head of the Irish faction that controlled the Democratic party in Philadelphia, handpicked Rizzo as his own successor in 1971 could easily be perceived as a sort of legitimization of the ethnic succession in power in the city administration. Furthermore, by allotting a significant share of his patronage among his own fellow ethnics, Rizzo himself helped accommodate a few Italian Americans within the payroll of the local government.[47]

Rizzo's 1971 victory was the product of a coalition of white voters who belonged to different nationality groups. It therefore demonstrated that ethnic cooperation was more productive than competition for providing effective solutions to such problems as crime and urban violence, which Rizzo's supporters deplored regardless of the different countries of birth of their southern and eastern European ancestors. Actually, Mayor Tate slated Rizzo for City Hall because he thought that his own police commissioner's law-and-order image as a nonsense law enforcement officer would keep Philadelphia's white voters in the Democratic fold. In Tate's opinion, Rizzo's candidacy would counteract the racial pressures that tended to encourage the voters of European descent to go over to the GOP as a response to the supposed identification of the Democratic Party with the interests of African Americans at the national level. As Tate himself acknowledged, "[T]he old Democratic coalition of ... organized labor, the working class whites, liberals, blacks and other minorities was breaking down. The working class whites ... were developing increasingly Republican tendencies. ... I felt that Rizzo could bring the white working class vote back into the Democratic Party."[48]

After all, four years earlier, Tate had named Rizzo as police commissioner to keep the support of the city's white voters and to secure his own reelection in 1967. It was hardly by chance that Tate announced the appointment of Rizzo on the very night of the primary polls. Republican Arlen Specter, the incumbent district attorney, was to oppose the mayor in the race for City Hall in November. Tate, therefore, needed to associate his own administration with a public figure who was well-known for his toughness on crime in order to prevent the GOP from capturing the law-and-order issue and taking advantage of the fears of the white electorate. Tate's decision paid off. Specter's failure to state clearly whether he, as mayor, would retain Rizzo as his police commissioner helped alienate white voters from the Republican Party, and contributed to Tate's reelection.[49]

Indeed, esteem for Rizzo extended beyond his nationality group and could be found among other white minorities. The response to his selection as police commissioner offer a case in point. Rizzo's appointment came under heavy criticism from Americans for Democratic Action because of his poor civil rights record. At that time, Rizzo was a member of the Germantown lodge 683 of the OSIA. Yet, Italian American associations were not alone in endorsing his nomination. The Philadelphia chapter of B'nai B'rith, the oldest and largest Jewish service organization nationwide, and the Lutheran Men, a club of Philadelphians of German descent, also backed the mayor's choice for police commissioner. Rizzo further benefited from trans-ethnic white support after the 1967 incident at the School Administration Building. The city's leadership of the National Association for the Advancement of Colored People denounced Rizzo for his "Gestapo-like" tactics in quelling this demonstration and called for his "immediate" dismissal. However, non-Italian whites joined the *Sons of Italy Times* in praising the work the police commissioner had done on 17 November 1967. For instance, a Jewish reader of the *Philadelphia Inquirer* wrote in a letter to the editor that "the people of Philadelphia once again owe Commissioner Rizzo a debt of gratitude for his prompt action which resulted in the prevention of what probably would have been a riot." Moreover, two other white members of the Board of Public Education, William Ross and William Goldman, sided with Robert Sebastian in defending Rizzo and blaming the incident on black "adult agitators" who, in their opinion, had turned otherwise inoffensive young students into "the pawns of pressure groups." As African American organizations called for a boycott of the city's white merchants until the

Tate administration removed Rizzo from the position of police commissioner, the School Board demonstration and its aftermath helped polarize the people of Philadelphia along racial lines. These events also helped Rizzo to stand out as a symbol of the white cohorts of the local population.[50]

Rizzo continued to enjoy trans-ethnic white support in the following years. In early 1976, a few months after his re-election to City Hall in November 1975, under the auspices of the Philadelphia chapter of Americans for Democratic Action, former Democratic mayor Joseph S. Clark Jr. and defeated independent African American mayoral candidate Charles W. Bowser started a citywide drive to hold a recall referendum on Rizzo. Their attempt was unsuccessful. According to the City Charter, the petition for a recall election required the signatures of at least one fourth of the 564,636 voters who had cast their ballots in the 1975 mayoral contest. The Citizens' Committee to Recall Rizzo collected 211,190 signatures, but a court eventually ruled that only 88,894 were valid. Although technicalities prevented Rizzo from facing the referendum, it is significant that the opponents of the recall movement were not confined to the mayor's fellow ethnics. A number of rank and file Philadelphians came out for Rizzo by means of letters to the local newspapers. They praised the mayor for his skill in running Philadelphia and accused the recallers of being "interested only in the disruption of the city." These individuals had not only Italian-sounding names, like Leonora Riccinti. They also included such people of other white European backgrounds as Thomas F. Gillepsie, Bill Wible, or Jack Downes.[51]

Scholars have argued that voters' identification with the ethnicity of politicians running for local offices has replaced party allegiance as a clue to the electorate's choice of candidates in municipal and county contests, following the steady decline of partisanship in U.S. politics since the late 1960s. Indeed, Philadelphia's Italian Americans usually demonstrated disproportionate support for politicians of Italian descent throughout the 1970s. The tendency to cast ballots for fellow ethnics was so widespread in their community that even politicians from other minority groups, such as African American would-be Councilman Henry De Bernardo or Japanese American Judge William Marutani, made impressive electoral showings among Italian American voters in the late 1970s thanks to their own misleadingly Italian-sounding last names.[52]

For this reason, the Italian origin of Rizzo's parents helped him gain the votes of many Italian Americans. Ernest L. Biagi, a former grand secretary of the Pennsylvania Grand Lodge of the OSIA, came out for Rizzo because of his Italian identity. He endorsed Rizzo on the grounds of his Italian background in a statement for the *Philadelphia Exclusive*, an English-language weekly for the local Italian American community. Biagi affirmed that he backed him "because I don't like the people who are ganging up against him. . . . They are haters who have never shown any understanding and sympathy towards the Italians." Yet, an examination of the editorial position and news coverage among the local Italian American press reveals that appeals like Biagi's to the national pride of Italian American voters had diminished by the early 1970s. For instance, in the same issue of the *Philadelphia Exclusive*, just below Biagi's statement, Ralph Cingolo—another prominent Italian American—placed the significance of Rizzo's candidacy within a broader trans-ethnic context and declared that "Rizzo will make a great mayor of Philadelphia, fair to all people regardless of their nationality of origin." As the president of the South Philadelphia Businessmen's Association, an organization that included not only Italian Americans but also members from other European national backgrounds, Cingolo viewed at Rizzo's bid for mayor from a broader perspective than Biagi did.[53]

Several immigrants, such as Father Mazzone, could still proclaim, "I am proud to be an Italian" in the early 1970s. Nonetheless, by then, the number of Italian-born residents in Philadelphia had been cut almost in half since the end of World War II. It actually dropped from 48,721 individuals in 1950 to 25,629 in 1970. The presence of Italian immigrants underwent a further decline in the following two decades. Indeed, Philadelphia was home to 17,262 Italian immigrants in 1980 and to only 9,279 in 1990. The number of people who spoke Italian at home also decreased, from 36,316 in 1980 to 23,974 in 1990. Conversely, the size of the population of Italian ancestry—a category that included not only immigrants but also their offspring—was on the increase. It rose from 132,630 in 1980 to 178,315 in 1990.[54]

Biagi was an Italian immigrant with strong ties to a nationally-oriented ethnic association such as the OSIA. The membership of this organization throughout the United States increased from 125,000 individuals in 1918 to nearly 300,000 in the early 1920s but dropped to 98,000 in 1977. It was to fall farther, to 90,000 people in the early 1980s. Biagi, therefore, was not representative of the rising third- and fourth-generation Italian Americans who did not speak the language of their grandparents, married outside their nationality group, and left South

Philadelphia for the suburbs in the wake of both the influx of African Americans to their neighborhoods and the decay of Philadelphia as a leading manufacturing center. Between 1950 and 1985, the city lost about 250,000 industrial jobs out of a total of 350,000. This figure included more than 30,000 federal positions with the Signal Corps Supply Center, the Marine Corps Supply Center, and the Navy Engineering Group. More specifically, from 1970 to 1978 the city suffered a loss of as many as 130,000 jobs. In those years, the development of the service sector failed to compensate the decline in manufacturing positions, as employers relocated their plants to areas outside Philadelphia that had lower taxes and a nonunionized work force.[55]

Suburban residence did not necessary constitute a postwar melting pot for Italian Americans in the Philadelphia metropolitan area, as aggregation along lines of national extraction sometimes persisted outside the inner city. For example, in Ardmore, a few miles west of Philadelphia, the population of Italian ancestry did not scatter throughout this suburb but concentrated south of Lancaster Avenue. This phenomenon was not specific to the Philadelphia area. Indeed, scholars of the Italian American experience in Long Island, New York, have indicated that social homogenization did not follow suburban resettlement. Similarly, a study of the New York City metropolitan area based on the 1980 and 1990 Censuses has revealed that, in those years, there were more Italian American neighborhoods in the suburbs than there were in the central city.[56]

Many Italian American suburbanites also retained links to their former Italian neighborhoods in Philadelphia, attended Italian festivals, and ate Italian food. So did their fellow ethnics who had previously left Boston's North End, Chicago's Near West Side, or Manhattan's Lower East Side. In particular, in the mid 1970s, Italian Americans from the suburban areas continued to go to the 9th Street market in the heart of South Philadelphia's historic "Little Italy" to buy their meat and vegetables.[57]

Even in the case of Italian-oriented leisure activities, the national descent of the Philadelphians of Italian ancestry no longer coincided with their ethnic identity. This latter had developed beyond the borders of the mother country and now embraced the broader contours of a white European self-referential group that was almost constantly on the defensive against the alleged encroachments of African Americans.

Remarkably enough, the Italian events that had formerly galvanized Philadelphians from Italian background into action in the postwar years no longer stimulated an ethnic commitment in the 1970s. In the late 1950s, Democratic activists were still able to exploit the similarity in names between the Christian Democrats, the leading party in Italy's coalition government, and the Democratic Party of the United States to register Italian immigrants who had arrived in Philadelphia after World War II as Democratic voters. Yet, unlike what had happened between the late 1940s and the early 1950s, Italy-related anticommunism was no longer a stimulus for mobilization among Italian Americans in the mid 1970s. Ralph Borrelli suggested that a "letter to Italy" campaign similar to the propagandistic operations of 1948 and 1953 should be launched again in 1976 in order to prevent the Communist Party from winning that year's parliamentary elections in Italy and to keep the Christian Democrats in power. This time, however, his appeal fell on deaf ears among his fellow ethnics. It is significant, for instance, that the Citizens Alliance for Mediterranean Freedom had no relevant following in Philadelphia's community. Former Texas Governor John B. Connally established this private organization to involve Italian Americans in the attempt to discourage Italian voters from electing a communist majority in the 1976 parliamentary contests. But the Citizens Alliance for Mediterranean Freedom could not list a single prominent Philadelphian of Italian descent among its prospective adherents.[58]

The outcome of the 1975 mayoral contest offers further evidence that, by then, whiteness had become more influential than Italianness in shaping the political behavior of Italian Americans in Philadelphia. In 1975, the Republican Party slated Italian American Councilman Thomas M. Foglietta for mayor in an attempt to recapture the votes of the Italian Americans who had cast their ballots for Rizzo in 1971. Foglietta enjoyed a reputation as a relatively liberal politician despite his Republican affiliation. He endeavored to strengthen the coalition between African Americans and the more progressive segments of the white electorate. For this very reason, however, his candidacy could hardly attract those Italian Americans who had become warier and warier of black militancy and its claims. Foglietta was of Italian ancestry and had been the top Republican vote getter in the 1971 elections for the city council. Yet, his failure to address the concerns of whites in the field of racial relations prevented him from securing the support of many of the Italian Americans who traditionally sided with the Republican party. Rizzo's boast that "Foglietta couldn't beat me in South Philadelphia if I gave him the voting machine tonight" was hardly an exaggeration. Even though 31 percent of Philadelphia's eligible Italian American voters were registered as Republicans in 1975, Rizzo carried the community by a 83-percent landslide. Foglietta's share of the Italian American vote did not exceed even the 18 percent that he managed to obtain citywide. In 1975, African American Charles W. Bowser, a deputy mayor in the Tate Administration, made an independent bid for City Hall on the ticket of a newly formed third party. Consequently, as Foglietta himself has acknowledged, a few Republicans of Italian ancestry also cast their ballots for Rizzo for fear that support for Foglietta would split the white vote and let a black candidate become mayor of Philadelphia.[59]

The re-elaboration of the self-identity of Philadelphia's Italian Americans as white ethnics consolidated in 1978. After winning re-election in 1975, Rizzo wanted to remain in office past 1979. For this reason, in 1978, he promoted a referendum to amend the City Charter and enable the mayor to serve more than two consecutive terms. The Rizzo administration helped exacerbate the polarization of Philadelphia along racial lines. In particular, the mayor let a contract with Multicon Corporation expire. Multicon was a private developer that had agree to build 120 homes for low-income families in Whitman Park. The breach of contract cost the city $626,000 in damages. But, by fighting against the Whitman Park public housing project, Rizzo championed the call of white residents for the preservation of the racial integrity of their neighborhoods. Rizzo's second term at City Hall also put a temporary end to a five-year confrontation between the municipal government and MOVE, a back-to-nature, predominantly African American, counterculture group that had settled at 33rd and Pearl Streets in the Powelton Village section of the West Philadelphia district in 1973. MOVE members, who included a few former Black Panthers, kept fifty to sixty unvaccinated dogs, dumped garbage in their backyard, drawing rats, stockpiled guns, and used a loudspeaker to hurl obscenities at their neighbors. Their lifestyle and behavior worried a number of local residents who had been complaining to city officials for years. Eventually, on 8 August 1978, the Philadelphia police stormed the MOVE compound and razed its headquarters in an early-morning bloody shootout that left an officer dead.[60]

In the attempt to capitalize on his own record, Rizzo waged the 1978 referendum campaign posing as the champion of law-abiding whites, planning to cash in on their fear of African American radicalism. He himself outlined his own interpretation of the paramount issue at stake in the vote on the City Charter: "This is an election between the social extremists and the social radicals against the people who live within the law. What am I talking about? The Black Panthers." Rizzo also argued at a press conference that "whites must join hands." Similarly, in an emotional appeal to the electorate of European descent, he stated that he was tired of hearing his political opponents encourage African Americans to "vote black" and urged his own supporters to "vote white."[61]

Sixty-six percent of the Philadelphia electorate rejected Rizzo's proposed amendment in 1978. Yet, while the mayor had repeatedly emphasized the need for interethnic cohesion among the city's whites, 85 percent of Italian American voters cast their ballots to remove the two-term limit on the mayoralty. This outcome represented a 2 percent increase over the 83 percent that Rizzo had received in their community in 1975. Significantly, Italian Americans had also the highest turnout among all Philadelphia's ethnic groups. The percentage of eligible voters of Italian ancestry who participated in the term-limit referendum was 75 percent, as opposed to 72 percent of Jews, 70 percent of both Poles and Irish, and 63 percent of African Americans. Turnout was 63 percent citywide.[62]

Italian American support for Rizzo increased as the white-versus-black polarization in Philadelphia became more and more evident even in symbolic terms. In 1983, Rizzo made a political comeback to challenge W. Wilson Goode—an African American civic leader and the managing director of the city administration—for the Democratic mayoral nomination in a racially divisive primary campaign in which Rizzo re-emphasized the "white" characterization of his own candidacy. Rizzo made a point of attacking Reverend Jesse Jackson and endorsed Republican Bernard Epton against African American Harold Washington for mayor of Chicago, even though this latter contest was completely unrelated to the mayoral campaign in Philadelphia. Undaunted by his defeat by Goode in the 1983 Democratic primaries, Rizzo went over to the Republican Party four years later and challenge him again in the 1987 election. During this latter campaign, Rizzo also tried to link Goode to Louis Farrakhan to consolidate the Jewish component of his own white coalition and win the support of liberal Jews by playing on their racial concerns. Indeed, racial issues shaped the 1987 mayoral contest. At that time, African American officials held the positions not only of mayor but also of school superintendent, managing director at City Hall, and City Council president.

White Philadelphians feared the loss of all their political power to the black community in the local government.[63]

Rizzo's bids for City Hall were unsuccessful in both 1983 and 1987, although his candidacy caused an estimated 40,000 white Democratic voters to switch to the GOP in the latter year. And as the fight between a white and a black politician epitomized the persisting antipathies between these two groups in Philadelphia, Rizzo's political following among Italian American voters reached 95 percent in 1983 and 92 percent in 1987. The electorate of Italian ancestry did not identify itself with Rizzo because he was of Italian extraction. Italian Americans voted for him because he was a symbol of white assertiveness. Thus, although another candidate of Italian origin—Frank Lomento—ran in the 1983 Democratic mayoral primary, his fate among Italian Americans was similar to Foglietta's eight years earlier. Lomento received only 2.6 percent of the vote in South Philadelphia, as opposed to 3.0 percent citywide. Mayor Goode ordered another assault on MOVE's headquarters on 13 May 1985. A police helicopter dropped a bomb, killing five members of the organization and six children. However, in the mid-1980s, Italian Americans were still the ethnic group in Philadelphia least positive in their evaluation of both the state of race relations and the effectiveness of police protection.[64]

Even the *Sons of Italy Times* showed scant sense of ethnic pride based on Italian descent when it endorsed Rizzo for mayor in 1987. This newspaper had hailed Rizzo's 1975 reelection in ethnic tones: "We supported him as one of our own—a Sons of Italy man—and a respected son of Italian parents, who as Mayor has enormously boosted the Italian image in this city, as none before has ever done." Twelve years later, however, it confined itself to routinely reminding its readers that Rizzo "made history by being the first Italian-American to become Police Commissioner. He made history again when he was elected the first Italian-American Mayor of Philadelphia." Nonetheless, the reasons the *Sons of Italy Times* offered to explain why it supported Rizzo's fourth bid for City Hall did not concern the national ancestry of the would-be mayor. As the organ of the OSIA put it, "[reelecting Rizzo] is your duty as a citizen. It's your right as an American. It's your salvation as a Philadelphian.... In South Philadelphia our members are crying about how the Goode administration wants to make them a dumping ground. In Germantown and West Philadelphia our members are crying out for more police protection." Moreover, the *Sons of Italy Times* never mentioned Rizzo's Italian extraction when it called on Italian Americans to cast their ballots in favor of the amendment to the City Charter during the 1978 "vote white" referendum campaign.[65]

Significantly enough, support for Rizzo among Italian American voters dropped as soon as he no longer faced an African American opponent, such as Goode. In 1991, Rizzo challenged two white candidates, incumbent District Attorney Roland Castille and former school board member Samuel Katz, in a successful bid for the Republican nomination for mayor. This time, he received only 62.5 percent of the Italian American vote in contrast to the 92 percent of the Fall 1987 election. In addition, after having enthusiastically endorsed Rizzo in 1987, the *Sons of Italy Times* remained silent about his candidacy in the 1991 primaries. However, both the size of the support by Italian American voters for Rizzo in the general election and the attitude of the organ of the OSIA toward him during this latter campaign are a matter of speculation. Rizzo died after securing the Republican nomination and, therefore, was not on the ballot in November, when Democrat Edward G. Rendell was elected mayor.[66]

Racial concerns did not influence the voting behavior of Philadelphia's Italian Americans just in local elections. In presidential politics, Philadelphians of Italian descent also participated in the white backlash that enlisted their fellow ethnics throughout the United States. They began by joining the race-motivated white ethnic members of the Silent Majority in 1968 and later moved on to swell the ranks of the Reagan Democrats who went over to the GOP because they thought that the Democratic Party had neglected their needs in favor of African Americans.[67]

Italian American support for the Democratic Party in elections for the White House declined nationwide from 77 percent in 1964 to 50 percent four years later. It reached a low of 39 percent in 1984. As a case in point, between 1960 and 1968, Republican presidential candidate Richard M. Nixon increased his own following among Italian Americans by 2 percent in Chicago, 3 percent in Boston, 10 percent in Cleveland, 13 percent in Brooklyn, and 15 percent in Newark. His gains were especially high in racially tense cities. The electoral behavior of Philadelphians of Italian ancestry mirrored this trend.[68]

When Alabama's Governor George Wallace ran for the White House as the candidate of the American Independent Party on a substantially white supremacist platform in 1968, he received only 7.5 percent of the vote in Philadelphia at large. His support, however, was greater among local Italian Americans and he won 12.8 percent of the ballots cast in their community. Another 44.1 percent of the Italian American vote went to Nixon. The Democratic standard bearer, incumbent Vice President Hubert H. Humphrey, won 43.1 percent.[69]

Democratic Mayor Rizzo endorsed Nixon in his 1972 reelection bid. He later expressed regret for the president's resignation in the wake of the Watergate investigation. Only one day after Nixon left the White House in disgrace, Rizzo hurried to write him: "As one who is privileged to know you personally, I have witnessed the recent events with sadness. I am truly sorry for what has happened, and I know that in your heart you did what you believed to be right for the nation." Nonetheless, Rizzo went back to the Democratic camp in 1976 and endorsed presidential candidate Jimmy Carter.[70]

Rizzo's long and diehard allegiance to Nixon may not have been representative of the political attitude of his fellow ethnics in Philadelphia. However, a number of prominent Philadelphians of Italian descent pledged their support to the president at the time of his bid for a second term in the White House in 1972 and 64.8 percent of the city's Italian American voters cast their ballots for Nixon on election day.[71]

Furthermore, Republican Ronald Reagan carried the community in the 1984 presidential race. That year, the Democratic Party chose Congresswoman Geraldine Ferraro as its candidate for vice president and made her the first politician of Italian ancestry to run for this office on the ticket of either major party. Ferraro's nomination was intended to help Democratic presidential candidate Walter Mondale win the votes of both women and Italian American voters. Her pro-choice stand on abortion, however, while pleasing the former portion of the electorate, may have antagonized the latter owing to their socially conservative tendencies. Actually, commenting on the rise of Italian Americans in politics in 1984, the *Sons of Italy Times* pointed to Mario Cuomo, the governor of New York State and the keynote speaker at the 1984 Democratic convention, as the politician who "well brings to government the Italian idea of family." The newspaper made no attempt to compare Ferraro's stand on family values and related issues with Cuomo's.[72]

Ferraro was a member of the Board of Directors of the National Italian American Foundation, a Washington-based organization formed for the purpose of advancing Italian American concerns, culture, and heritage in the United States. She appealed to Italian American ethnic pride in her acceptance speech and, whenever it was possible, throughout the election campaign. That her bid for vice president was a major achievement for the U.S. population of Italian descent as a whole was obvious. The *Sons of Italy Times*, for instance, hailed her candidacy as "a breakthrough" for Italian Americans. Furthermore, the election campaign allegations that Ferraro's family—and specifically her husband, real estate developer John Zaccaro—was linked to organized crime might have touched a sensitive nerve among Italian Americans sufficient to have induced them to lash back at that traditional anti-Italian stereotype by showing solidarity for their fellow-ethnic candidate while casting their ballots at the polls.[73]

In 1984, many voters analyzed the Democratic program through a racial filter that pitted blacks against whites. They, therefore, read the "fairness" emphasized in the Democratic platform as federal intervention to favor African Americans to the detriment of European minorities. In this context, the bulk of Philadelphia's Italian American voters chose to identify themselves as whites, not as Italian Americans. The Mondale-Ferraro Democratic ticket carried Philadelphia with 64.9 percent of the vote but received only 43 percent within the local Italian American electorate. The backlash in Philadelphia's Italian American community against the Democratic Party because of its supposed pro–African American bias is unsurprising. After all, in 1984, many Italian American families in South Philadelphia lived in neighborhoods in which income levels were lower than in the city's predominantly black districts, although deindustrialization had deeply affected the wage and employment levels of local African Americans.[74]

Italian Americans' reaction against the supposed encroachments of blacks further consolidated as opposition to affirmative action policies mounted nationwide and the United States began to back away from these programs in the 1990s. A characteristic stereotypical perception of the same ilk as the notorious welfare-queen paradigm, for instance, can be seen in the remarks of a Philadelphia firefighter of Italian ancestry on the subject of affirmative action in 1995. Interviewed in a *New York Times* report on preferential programs for minorities, he admitted that "affirmative action and even welfare, at the beginning, was a great idea." But he added that, later, "it got out of hand" and, as a result, "it's gotten to be some kind of entitlement. Everybody thinks they're entitled to everything. No one wants to work hard any more."[75]

While this kind of attitude helped to bring Italian Americans closer to other immigrant groups from European backgrounds, Philadelphians of Italian descent kept at least emotional and sentimental ties to their ancestral country in the postwar years. For instance, when an earthquake struck the Italian region of Friuli in May 1976, they hurried to raise money for the victims and to start an early reconstruction of the area. The financial effort involved not only such ethnic associations as the local lodges of the OSIA and *prominenti* like Mayor Rizzo but also a number of rank and file members of the community who were glad to contribute their own money. Others, such as Court of Common Pleas Judge Armand Della Porta, lobbied Washington and urged the U.S. government to "go to the aid of the Italian people" in Friuli.[76]

Philadelphians of Italian descent also made a point of proclaiming Italian contributions to the history and culture of the United States. They organized a two-week Italo-American Bicentennial Celelebration in 1976 on the occasion of the nation's Bicentennial. Ethnic pride based on national extraction surfaced again among them on 21 August 1992, when several leaders of local Italian American organizations called for the dismissal of the head of the city's art commission on the grounds that he had anti-Italian prejudices because he harbored referred to a color as "dago red" instead of "day-glo red."[77]

Likewise, five years later, attorney Joseph V. Del Raso and a few other Philadelphians of Italian descent joined about fifty-thousand fellow ethnics to petition President William Jefferson Clinton and Vice President Albert Gore on behalf of Italy. Specifically, they urged the U.S. government not to deny their ancestral country a permanent seat on the United Nations Security Council within a proposed reform for the expansion of this organ that would initially benefit Germany and Japan alone to the exclusion of Italy. The Conference of Presidents of Major Italian American Organizations helped launch this movement. Yet, the number of individuals who eventually signed the petition nationwide, out of an ethnic group that numbered almost fifteen million members throughout the United States, indicates that the drive failed to enjoy mass approval among Italian Americans.[78]

More significantly, the 1980s saw a resurgence of the establishment of Italian associations along localistic lines in Philadelphia, for instance, the Associazione Regionale Abruzzese, which was founded in 1988. Many of these clubs, however, were created at the urging of the Italian government and did not result from the initiative of Philadelphia's community itself. They also provided services almost exclusively for those Italian newcomers who arrived in the city after World War II. Actually, besides being restricted to people with origins in specific towns or regions like their counterparts of the early twentieth century, membership in a number of these associations was open to Italian citizens only. Yet, the newly arrived Italians accounted for a negligible percentage of the members of the Italian American community as a whole. Italian immigrants to the Philadelphia area between 1960 and 1965, for instance, made up only 1.2 percent of the total population of Italian ancestry in those years.[79]

The creation of subnational Italian American ethnic clubs was not specific to Philadelphia alone. A local chapter of the Associazione Lucchesi nel Mondo (Italians in the World Association) was founded in San Francisco in 1972. The promoter of this chapter, however, was not an Italian American or an immigrant to San Francisco but a resident of Lucca who had briefly come to San Francisco to visit relatives. The Italian city of Lucca was also home to the headquarters of this organization.[80]

In addition, while the more recent Italian immigrants tended to reproduce the social aggregation, based on subnational descent, of their turn of the century predecessors, the offspring of these latter were glad to accept individuals who were not of Italian ancestry within their own ethnic organizations. Noticeably enough, as Richard N. Juliani has reported, an initially Italian American club in suburban Philadelphia ended up having more Irish American affiliates than Italian American members in the early 1990s. Its most relevant social event was an annual softball match between the representatives of these two groups.[81]

This transformation of the ethnic makeup of Italian American social organizations was not confined to Philadelphia. For example, nearly one third of the members of the Aurora Club in Providence were not of Italian extraction in 1972.[82]

Examples such as these of mass trans-Italian membership in Italian American ethnic associations would have been impossible in the interwar years. Multiethnic white membership in nominally Italian American clubs contributes to offer further evidence of the extent to which Philadelphians of Italian descent have broadened the boundaries of their self-referential community and reached out to other nationality groups of European origin since the end of World War II.

Chapter 7

Conclusion

This book has outlined the process by which people of Italian descent renegotiated their ethnic identity in Philadelphia between the late nineteenth century and the early 1990s. The findings of the research can be summarized as follows.

Aggregation along localistic, provincial, or regional lines usually shaped the self-perception and social clustering of the Italian immigrants who arrived in Philadelphia in mass tides in the late nineteenth and early twentieth centuries. By the outbreak of World War II, however, this situation had begun to change. The emergence of Italian nationalism in the wake of both the beginning of World War I and the rise of Fascism to power in Italy, the common experience of persistent anti-Italian sentiments, the end of mass immigration from their ancestral country, and the appearance of an American-born second generation of individuals with loose ties to the land of their parents contributed to bring together Italian Americans from disparate local backgrounds. These circumstances also helped Philadelphians of Italian origin develop a sense of ethnic identity based on national descent which they had lacked upon their arrival in the United States.

Italy's international prominence under Mussolini's regime was a key event in the rise of an Italian self-perception on the part of the population of Italian ancestry in Philadelphia during the interwar years.

This sense of ethnicity emerged because the prestige of Fascist Italy outweighed decades of anti-Italian intolerance and bigotry in the United States that had often been motivated by the perceived inferiority of the Italian people. The Italo-Ethiopian War heightened racial conflicts between African Americans and Italian Americans. Nonetheless, events during the interwar decades failed to stimulate the latter to think of themselves as white Americans, because the Depression and the local repercussions of Fascist policies isolated Italian Americans from other white minority groups such as the Irish and the Jews.

Most Philadelphian voters of Italian descent joined the Democratic Party in the mid-1930s although they regarded it less as a cross-ethnic institution through which they could defend their class interests than as a means of asserting their rise as a nationality group in the country of their adoption. Actually, when local Democratic officials no longer pandered to the ethnic claims of their Italian American constituents, voters of Italian descent began to go back to the Republican camp. The outbreak of hostilities between the United States and Italy as well as growing concerns for the policy of the United States toward their mother country in the postwar years consolidated the Republican allegiance of Italian Americans in the 1940s based on their persisting Italian ethnic identity.

Even the early postwar anticommunist attitude of Philadelphians of Italian descent shows that they retained an Italian-oriented self-image and continued to identify themselves with their ancestral country. The participation of Italian Americans in the efforts of the Truman administration to secure the defeat of the Communist Party in Italy's 1948 parliamentary elections hardly resulted from the Americanization of the Italian immigrants and their offspring. Rather, it arose from their desire to position themselves to serve the interests of their motherland more effectively. Italian Americans endorsed the anticommunist crusade of the U.S. government for two main purposes. They wanted to erase the suspicion of disloyalty toward the United States, which had haunted them since the outbreak of World War II, and they wished to gain a more authoritative voice in order to advance Italy's postwar claims.

Since the sense of Italianness among the Philadelphians of Italian extraction did not decline during the Depression decade or in the wake of both World War II and its aftermath, it could hardly resurge in the 1970s. Italian Americans had continued to distance themselves from other European minorities throughout World War II. But ethnic defensiveness against African American assertiveness and racial tensions over housing and schooling caused them to extend the boundaries of their ethnic identity and to redefine it within the broader white ethnic movement in the postwar decades. This new sense of ethnic self-perception climaxed as the population of Philadelphia polarized along racial lines on issues such as public education and crime in the late 1960s, at the time of Rizzo's bids for mayor during the 1970s and 1980s, and on the occasion of the 1978 "vote white" referendum campaign.

The shift from a localistic sense of affiliation to a self-image based on the awareness of a common national ancestry characterized not only the Italian immigrants and their offspring but also a number of minorities of European descent such as the Poles, the Lithuanians, and other nationality groups that arrived in the United States from lands that were still struggling to become states in the late nineteenth and early twentieth centuries. In these cases, as Nathan Glazer has pointed out, "the newcomers became nations in America."[1]

However, the mechanics of the formation of this identity has been a matter of scholarly disagreement. In a pioneer 1921 study, Robert E. Park and Herbert A. Miller argued that immigrants developed a broader sense of group solidarity than their initial localistic self-perceptions in response to the discrimination that they experienced in their host society. While another major work published in the interwar years pointed to ethnic defensiveness in order to account for the development of group consciousness, a few scholars have recently restated that thesis. For instance, Rudolph J. Vecoli has maintained that the ostracism endured in America was pivotal to turn the parochial cohorts of immigrants from any given country into a single ethnic group. Likewise, in David G. Gutierrez's opinion, the persistence of anti-Mexican prejudice in present-day United States has contributed to break down divisions within Mexican American communities and to strengthen the Mexican identity of their members as something distinct from mainstream Anglo-Americanism. Similarly, in the specific case of Italian Americans, Robert Viscusi has maintained that it was only after they had suffered humiliation in their adoptive country because of their mutual national origin that people from such disparate towns and villages as Caltanisetta or Muro Lucano came to think of themselves as Italians.[2]

Nevertheless, a detailed study of Italian immigration to Toronto before World War II has concluded that it was isolation from the mainstream society rather than ethnic discrimination or intolerance that induced Italian newcomers to the New World to acquire a fuller sense of their being Italians. Moreover, it has been argued that nativist attacks played a lesser role than Prohibition in solidifying the Italian American community in St. Louis across regional lines. In this view, the intense subnational antipathies that had affected Lombards and Sicilians for decades dissolved into a symbiotic relationship when they envisaged the chance of producing and retailing illegally distilled liquor.[3]

In Philadelphia, however, the strong-arm methods of the Lanzetti brothers—rather than any common sense of purpose in violating the Volstead Act—settled differences in the Italian American community during the Prohibition era. The same occurred, for instance, in Chicago under the rule of the Genna brothers and Al Capone.[4] Indeed, evidence from Philadelphia suggests that ethnic defensiveness was central to the development of an Italian self-perception on the part of the local population of Italian descent in the interwar years. This main determinant of ethnicization, however, did not confine itself to merging the disparate localistic loyalties of the Old World into a common sense of Italianness in the face of anti-Italian prejudice and intolerance between the end of World War I and the beginning of World War II. Such a stimulus also led Italian Americans to forge a white ethnic identity, which they could share with other minorities of European extraction, as a reaction to supposed African American encroachments in the postwar decades.

In San Francisco, the local Anti-Defamation Commission of the OSIA joined forces with the city's chapter of the B'nai B'rith to denounce a case of "reverse discrimination" in 1975. Specifically, they stood by the claims of unfair treatment made by a white student who had been excluded from a medical school under special admission programs that favored underprivileged minorities such as African Americans. Remarkably enough, the student was not of Italian ancestry.[5]

Politics provides further instances of the progressive growth of the significance of a white identity among Italian Americans nationwide. Some of them gave in to the white supremacist appeal of George C. Wallace to race-sensitive working-class ethnics in Baltimore as early as 1964. Two years later, Democrat George P. Mahoney capitalized on antiblack feelings to capture almost 75 percent of that city's Italian American vote in his unsuccessful bid for governor of Maryland against

Spiro Agnew. A few voters of Italian and Polish descent were also side by side in Chicago to support Wallace's 1968 campaign for the White House. Similarly, Italian Americans and other European groups organized politically around their common white ethnic ancestry in Newark, New Jersey, in the late 1960s and early 1970s. White Newarkers deeply resented the rise of blacks to power in the local government in the wake of a significant rise in the number of African Americans and Puerto Ricans in the city's population. They also increasingly feared African Americans after the 1967 black riots.[6]

The case of Philadelphia further corroborates the hypothesis that points to the antiblack backlash as the leading factor that induced Italian Americans to develop a white ethnic identity after World War II. In Philadelphia, too, the struggles over housing and schooling were among the issues that pitted Italian Americans against African Americans and Puerto Ricans. This conflict polarized the contenders along racial lines and caused Italian Americans to reach out to other minorities of European descent. As a result, the experience of Italian American resistance to urban blight in Philadelphia in the 1970s and 1980s cannot be interpreted in terms of the mere resurgence of the Italian identity among the descendants of the turn-of-the-century immigrants. Nor was it confined only to the revitalization of the Italian neighborhoods, which allegedly characterized other Italian American communities such as Bloomfield in Pittsburgh, the "Hill" in St. Louis, the "Little Italy" of Baltimore, or "Federal Hill" in Providence in those years.[7]

Italian Americans' overwhelming support for Rizzo in the 1970s and 1980s was the epitome of the development of a white ethnic consciousness among a majority of the Philadelphians of Italian descent. Like Rizzo, Hugh J. Addonizio, Mario Procaccino, and John Marchi capitalized on the antiblack resentment of their fellow ethnics to make impressive showings among Italian Americans. In 1969, Addonizio, Newark's first mayor of Italian ancestry, gained 87.5 percent of the Italian American vote in his unsuccessful reelection bid against Kenneth A. Gibson, an African American highway engineer. In New York City's mayoral election of the same year, the combined Italian American vote for Democrat Procaccino and Republican Marchi was 85.7 percent, although incumbent mayor John Lindsay came out on top citywide running as the candidate of the Liberal Party. Procaccino was a native of Bisaccia, Italy. Marchi's ancestors were from Lucca. Yet, Procaccino's and Marchi's Italian extraction was not a paramount issue in Italian American neighborhoods. New Yorkers of Italian descent were accustomed to fellow ethnics running for high office. After all, New York City had already had two Italian American mayors, Fiorello H. La Guardia (1934–1945) and Vincent R. Impellitteri (1950–1953). Significantly, when Impellitteri was elected in 1950, all three major candidates for mayor were of Italian origin. In addition, Procaccino had a record of failures to carry the Italian American vote prior to 1969. This year, it was Procaccino's and Marchi's criticism of mayor Lindsay's liberal approach to African American claims that secured them the support of their fellow ethnics at the polls. Procaccino also became the spokesperson for the racial grievances of many white blue-collar workers of both Italian and other European backgrounds.[8]

Of course, the re-elaboration of the ethnic identity of Italian immigrants and their offspring was not one-dimensional and offers some remarkable exceptions to the pattern outlined for Philadelphia. In turn-of-the-century New Orleans, for example, Sicilians established social ties to African Americans because both groups were marginalized in southern society. Indeed, other white cohorts of the population discriminated against the Italian newcomers on the grounds of their alleged Mafia connections. Furthermore, not only the experience of a similar economic status to that of blacks in their adoptive city but also centuries of alien domination, specifically, nearly two hundred years of Arab rule, in their native land made Sicilians tolerant of African Americans and even friendly with them in New Orleans between the 1880s and the 1920s. As George E. Cunningham has pointed out, Italian immigrants to New Orleans were "a hindrance to white solidarity" at the turn of the century as they usually antagonized white supremacists in the 1890s. Likewise, in Tampa, Florida, working-class Cubans, Spaniards, and Italians developed a single Latin self-perception out of a commonly shared radical culture in response to the hostility of the local establishment.[9]

Nonetheless, the two latter examples are also extreme cases. The great bulk of the plantation owners in Louisiana failed to consider Italians as white people. Therefore, the state's Italian Americans were generally so eager to distance themselves from African Americans that they gave up working in the cane fields in order to avoid identification with the black labor force in the eyes of other white groups. Similarly, while an unusually strong radical culture among cigar workers brought Italians and their Latin co-workers together in Tampa, Italians generally set themselves aside from the local population of Mexican origin in Texas. Indeed, in southern states such as Alabama,

Louisiana, North Carolina, and Texas, Italian Americans often occupied a rather precarious racial middle ground between African Americans and whites into the early twentieth century. Actually, in those decades, the color line in the South was so vague that—as if they had been people of African descent—Italian Americans were often lynched for infringements of the law or for merely befriending blacks in the states of Louisiana, Mississippi, and West Virginia.[10]

Something similar occurred in Baltimore at the turn of the century. Opposition to both disfranchisement and segregation in housing could have potentially brought together African Americans and Italian Americans. These latter, however, quickly learnt that they had to separate themselves from the black population if they wanted to be accepted by the broader society.[11]

The experience of Italian Americans in Roseto, which has already been mentioned in the introduction, was unconventional, too. Roseto, Pennsylvania, was almost exclusively populated by Italian immigrants from Roseto Valforte, a village in Puglia. Of course, the offspring of the *Pugliesi* immigrants could not avoid contacts with the descendants of newcomers from other Italian areas such as the *Abruzzesi* of nearby Martin's Creek or the Venetians of adjacent Pen Argyl. Nevertheless, they had fewer chances of significant interaction with other Italian Americans than the average dweller of any multiregional "Little Italy." Therefore, they were able to retain their subnational identity longer than their fellow countrymen did elsewhere. Rudolph J. Vecoli has also shown that the localistic sense of affinity among Italian immigrants in Chicago was much more complex than the northern-southern dichotomy outlined by Nelli and that subnational self-images were slow to die in that city.[12]

The last few years have seen the increasing gentrification of the old Italian district north of Christian Street in South Philadelphia with the result that affluent home buyers who are not of Italian ancestry have begun to replace the Italian American population that has moved to the suburbs. In addition, merchants of Asian origin have progressively taken over many retail stores in the local Italian market in 9th Street. National chain corporations have also started to make inroads into this area, while the Italian restaurants have been catering to an increasing number of non-Italian patrons. Even St. Mary Magdalen de Pazzi's has lost its Italian ethnic flavor as more and more Asian Americans have moved into the parish in the 1990s.[13]

Urban "Little Italies" have undergone a contraction not only in Philadelphia but throughout the United States. For instance, residential dispersion from the inner city to suburban areas in Catonsville, Parkville, Essex, and Dundalk has occurred among Italian Americans in Baltimore since the 1950s and has intensified since the 1970s. Similarly, in this latter decade, the renovation of adjoining districts made Boston's North End fashionable to outsiders while its Italian American residents moved to the suburbs. Although the ethnic traditions of the neighborhood have somehow survived, they have lost most of their authenticity and serve primarily commercial purposes to attract tourists and prospective residents from the outside. Likewise, Asian Americans, Hispanics, and African Americans work nowadays in restaurants, coffee shops, and stores with Italian-sounding names in New York City's "Little Italy" along Mulberry Street. As Jerome Krase has argued, Italian American neighborhoods in the country risk surviving as mere "Ethnic Disneylands" or as "Pompeian-like ruins." Thus, the market in 9th Street and South Philadelphia has retained its Italian flavor at least for tourists.[14]

Nonetheless, against the backdrop of the transformations that have recently reshaped this district, the fires that engulfed Palumbo's restaurant in 1994 may really have ended an era for the ethnic identity of Italian Americans in Philadelphia. As Richard D. Alba has maintained, it is "the concentration of Italian-American loyalists in neighborhoods with a definite ethnic character [which] keeps alive the notion of an Italian-American ethnicity, even in the midst of widespread assimilation."[15]

This work has provided an interpretation of the changing meaning of that sense of ethnicity over time. In particular, it has stressed the process by which the emergence of some concept of Italianness began to replace the subnational parochialism of the turn-of-the-century immigrants during World War I. This study has also demonstrated that such a new Italian self-perception consolidated in the interwar years but has yielded to a growing white ethnic consciousness since the 1960s.

Of course, the timing and the mechanics of the redefinition of the self-image of the population of Italian extraction in Philadelphia have had peculiarities of their own. Nonetheless, they have also reflected a pattern that has characterized a number of other Italian American communities in the United States.

In the late 1970s and 1980s, a few Italian Americans contended that people of Italian ancestry were entitled to special assistance programs and affirmative action protection as members of an ethnic minority in its own right. Ethnic activists even made the case for the categorization of Italian Americans as a "cognizable racial group." More recently, with reference to Italian Americans, Richard N. Juliani has also argued that "the final eradication of all traces of their ethnicity as well as their visibility as a subpopulation in American society remains to be seen." Still, even advocates of the alleged persistence of an Italian ethnicity among present-day Americans of Italian descent such as Richard Gambino have acknowledged that the Italian American identity is at least in crisis nowadays.[16]

It has been suggested that "the making of new affiliations" is the main feature that distinguishes American society from many other societies in the world. Most Philadelphians of Italian descent have actually widened their own "circle of the We," as David A. Hollinger has called it, over the last century.[17] They no longer confine their self-referential ethnic group to the small communities of their own *paesani* or fellow countrymen but have extended it to include other white peoples of European ancestry. The re-elaboration of their self-image has gone beyond the boundaries of their nationality group but has failed to cross the borderlines of their race. Indeed, it was the development of a racial consciousness as a form of ethnic defensiveness against the alleged encroachments of African Americans that has progressively caused many Italian Americans to reach out to other minorities of European extraction and to become aware of their common whiteness since the 1960s.

By the early 1990s, Italian Americans in Philadelphia had renegotiated their ethnic identity to an extent that Alba's "twilight" notion can summarize better than Vecoli's "not just white folks" thesis can. Contrary to their grandparents, they have superseded a localistic sense of affiliation. Unlike their parents, they have overcome an ethnic segmentation along nationality lines *à la* Polenberg. But they have not passed over the fault line of race, and white racial consciousness bulks large in their current self-perception.

Notes

Chapter 1. Introduction

1. *Philadelphia Inquirer,* 21, 22, 24 June, 14 July, 4, 26 Aug., 2, 13 Sept. 1994. Vignola's quotation is from the issue of 24 June. For the Italian flavor of Palumbo's, see also Richard N. Juliani, "The Social Development of Italian-American Communities," paper presented at the 28th annual conference of the American Italian Historical Association, Lowell MA, 9–12 Nov. 1995; Murray Dubin, *South Philadelphia: Mummers, Memories, and the Melrose Diner* (Philadelphia: Temple University Press, 1996), 46–48, 94–95.

2. Albert Di Bartolomeo, "A South Philly Tradition Went Up with Palumbo's," *Philadelphia Inquirer* (1 July 1994): A15.

3. Ibid.

4. Anna Maria Martellone, "Italo-American Ethnic Identity: A Plea against the Deconstruction of Ethnicity and in Favor of Political History," *Altreitalie* 3, no. 6 (Nov. 1991): 106–13.

5. Fredrick Barth, "Introduction," in *Ethnic Groups and Boundaries: The Social Organization of Cultural Differences,* ed. Fredrick Barth (Boston: Little, Brown, 1969), 9–38; Talcott Parsons, "Some Theoretical Considerations on the Nature and Trends of Change of Ethnicity," in *Ethnicity: Theory and Experience,* ed. Nathan Glazer and Daniel Patrick Moynihan (Cambridge MA: Harvard University Press, 1975), 53–83; Charles F. Keyes, "The Dialectics of Ethnic Change," in *Ethnic Change,* ed. Charles F. Keyes (Seattle: University of Washington Press, 1981), 4–30; Brackette F. Williams, "A Class Act: Anthropology and the Race to Nation Across Ethnic Terrain," *Annual Review of Anthropology* 18 (1989): 401–44; Eugeen E. Roosens, *Creating Ethnicity: The Process of Ethnogenesis* (Newbury Park CA: Sage, 1989); Anthony Cohen, "Culture as

Identity: An Anthropologist's View," *New Literary History* 24, no. 2 (Winter 1993): 195–209. For emblematic case studies worldwide, see Jay O'Brien, "Towards a Reconstruction of Ethnicity: Capitalist Expansion and Cultural Dynamics in Sudan," in *Golden Ages, Dark Ages: Imagining the Past in Anthropology and History*, ed. Jay O'Brien and William Roseberry (Berkeley: University of California Press, 1991), 126–38; Mary E. Kelly and Tracy X. Karner, "Reclaiming and Inventing Ethnic Identity: Lithuanians and Finns at the Turn of the Twentieth Century," *Ethnic Forum* 14, no. 2 (Summer 1994): 5–21; Jeffrey Lesser, "(Re) Creating Ethnicity: Middle Eastern Immigration to Brazil," *Americas* 53, no. 1 (July 1996): 45–65; Rina Cohen and Gerald Gold, "Constructing Ethnicity: Myth of Return and Modes of Exclusion among Israelis in Toronto," *International Migration* 35, no. 3 (1997): 373–92; Laurie Kroshus Medina, "Defining Difference, Forging Unity: The Co-Construction of Race, Ethnicity and Nation in Belize," *Ethnic and Racial Studies* 20, no. 4 (Oct. 1997): 757–80.

6. William L. Yancey, Eugene P. Ericksen, and Richard N. Juliani, "Emergent Ethnicity: A Review and Reformulation," *American Sociological Review* 41, no. 3 (June 1976): 391–403; Werner Sollors, *Beyond Ethnicity: Consent and Descent in American Culture* (New York: Oxford University Press, 1986); *The Invention of Ethnicity*, ed. Werner Sollors (New York: Oxford University Press, 1989); Mary C. Waters, *Ethnic Options: Choosing Identities in America* (Berkeley: University of California Press, 1990); Kathleen N. Conzen et al., "The Invention of Ethnicity: A Perspective from the USA," *Journal of American Ethnic History* 12, no. 1 (Fall 1992): 3–41; Russell A. Kazal, "Revisiting Assimilation: The Rise, Fall, and Reappraisal of a Concept in American Ethnic History," *American Historical Review* 100, no. 2 (Apr. 1995): 437–71. For an intriguing test case of the redescription of ethnic identity on the part of Punjabi immigrants to California, see Karen Isaksen Leonard, *Making Ethnic Choices: California's Punjabi Mexican Americans* (Philadelphia: Temple University Press, 1992). For Mexican Americans, see George J. Sanchez, *Becoming Mexican American: Ethnicity and Identity in Chicano Los Angeles, 1900–1945* (New York: Oxford University Press, 1993). For Norwegian Americans, see April R. Schultz, *Ethnicity on Parade: Inventing the Norwegian American through Celebration* (Amherst, MA: University of Massachusetts Press, 1994).

7. Richard Polenberg, *One Nation Divisible: Class, Race, and Ethnicity in the United States Since 1938* (New York: Viking Press, 1980), 251–92.

8. David A. Hollinger, *Postethnic America: Beyond Multiculturalism* (New York: Basic Books, 1995), 19–50; Kwame Anthony Appiah, *In My Father's House: Africa in the Philosophy of Culture* (New York: Oxford University Press, 1992); Jae-Hyup Lee, "Identity and Social Dynamics in Ethnic Community: Comparative Study on Boundary Making among Asian Americans in Philadelphia" (Ph.D. diss., University of Pennsylvania, 1994); LeiLani Linda Nishime, "Creating Race: Genre and Cultural Construction of Asian-American Identity" (Ph.D. diss., University of Michigan, 1997); Nazli Kibria, "The Construction of

'Asian American': Reflections on Intermarriage and Ethnic Identity among Second-Generation Chinese and Korean Americans," *Ethnic and Racial Studies* 20, no. 3 (July 1997): 523–44; Susan Renee Dauria, "Deindustrialization and the Construction of History and Ethnic Identity: A Case in Upstate New York" (Ph.D. diss., State University of New York at Albany, 1994); John McDonald Hartigan Jr., "Cultural Construction of Whiteness: Racial and Class Formation in Detroit" (Ph.D. diss., University of California, Santa Cruz, 1995); Peter Binzen, *Whitetown, U.S.A.* (New York: Random House, 1971); Perry L. Weed, *The White Ethnic Movement and Ethnic Politics* (New York: Praeger, 1973); Richard D. Alba, *Ethnic Identity: The Transformation of White America* (New Haven: Yale University Press, 1990); Jonathan W. Warren and France Winddance Twine, "White Americans, the New Minority? Non-Blacks and the Ever-Expanding Boundaries of Whiteness," *Journal of Black Studies* 28, no. 2 (Nov. 1997): 200–18; Karen Brodkin, *How Jews Became White Folks and What That Says about Race in America* (New Brunswick NJ: Rutgers University Press, 1998).

9. Mary Patrice Erdmans, *Opposite Poles: Immigrants and Ethnics in Polish Chicago, 1976–1990* (University Park PA: Pennsylvania State University Press, 1998).

10. Barbara Jeanne Fields, "Slavery, Race, and Ideology in the United States of America," *New Left Review* no. 181 (May–June 1990): 95–118; David R. Roediger, *The Wages of Whiteness: Race and the American Working Class* (New York: Verso, 1991); David R. Roediger, *Toward the Abolition of Whiteness: Essays on Race, Politics, and Working Class History* (New York: Verso, 1994); Theodore W. Allen, *The Invention of the White Race: Racial Oppression and Social Control* (New York: Verso, 1994); Theodore W. Allen, *The Invention of the White Race: The Origin of Racial Oppression in Anglo-America* (New York: Verso, 1997); Noel Ignatiev, *How the Irish Became White* (New York: Routledge, 1995); George Lipsitz, *The Possessive Investment in Whiteness: How White People Profit from Identity Politics* (Philadelphia: Temple University Press, 1998); Gary Gerstle, "Working-Class Racism: Broaden the Focus," *International Labor and Working Class History* 44, no. 2 (Fall 1993): 33–40; Paul R. Spikard, "Mapping Race: Multiracial People and Racial Category Construction in the United States and Britain," *Immigrants & Minorities* 15, no. 2 (July 1996): 107–19; Bruce Nelson, "Class, Race, and Democracy in the CIO: The 'New' Labor History Meets the 'Wages of Whiteness,'" *International Review of Social History* 41, no. 3 (Dec. 1996): 351–74.

11. Matthew Frye Jacobson, *Whiteness of a Different Color: European Immigrants and the Alchemy of Race* (Cambridge MA: Harvard University Press, 1998); Ian F. Harney Lopez, *White by Law: The Legal Construction of Race* (New York: New York University Press, 1998).

12. Herbert J. Gans, *The Urban Villagers: Group and Class in the Life of Italian Americans* (New York: Free Press, 1962); Rudolph J. Vecoli, "The Search for an Italian American Identity: Continuity and Change," in *Italian Americans:*

New Perspectives in Italian Immigration and Ethnicity, ed. Lydio F. Tomasi (New York: Center for Migration Studies, 1985), 88–112; Joan Savereno, "The Italians of Reading: Forging an Identity in the 1920s," *Historical Review of Berks County* 56, no. 3 (Fall 1991): 172–97; Emilio Franzina, *Gli Italiani al Nuovo Mondo: L'emigrazione italiana in America, 1492–1942* (Milan: Mondadori, 1995).

13. Humbert S. Nelli, *Italians in Chicago, 1880–1930: A Study in Ethnic Mobility* (New York: Oxford University Press, 1970); John W. Briggs, *An Italian Passage: Immigrants to Three American Cities, 1890–1930* (New Haven: Yale University Press, 1978); Carla Bianco, *The Two Rosetos* (Bloomington: Indiana University Press, 1974), 53–59; Michela Di Leonardo, *The Varieties of Ethnic Experience: Kinship, Class, and Gender among California Italian Americans* (Ithaca NY: Cornell University Press, 1984), 168–78.

14. Richard D. Alba, *Italian Americans: Into the Twilight of Ethnicity* (Englewood Cliffs NJ: Prentice Hall, 1985); Richard D. Alba, "Identity and Ethnicity among Italians and Other Americans of European Ancestry," in *The Columbus People: Perspectives in Italian Immigration to the Americas and Australia*, ed. Lydio F. Tomasi, Piero Gastaldo, and Thomas Row (Staten Island: Center for Migration Studies, 1994), 21–44; Richard D. Alba, "Italian Americans: A Century of Ethnic Change," in *Origins and Destinies: Immigration, Race, and Ethnicity in America*, ed. Silvia Pedraza and Ruben G. Rumbaut (Belmont CA: Wadsworth, 1996), 172–81; James A. Crispino, *The Assimilation of Ethnic Groups: The Italian Case* (Staten Island: Center for Migration Studies, 1979); John Patrick Roche, "Suburban Ethnicity: Ethnic Attitude and Behavior among Italian Americans in Two Suburban Communities," *Social Science Quarterly* 63, no. 1 (Mar. 1982): 145–53; Joseph J. Bentivegna, "Trends in Italian American Heritage," *Il Caffè* 10, no. 1 (April 1990): 23–27; Herbert J. Gans, "Symbolic Ethnicity: the Future of Ethnic Groups and Cultures in America," in Herbert J. Gans et al., *On the Making of Americans: Essays in Honor of David Riesman* (Philadelphia: University of Pennsylvania Press, 1979), 193–220.

15. Stephen Steinberg, *The Ethnic Myth: Race, Ethnicity, and Class in America* (New York: Atheneum, 1981).

16. Rudolph J. Vecoli, "The Italian Immigrants in the United States Labor Movement from 1880 to 1929," in Fondazione Giacomo Brodolini, *Gli italiani fuori d'Italia: Gli emigrati italiani nei movimenti operai dei paesi d'adozione (1880–1940)*, ed. Bruno Bezza (Milan: Franco Angeli, 1983), 257–306; Donna R. Gabaccia, *Militants and Migrants: Rural Sicilians Become American Workers* (New Brunswick NJ: Rutgers University Press, 1988); Bruno Cartosio, "Sicilian Radicals in Two Worlds," in *In the Shadow of the Statue of Liberty: Immigrants, Workers, and Citizens in the American Republic, 1880–1920*, ed. Marianne Debouzy (Saint-Denis: Presses Universitaires de Vincennes, 1988), 117–28; Michael Miller Topp, "The Italian-American Left: Transnationalism and the Quest for Unity," in *The Immigrant Left in the United States*, ed. Paul Buhle and Dan Georgakas (Albany: State University of New York Press, 1996), 119–47; Michael Miller

Topp, "The Transnationalism of the Italian-American Left: The Lawrence Strike of 1912 and the Italian Chamber of Labor of New York City," *Journal of American Ethnic History* 17, no. 1 (Fall 1997): 39–63; Carlo Sforza, *The Real Italians: A Study in European Psychology* (New York: Columbia University Press, 1942), 125.

17. Carla Bianco, "La politica culturale degli Stati Uniti," *Studi Emigrazione* 12, no. 37 (Mar. 1975): 97–108.

18. Nathan Glazer and Daniel Patrick Moynihan, *Beyond the Melting Pot: The Negroes, Puerto Ricans, Jews, Italians, and Irish of New York City* (Cambridge MA: MIT Press, 1963), 208–16; Michael Novak, *The Rise of Unmeltable Ethnics: Politics and Culture in the Seventies* (New York: Macmillan, 1972); Theodore H. White, *America in Search of Itself: The Making of the President, 1956–1980* (New York: Harper and Row, 1982), 371. See also the enlarged and updated edition of Novak's study, *Unmeltable Ethnics: Politics and Culture in American Life* (New Brunswick NJ: Transaction Publishers, 1996).

19. Robert Orsi, "The Religious Boundaries of an Inbetween People: Street *Feste* and the Problem of the Dark-Skinned Other in Italian Harlem, 1920–1990," *American Quarterly* 44, no. 3 (Sept. 1992): 313–47.

20. Lawrence H. Fuchs, " 'The Invention of Ethnicity': The Amen Corner," *Journal of American Ethnic History* 12, no. 1 (Fall 1992): 53–58; Geno Baroni, "Ethnicity and Public Policy," in *Pieces of a Dream: The Ethnic Worker's Crisis with America*, ed. Michael Wenk, Silvano M. Tomasi, and Geno Baroni (Staten Island: Center for Migration Studies, 1972), 9–10; Andrew M. Greeley, *Ethnicity in the United States: A Preliminary Reconnaissance* (New York: Wiley, 1974), 213–14, 284–86. For Baroni, see Lawrence O'Rourke, *Geno: The Life and Mission of Geno Baroni* (New York: Paulist Press, 1991); Frank J. Cavaioli, "Geno Baroni: Italian-American Civil Rights Priest," in *Shades of Black and White: Conflict and Collaboration Between Two Communities*, ed. Dan Ashyk, Fred Gardaphe, and Anthony Julian Tamburri (Staten Island: American Italian Historical Association, 1999), 45–54.

21. Richard N. Juliani, "The Position of Italian Americans in Contemporary Society," in *The Melting Pot and Beyond: Italian Americans in the Year 2000*, ed. Jerome Krase and William Egelman (Staten Island: American Italian Historical Association, 1987), 68; Rudolph J. Vecoli, "Ethnicity and Immigration," in *Encyclopedia of the United States in the Twentieth Century*, ed. Stanley I. Kutler, 4 vols. (New York: Charles Scribner's Sons, 1996), 1:180–81; William M. De Marco, *Ethnics and Enclaves: Boston's Italian North End* (Ann Arbor: UMI Research Press, 1980), 35–36; Fred Gardaphe, "Presidential Address," in *Shades of Black and White*, viii–x; Donna Gabaccia, "The 'Yellow Peril' and the 'Chinese of Europe': Global Perspectives on Race and Labor, 1815–1930," in *Migration, Migration History, History: Old Paradigms and New Perspectives*, ed. Jan Lucassen and Leo Lucassen (New York: Peter Lang, 1997), 189–90. For historical outlines of anti-Italian prejudice in the United States, see *Wop! A Documentary History*

of Anti-Italian Discrimination in the United States, ed. Salvatore J. LaGumina (San Francisco: Straight Arrow Books, 1973); Phylis Martinelli and Leonard Gordon, "Italian Americans: Images Across Half a Century," *Ethnic and Racial Studies* 11, no. 3 (July 1988): 319–31.

22. Rudolph J. Vecoli, "Born Italian: Color Me Red, White, and Green," *Soundings* 61, no. 1 (Spring 1973): 117–23; Rudolph J. Vecoli, "Italian Immigrants and Working-Class Movements in the United States: A Personal Reflection on Class and Ethnicity," *Journal of the Canadian Historical Association* 4 (1993): 293–305; Rudolph J. Vecoli, "Are Italian Americans Just White Folks?" *Italian Americana*, 13, no. 2 (Summer 1995): 149–61; Raymond A. Belliotti, *Seeking Identity: Individualism Versus Community in an Ethnic Context* (Lawrence: University Press of Kansas, 1995), 159–89; Richard Gambino, *Blood of My Blood: The Dilemma of the Italian Americans* (1974; rpt. Toronto: Guernica, 1996); Richard Gambino, "Are Italian Americans in 'the Twilight' of Ethnicity, or a New Dawn'?," in *Industry, Technology, Labor, and the Italian-American Communities,* ed. Mario Aste et al. (Staten Island: American Italian Historical Association, 1997), 161–74. For similar but more detached theses, see Donald Tricarico, "Contemporary Italian American Ethnicity: Into the Mainstream," in *Italian Americans: The Search for a Usable Past,* ed. Richard N. Juliani and Philip V. Cannistraro (Staten Island: American Italian Historical Association, 1989), 258–81; Daniel J. Monti Jr., "Some Sort of Americans: The Working and Reworking of Italian-American Ethnicity in the United States," in *Italian Americans in a Multicultural Society,* ed. Jerome Krase and Judith N. DeSena (New York: Forum Italicum, 1994), 19–32.

23. Rudolph J. Vecoli, "Ethnicity: A Neglected Dimension of American History," in *The State of American History,* ed. Herbert Jacob Bass (New York: Quadrangle Books, 1970), 70; Rudolph J. Vecoli, "From Pennsylvania Dutch to California Ethnic: The Odyssey of David Hollinger," *Reviews in American History* 24, no. 3 (Sept. 1996): 522; Fred Barbaro, "Ethnic Affirmation, Affirmative Action, and the Italian American," *Italian Americana* 1, no. 1 (Autumn 1974): 41–58; Alfred Aversa Jr., "Italian Neo-Ethnicity: The Search for Self-Identity," *Journal of Ethnic Studies* 6, no. 2 (Summer 1978): 49–56; Nicholas Pileggi, "Risorgimento: The Red, White, and Greening of New York," in *America and the New Ethnicity,* ed. David R. Colburn and George E. Pozzetta (Port Washington NY: Kennikat, 1979), 118–32; Humbert S. Nelli, *From Immigrants to Ethnics: The Italian Americans* (New York: Oxford University Press, 1983), vii–viii, 173–93.

24. Robert Viscusi, "Viaggio Continuo: Resisting Identity," in *Il sogno italoamericano: Realtà e immaginario dell'emigrazione negli Stati Uniti,* ed. Sebastiano Martelli (Naples: CUEN, 1998), 377–90.

25. *A Directory of Italian and Italian-American Organizations and Community Services,* ed. Andrew Brizzolara (Staten Island: Center for Migration Studies, 1976); Frank J. Cavaioli, "A Sociodemographic Analysis of Italian Americans

and the Twilight of Ethnicity," in *Italian Ethnics: Their Languages, Literatures and Lives*, ed. Dominic Candeloro, Fred L. Gardaphe, and Paolo A. Giordano (Staten Island: American Italian Historical Association, 1990), 191–99.

26. Paola Corti, *L'emigrazione* (Rome: Editori Riuniti, 1999), 17.

27. David A. J. Richards, *Italian American: The Racialization of an Ethnic Identity* (New York: New York University Press, 1999).

28. Anna Maria Martellone, "Tra memoria del passato e speranza del nuovo: L'identità italiana negli Stati Uniti," *Memoria e ricerca* 4, no. 8 (December 1996): 57–75; Patricia Boscia-Mulè, *Authentic Ethnicities: The Interaction of Ideology, Gender Power, and Class in the Italian-American Experience* (Westport CT: Greenwood Press, 1999), esp. 127–55.

29. For a recent critical review of studies on the Italian-American experience, see Donna Gabaccia, "Italian History and Gli Italiani nel Mondo, Part I," *Journal of Modern Italian Studies* 2, no. 1 (Spring 1997): 45–66.

30. Joan Lynn Savereno, "Private Lives, Public Identities: The Italians of Reading and Berks County, Pennsylvania, 1890–1940" (Ph.D. diss., University of Pennsylvania, 1996).

31. Richard N. Juliani, *Building Little Italy: Philadelphia's Italians Before Mass Migration* (University Park, PA: Pennsylvania State University Press, 1998), 286. Juliani has previously expressed a similar view in his "Images, Interactions, and Institutions: The Emergence of an Italian Community in Philadelphia," in *Origins and Transitions: Towards a Plural Citizenship*, ed. Mario Aldo Toscano (Naples: Ipermedium, 1996), 202.

32. Nelli, *From Immigrants to Ethnics*, 62; Fondazione Giovanni Agnelli, *The Italian-Americans: Who They Are, Where They Live, How Many They Are* (Turin: Fondazione Giovanni Agnelli, 1980), 9; Richard N. Juliani, "Philadelphia," in *The Italian American Experience: An Encyclopedia*, ed. Salvatore J. LaGumina et al. (New York: Garland, 2000), 462–63.

Chapter 2. The Transposition of Subnational Identities

1. Howard R. Marraro, "Italo-Americans in Pennsylvania in the Eighteenth Century," *Pennsylvania History* 7, no. 3 (July 1940): 159–66; Giambattista Scandella, "Journals, 1797–98," Giambattista Scandella Papers, box 1, folders 1–7, box 2, folders 1–2, BIES; Giovanni E. Schiavo, *Four Centuries of Italian-American History* (New York: Vigo Press, 1952), 11; Valentine J. Belfiglio, "Italian Culture in Eighteenth-Century Philadelphia," *Italian Quarterly* 23, no. 87 (Winter 1982): 77–81; M. Agnes Gertrude, "Italian Immigration into Philadelphia: I," *Records of the American Catholic Society of Philadelphia* 58, no. 2 (June 1947): 137; "Italians in Philadelphia," p. 1, unpublished typescript, Papers of the Pennsylvania Grand Lodge of the Order Sons of Italy in America, box 213, folder 34, IHRC.

2. Juliani, *Building Little Italy,* esp. 141–253.

3. U.S. Bureau of the Census, *Tenth Census of the United States: Statistics of Population* (Washington DC: U.S. Government Printing Office, 1882), 541; *Eleventh Census of the United States: Statistics of Population* (Washington DC: U.S. Government Printing Office, 1892), 672; *Twelfth Census of the United States Taken in the Year 1900: Population,* 2 vols. (Washington DC: U.S. Government Printing Office, 1902), 2:802, 877, 885, 901, 905; *Thirteenth Census of the United States Taken in the Year 1910: Population,* 3 vols. (Washington DC: U.S. Government Printing Office, 1913), 3:605; Bianca Arcangeli, "Le colonie italiane di Philadelphia," *Annali della Facoltà di Lettere e Filosofia dell'Università di Napoli* 16 (1973–74): 217–30.

4. Ira A. Glazier, "Ships and Passengers in Emigration from Italy to the US, 1880–1900," in *Le genti del mare Mediterraneo,* ed. Rosalba Ragosta, 2 vols. (Naples: Pironti, 1981), 2:1106; U.S. Treasury Department, *Annual Reports and Statements of the Chief of the Bureau of Statistics on the Foreign Commerce and Navigation, Immigration, and Tonnage of the United States,* 15 vols. (Washington DC: U.S. Government Printing Office, 1880–1894); Richard N. Juliani, "The Origin and Development of the Italian Community in Philadelphia," in *The Ethnic Experience in Pennsylvania,* ed. John E. Bodnar (Lewisburg PA: Bucknell University Press, 1973), 235–37.

5. Gaetano Ferro and Adele Maiello, "Un secolo e mezzo di flussi migratori," in Università degli Studi di Genova, *L'emigrazione nelle Americhe dalla provincia di Genova: Questioni generali e introduttive* (Bologna: Patron, 1990), 154; Juliani, *Building Little Italy,* 274.

6. B. R. Cassigoli and H. Chiariglione, *Libro d'oro degli italiani d'America: Con descrizioni e biografie* (Pueblo, 1904), 542–45; *La Colonia italiana di Filadelfia all'esposizione di Milano* (Philadelphia: Officine Tipografiche del Giornale "L'Opinione," 1906); Ernest L. Biagi, *The Italians of Philadelphia* (New York: Carlton Press, 1967), 162–64; John F. Sutherland, "Housing the Poor in the City of Homes: Philadelphia at the Turn of the Century," in *The Peoples of Philadelphia: A History of Ethnic Groups and Lower Class Life, 1790–1940,* ed. Allen D. Davis and Mark H. Haller (Philadelphia: Temple University Press, 1973), 191–92, 200; Richard A. Varbero, "Urbanization and Acculturation: Philadelphia's South Italians, 1918–1932" (Ph.D. diss., Temple University, 1975), 282–90; Richard N. Juliani, "The Italian Community of Philadelphia," in *Little Italies in North America,* ed. Robert F. Harney and J. Vincenza Scarpaci (Toronto: Multicultural Society of Ontario, 1981), 92–93; C. C. A. Baldi Middle School, *Handbook* (Philadelphia: C. C. A. Baldi Middle School, 1986), 6–7; Victor R. Greene, *American Immigrant Leaders, 1800–1910: Marginality and Identity* (Baltimore: Johns Hopkins University Press, 1987), 133–35; Giovanni E. Schiavo, *Italian-American History* (New York: Vigo Press, 1947), xv–xvi.

7. Anna Maria Martellone, "Prefazione," in Elisabetta Vezzosi, *Il socialismo indifferente: Immigrati italiani e Socialist Party negli Stati Uniti del primo Novecento*

(Rome: Edizioni Lavoro, 1991), xv–xvi; "Curriculum vitae del Gr. Uff. Giovanni Di Silvestro," SPD–DSG; CPC, box 1819, folder 73440 "Di Silvestro, Arpino Giuseppe"; Biagi, *The Italians of Philadelphia*, 181–82.

8. L. Aldrovandi, "Note sull'emigrazione italiana in Pennsylvania," *Bollettino dell'Emigrazione* no. 3 (1911): 42; U.S. Senate. 61st Cong., 3d Sess., *Reports of the Immigration Commission*, 41 vols. (1911; rpt. New York: Arno Press, 1969), 37:219–20.

9. Theodore Hershberg et al., "A Tale of Three Cities: Blacks, Immigrants, and Opportunity in Philadelphia, 1850–1880, 1930, 1970," in *Philadelphia: Work, Space, Family, and Group Experience in the Nineteenth Century: Essays Toward an Interdisciplinary History of the City*, ed. Theodore Hershberg (New York: Oxford University Press, 1981), 475.

10. Nathaniel Burt and Wallace E. Davies, "The Iron Age," in *Philadelphia: A 300-Year History*, ed. Russell F. Weigley (New York: Norton, 1982), 474–83; Philip Scranton, *Endless Novelty: Specialty Production and American Industrialization, 1865–1925* (Princeton: Princeton University Press, 1997), 90–99, 260–88.

11. Philip Scranton, "The Transition from Custom to Ready-to-Wear Clothing in Philadelphia, 1890–1930," *Textile History* 25, no. 2 (Autumn 1994): 258; Caroline Golab, *Immigrant Destinations* (Philadelphia: Temple University Press, 1977), 30–33.

12. Richard N. Juliani, *The Social Organization of Immigration: The Italians in Philadelphia* (New York: Arno Press, 1980), 188–91; Biagio Castagna, *Bozzetti americani e coloniali: Filadelfia, Stati Uniti d'America* (Salerno: Jovane, 1907), 57; S. A. Paolantonio, *Frank Rizzo: The Last Big Man in Big City America* (Philadelphia: Camino, 1993), 23.

13. Caroline Golab, "The Immigrant and the City: Poles, Italians, and Jews in Philadelphia, 1870–1920," in *The Peoples of Philadelphia*, 214–15.

14. Aurora Unti, "The Italians in Philadelphia," in International Institute, *Foreign Born in Philadelphia* (Philadelphia: International Institute, 1930), 8–9; Barbara Klaczynska, "Why Women Work: A Comparison of Various Groups—Philadelphia, 1910–1930," *Labor History* 17, no. 1 (Winter 1976): 77–79; Stephanie W. Greenberg, "Neighborhood Change, Racial Transition, and Work Location: A Case Study of an Industrial City, Philadelphia 1880–1930," *Journal of Urban History* 7, no. 3 (May 1981): 299; Rosara Lucy Passero, "Ethnicity in the Men's Ready-Made Clothing Industry, 1880–1950: The Italian Experience in Philadelphia" (Ph.D. diss., University of Pennsylvania, 1978), 151–56, 305–6, 314, 319; Juliani, *The Social Organization of Immigration*, 191, 198; Torry Dickinson, "Redivided Lives: The Formation of the Working Class in Philadelphia, 1870–1945" (Ph.D. diss., State University of New York at Binghamton, 1983), 231–51; Janet S. McKay, *Pennsylvania Children in New Jersey Cranberry Farms* (Philadelphia: Public Education and Child Labor Association of Pennsylvania, 1923).

15. Scranton, "The Transition from Custom to Ready-to-Wear Clothing in Philadelphia," 252, 257; Passero, "Ethnicity in the Men's Ready-Made Clothing

Industry," 322–25. For an insightful analysis of the development of small-size capitalism in Philadelphia's textile industry, see Philip Scranton, *Proprietary Capitalism: The Textile Manufacture at Philadelphia* (Philadelphia: Temple University Press, 1983).

16. Aldrovandi, "Note sull'emigrazione italiana in Pennsylvania," 42; Philip Rose, *The Italians in America* (New York: Doran, 1922), 57; Arcangeli, "Le colonie italiane di Philadelphia," 233–37.

17. Gladys L. Palmer, *Recent Trends in Employment and Unemployment in Philadelphia* (Philadelphia: Philadelphia Labor Market Studies, 1937), 26; Gladys L. Palmer and Ada M. Stoflet, *The Labor Force of the Philadelphia Radio Industry* (Philadelphia: Philadelphia Labor Market Studies, 1938), 15–16, 23, 53; Richard A. Varbero, "Workers in City and County: The South Italian Experience in Philadelphia, 1900–1950," in *Italian Americans: The Search for a Usable Past*, 23–25; Sam Bass Warner Jr., "If All the World Were Philadelphia: A Scaffolding for Urban History, 1774–1930," *American Historical Review* 74, no. 1 (Oct. 1968): 40–41.

18. Anna Maria Martellone, "Italian Mass Emigration to the United States, 1876–1930: A Historical Survey," *Perspectives in American History* 1 (1984): 389, 402–403; Ira A. Glazier, "Introduction," in *Italians to America: Lists of Passengers Arriving at U.S. Ports, 1880–1899*, ed. Ira A. Glazier and P. William Filby (Wilmington DE: Scholarly Resources Inc., 1992), xii–xiii.

19. Aldrovandi, "Note sulla emigrazione italiana in Pennsylvania," 3; Juliani, "The Origin and Development of the Italian Community in Philadelphia," 233–34, 241; Arcangeli, "Le colonie italiane di Philadelphia," 237–42. For the background of worldwide emigration from Chiavari with a focus, however, on the second half of the nineteenth century, see Adele Maiello, "L'emigrazione dal chiavarese: Sue origini e caratteristiche," *Annali della Facoltà di Scienze Politiche dell'Università degli Studi di Genova*, 11–13 (1983–86), 3 vols., 2:155–83.

20. U.S. Bureau of the Census, *Fourteenth Census of the United States Taken in the Year 1920: Population*, 3 vols. (Washington DC: U.S. Government Printing Office, 1922), 2:896, 944; *Fifteenth Census of the United States: 1930, Population*, 3 vols. (Washington DC: U.S. Government Printing Office, 1932), 3:671, 704, 707.

21. Giovanni E. Schiavo, *The Italians in America before the Civil War* (New York: Vigo Press, 1934), 211–14; Juliani, *Building Little Italy*, 73, 128–30; Angeline H. Lograsso, "Piero Maroncelli in Philadelphia," *Romanic Review* 24, no. 4 (Oct.–Dec. 1933): 323–29.

22. Alfonso Strafile, *"Memorandum" coloniale ossia sintesi storica di osservazioni e fatti che diano un'idea generale della vita coloniale degli Italiani nel Nord America con monografia illustrativa della colonia di Philadelphia* (Philadelphia: "Mastro Paolo" Printing House, 1910), 20–21; Joanne Pellegrino, "An Effective School of Patriotism," in *Studies in Italian American Social History:*

Essays in Honor of Leonard Covello, ed. Francesco Cordasco (Totowa NJ: Rowan and Littlefield, 1975), 84–104; Catherine L. Albanese, *A Cobbler's Universe: Religion, Poetry, and Performance in the Life of a South Italian Immigrant* (New York: Continuum, 1997).

    23. Martin Clark, *Modern Italy, 1871–1982* (London: Longman, 1984), 1–2; Ruggiero Romano, *Paese Italia: Venti secoli di identità* (Rome: Donzelli, 1994); Robert D. Putnam, *Making Democracy Work: Civic Traditions in Modern Italy* (Princeton: Princeton University Press, 1993), 121–37.

    24. William Dean Howells, *Italian Journeys* (London: William Heinemann, 1901), 5.

    25. John S. MacDonald and Leatrice D. MacDonald, "Urbanization, Ethnic Groups, and Social Segmentation," *Social Research* 29, no. 4 (Winter 1962): 445–46; Marie Hall Ets, *Rosa: The Life of an Italian Immigrant* (Minneapolis: University of Minnesota Press, 1970), 209, 232.

    26. Robert A. Park and Herbert A. Miller, *Old World Traits Transplanted* (Chicago: University of Chicago Press, 1921), 145–59; John S. MacDonald and Leatrice D. MacDonald, "Migration, Ethnic Neighborhood Formation, and Social Networks," *Milbank Memorial Fund Quarterly* 42, no. 1 (Jan. 1964): 82–97; Riccardo Scartezzini, Roberto Guidi, and Anna Maria Zaccaria, *Tra due mondi: L'avventura americana tra i migranti italiani di fine secolo: Un approccio analitico* (Milan: Franco Angeli, 1994); Judith E. Smith, *Family Connections: A History of Italian and Jewish Immigrant Lives in Providence, Rhode Island, 1900–1940* (Albany: State University of New York Press, 1985), 132–33; John E. Zucchi, *Italians in Toronto: Development of a National Identity, 1875–1935* (Kingston and Montreal: McGill-Queen's University, 1988); Franc Sturino, *Forging the Chain: Italian Migration to North America* (Toronto: Multicultural History Society of Ontario, 1990); Joseph J. Barton, *Peasants and Strangers: Italians, Rumanians, and Slovaks in an American City, 1890–1950* (Cambridge MA: Harvard University Press, 1975), 60–63; Andreina De Clementi, "La sfida dell'insularità: Generazioni e differenze etniche tra gli emigranti italiani negli Stati Uniti," *Memoria e ricerca* 4, no. 8 (Dec. 1996): 100–1; Antonio Mangano, "The Associated Life of the Italians in New York City" [1904], in *The Italian in America: The Progressive View,* ed. Lydio F. Tomasi (Staten Island: Center for Migration Studies. 1978), 154; Amy Bernardi, *America Vissuta* (Turin: Bocca, 1911), 331; William Foote Whyte, *Street Corner Society: The Social Structure of an Italian Slum* (1943; Chicago: University of Chicago Press, 1955), xvii.

    27. Francis Anthony Ianni, "The Acculturation of the Italo-Americans in Norristown, Pennsylvania: 1900 to 1950" (Ph.D. diss., Pennsylvania State College, 1952), 129–33; Jere Downs, "Procession Carries on Sicilian Traditions," *Philadelphia Inquirer* (25 Aug. 1994), section C: 2; Diane Vecchio Wilson, "Assimilation and Ethnic Consolidation of Italians in Cortland, New York: 1892–1930," in *The Family and Community Life of Italian Americans,* ed. Richard N. Juliani (Staten Island: American Italian Historical Association, 1983), 183, 186.

28. Enrico Moretti, "Social Networks and Migrations: Italy, 1876–1913," *International Migration Review* 33, no. 127 (Fall 1999): 640–57; Ira A. Glazier and Robert Kleiner, "Analisi comparata degli emigranti dall'Europa meridionale e orientale attraverso le liste passeggeri delle navi statunitensi," *Altreitalie* 4, no. 7 (Jan.–June 1992): 119, 125; Gianfausto Rosoli, "From 'Promised Land' to 'Bitter Land': Italian Migrants and the Transformation of a Myth," in *Distant Magnets: Expectations and Realities in the Immigrant Experience, 1840–1930*, ed. Dirk Hoerder and Horst Roessner (New York: Holmes & Meier, 1993), 225–26; Juliani, "The Italian Community of Philadelphia," 93–95.

29. Joan Younger Dickinson, "Aspects of Italian Immigration to Philadelphia," *Pennsylvania Magazine of History and Biography* 90, no. 4 (Oct. 1966): 463; Ellen Ginzburg Migliorino, "Il proletariato italiano di Filadelfia all'inizio del secolo," *Studi Emigrazione* 13, no. 41 (Mar. 1976): 35; Golab, *Immigrant Destinations*, 116; Maria Rizzo "L'emigrazione italiana negli Stati Uniti d'America dal 1880 alla prima guerra mondiale: I problemi dell'adattamento in un case study: Gli italiani a Philadelphia" (Ph.D. diss., University of Naples, 1985–86), 124–25; Walter Licht, *Getting Work: Philadelphia, 1840–1950* (Cambridge MA: Harvard University Press, 1992), 36 (to which the percentage refers); transcript of an interview with Josephine Reale by Nancy Dallett, Haverton PA, 25 Oct. 1985, Ellis Island Oral History Project, interview no. 71, p. 11.

30. Emily Wayland Dinwiddle, "Some Aspects of Italian Housing and Social Conditions in Philadelphia," *Charities* 12, no. 5 (May 1904): 490–94; Sutherland, "Housing the Poor in the City of Homes," 189.

31. Donna R. Gabaccia, *From Sicily to Elizabeth Street: Housing and Social Change among Italian Immigrants, 1880–1930* (Albany: State University of New York Press, 1984), 103–5.

32. Gertrude, "Italian Immigration into Philadelphia: I," 190; Pietro Militello, *Italians in America* (Philadelphia: Franklin, 1973), 2; Juliani, *The Social Organization of Immigration*, 168–72, 178–82; Nicholas V. DeLeo, "A Look at the Early Years of Philadelphia's Little Italy," *Pennsylvania Folklife* 45, no. 1 (Autumn 1995): 36.

33. Jim Riggio, "Tales of Little Italy," *Philadelphia Magazine* 62, no. 3 (Mar. 1971): 74; Dorothy Noyes, *Uses of Tradition: Arts of Italian Americans in Philadelphia* (Philadelphia: Samuel S. Fleisher Museum, 1989), 15.

34. Dickinson, "Aspects of Italian Immigration to Philadelphia," 463; transcript of an interview with Joseph Talese by Nancy Dallett, Ocean City, NJ, 25 Oct. 1985, Ellis Island Oral History Project, interview no. 61, p. 13; Biagi, *The Italians of Philadelphia*, 26–27, 76. Information about restaurants and pharmacies come from ads published in *Il Popolo*, 23 Sept., 9 Dec. 1905; 7 April 1906. For Casciato, Di Bernardino, and Melocchi, see *Giuseppe Garibaldi*, 7 July 1907.

35. "Avventure degli italiani in America," *L'Eco del Rhode Island* (6 Nov. 1915): 1 (reprinted from *Mastro Paolo*); Hugo Maiale, "The Italian Vote in Philadelphia between 1928 and 1946" (Ph.D. diss., University of Pennsylvania, 1950), 276.

36. Presbyterian Church of St. Andrew and St. Philip, *Commemorating Seventy-Five Years Work and Worship* (Philadelphia, 1980); DeLeo, "A Look at the Early Years," 33. Scattered issues of *L'Aurora* for the years 1935 and 1936, when the newspaper was published by reverend Angelo Di Domenica, are available at ACS.

37. Richard N. Juliani, "The Parish as an Urban Institution: Italian Catholics in Philadelphia," *Records of the American Catholic Historical Society of Philadelphia* 96 (1986): 49–65; Antonio Isoleri, *"Pati, Non Mori!"* (Philadelphia: Penn Printing House, 1891), 15–17; Vito C. Mazzone, *The Oldest Italian Church in the U.S.A.: Saint Magdalen de Pazzi, Philadelphia, PA* (Philadelphia: Farr-Welt, 1983); Alfred M. Natali, *St. Mary Magdalen de Pazzi: First Italian Parish in the U.S.A.* (Philadelphia, 1991), 15–18; Celeste A. Morello, *Beyond History: The Times and Peoples of St. Paul's Roman Catholic Church, 1843 to 1993* (Philadelphia: Jeffries & Manz, 1992), 99–100, 109, 111, 128.

38. Varbero, "Urbanization and Acculturation," 65, 203–11. For the role of the saints in Italian Americans' religious devotion, see *The Saints in the Lives of Italian Americans*, ed. Joseph A. Varacalli et al. (Stony Brook NY: Forum Italicum, 1999).

39. Franzina, *Gli italiani al Nuovo Mondo*, 228–29; Maria Susanna Garroni, "Italian Parishes in a Burgeoning City: Buffalo, 1880–1920," *Studi Emigrazione* 28, no. 103 (Sept. 1991): 356; Gary Ross Mormino, *Immigrants on the Hill: Italian Americans in St. Louis, 1882–1982* (Urbana: University of Illinois Press, 1986), 154; Peter W. Bardaglio, "Italian Immigrants and the Catholic Church in Providence, 1890–1930," *Rhode Island History* 34, no. 1 (Feb. 1975): 46–57; Smith, *Family Connections*, 147–52.

40. M. Agnes Gertrude, "Italian Immigration into Philadelphia: II," *Records of the American Catholic Historical Society of Philadelphia* 58, no. 3 (Sept. 1947): 189–90; Elizabeth Lay Mathias, "From Folklore to Mass Culture: Dynamics of Acculturation in the Games of Italian-American Men" (Ph.D. diss., University of Pennsylvania, 1974), 81–83; Joseph R. Daughen and Peter Binzen, *The Cop Who Would Be King: Mayor Frank Rizzo* (Boston: Little, Brown, 1977), 53; Rizzo, "L'emigrazione italiana," 125; Orsi, "The Religious Boundaries," 315; Pasquale Verdicchio, *Bound by Distance: Rethinking Nationalism through the Italian Diaspora* (Madison NJ: Fairleigh Dickinson University Press, 1997), 100, 103.

41. Robert F. Foerster, *The Italian Emigration of Our Times* (New York: Russell and Russell, 1919), 393; Lawrence F. Pisani, *The Italian in America: A Social Study and History* (New York: Exposition Press, 1957), 126; Virginia Yans-McLaughlin, *Family and Community: Italian Immigrants in Buffalo, 1880–1930* (Ithaca: Cornell University Press, 1971), 110–11, 130–31; Barton, *Peasants and Strangers*, 74; Dino Cinel, *From Italy to San Francisco: The Immigrant Experience* (Stanford: Stanford University Press, 1982), 201; Mormino, *Immigrants on the Hill*, 75–80; Joseph Salituro, "The Italians in Kenosha, Wisconsin," in *Italian Americans and Their Public and Private Life*, ed. Frank J. Cavaioli, Angela Danzi,

and Salvatore J. LaGumina (Staten Island: Italian American Historical Association, 1993), 57.

42. Order Sons of Italy in America, *By-Laws of the Grand Lodge of Pennsylvania* (Philadelphia: Model Printing House, 1936); Ernest L. Biagi, *The Purple Aster: A History of the Sons of Italy in America* (n.p.: Veritas Press, 1961); John Andreozzi, "The Order Sons of Italy in America: Historical Summary," in *Guide to the Records of the Order Sons of Italy in America*, ed. John Andreozzi (St. Paul: Immigration History Research Center, 1989), 7–14.

43. *History of the Società di Unione e Fratellanza Italiana* (Philadelphia, 1929); Richard N. Juliani, "Immigrants in Philadelphia: The World of 1886," in *Italian Americans: The Search for a Usable Past*, 11; Juliani, *Building Little Italy*, 223–25; Fred Hamilton, *Rizzo* (New York: Viking Press, 1973), 23. For specific information about the Cuneos and their migration strategies, see Antonio Gibelli, "La risorsa America," in *Storia d'Italia: Le regioni dall'Unità a oggi: La Liguria*, ed. Antonio Gibelli and Paride Rugafiori (Turin: Einaudi, 1994), 618–24.

44. Interviews with Severino Verna and Stephen Diorio, WPA-ES, roll 3; *Constitution and By-Laws of the Christopher Columbus Mutual Aid Society* (Philadelphia, 1901), BIES; "Regolamento," p. 9, Papers of the Società di Mutuo Soccorso fra Castrogiovannesi e Provinciali, box 1, folder 1, BIES; Juliani, "Italian Organizations in Philadelphia," in *Invisible Philadelphia: Community through Voluntary Organizations*, ed. Jean Barth Toll and Mildred S. Gillam (Philadelphia: Atwater Kent Museum, 1995), 110–12.

45. *Il Popolo*, 28 Apr. 1906.

46. Briggs, *An Italian Passage*, 141; Mormino, *Immigrants on the Hill*, 128, 131; Juliani, *The Social Organization of Immigration*, 170–72; *Philadelphia Inquirer*, 3 Feb. 1947.

47. Joseph Velikonja, "The Periodical Press and Italian Communities," in *The Family and Community Life of Italian Americans*, 53; Paul Palazzi, "Spires of Influence," 1–5, WPA-ES, roll 3.

48. John Higham, "Introduction: The Forms of Ethnic Leadership," in *Ethnic Leadership in America*, ed. John Higham (Baltimore: Johns Hopkins University Press, 1978), 1–18; Greene, *American Immigrant Leaders*.

49. Letter by the prefect of L'Aquila to the Ministry of Interior, L'Aquila, 26 June 1908, CPC, box 1819, folder 73440 "Di Silvestro, Arpino Giuseppe"; Baldo Aquilano, *L'Ordine Figli d'Italia in America* (New York: Società Tipografica Italiana, 1925), 247–48; Palazzi, "Spires of Influence," 7–10; Biagi, *The Purple Aster*, 19, 21, 35, 135; Varbero, "Urbanization and Acculturation," 306–7. For the role of the publishers of Italian-language newspapers in spreading nationalistic rhetoric among Italian immigrants, see in general Rudolph J. Vecoli, "The Italian Immigrant Press and the Construction of Social Reality, 1850–1920," in *Print Culture in a Diverse America*, ed. James P. Danky and Wayne A. Wiegand (Urbana: University of Illinois Press, 1998), 22–23.

50. *Il Popolo*, 28 Apr. 1906; *La Rassegna* 7 Apr., 7 July 1917; *La Ragione*, 25 Apr. 24 July, 23 Aug. 1917.

51. *L'Opinione*, 10 June 1906; A. Frangini, *Italiani in Filadelfia: Strenna nazionale: Cenni biografici* (Philadelphia: Stabilimento Tipografico "L'Opinione," 1907), 20–21; Strafile, *"Memorandum" coloniale*, 29. For illiteracy rates among Italian immigrants, see Luigi Di Comite and Ira A. Glazier, "Socio-Demographic Characteristics of Italian Emigration to the United States from Ship Passenger Lists: 1880–1914," *Ethnic Forum* 4, no. 1–2 (Spring 1984): 86–87.

52. Annette Wheeler Cafarelli, "The Making of Tradition," in *Shades of Black and White*, 35; John F. Lewis, *Christopher Columbus: A Short Oration by John F. Lewis before the United Italian Societies of Philadelphia, October 12, 1892* (Philadelphia: George H. Buchanan, 1892), 2; Antonio Isoleri, *Un ricordo delle feste colombiane celebrate in Philadelphia, Stati Uniti d'America, nell'ottobre del 1892* (Philadelphia: Penn Printing House, 1893), 19–59; Richard D. Grifo and Anthony F. Noto, *Italian Presence in Pennsylvania* (University Park PA: Pennsylvania Historical Association, 1990), 29; *Giuseppe Garibaldi*, 7 July 1907; Strafile, *"Memorandum" coloniale*, 13, 29; *L'Opinione*, 19 Feb. 1907.

53. *Il Popolo*, 23 Sept. 1905; 14 Apr. 1906.

54. "Elenco delle società italiane esistenti negli Stati Uniti alla fine del 1910," *Bollettino dell'Emigrazione* no. 4 (1912): 514–16; Silvano M. Tomasi, "Militantism and Italian-American Unity," in *Power and Class: The Italian American Experience Today*, ed. Francis X. Femminella (Staten Island: American Italian Historical Association, 1973), 22; Biagi, *The Italians of Philadelphia*, 208–9, 222–23, 37.

55. See the related documentation in Order Sons of Italy in America, Giovanni Di Silvestro Papers, box 12, folder 15, IHRC.

56. *Il Popolo*, 21, 28 Apr. 1906; *La Plebe*, 18 June 1908.

Chapter 3. The Development of a National Identity

1. *Philadelphia Inquirer*, 25, 26 May 1915; *Il Momento*, 27 Jan., 10 Mar., 2 June 1917; 19 Jan. 1918; *La Rassegna*, 25 Aug. 1917; *La Ragione*, 26 May 1917; *La Libera Parola*, 15, 29 June 1918; Aquilano, *L'Ordine Figli d'Italia*, 252–56; Biagi, *The Purple Aster*, 137.

2. Frangini, *Italiani in Filadelfia*, 7; Harry C. Silcox, *Philadelphia Politics from the Bottom Up: The Life of Irishman William McMullen* (Philadelphia: Balch Institute Press, 1989), 109; Gaeton J. Fonzi, "Philadelphia's Italians: A Bubbly Minestrone," *Philadelphia Magazine* 52, no. 1 (Jan. 1961): 28; Paolantonio, *Frank Rizzo*, 21–23; Steve Fraser, "Dress Rehearsal for the New Deal: Shop-Floor Insurgents, Political Elites, and Industrial Democracy in the Amalgamated Clothing Workers," in *Working-Class America: Essays on Labor, Community, and*

American Society, ed. Michael H. Frish and Daniel J. Walkowitz (Urbana: University of Illinois Press, 1983), 231–32; Steve Fraser, "*Landslayt* and *Paesani*: Ethnic Conflict and Cooperation in the Amalgamated Clothing Workers of America," in *"Struggle a Hard Battle": Essays on Working-Class Immigrants*, ed. Dirk Hoerder (DeKalb: Northern Illinois University Press, 1986), 287–89; Strafile, *"Memorandum" coloniale*, 12; Jerre Mangione and Ben Morreale, *La Storia: Five Centuries of the Italian American Experience* (New York: Harper-Collins, 1992), 153; Daughen and Binzen, *The Cop Who Would Be King*, 49–50.

3. Castagna, *Bozzetti americani e coloniali*, 64; Richard A. Varbero, "Philadelphia's South Italians and the Irish Church: A History of Cultural Conflict," in *The Religious Experience of Italian Americans*, ed. Silvano M. Tomasi (Staten Island: American Italian Historical Association, 1975), 31–52; Richard N. Juliani, "The Interaction of Irish and Italians: From Conflict to Integration," in *Italians and Irish in America*, ed. Francis X. Femminella (Staten Island: American Italian Historical Association, 1985), 28–30.

4. Rudolph J. Vecoli, "Prelates and Peasants: Italian Immigrants and the Catholic Church," *Journal of Social History* 2, no. 3 (Spring 1969): 230; interview with Rita R. by the author, Philadelphia, 12 Nov. 1989.

5. Morello, *Beyond History*, 91–97.

6. Gerald Meyer, "Italian Harlem: Portrait of a Community," in *The Italians of New York: Four Centuries of Struggle and Achievement*, ed. Philip V. Cannistraro (New York: New York Historical Society, 1999), 59.

7. Luigi Villari, *Gli Stati Uniti e l'emigrazione italiana* (Milan: Treves, 1912), 290; *Public Ledger*, 24 May 1918; *Il Momento*, 12 May 1917; 1 June 1918.

8. *Philadelphia Inquirer*, 5 Nov. 1918.

9. *Public Ledger*, 5 Nov. 1918.

10. *Cronaca Sovversiva*, 31 July 1915; *La Comune*, 6 (1915): 1; Filippo Bocchini, "Alle madri," ibid., 3 (Jan. 1912): 1; Mario De Ciampis, "Storia del movimento socialista rivoluzionario italiano," *La Parola del Popolo* 50, no. 37 (Dec. 1958–Jan. 1959): 161. No issues of *Mastro Paolo*, *L'Opinione*, and *La Voce del Popolo* are nowadays available for the war years. The editorial stances of these newspapers in this period are, however, outlined by Palazzi, "Spires of Influence," 5–6, 11–12.

11. Vecoli, "The Search for an Italian American Identity," 93; *Il Momento*, 8 Mar., 5 Apr., 1, 15 Nov. 1919; *La Libera Parola*, 8, 15 Feb., 1, 8, 29 Mar. 1919; 7, 14, 21, 28 Mar. 1920; 5, 12 Nov. 1921.

12. *La Libera Parola*, 20 Apr., 29 June 1918.

13. John B. Duff, "The Italians," in *The Immigrants' Influence on Wilson's Peace Policies*, ed. Joseph P. O'Grady (Lexington: University of Kentucky Press, 1967), 111–39; Joseph T. Makarewicz, "The Impact of World War I on Pennsylvania Politics with Emphasis on the Election of 1920" (Ph.D. diss., University of Pittsburgh, 1972), 231; *La Libera Parola*, 5 Sept. 31 Oct. 1920; *American Newspaper Annual & Directory* (Philadelphia: N.W. Ayer and Son, 1920), 857.

14. "Mr. Moore and the Italians," undated press release, J. Hampton Moore Papers, box 303-168C, folder "1 Sept.–31 Oct. 1927," HSP.

15. *Il Momento*, 21 Apr., 4 Aug. 1917; Philadelphia Chamber of Commerce, *Americanization in Philadelphia: A City-Wide Plan of Co-Ordinated Agencies under the Direction of the Americanization Committee* (Philadelphia: Edwin E. Bach, 1923); Varbero, "Urbanization and Acculturation," 10–12; Robert K. Murray, *Red Scare: A Study in National Hysteria, 1919–1920* (Minneapolis: University of Minnesota Press, 1955); Roberta Strauss Feuerlicht, *Justice Crucified: The Story of Sacco and Vanzetti* (New York: McGraw-Hill, 1977); Vecoli, "The Italian Immigrants in the United States Labor Movement," 305–6; William Preston Jr., *Aliens and Dissenters: Federal Suppression of Radicals, 1903–1933* (1963; Urbana: University of Illinois Press, 1994), 63–87; Ellen Ginzburg Migliorino, "La comunità italo-americana nel clima conservatore di Filadelfia agli inizi del Novecento," in *Italia e Stati Uniti dall'indipendenza americana ad oggi (1776–1976): Atti del I congresso internazionale di storia americana* (Genoa: Tilgher, 1978), 318–19; Augusta Molinari, "I giornali delle comunità anarchiche italo-americane," *Movimento operaio e socialista* 4, no. 1–2 (Jan.–June 1981): 129.

16. Anna Maria Martellone, "Introduzione," in *La "questione" dell'immigrazione negli Stati Uniti*, ed. Anna Maria Martellone (Bologna: Il Mulino, 1980), 63–65; Edward Prince Hutchinson, *Legislative History of American Immigration Policy, 1798–1965* (Philadelphia: Balch Institute Press, 1981), 187–92; Mae M. Ngai, "The Architecture of Race in American Immigration Law: A Reexamination of the Immigration Act of 1924," *Journal of American History* 86, no. 1 (June 1999): 67–92; Ercole Sori, *L'emigrazione italiana dall'Unità alla seconda guerra mondiale* (Bologna: Il Mulino, 1979), 419; Mario Arpea, *Alle origini dell'emigrazione abruzzese: La vicenda dell'altipiano delle Rocche* (Milan: Franco Angeli, 1987), 118; U.S. Bureau of the Census, *Statistical Abstract of the United States: 1966* (Washington DC: U.S. Government Printing Office, 1966), 92.

17. *Evening Bulletin*, 3 June 1924; *L'Opinione*, 9 June 1929.

18. Emerson Hunsberger Loucks, *The Ku Klux Klan in Pennsylvania: A Study in Nativism* (Harrisburg PA: Telegraph Press, 1936); Kenneth T. Jackson, *The Ku Klux Klan in the City, 1915–1930* (New York: Oxford University Press, 1967), 170–73, 180, 184, 237, 239; Philip Jenkins, *Hoods and Shirts: The Extreme Right in Pennsylvania, 1925–1950* (Chapel Hill: University of North Carolina Press, 1997), 62–88.

19. "Ku Klux Klan Rides Again," flyer reproduced in *Discovery: The Columbus Legacy* (Harrisburg, PA: Pennsylvania Historical and Museum Commission, 1989), 23; Patrick J. Gallo, *Old Bread, New Wine: A Portrait of the Italian Americans* (Chicago: Nelson-Hall, 1981), 121; *La Libera Parola*, 31 Oct. 1925.

20. David M. Chalmers, *Hooded Americanism: The First Century of the Ku Klux Klan, 1865–1965* (Garden City NY: Doubleday, 1965), 236–42; *La Libera Parola*, 7 Aug. 1921; 24 Aug. 1924.

21. *Evening Bulletin*, 31 May 1921; *Evening Ledger*, 30 Mar. 1922; Carolyn Adams et al., *Neighborhoods, Division, and Conflict in a Postindustrial City* (Philadelphia: Temple University Press, 1991), 10.

22. Margaret B. Tinkcom, "Depression and War, 1919–1946," in *Philadelphia*, 629; Hamilton, *Rizzo*, 32. A typewritten copy of the report of the Grand Jury investigation is available in Papers of the Committee of Seventy, series 3, folder 1, TUUA.

23. *The Bulletin Almanac and Year Book* (Philadelphia: Evening Bulletin, 1937), 486; ibid. (1938), 472; Gary W. Potter and Philip Jenkins, *The City and the Syndicate: Organizing Crime in Philadelphia* (Lexington, MA: Ginn Press, 1985), 14.

24. *Evening Bulletin*, 3 July 1939; Luigi Villari, "L'emigrazione italiana nel distretto consolare di Filadelfia," *Bollettino dell'emigrazione* no. 16 (1908): 1867–68, 1877–78; "Curriculum vitae del Gr. Uff. Giovanni Di Silvestro," SPD-DSG; *Philadelphia Daily News*, 20 May 1934.

25. Mark H. Haller, "Recurring Themes," in *The Peoples of Philadelphia*, 286; *Evening Bulletin*, 3 July 1939; 15 Sept. 1924; 27 Apr. 1928; 3 July 1929; *Philadelphia Record*, 1 Sept. 1935; *Public Ledger*, 28, 29 Jan. 1933; *Philadelphia Inquirer*, 28, 29, 30 Jan. 1933.

26. DeLeo, "A Look at the Early Years," 31; *Evening Bulletin*, 21, 25 Feb. 1924; Richard A. Varbero, "The Politics of Ethnicity: Philadelphia's Italians in the 1920's," in *Studies in Italian American Social History*, 175–76; *La Libera Parola*, 23 Jan., 24 July, 21 Aug. 1921; 24 June 1922; *L'Opinione*, 1 July–23 Aug. 1927; interviews with Peter Coppozi, Joseph Canazara, Ernest Strolla, and Carl Reeve, WPA-ES, roll 3; Philip V. Cannistraro, "Mussolini, Sacco-Vanzetti, and the Anarchists: The Transatlantic Context," *Journal of Modern History* 68, no. 1 (Mar. 1996): 51; Antonio Margariti, *America! America!* (Casalvelino Scalo: Galzerano, 1980), 67.

27. Martellone, "Italian Mass Emigration to the United States," 392; U.S. Bureau of the Census, *Fifteenth Census of the United States, 1930: Population*, 2:551.

28. Golab, *Immigrant Destinations*, 58; Giovanni Di Silvestro, *Note e appunti sulle colonie italiane degli Stati Uniti del Nord* (Philadelphia: Stabilimento Tipografico de "La Voce del Popolo," 1908), 18; Michele Renzulli, *L'Italia e il Fascismo negli Stati Uniti d'America* (Rome: Poliglotta, 1938), 141; *Relazione del Primo e Secondo Congresso degli Italiani degli Stati Uniti* (Philadelphia: Nardello Press, 1913), 15–16, 19, 21, 31, 40; Castagna, *Bozzetti americani e coloniali*, 57; Richard N. Juliani, "Una comunità in transizione: Il caso italiano a Filadelfia," in *Atti del Convegno "Le società in transizione: italiani e italo-americani negli anni Ottanta," Balch Institute, Philadelphia, 11–12 ottobre 1985* (Rome: Ministero degli Affari Esteri, n.d.), 310.

29. Dino Cinel, *The National Integration of Italian Return Migration, 1870–1929* (New York: Cambridge University Press, 1991), 105–6; Francesco Paolo

Cerase, *L'emigrazione di ritorno: Innovazione o reazione? L'esperienza dell'emigrazione di ritorno dagli Stati Uniti d'America* (Rome: Facoltà di scienze statistiche demografiche e attuariali dell'Università di Roma, 1971), 90; Massimo Livi Bacci, *L'immigrazione e l'assimilazione degli italiani negli Stati Uniti secondo le statistiche demografiche americane* (Milan: Giuffrè, 1961), 35–37. For Italian returnees in general, see also George R. Gilkey, "The United States and Italy: Migration and Repatriation," *Journal of Developing Areas* 2, no. 1 (Oct. 1967): 25–30; Anna Maria Martellone, "Italian Immigrant Settlement and Repatriation," in *The United States and Italy: The First Two Hundred Years*, ed. Humbert S. Nelli (Staten Island: American Italian Historical Association, 1977), 150–52; Andrew Rolle, *The Italian Americans: Troubled Roots* (Norman: University of Oklahoma Press, 1980), 47–55.

30. Dorothy Noyes, "From the *Paese* to the *Patria*: An Italian American Pilgrimage to Rome in 1929," in *Studies in Italian American Folklore*, ed. Luisa Del Giudice (Logan: Utah State University Press, 1993), 150; Barton, *Peasants and Strangers*, 85; "Programma ricordo della Loggia Piave no. 364," Luigi Cipolla Papers, folder 1, IHRC; Rose Doris Scherini, *The Italian-American Community of San Francisco: A Descriptive Study* (New York: Arno Press, 1980), 122; Briggs, *An Italian Passage*, 151–53; *L'Opinione*, 16 Mar. 1933.

31. Interviews with Severino Verna, Stephen Diorio, C. Erminio, and F. Ragozzino, WPA-ES, roll 3; *L'Opinione*, 29 Mar. 1933.

32. Juliani, *The Social Organization of Immigration*, 185–87; Passero, "Ethnicity in the Men's Ready-Made Clothing Industry," 294, 304–5; Golab, "The Immigrant and the City," 210–11.

33. Juliani, "Italian Organizations in Philadelphia," 113; Dubin, *South Philadelphia*, 111.

34. Antonio Valeo, "Ai membri del Circolo Maidese ed ai nostri amici," in Circolo Maidese in Philadelphia, *Atti ufficiali del banchetto inaugurale, 14 marzo 1934–XII* (Philadelphia, 1934), 19, pamphlet in Social and Educational Circles in Philadelphia Collection, BIES; Juliani, "The Origin and Development of the Italian Community in Philadelphia," 242.

35. Salituro, "The Italians in Kenosha," 60; letter by Giuseppe Castruccio, Italian consul general, to the Italian ambassador, Chicago, 16 July 1935, MCP, box 447, folder "Propaganda italiana a Chicago;" Nicholas Ruggieri, "Italian Provincial Groups Give Way to Nationalism," *Providence Evening Bulletin* (16 Mar. 1936): 15; Paul R. Campbell and Patrick T. Conley, *The Aurora Club of Rhode Island: A Fifty Year History* (Providence: Aurora Civic Association, 1982), 29–38.

36. Francesco Saracco, unpublished journals, 19, Francesco Saracco Papers, BIES; *L'Opinione*, 15, 17 Feb. 1934.

37. Circular by Louis Verna to the members of the Unione Abruzzese, n.d., Di Silvestro Papers, box 1, folder 1; letters to J. Hampton Moore, by Pietro Rosoni, R. Rogomo, Thomas G. Martin, Nicola Di Salvo, Antonio Decimo,

Vincenzo Di Natale, S. Serraini, Filippo Freda, Michael Buonanno, Philadelphia, various dates, Sept. and Oct. 1931, Moore Papers, box 318-168E; *La Libera Parola*, 1 Oct. 1921; *L'Opinione*, 3 Apr. 1933; 25, 27, 28 Jan., 3, 4, 6, 13, 14 Feb. 1934. For data about the percentage of Italian Americans on the municipal payroll, see John L. Shover, "Ethnicity and Religion in Philadelphia Politics, 1924–1940," *American Quarterly* 25, no. 5 (Dec. 1973): 513.

38. St. Rita's Parish, *Golden Jubilee Souvenir* (Philadelphia, 1957); *Open House: St. Rita's Parish* (Philadelphia, 1972); *L'Opinione*, 20, 21, 23 May 1933; *Evening Bulletin*, 21 May, 1933; Varbero, "Philadelphia's South Italians and the Irish Church," 45–47; Morello, *Beyond History*, 122–24. For Cardinal Dougherty, see also Hugh J. Nolan, "Cardinal Dougherty: An Appreciation," *Records of the American Catholic Historical Society of Philadelphia* 62, no. 3 (Sept. 1951): 135–41.

39. Letter by Giuseppe Castruccio, Italian consul general, to the Italian ambassador, Chicago, 19 August 1935, MCP, box 447, folder "Propaganda italiana a Chicago."

40. *Centennial Jubilee: St. Mary Magdalen De Pazzi Parish* (Philadelphia: Morgan Printing Co., 1952), unpaginated; "Questions for Msgr. Mazzone," undated manuscript, Vito C. Mazzone Papers, BIES.

Chapter 4. Italianness in the Depression Years

1. Thomas Gobel, "Becoming American: Ethnic Workers and the Rise of the CIO," *Labor History* 29, no. 1 (Spring 1988): 173–98; Gary Gerstle, *Working-Class Americanism: The Politics of Labor in a Textile City, 1914–1960* (New York: Cambridge University Press, 1989), 95–195; Lizabeth Cohen, *Making a New Deal: Industrial Workers in Chicago, 1919–1939* (New York: Cambridge University Press, 1990), 251–360; James R. Barrett, "Americanization from the Bottom Up: Immigration and the Remaking of the Working Class in the United States, 1880–1930," *Journal of American History* 79, no. 3 (Dec. 1992): 996–1020; Gary Gerstle, "The Protean Character of American Liberalism," *American Historical Review* 99, no. 4 (Oct. 1994): 1044–45.

2. "Unemployment Survey of Philadelphia, 1929," *Monthly Labor Review* 30, no. 2 (Feb. 1930): 21; "Unemployment in Philadelphia, Apr., 1930," ibid. 31, no. 1 (July 1930): 36; "Unemployment Survey of Metropolitan Life Insurance Co.," ibid. 32, no. 3 (Mar. 1931): 54; "Unemployment in Philadelphia, April, 1931," ibid. 33, no. 1 (July 1931): 68; Unemployment Committee of the National Federation of Settlements, *Case Studies of Unemployment*, ed. Marion Elderton (Philadelphia: University of Pennsylvania Press, 1931); letter by Lena Giannini to Franklin D. Roosevelt, Philadelphia, 10 Nov. 1932, Papers of the National Committee of the Democratic Party, box 682, folder "G," FDRL.

3. Donald Winfield Jarrell, "A History of Collective Bargaining at the Camden-Area Plants of the Radio Corporation of America with Special Atten-

tion to Bargaining Power" (Ph.D. diss., University of Pennsylvania, 1967), 44; John F. Bauman and Thomas H. Coode, *In the Eye of the Great Depression: New Deal Reporters and the Agony of the American People* (DeKalb IL: Northern Illinois University Press, 1988), 42; Karl De Schweinitz, "Philadelphia Takes Heart," *Survey* (15 May 1931): 217; Dickinson, "Redivided Lives," 236; *Polk's (Boyd's) Philadelphia (Pennsylvania) City Directories* (Philadelphia: R. L. Polk & Co., 1927), 1175–77; ibid. (1930), 1999–2000 (figures based on a check of the Italian-sounding names of companies).

    4. Philip Scranton and Walter Licht, *Work Sights: Industrial Philadelphia, 1890–1950* (Philadelphia: Temple University Press, 1986), 27 (to which the quotation refers); Howell John Harris, "The Deluge: The New Deal and the Open Shop Era," paper presented at the "New Deal Conference," Sidney Sussex College, Cambridge, England, 21–23 Sept. 1993; Walter Licht, "Studying Work: Personnel Policies in Philadelphia Firms, 1850–1950," in *Masters to Managers: Historical and Comparative Perspectives on American Employers*, ed. Sanford M. Jacoby (New York: Columbia University Press, 1991), 62–63.

    5. The sample to which the following paragraphs refer has drawn upon *La Libera Parola*, 1920–1942; *L'Opinione*, 1927–1935; and *Il Popolo Italiano*, 1935–1942. Philadelphia's City Directories could have provided a better source for such an analysis but they were no longer published after 1936.

    6. *Polk's (Boyd's) Philadelphia (Pennsylvania) City Directories* (1930), 1967; *L'Opinione*, 16, 19, 25 Mar. 1933.

    7. John M. Allswang, *A House for All Peoples: Ethnic Politics in Chicago, 1890–1936* (Lexington: University Press of Kentucky, 1971); Richard Jensen, "The Cities Reelect Roosevelt: Ethnicity, Religion, and Class in 1940," *Ethnicity* 8, no. 2 (June 1981): 189–95; Gerald H. Gamm, *The Making of New Deal Democrats: Voting Behavior and Realignment in Boston, 1920–1940* (Chicago: University of Chicago Press, 1989).

    8. David H. Kurtzman, *Methods of Controlling Votes in Philadelphia* (Philadelphia: University of Pennsylvania Press, 1935); John T. Salter, *The People's Choice: Philadelphia's William Vare* (New York: Exposition Press, 1971); Varbero, "The Politics of Ethnicity," 164–81; John Koren, "The Padrone System and Padrone Banks," *Bulletin of the Bureau of Labor* 9 (Mar. 1897): 123; *La Comune*, 4 (Feb. 1914): 2; Sam Bass Warner Jr., *The Private City: Philadelphia in Three Periods of Its Growth* (Philadelphia: University of Pennsylvania Press, 1968), 217; Varbero, "Workers in City and County," 17; Peter McCaffery, *When Bosses Ruled Philadelphia: The Emergence of the Republican Machine, 1867–1933* (University Park PA: Pennsylvania State University Press, 1993).

    9. Philadelphia voting statistics offer no ethnic breakdown. Figures on Italian American electoral behavior have, therefore, been inferred from aggregate data. A sample of the Italian American vote has been made by including the voting divisions where at least 80 percent of the registered voters were of Italian ancestry and no other ethnic group had more than 10 percent of the

remaining registrants. It has been assumed that the election returns of the divisions meeting these criteria were representative of the vote of the Italian American community. The ethnic concentration of voting divisions has been identified through a check of the Italian-sounding names of eligible voters conducted on the incomplete collection of the *Street Lists of Voters*, PCA. Census data on the nativity and ancestry of the residents of the voting divisions—obtained by checking the maps of the census tract against the maps of the voting divisions—have supplemented the name-check of the *Street Lists of Voters* for the missing years. The row votes by division have been drawn from the *Annual Reports of the Registration Commission for the City of Philadelphia* (Philadelphia: Dunlap, 1928, 1930, 1931, 1932) for the 1928 and 1932 presidential elections, for the 1930 senatorial race, and for the 1931 mayoral contest; from *The Pennsylvania State Manual* (Harrisburg: Commonwealth of Pennsylvania, 1927) for the 1926 senatorial election; and from the *Manual of the City Council of Philadelphia* (Philadelphia: Dunlap, 1935) for the 1934 senatorial race. Such row votes have been converted into the percentages that appear in the text. Unless stated otherwise, here and hereafter all the percentages of the Italian American vote refer to the above-mentioned sample, while the row votes have been obtained from the sources listed in the notes each time.

10. Pennsylvania Committee on Public Assistance and Relief, *The Relief Population of Pennsylvania: Report of a Statistical Study of Relief Recipients* (Harrisburg PA: Commonwealth of Pennsylvania, 1936), 34; Tinkcom, "Depression and War," 613; Records of the Department of Public Works, Director's office, Correspondence and Reports: 1926–1936, 1936–1939, 1950, series A–658, folder "WPA Projects: Jan. '36–Dec. '39," PCA (ratio based on a check of the Italian-sounding names of the foremen); testimony of E. Rosemberg, member of the Philadelphia County Board of Assistance, as quoted in Maiale, "The Italian Vote in Philadelphia," 170; Scranton and Licht, *Work Sights,* 237; report by Lorena Hickok to Harry Hopkins, Washington DC, 6 Aug. 1933, Lorena Hickok Papers, box 11, folder "Aug. through Oct. 1933," FDRL; John F. Bauman, "Public Housing in the Depression: Slum Reform in Philadelphia Neighborhoods in the 1930s," in *The Divided Metropolis: Social and Spatial Dimension of Philadelphia, 1800–1975,* ed. William W. Cutler III and Howard Gillette Jr. (Westport, CT: Greenwood Press, 1980), 242.

11. Letter by Angelo Caligiuri to Franklin D. Roosevelt, Philadelphia, 21 Sept. 1936, Franklin D. Roosevelt Papers, President's Alphabetical File, box 22, FDRL; Maiale, "The Italian Vote in Philadelphia," 175; John T. Salter, "Letters from Men in Action," *National Municipal Review* 26, no. 9 (Sept. 1937): 423–24.

12. William F. Ogburn and Nell Snow Talbot, "A Measurement of the Factors in the Presidential Elections of 1928," *Social Forces* 8, no. 2 (Dec. 1929): 175–83; Samuel Lubell, *The Future of American Politics* (1952; New York: Harper Colophon Books, 1965), 28–57; Ruth C. Silva, *Rum, Religion, and Votes: 1928 Re-Examined* (University Park, PA: Pennsylvania State University Press, 1962),

41–49; David Burner, *The Politics of Provincialism: The Democratic Party in Transition, 1918–1932* (New York: Alfred A. Knopf, 1967), esp. 183–84, 198–201; Lawrence Fuchs, "Election of 1928," in *History of American Presidential Elections, 1789–1984*, ed. Arthur M. Schlesinger Jr. and Fred L. Israel, 5 vols. (New York: Chelsea, 1971), 3:2593; David E. Kyvig, "Raskob, Roosevelt, and Repeal," *Historian* 37, no. 3 (May 1975): 470–72; Allan J. Lichtman, *Prejudice and the Old Politics: The Presidential Election of 1928* (Chapel Hill: University of North Carolina Press, 1979).

13. *La Libera Parola*, 1 Feb. 1919; 31 Oct. 1920; 9 Jan. 1921; 19 Dec. 1925; 25 Aug., 15 Sept. 1928; *L'Opinione*, 29 July 1927; *Evening Bulletin*, 7 Nov. 1928; *Philadelphia Daily News*, 8 Nov. 1928; *Indiana Democrat*, 31 Oct. 1928.

14. John Higham, *Strangers in the Land: Patterns of American Nativism* (New Brunswick NJ: Rutgers University Press, 1955), 313–24; Robert A. Divine, *American Immigration Policy, 1924–1952* (New Haven: Yale University Press, 1957), 145–46; *Congressional Record* (1 Feb. 1927): 2683; *La Libera Parola*, 8 Mar. 1924; *L'Opinione*, 30 Oct., 9, 11 Nov. 1927; *Evening Bulletin*, 25 Oct. 1928; *A Record of Service to Pennsylvania and the Nation* (1928), 6, election campaign pamphlet, David A. Reed Papers, box 4, folder "Speeches and pamphlets," Seedley G. Mudd Library, Princeton University, Princeton NJ.

15. *Philadelphia Record*, 8 Nov. 1928; circular letter by Eugene V. Alessandroni to OSIA members, Philadelphia, 30 Oct. 1926, Di Silvestro Papers, box 1, folder 22; *Corriere d'America*, 1 Nov. 1927; letter by W. W. Roper to George W. Pepper, Philadelphia, 30 Mar. 1926, George W. Pepper Papers, box 70, folder "100-31," University of Pennsylvania Archives, Philadelphia. For Vare anti-restriction stand, see also *Evening Bulletin*, 14 Aug. 1924; Robert H. Zieger, *Republicans and Labor, 1919–1929* (Lexington: University of Kentucky Press, 1969), 83.

16. Transcript of an interview with Paul D'Ortona by Walter M. Phillips, p. 1, Philadelphia, 17 May 1977, Walter M. Phillips Oral History Project Transcripts, box 3, TUUA.

17. Information concerning Italian American members of legislative bodies are from *Journal of the Selected Council of the City of Philadelphia*, 40 vols. (Philadelphia, 1880–1919); *Journal of the Common Council of the City of Philadelphia*, 40 vols. (Philadelphia, 1880–1919); *Smull's Legislative Hand Book and Manual of the State of Pennsylvania*, 22 vols. (Harrisburg PA: J. L. L. Kuhn, 1881–82 – 1923–24); *The Pennsylvania State Manual*, 2 vols. (Harrisburg PA: Commonwealth of Pennsylvania, 1925–26 – 1927); *Manual of the City Council of Philadelphia*, 8 vols. (Philadelphia: Dunlap Printing Company, 1920–1927).

18. Irwin F. Greenberg, "The Philadelphia Democratic Party, 1911–1934" (Ph.D. diss., Temple University, 1972), 235–40; J. David Stern, *Memoirs of a Maverick Publisher* (New York: Simon and Schuster, 1962), 200; letter by Charles Pellegrino to Franklin D. Roosevelt, Philadelphia, 5 Oct. 1932, Papers of the National Committee of the Democratic Party, box 665, folder "P (cont.)."

19. *Evening Bulletin,* 7 Nov. 1928; *The Pennsylvania Manual* (1929), 524; *La Libera Parola,* 23 Apr. 1932; *The Pennsylvania Manual* (1933), 427–28.

20. Irwin F. Greenberg, "Philadelphia Democrats Get a New Deal: The Election of 1933," *Pennsylvania Magazine of History and Biography* 97, no. 2 (Apr. 1973): 210–32; Stern, *Memoirs of a Maverick Publisher,* 205; *Public Ledger,* 14 Sept. 1933.

21. *Manual of the City Council of Philadelphia* (1934), 288–89; *L'Opinione,* 23, 26 Aug. 1933; Community Council of Philadelphia, *Neighborhood Relief in Philadelphia: A Study of Sixty Local Relief Agencies Active During the Winter of 1930–1931* (Philadelphia: Community Council of Philadelphia, 1931), 32–33; John F. Bauman, "The City, the Depression, and Relief: The Philadelphia Experience, 1929–1939" (Ph.D. diss., Rutgers University, 1969), 54–55, 217; James J. N. Henwood, "Politics and Unemployment Relief, Pennsylvania, 1931–1939" (Ph.D. diss., University of Pennsylvania, 1975), 44–46, 54–59.

22. *L'Opinione,* 28 Apr. 1934; *Philadelphia Inquirer,* 29 Apr. 1936; *Philadelphia Record,* 5 Sept. 1936; *La Libera Parola,* 12 Sept. 1936. The row votes for the 1933 elections are from the *Annual Report of the Registration Commission for the City of Philadelphia* (1933). For Anthony Di Silvestro's biographical sketch, see Biagi, *The Italians of Philadelphia,* 181–83.

23. *Philadelphia Inquirer,* 14 May 1934; Petitions for Nominations, 1934, Records of the Department of State, Commonwealth of Pennsylvania, Pennsylvania State Archives, Harrisburg PA; interview with Frank C. by the author, Philadelphia, 12 Aug. 1989; *L'Opinione,* 21, 22, 23, 24, 25, 26, 27 May, 22, 23, 24 Oct. 1934; *Manual of the City Council of Philadelphia* (1935), 319–20.

24. The row votes are from *Manual of the City Council of Philadelphia* (1937), 288.

25. "The following wire or write urging the president to make more campaign speeches," 9 Oct. 1932, Herbert Hoover Presidential Papers, box 646, folder "Italian," Herbert Hoover Presidential Library, West Branch IA.

26. *L'Opinione,* 13 Sept., 3 Oct. 1934; Chester Harris, *Tiger at the Bar: The Life Story of Charles J. Margiotti* (New York: Vantage Press, 1956), 320–29; report by Lorena Hickok to Harry Hopkins, Hickok Papers, box 11, folder "1935." The row votes are from County Board of Elections of Philadelphia, tabulation sheets of the election returns (hereafter CBEP), 1934 primary election for governor, Republican Party, PCA.

27. *La Libera Parola,* 24 Nov. 1934; *L'Opinione,* 23 Nov. 1934; 15, 17 Jan., 6, 14 Feb., 27 Mar. 1935. The ethnic background of the appointees has been identified through a name check conducted on the personnel directory published in *The Pennsylvania Manual* (1933), 1031–32; ibid. (1935–1936), 624–25; ibid. (1937), 945–46.

28. *Il Progresso Italo-Americano,* 7, 21 Sept., 5 Oct. 1937; *La Libera Parola,* 18 Dec. 1937.

29. Alfred L. Morgan, "The Significance of Pennsylvania's 1938 Gubernatorial Election," *Pennsylvania Magazine of History and Biography* 102, no. 2 (Apr. 1978): 189–98; Joseph F. Guffey, *Seventy Years on the Red-Fire Wagon: From Tilden to Truman through New Freedom and New Deal* (n.p.: privately printed, 1952), 103–9; Harris, *Tiger at the Bar*, 367–70.

30. Philip S. Klein and Ari Hoogenboom, *A History of Pennsylvania* (New York: McGraw-Hill, 1973), 412–18; Richard C. Keller, "Pennsylvania's Little New Deal," in *The New Deal: The State and Local Levels*, ed. John Braeman, Robert H. Bremner, and David Brody, 2 vols. (Columbus: Ohio State University Press, 1975), 2:45–76.

31. The row votes are from CBEP, 1938 primary elections for governor, lieutenant governor, and U.S. Senator, Democratic Party.

32. *Philadelphia Inquirer*, 28 Apr. 1938; "Italiani: Rivendicate [sic!] Charles J. Margiotti," electoral handout, Nicholas J. A. Tumolo Papers, box 7, BIES. The row votes are from *The Pennsylvania Manual* (1939).

33. *Philadelphia Inquirer*, 29 Mar. 1938; *Il Popolo Italiano*, 1 Apr., 15, 19 May 1938; 23 Apr. 1940. The row votes are from CBEP, 1938 elections for Representatives in Congress and 1940 elections for State Senators; *The Pennsylvania Manual* (1939, 1941).

34. Murray Friedman and Carolyn Beck, "An Ambivalent Alliance: Blacks and Jews in Philadelphia, 1940 to 1985," in *Philadelphia Jewish Life, 1940–1985*, ed. Friedman (Ardmore PA: Seth Press, 1986), 144–46; Charles Pete T. Banner-Haley, *To Do Good and To Do Well: Middle-Class Blacks and the Depression, Philadelphia, 1929–1941* (New York: Garland, 1993), 163–66; *L'Opinione*, 28 Feb. 1935; *La Libera Parola*, 5, 19 Oct. 1935; *Philadelphia Daily News*, 9 May 1936; letter by Koch to Italian embassy, Washington DC, 25 July 1940, MCP, box 19, folder 61. For Italy's 1938 antisemitic decrees, see Renzo De Felice, *Storia degli ebrei italiani sotto il fascismo* (1961; Turin: Einaudi, 1993), 278–84; Michele Sarfatti, *Mussolini contro gli ebrei: Cronaca dell'elaborazione delle leggi del 1938* (Turin: Zamorani, 1994).

35. William R. Scott, "Black Nationalism and the Italo-Ethiopian Conflict, 1935–1936," *Journal of Negro History* 63, no. 2 (April 1978): 129–31; Ronald H. Bayor, *Neighbors in Conflict: The Irish, Germans, Jews, and Italians of New York City, 1929–1941* (Baltimore: Johns Hopkins University Press, 1978), 80–85; John F. Stack Jr., *International Conflict in an American City: Boston's Irish, Italians, and Jews, 1935–1944* (Westport CT: Greenwood Press, 1979), 78–103; Nadia Venturini, *Neri e Italiani ad Harlem: Gli anni Trenta e la guerra d'Etiopia* (Rome: Edizioni Lavoro, 1990), esp. 159–65, 183–84, 194–95.

36. *La Libera Parola*, 31 Oct. 1936; *Manual of the City Council of Philadelphia* (1937), 286; CBEP, 1938 elections for Representatives in Congress; "Spilli e Spilloni," *La Voce Indipendente* 1, no. 9 (Nov. 1938): 3; *South Phila American Weekly*, 10 Nov. 1938. Data for the 1935 councilman election have been correlated at the ward level. The number of residents of Italian origin and parentage in the city's

wards are from U.S. Bureau of the Census, unpublished work sheets for the fifteenth Census of the United States, 1930, TUUA. The row votes at the ward level are from *Evening Bulletin*, 6 Nov. 1935.

37. Bauman, "Public Housing in the Depression," 241–42.

38. *La Libera Parola*, 2, 23 Nov. 1935.

39. Edwin Fenton, "Italians in the Labor Movement," *Pennsylvania History* 26, no. 2 (Apr. 1959): 136; Rudolph J. Vecoli, "Italian-American Workers, 1880–1920: Padrone Slaves or Primitive Rebels?," in *Perspectives in Italian Immigration and Ethnicity*, ed. Silvano M. Tomasi (New York: Center for Migration Studies, 1977), 41; *La Plebe*, 24 Aug, 9 Nov., 8 Dec. 1907; 18 Jan., 22 Feb., 30 May, 18 June 1908; *Il Proletario*, 17 Dec. 1905; Vezzosi, *Il socialismo indifferente*, 33, Carlo Tresca, "Autobiography," 91, 94–101, 105–6 (quotes 91, 95), unpublished typescript, Biblioteca di Storia e Letteratura Nordamericana, University of Florence, Florence, Italy. For Tresca, see Dorothy Gallagher, *All the Right Enemies: The Life and Murder of Carlo Tresca* (New Brunswick NJ: Rutgers University Press, 1988).

40. Vecoli, "The Italian Immigrants in the United States Labor Movement," 294; Maxwell Whiteman, "Out of the Sweatshop," in *Jewish Life in Philadelphia, 1830–1940*, ed. Murray Friedman (Philadelphia: Institute for the Study of Human Issues, 1983), 74–75; Patrick Renshaw, *Il sindacalismo rivoluzionario negli Stati Uniti* (1967; Bari: Laterza, 1970), 149–50; Lisa McGirr, "Black and White Longshoremen in the IWW: A History of the Philadelphia Marine Transport Workers Industrial Union Local 8," *Labor History* 36, no. 3 (Summer 1995): 383–84.

41. Varbero, "Workers in City and County," 20–22; Elden La Mar, *The Clothing Workers in Philadelphia: History of Their Struggles for Union and Security* (Philadelphia: Philadelphia Joint Board of the Amalgamated Clothing Workers of America, 1940), 79; Emilio Grandinetti, "Amalgamated Clothing Workers of America: Il contributo degli italiani al sindacato dell'abbigliamento maschile," *La Parola del Popolo* 50, no. 37 (Dec. 1958—Jan. 1959): 173.

42. Jarrell, "A History of Collective Bargaining at the Camden-Area Plants of the Radio Corporation of America," 43–45; Passero, "Ethnicity in the Men's Ready-Made Clothing Industry," 301–2, 313; Fred Thompson, *The I.W.W.: Its First Fifty Years, 1905–1955* (Chicago: Industrial Workers of the World, 1955), 161.

43. Passero, "Ethnicity in the Men's Ready-Made Clothing Industry," 302–3; Richard N. Juliani, "Italians and Other Americans: The Parish, the Union, and the Settlement House," in *Perspectives in Italian Immigration and Ethnicity*, ed. Silvano M. Tomasi (New York: Center for Migration Studies, 1977), 182.

44. Letter by Louis Verna to Ralph Borrelli, Philadelphia, 16 May 1936, Ralph Borrelli Papers, box 2, BIES; Elizabeth Fones-Wolf, "Industrial Unionism and Labor Movement Culture in Depression-Era Philadelphia," *Pennsylvania Magazine of History and Biography* 109, no. 1 (Jan. 1985): 22; letter by Leon Sacks

to Charles Weinstein, chairperson, Philadelphia Joint Board of the ACWA, Philadelphia, 10 Oct. 1938, Papers of the Philadelphia Joint Board of the ACWA, box 9, folder "Labor's Non-Partisan League, General Correspondence, 1938," TUUA.

45. Fones-Wolf, "Industrial Unionism," 3–26; *News Bulletin,* 16 Oct. 1939, 4; Thomas T. Spencer, " 'Labor Is with Roosevelt': The Pennsylvania Labor's Non-Partisan League and the Election of 1936," *Pennsylvania History* 46, no. 1 (Jan. 1979): 3–16; *L'Opinione,* 25 Aug. 1929; 1, 2, 3 Apr., 25 Sept. 1932; 10 Apr. 1934; *La Libera Parola,* 8 Nov. 1930; 22 Aug., 26 Sept., 31 Oct. 1936; *Il Progresso Italo-Americano,* 6 Oct. 1936.

46. Statistics for Philadelphia's voting districts list neither ethnic information nor demographic data. However, the extent of the city's Census tracts was small enough to assume that the variations in the percentage of the population of voting age (twenty-one years old and over) were the same in both a Census tract and each of its voting districts. The Italian-American electoral participation has been calculated through the sample that has already been discussed in note 9 of this chapter. The trend of the Italian American turnout has been derived from the absolute numbers of votes cast, rather than from the proportion of the eligible electorate, because birth and death rates did not change appreciably within the sample in the years to which the analysis refers. Actually, the total growth of the adult population of the districts included in the sample during the decade between the 1930 Census and the 1940 Census was as little as 9.5 percent. Such a percentage cannot compare with the increase of 70.1 percent in the total number of votes cast in the districts of the sample in these years. Therefore, the rise in the participating electorate clearly outweighed the augmentation of the adult population as the paramount determinant of the growth in the number of votes cast. The row votes are from the *Annual Reports of the Registration Commission for the City of Philadelphia* (1926–1936). Brancato's words are cited in Frances L. Reinhold, "Anna Brancato: State Representative," in *The American Politician,* ed. John T. Salter (Chapel Hill: University of North Carolina Press, 1938), 348.

47. The row votes are from the *Annual Reports of the Registration Commission for the City of Philadelphia* (1936, 1940).

48. Daria Frezza Bicocchi, "Propaganda fascista e comunità italiane in USA: La Casa Italiana della Columbia University," *Studi Storici* 11, no. 4 (Oct. 1970): 672–74; Nadia Venturini, "Le comunità italiane negli Stati Uniti tra storia sociale e storia politica," *Rivista di storia contemporanea* 13, no. 2 (Apr. 1984): 204–5; Paolo Nello, *Dino Grandi: La formazione di un leader fascista* (Bologna: Il Mulino, 1987), 264; Dino Grandi, "Ai Figli d'Italia: Discorso agli italo-americani in Filadelfia," in his *La politica estera dell'Italia dal 1929 al 1932,* ed. Paolo Nello, 2 vols. (Rome: Bonacci, 1985), 2:569–76; Giovanni Di Silvestro, "Note sulla cittadinanza americana," SPD-DSG; Eastern District of Pennsylvania, Naturalization Records, petition 48817 (Bocchini, Filippo), series M-1522, roll 214, National Archives, Mid Atlantic Region Branch, Philadelphia.

49. Cohen, *Making a New Deal*, 99–158; Pietro Russo, "La stampa periodica italo-americana," in Rudolph J. Vecoli et al., *Gli italiani negli Stati Uniti: L'emigrazione e l'opera degli italiani negli Stati Uniti d'America* (Florence: Istituto di Studi Americani, 1972), 507; Michael E. Parrish, *Anxious Decades: America in Prosperity and Depression, 1920–1941* (New York: Norton, 1992), 74–78; Susan Smulyan, *Selling the Radio: The Commercialization of American Broadcasting* (Washington DC: Smithsonian Institution Press, 1994), 10, 30–31, 63–64, 120, 129.

50. *Directory of Newspapers and Periodicals* (Philadelphia, N. W. Ayer & Son, 1930), 874, 875.

51. Interview with Remo Zuecca, in WPA-ES, roll 3; *Il Popolo Italiano*, 8 June 1935. *L'Opinione-Il Progresso Italo-Americano* reported a circulation of 72,080 copies for the weekday edition and 67,731 for the Sunday edition but these figures are misleading because they refer to the number of copies sold by *Il Progresso Italo-Americano* in Philadelphia. See *Directory of Newspapers and Periodicals* (Philadelphia: N. W. Ayer & Son, 1936), 637.

52. Order Sons of Italy in America, *By-Laws*, 165; memorandum about a telephone call by Antonio Ferrari from Philadelphia, 2 Oct. 1924, Calvin Coolidge Papers, microfilm edition, series 1, file 178A, roll 90, Library of Congress, Washington DC; letter by Edward Corsi to Giovanni Di Silvestro, New York, 19 Apr. 1932, Di Silvestro Papers, box 11, folder 22; certificate of election, ibid., box 12, folder 13; letter by James V. Donnaruma to Giovanni Di Silvestro, Boston, 10 Feb. 1936, ibid., box 10, folder 11; Biagi, *The Italians of Philadelphia*, 154–55; *Public Ledger*, 4, 5, Oct. 1927; index card "Di Silvestro, Anthony," Papers of the Pennsylvania Grand Lodge of the Order Sons of Italy in America, box 70; Palazzi, "Spires of Influence," 24–26; interview with Frank C. by the author, Philadelphia, 12 Aug. 1989; *Ordine Nuovo*, 24 May 1936. For the Columbia Republican League, see Anna Maria Martellone, "Italian Immigrants, Party Machines, Ethnic Brokers in City Politics, from the 1880s to the 1930s," in *The European Emigrant Experience in the U.S.A.*, ed. Walter Hölbling and Reinhold Wagnleitner (Tübingen: Gunter Narr Verlag, 1992), 178–80.

53. Joseph William Carnevale, *Americans of Italian Descent in Philadelphia and Vicinity* (Philadelphia: Ferguson, 1954), 385.

54. Theodore N. Beckman and Herman C. Nolen, *The Chain Store Problem: A Critical Analysis* (New York: McGraw-Hill, 1938), 39; *Polk's (Boyd's) Philadelphia (Pennsylvania) City Directories* (Philadelphia: R. L. Polk, 1935–1936), 2037, 2039.

55. Felicita Taormina and Irina Smith, *To the Market, To the Market: Philadelphia's Italian Market* (Philadelphia: privately printed, 1979), 4; Gertrude, "Italian Immigration into Philadelphia: II," 191.

56. Dan Fricker, "Radio Broadcasts Italian Style," unidentified and undated newspaper clipping, Borrelli Papers, box 1; letter by Rigg Banco to Ralph Borrelli, Philadelphia, 30 Oct. 1935, ibid., box 2.

57. Fricker, "Radio Broadcasts Italian Style."

58. Ralph Borrelli, untitled memoirs, 9, Borrelli Papers, box 1; Cesare Mattioli, untitled manuscript, 1933, 3–7, ibid.; *La Libera Parola*, 9 Jan. 1936.

59. "Fascist Radio Propaganda," report dated 20 June 1940, DS-RG59, 811.00F/280A. For Conte Luna Products Inc., see "Arena Factory Addition Will Raise Output," *Norristown Times Herald* (13 Sept. 1937): 29.

60. Fricker, "Radio Broadcasts Italian Style"; letter by Joseph Velinote to WRAX, Philadelphia, 19 Dec. 1935, Borrelli Papers, box 2; letter by Donato Iverso and Amato Prudente to Ralph Borrelli, Philadelphia, 2 Jan. 1936, ibid.

61. Renzo De Felice, "Alcuni temi per la storia dell'emigrazione italiana," *Affari Sociali Internazionali* 1, no. 3 (Sept. 1973): 7; Cannistraro, "Mussolini, Sacco-Vanzetti, and the Anarchists," 31–62; Claudia Damiani, *Mussolini e gli Stati Uniti, 1922–1935* (Bologna: Cappelli, 1980), 51–73, 277–78; Philip V. Cannistraro and Gianfausto Rosoli, "Fascist Emigration Policy in the 1920s: An Interpretative Framework," *International Migration Review* 13, no. 4 (Winter 1979): 683–89; Monte S. Finkelstein, "The Johnson Act, Mussolini and Fascist Emigration Policy: 1921–1930," *Journal of American Ethnic History* 8, no. 1 (Fall 1988): 38–55.

62. The initial response of Philadelphia's Italian Americans to Fascism and its nationalistic appeal can easily be perceived in the articles that Michele Renzulli published in the Italian-language newspaper *La Voce della Colonia* in the early 1920s and later reprinted in his *L'Italia e il Fascismo negli Stati Uniti d'America*.

63. "Relazione," 29 July 1923, MCP, Gabinetto, Reports 7/A–71/A.

64. Agostino De Biasi, *La battaglia dell'Italia negli Stati Uniti: Articoli e note polemiche* (New York: Il Carroccio, 1927); Philip V. Cannistraro, "Per una storia dei Fasci negli Stati Uniti (1921–1929)," *Storia Contemporanea* 25, no. 6 (Dec. 1995): 1063, 1066–69.

65. Gaetano Salvemini, *Italian Fascist Activities in the United States*, ed. Philip V. Cannistraro (New York: Center for Migration Studies, 1977), 11–16; Domenico Saudino, "Il Fascismo alla conquista dell'Ordine Figli d'Italia," *La Parola del Popolo* 50, no. 37 (Dec. 1958–Jan. 1959): 247–56; Nadia Venturini, "Prominenti at War: The Order Sons of Italy in America," *Rivista di Studi Anglo-Americani* 3, no. 4–5 (1984–1985): 448–49; Domenico Fabiano, "La Lega Italiana per la Tutela degli Interessi Nazionali e le origini dei Fasci italiani all'estero (1920–1923)," *Storia Contemporanea* 16, no. 2 (Apr. 1985): 212; Cannistraro, "Per una storia dei Fasci negli Stati Uniti," 1069–71, 1130–31; Louis C. Anthes, " 'The Search for the Order': The Order Sons of Italy in America and the Politics of Ethnicity," in *Industry, Technology, Labor*, 26–27; *La Libera Parola*, 28 Oct. 1922; Giuseppe Bastianini, *Gli italiani all'estero* (Milan: Mondadori, 1939), 51–52; Giovanni Di Silvestro, "Gli italiani e le cose americane," *L'Opinione*, undated clipping, Di Silvestro Papers, box 12, folder 5.

66. Report by the Italian consul to Gelasio Caetani, Philadelphia, 18 Mar. 1923, MCP, box 163, folder 18; *Il Martello*, 23 Mar., 16 June 1923; tele-

gram by Sillitti to Ministry of Foreign Affairs, Philadelphia, 25 Nov. 1923, Papers of the Ministry of Foreign Affairs, Affari Politici, 1919–1930, Stati Uniti, box 1598, Archivio Storico del Ministero degli Affari Esteri, Rome, Italy; *La Libera Parola,* 1 Dec. 1923; report by Molossi to Benito Mussolini, Rome, 6 June 1923, MCP, Gabinetto, Reports 7/A–71/A; Ministero dell'Interno, Direzione Generale di Pubblica Sicurezza, Divisione Affari Generali e Riservati, series G1, box 225, folder 610, ACS; circular letter by the Philadelphia Branch of the Anti-Fascist Alliance of North America, Philadelphia, 22 May 1927, Di Silvestro Papers, box 11, folder 17; *Philadelphia Inquirer,* 4 Sept. 1935; unidentified and undated newspaper clipping, Mazzone Papers; *Philadelphia Daily News,* 11 May 1936: For the Anti-Fascist Alliance of North America, see Pellegino Nazzaro, "Il manifesto dell'Alleanza Anti-Fascista del Nord America," *Affari Sociali Internazionali* 2, no. 1–2 (June 1974): 171–85; Adriana Dadà, "Contributo metodologico per una storia dell'emigrazione e dell'antifascismo italiani negli Stati Uniti," *Annali dell'Istituto di Storia dell'Università di Firenze* 1 (1979): 202–4.

67. Letter by Giovanni Di Silvestro to Osvaldo Sebastiani, Rome, 16 Jan. 1939, SPD-DSG; *Observer,* 25 Sept. 1938; Ellen Ginzburg Migliorino, "Jewish Emigration from Trieste to the United States after 1938, with Special Reference to New York, Philadelphia, and Wilmington," *Studi Emigrazione* 28, no. 103 (Sept. 1991): 369–77.

68. Annamaria Tasca, "Italians," in *The Immigrant Labor Press in North America, 1840s–1970s: An Annotated Bibliography,* ed. Dirk Hoerder, 3 vols. (Westport CT: Greenwood Press, 1987), 3:72, 127.

69. Circular letter by the Philadelphia branch of the Anti-Fascist Alliance of North America, Philadelphia, 22 May 1927, Di Silvestro Papers, box 11, folder 17.

70. Salvemini, *Italian Fascist Activities,* 11–13, 16, 99; letter by Di Vincenzo, acting Italian consul, to Gelasio Caetani, Italian ambassador, Philadelphia, 23 Mar. 1923, MCP, Gabinetto, Reports 7/A–71/A; "Relazione," 29 July 1923, ibid.; letter by Luigi Borgo to Dino Grandi, Philadelphia, 4 Aug. 1925, ibid.; *Observer,* 23 Aug., 31 Oct. 1938; *Philadelphia Inquirer,* 21 Nov. 1931; *La Libera Parola,* 5 Dec. 1931; Dino Grandi, *Il mio paese: Ricordi autobiografici,* ed. Renzo De Felice (Bologna: Il Mulino, 1985), 320.

71. *Il Progresso Italo-Americano,* 20 Sept. 1935; *Il Popolo Italiano,* 13 Oct., 1, 11, 12, 29 Nov. 1935; 31 Jan. 1936; *La Libera Parola,* 19 Oct., 2, 9, 23 Nov., 7, 28 Dec. 1935; 14 Mar., 11, 25 Apr., 15 Aug. 1936; letter by Domenico De Gregoris to Benito Mussolini, Philadelphia, 20 Jan. 1936, MCP, box 451, folder "Invio di pellicole di propaganda negli Stati Uniti;" FBI report dated 28 June 1941, DS-RG59, 865.20211/Federation of Italian World War Veterans/6; telegram by Zeffirino Aversa, President, Comitato Amici dell'Italia, to Franklin D. Roosevelt, Philadelphia, 18 Oct. 1935, Roosevelt Papers, Official File, 547a. For the real

purpose of Italian American contributions to the Italian Red Cross, see Fiorello B. Ventresco, "Italian Americans and the Ethiopian Crisis," *Italian Americana* 6, no. 1 (Fall–Winter 1980): 16–17. For the President's warning against travel on belligerent vessels, see *The Public Papers and Addresses of Franklin D. Roosevelt*, ed. Samuel I. Rosenman, 13 vols. (New York: Macmillan, 1938), 4:416–17.

72. *Il Popolo Italiano*, 10, 16, 19, 23, 30 Jan. 1936; *La Libera Parola*, 18, 25 Jan., 8, 22 Feb. 1936; U.S. House of Representatives, 74th Cong., 2d Sess., *Hearings before the Committee on Foreign Affairs on H. J. Res. 422 to Maintain the Neutrality of the United States in the Event of War or Threat of War between or among Foreign Nations* (Washington DC: U.S. Government Printing Office, 1936), 208–14; Giovanni Di Silvestro, "The Neutrality Measure Now Pending in Congress Have the Mark of Hostility Against a Friendly Nation," *Philadelphia Inquirer* (26 Jan. 1936), Di Silvestro Papers, box 3, folder 1. For the Italian American campaign against the Pittman-McReynolds Bill in the United States, see Gian Giacomo Migone, *Gli Stati Uniti e il Fascismo: Alle origini dell'egemonia americana in Italia* (Milan: Feltrinelli, 1980), 343–57; Leo V. Kanawada Jr., *Franklin D. Roosevelt Diplomacy and American Catholics, Italians, and Jews* (Ann Arbor MI: UMI Research Press, 1982), 82–89. For the case of Pennsylvania, see also Jenkins, *Hoods and Shirts*, 104–5, 107.

73. *Il Popolo Italiano*, 5, 6 May 1936; *La Libera Parola*, 9, 16, 30 May 1936; "Goodwill Pilgrimage to Italy," brochure, Papers of the Pennsylvania Grand Lodge of the OSIA, box 5, folder 12; *Il Progresso Italo-Americano*, 3 Nov. 1936; 21 Nov. 1937.

74. *Il Martello*, 10 Feb. 1934; memorandum by Pierrepont Moffat, 21 Sept. 1933, DS-RG59, 811.00F/161; *La Libera Parola*, 3 Nov. 1934; James P. Shenton, "Fascism and Father Coughlin," *Wisconsin Magazine of History* 44, no. 1 (Autumn 1960): 6–11; Charles J. Tull, *Father Coughlin and the New Deal* (Syracuse: Syracuse University Press, 1965), 112; David H. Bennet, *Demagogues in the Depression: American Radicals and the Union Party, 1932–1936* (New Brunswick NJ: Rutgers University Press, 1969), 75, 230–31; Philip V. Cannistraro and Theodore P. Kovaleff, "Father Coughlin and Mussolini: Impossible Allies," *Journal of Church and State* 13, no. 3 (Autumn 1971): 427–43; Alan Brinkley, *Voices of Protest: Huey Long, Father Coughlin, and the Great Depression* (New York: Alfred A. Knopf, 1982), 134–37, 152; Eric Asard, "Father Coughlin and Populist Insurgency Against the New Deal," *Storia Nordamericana* 6, no. 1–2 (1989): 100–2. The row votes are from *The Pennsylvania Manual* (1935), 447; CBEP, 1936 election for president.

75. Biagi, *The Italians of Philadelphia*, 124–26; *Il Popolc Italiano*, 17 Oct. 1936; Giovanni Di Silvestro, "The Idea of an American 'Fascismo' " and "Gli italiani e le cose americane," *L'Opinione*, undated clippings, Di Silvestro Papers, box 12, folder 5; *Testimonial Dinner Tendered to His Excellency Fulvio Suvich* (1938), unpaginated brochure, Borrelli Papers, box 1.

76. *Il Popolo Italiano,* 28, 31 Jan. 1936; 21 Feb. 1936; *La Libera Parola,* 7 Dec. 1935; *Il Progresso Italo-Americano,* 20 Feb. 1936.

77. Vincent M. Lombardi, "Italian-American Workers and the Response to Fascism," in *Pane e Lavoro: The Italian-American Working Class,* ed. George E. Pozzetta (Toronto: Multicultural Society of Ontario, 1980), 141–57; Madeline Jane Goodman, "The Evolution of Ethnicity: Fascism and Anti-Fascism in the Italian-American Community" (Ph.D. diss., Carnegie Mellon University, 1993); Gaetano Salvemini, *Memorie di un fuoruscito,* ed. Gaetano Arfè (Milan: Feltrinelli, 1960), 110; Massimo Salvadori, *Resistenza ed azione (Ricordi di un liberale)* (Bari: Laterza, 1951), 163. The third quotation is from Caroline F. Ware, "Cultural Groups in the United States," in *The Cultural Approach to History,* ed. Ware (New York: Columbia University Press, 1940), 63. In general, see also Louis Gerson, *The Hyphenate in Recent American Politics and Diplomacy* (Lawrence: University of Kansas Press, 1964), 11, 122; Philip V. Cannistraro, "Fascism and Italian Americans," in *Perspectives in Italian Immigration and Ethnicity,* ed. Silvano M. Tomasi (New York: Center for Migration Studies, 1977), 51–66; Philip A. Bean, "Fascism and Italian-American Identity: A Case Study: Utica New York," *Journal of Ethnic Studies* 17, no. 1 (Summer 1989): 101–19; Stanislao G. Pugliese, "The Culture of Nostalgia: Fascism in the Memory of Italian Americans," *Italian American Review* 5, no. 2 (Autumn–Winter 1996–97): 21–22.

78. *L'Opinione,* 21 Nov. 1931; Mattioli, untitled manuscript, 4; Borrelli, untitled memoirs, 9–10; appunto personale per il dott. Crolla, n.d. [but 1935], MCP, box 447, folder "Dante Alighieri negli Stati Uniti;" letter by Frank Palumbo to Ralph Borrelli, Philadelphia, 22 Apr. 1936, Borrelli Papers, box 2; *Il Popolo Italiano,* 28 Oct. 1933; 10 Jan., 24 Apr. 1936.

79. *Il Popolo Italiano,* 23 Apr. 1936. For the interest of Mussolini's regime in movies as vehicles for the diffusion of Fascist propaganda in both Italy and the United States, see Gian Piero Brunetta, "Il sogno a stelle e strisce di Mussolini," in *L'estetica della politica,* ed. Maurizio Vaudagna (Rome and Bari: Laterza, 1989), 173–86. For the reception of EIAR's broadcasts in Philadelphia, see *La Libera Parola,* 14 Dec. 1935; *Il Popolo Italiano,* 1 Mar. 1939. Extensive coverage of the Italian "pilgrimages" of the OSIA can be found in SPD-DSG and Di Silvestro Papers, box 4, folders 1–8. See also Noyes, "From the *Paese* to the *Patria,*" 127–52.

80. Joan Savereno, " 'Domani Ci [sic] Zappa': Italian Immigration and Ethnicity in Pennsylvania," *Pennsylvania Folklife* 45, no. 1 (Autumn 1995): 20; telegrams to Franklin D. Roosevelt by Generoso Pope, New York, 28 Apr. 1934 and by Domenico Dalfonso, Venerable, OSIA lodge Gugliermo Marconi, Philadelphia, 10 May 1934, Roosevelt Papers, Official File 781, folder "Columbus Day, 1933–34;" *Evening Bulletin,* 12 Oct. 1920; Joseph Salituro, "Italian American and Nationalism: A Case of Mixed Loyalties," in *To See the Past More Clearly: The Enrichment of the Italian Heritage, 1890–1990,* ed. Harral E. Landry (Austin TX: Nortex Press, 1994), 264; *La Libera Parola,* 5 Oct. 1935. For Bartilucci's appointment, see *Philadelphia Inquirer,* 19 May 1920.

81. Letter by Domenico De Gregoris to Dino Alfieri, Philadelphia, 6 Aug. 1937, MCP, box 449, folder "Centro Educativo 'A. Mussolini' di Filadelfia"; letter by the Italian consul to Ministero della Cultura Popolare, Philadelphia, 27 Sept. 1937, ibid.; undated circular letter by the Biblioteca Circolante del Littorio, DS-RG59, 811.00F/58.

82. John F. McClymer, "The Americanization Movement and the Education of the Foreign-Born Adult, 1914–1925," in *American Education and the European Immigrant, 1840–1940,* ed. Bernard J. Weiss (Urbana: University of Illinois Press, 1982), 96–116; Savereno, " 'Domani Ci Zappa,' " 11–12; Patrizia Salvetti, "La comunità italiana di S. Francisco tra italianità e americanizzazione negli anni '30 e '40," *Studi Emigrazione* 19, no. 65 (Mar. 1982): 24–25; memorandum by Joseph C. Green, 7 Feb. 1935, DS-RG59, 811.00F/190; *Foreign Relations of the United States: Diplomatic Papers, 1935,* 4 vols. (Washington DC: U.S. Government Printing Office, 1952), 2:544–45; Richard A. Varbero, "Philadelphia's South Italians in the 1920s," in *The Peoples of Philadelphia,* 255–64; Ellen Ginzburg Migliorino, "Immigrati italiani nelle scuole di Filadelfia (Pennsylvania)," in *Il movimento migratorio italiano dall'unità nazionale ai giorni nostri,* ed. Franca Assante, 2 vols. (Geneva: Droz, 1978), 2:165–80. For Italian American preference for public schools in general, see Vecoli, "Prelates and Peasants," 249–51.

83. Memorandum for Joseph C. Green, 31 Jan. 1935, DS-RG59, 811.00F/195; memorandum by Renzo Sereno for David Karr, 9 Sept. 1942, Philleo Nash Papers, box 23, folder "Italian-American memoranda," HSTL; Leonard Covello and Anita E. Giacobbe, *First Book in Italian* (New York: Macmillan, 1938), 400 (to which the quote refers); Peter Sammartino and Tommaso Russo, *Il primo libro* (New York: Harper, 1936), 159.

84. Peter R. D'Agostino, "The Triad of Roman Authority: Fascism, the Vatican, and Italian Religious Clergy in the Italian Emigrant Church," *Journal of American Ethnic History* 17, no. 3 (Spring 1998): 8.

85. Daniel A. Binchy, *Church and State in Fascist Italy* (London: Oxford University Press, 1970).

86. Luciano J. Iorizzo and Salvatore Mondello, *The Italian Americans* (1971; Boston: Twayne, 1980), 252; Humbert S. Nelli, "Italians," in *Harvard Encyclopedia of American Ethnic Groups,* ed. Stephan Thernstrom (Cambridge MA: Belknap Press of Harvard University Press, 1980), 553–54; Philip V. Cannistraro, "Fascism and Italian Americans in Detroit, 1933–1935," *International Migration Review* 9, no. 1 (Spring 1975): 35–37; Franzina, *Gli Italiani al Nuovo Mondo,* 209; Peter R. D'Agostino, "The Scalabrini Fathers, the Italian Emigrant Church, and Ethnic Nationalism in America," *Religion and American Culture* 7, no. 1 (Winter 1997): 141–45; D'Agostino, "The Triad of Roman Authority," 3–37; Nelli, *Italians in Chicago,* 239, 241; Salvetti, "La comunità italiana di S. Francisco," 21; Mormino, *Immigrants on the Hill,* 217. For the pro-Fascist propaganda of the Catholic Church among Italian emigrants, see in general Gianfausto Rosoli, "Santa Sede e propaganda fascista all'estero tra i figli degli emigranti italiani," *Storia Contemporanea* 17, no. 4 (Apr. 1986): 293–318.

87. *Il Popolo Italiano*, 19 Jan., 10, 21, 28 Feb., 2 Nov. 1936; *La Libera Parola*, 13 May 1939; Varbero, "Urbanization and Acculturation," 330 (to which the quotation refers); Jenkins, *Hoods and Shirts*, 99–100.

Chapter 5. The Impact of World War II and Its Aftermath

1. *The Public Papers and Addresses of Franklin D. Roosevelt* (1941), 9:263; Alexander De Conde, *Half Bitter, Half Sweet: An Excursion into Italian-American History* (New York: Charles Scribner's Sons, 1971), 240–41; Jensen, "The Cities Reelect Roosevelt," 192; Robert A. Dahl, *Who Governs? Democracy and Power in an American City* (New Haven: Yale University Press, 1961), 49, 51; Frederick M. Wirt, *Power in the City: Decision Making in San Francisco* (Berkeley: University of California Press, 1974), 234–35; Stack, *International Conflict*, 114–16; John W. Jeffries, *Testing the Roosevelt Coalition: Connecticut Society and Politics in the Era of World War II* (Knoxville: University of Tennessee Press, 1979), 63–64, 81–83, 88–89, 201; Bayor, *Neighbors in Conflict*, 147–48; *F.D.R.: His Personal Letters, 1928–1945*, ed. Elliott Roosevelt, 3 vols. (New York: Duell, Sloane and Pearce, 1950), 2:1072.

2. *Philadelphia Inquirer*, 11 June 1940; *Philadelphia Record*, 11 June 1940; *Il Popolo Italiano*, 11 June, 20 Oct. 1940; *Observer*, 24 June 1940. The row votes are from *The Pennsylvania Manual* (1937, 1941).

3. *Il Popolo Italiano*, 15, 20, 26 June 1940; 8, 29, 30, 31 Jan., 1, 2, 4, 7, 8, 10, 15, 20, 23, 24 Feb., 2, 4 Mar. 1941; "Funds for Fascism," Italian News Service Press Release, 11 Mar. 1941, Roosevelt Papers, Official File 233a, folder "Miscellaneous 1941"; letter by Adolf A. Berle to Luigi Antonini, Washington DC, 21 Feb. 1941, Adolf A. Berle Papers, box 28, folder "Antonini, Luigi," FDRL; FBI report by J. H. Lee, 28 June 1941, DS-RG59, 865.20211/Federation of Italian World War Veterans/6, microfilm series LM 142, reel 39.

4. *Observer*, 29 July, 5 Aug. 1940; Mr. Bee, "Buzzes," *South Philadelphia Times*, 21 Feb. 1941, newspaper clipping, James Westbrook Papers, box 33, folder "Fascism, Italian Americans, 1941," Hoover Library (for Baldi's identification with "Mr. Bee," see letter by Umberto Gualtieri to James Westbrook, Brooklyn NY, 24 Mar. 1941, ibid.); letter by Giovanni Di Silvestro to Peppino Di Sarra, Philadelphia, 16 June 1941, Di Silvestro Papers, box 9, folder 15.

5. *Ordine Nuovo*, 11 May 1940; 29 Nov. 1941.

6. Paul Lyons, *Philadelphia Communists, 1936–1956* (Philadelphia: Temple University Press, 1982), 84–85; *Il Popolo Italiano*, 6, 12 July 1940.

7. Philip Gleason, "Americans All: World War II and the Shaping of American Identity," *Review of Politics* 43, no. 4 (Oct. 1981): 483–518; John Morton Blum, *V Was for Victory: Politics and American Culture during World War II* (New York: Harcourt Brace Jovanovich, 1976), 154 (to which Ascoli's quote refers);

John P. Diggins, *Mussolini and Fascism: The View from America* (Princeton: Princeton University Press, 1972), 352; Lawrence Di Stasi, "How World War II Iced Italian American Culture," in *Multi America: Essays on Cultural Wars and Cultural Peace,* ed. Ishmael Reed (New York: Viking, 1997), 169–78.

8. Memorandum for the president, 4 Sept. 1942, Roosevelt Papers, Official File 233a, folder "Miscellaneous 1942."

9. U.S. Bureau of the Census, *16th Census of the United States: Population and Housing, Statistics for Census Tracts, Philadelphia* (Washington DC: U.S. Government Printing Office, 1942); Sylvester K. Stevens, *Pennsylvania: The Heritage of a Commonwealth,* 2 vols. (West Palm Beach FL: American Historical Company, 1968), 2:885–86; Klein and Hoogenboom, *A History of Pennsylvania,* 425–26; Tinkcom, "Depression and War," 635–37, 641–42; minutes of the executive board meeting of local 122, 19 Jan. 1942, Papers of the Philadelphia Joint Board of the ACWA, box 63, folder "Membership Meeting Minutes, 1940–1959"; Licht, *Getting Work,* 11.

10. "The Foreign Language Press," *Fortune* 22, no. 5 (Nov. 1940): 102, 108; "Lay Off the Italians," *Collier's* (3 Aug. 1940): 54; Richard W. Steele, " 'No Racials': Discrimination Against Ethnics in American Defense Industry, 1940–42," *Labor History* 32, no. 2 (Winter 1991): 66–90; report by Harold B. Hoskins to Adolf A. Berle, Washington DC, 14 Apr. 1941, DS-RG59, 811.00/841. No issue of *L'Osservatore* is nowadays available to check the accusations of *Fortune* magazine.

11. *Il Progresso Italo-Americano,* 26 June 1941; Borrelli, untitled memoirs, 12–13; Fricker, "Radio Broadcasts Italian Style"; undated report on Ralph Borrelli by the Federal Bureau of Investigation, DS-RG59, 865.20211/Borrelli, microfilm series LM 142, reel 38; letter by Emory S. Land to Franklin D. Roosevelt, Washington DC, 18 Feb. 1942, Roosevelt Papers, Official File 233a, folder "Miscellaneous 1942"; telegram by Browning to Philleo Nash, n.d. [but 1944], Philleo Nash Papers, box 28, folder "Race Tension, Pennsylvania," Nash Papers.

12. "Act No. 304," in *Laws of the General Assembly of the Commonwealth of Pennsylvania Passed at the Session of 1939 in the One Hundred and Sixty-Third Year of Independence* (Harrisburg PA: Commonwealth of Pennsylvania, 1939), 652–53; *Journal of the Senate of the Commonwealth of Pennsylvania,* 3 vols. (Harrisburg PA: Commonwealth of Pennsylvania, 1939), 3:741–44, 3532–33; *Journal of the House of Representatives of the Commonwealth of Pennsylvania,* 3 vols. (Harrisburg PA: Commonwealth of Pennsylvania, 1939), 3:3415–18; ibid. (1942), 349–50.

13. Press release of the Comitato Italiano per la Difesa degli Immigrati, July 1939, Leonrad Covello Papers, box 87, folder 5, BIES; letter by Paul D'Ortona to Franklin D. Roosevelt, Philadelphia, 9 Sept. 1943, Roosevelt Papers, Official File 233, folder "Italy, Government of: 1937–1943."

14. Richard Weiss, "Ethnicity and Reform: Minorities and the Ambience of the Depression Years," *Journal of American History* 66, no. 3 (Dec. 1979): 566–

85; memorandum for the Solicitor General by Lawrence M. C. Smith, 12 May 1941, Francis Biddle Papers, box 1, folder "Aliens and Immigration," FDRL.

15. *Il Popolo Italiano*, 9, 12 Dec. 1941; *La Libera Parola*, 12 Dec. 1941; *Ordine Nuovo*, 13 Dec. 1941; telegrams by Eugene V. Alesandroni to J. Edgar Hoover, Philadelphia, 12 Dec. 1941, DS-RG59, 865.20211/173, microfilm series 142, reel 37 and to Franklin D. Roosevelt, Philadelphia, 15 Dec. 1941, Roosevelt Papers, Official File, 233a, folder "Miscellaneous 1941"; *Il Popolo Italiano*, 9 March 1943. Manerba's statement was also brought to the attention of the Office of War Information (see Marjorie Ferguson et al., "Highlights in the Italian-Language Press," 23 Mar. 1943, Nash Papers, box 16, folder "Italian-Language Press").

16. Report by Augusto Rosso to the Ministry for Press and Propaganda, MCP, box 449, folder "Saturday Evening Post di Filadelfia"; George E. Pozzetta and Gary R. Mormino, "The Politics of Christopher Columbus and World War II," *Altreitalie* 10, no. 17 (Jan.–June 1998): 10, 14.

17. Memorandum for the president by Attorney General Francis Biddle, 7 Oct. 1942, Biddle Papers, box 1, folder "Aliens and Immigration"; Stephen Fox, *The Unknown Internment: An Oral History of the Relocation of Italian Americans during World War II* (Boston: Twayne, 1990); Rose D. Scherini, "Executive Order 9066 and Italian Americans: The San Francisco Story," *California History* 70, no. 4 (Winter 1991–92): 367–77; Carol Bulger Van Valkenburg, *An Alien Place: The Fort Missoula, Montana, Detention Camp, 1941–1944* (Missoula MT: Pictorial Histories, 1995); Roger Daniels, "L'internamento di 'Alien Enemies' negli Stati Uniti durante la seconda guerra mondiale," *Acoma* 4, no. 11 (Summer–Autumn 1997): 42, 46; Dan A. D'Amelio, "A Season of Panic: The Internments of World War II," *Italian Americana* 17, no. 2 (Summer 1999): 147–62; *South Philadelphian*, 28 June 1940; *Il Popolo Italiano*, 12 Oct. 1940; Marjorie Ferguson et al., "Survey of the Italian-Language Press," 14 Dec. 1942, Nash Papers, box 16, folder "Italian-Language Press."

18. *Ordine Nuovo*, 8 Mar., 31 Aug. 1941.

19. *Il Progresso Italo-Americano*, 28, 31 Dec. 1941; *Il Popolo Italiano*, 16 Apr., 16, 27, 30 Sept., 11 Oct. 1942; *Ordine Nuovo*, 3, 17, 24, Jan. 1942; 11 Sept. 1943; 15 July, 12, 15, 17 Aug. 1944; *La Libera Parola*, 25 July 1942; *Philadelphia Inquirer*, 12 Oct. 1942; letter by Vincent F. Callahan, director of the U.S. Treasury Department Radio and Press War Savings Staff, to Ralph Borrelli, Washington, DC, 25 June 1942, Borrelli Papers, box 1; *Observer*, 9 Feb. 1942; Papers of the Philadelphia Joint Board of the ACWA, box 101, folder "Clippings: Italians, 1942."

20. *Il Progresso Italo-Americano*, 25 Oct. 1942. The row votes are from *The Pennsylvania Manual* (1943).

21. *The Public Papers and Addresses of Franklin D. Roosevelt* (1950), 11:80; Stephen Brian Grove, "The Decline of the Republican Machine in Philadelphia, 1936–52" (Ph.D. diss., University of Pennsylvania, 1976), 332–33; address of U.S. Senator Joseph F. Guffey of Pennsylvania, Academy of Music, Philadelphia, 11 Oct. 1942, Joseph F. Guffey Papers, box "Speeches and Press Releases,

III," folder "1942," Washington and Jefferson College, Washington PA. For the 1942 election campaign strategy of the Democratic party, see also Robert E. Ficken, "Political Leadership in Wartime: Franklin D. Roosevelt and the Elections of 1942," *Mid-America* 57, no. 1 (Jan. 1975): 20–21.

22. *Il Popolo Italiano,* 28 Jan. 1943.

23. The row votes are from *The Pennsylvania Manual* (1945).

24. Report by Ascanio Colonna to the Ministry for Foreign Affairs, Washington DC, 5 July 1940, as published in Philip V. Cannistraro, "Gli Italo-Americani di fronte all'ingresso dell'Italia nella Seconda Guerra Mondiale," *Storia Contemporanea* 7, no. 4 (Dec. 1976): 861; *Il Popolo Italiano,* 26, 27 July 1943; abstract of a telephone call by Damiano Sassi, National Commander, Italian American World War Veterans of the United States, to Franklin D. Roosevelt, Philadelphia, 26 July 1943, Roosevelt Papers, President's Alphabetical File, box 216; *Philadelphia Record,* 9 Sept. 1943.

25. August Meier and Elliott Rudwick, *Black Detroit and the Rise of UAM* (New York: Oxford University Press, 1979), 162–74; George Lipsitz, *Rainbow at Midnight: Labor and Culture in the 1940s* (Urbana: University of Illinois Press, 1994), 69–83; Robert H. Zieger, *The CIO, 1935–1955* (Chapel Hill: University of North Carolina Press, 1995), 152–55; James R. Barrett and David Roediger, "Inbetween Peoples: Race, Nationality, and the 'New Immigrant' Working Class," *Journal of American Ethnic History* 16, no. 3 (Spring 1997): 33–34.

26. Memoranda by the correspondence panels section for Philleo Nash, Washington DC, 10, 24 Aug. 1944, Nash Papers, box 28, folder "Philadelphia Strike"; *Philadelphia Inquirer,* 2 Aug. 1944; "Hate Strike, Philadelphia," *Monthly Summary of Events and Trends in Race Relations* 2, no. 1–2 (Aug.–Sept. 1944): 6–7; Allan M. Winkler, "The Philadelphia Transit Strike of 1944," *Journal of American History* 59, no. 1 (June 1972): 73–89; Roland L. Filippelli, "Philadelphia Transit Strike of 1944," in *Labor Conflict in the United States: An Encyclopedia,* ed. Roland L. Filippelli (New York: Garland, 1990). 419–21.

27. *Evening Bulletin,* 1, 2, 3, 4, 5, 7, 9, 14 Aug. 1944; press release by the Department of Justice, 4 Oct. 1944, Nash Papers, box 28, folder "Philadelphia Strike"; *Il Popolo Italiano,* 2, 3, 4, 5, 6, 7, 8 Aug. 1944.

28. *Philadelphia Inquirer,* 9 Sept. 1943.

29. *Philadelphia Inquirer,* 9 Sept. 1943; *Southwark Courier,* 11 Sept. 1943; U.S. House of Representatives, 79th Cong., 1st Sess., *Hearings before the Committee of Foreign Affairs Pursuant to H. J. Res. 99, a Joint Resolution Requesting the President to Recognize Italy as an Ally and to Extend Lend-Lease Aid* (Washington DC: U.S. Government Printing Office, 1945), 51, 54–56, 85, 89, 90–91, 96; *Il Popolo Italiano,* 21, 23 Sept., 27 Oct. 1944; letter by Cornelia Bryce Pinchot to Edwin M. Watson, Harrisburg PA, 17 Oct. 1944, Papers of the National Committee of the Democratic Party, box 29, folder "Pennsylvania, I-O," FDRL.

30. Blum, *V Was for Victory,* 152–54; Venturini, "Prominenti at War," 462; Francis Biddle, *In Brief Authority* (Garden City NY: Doubleday, 1962), 229.

31. *Philadelphia Record*, 14, 19 Oct. 1942; *South Phila American*, 18 Oct. 1942; *Observer*, 19 Oct. 1942.

32. *Evening Bulletin*, 13 Oct. 1942; *Ordine Nuovo*, 24 Oct. 1942.

33. *Observer*, 11 May 1942; *Il Popolo Italiano*, 26 Oct. 1942.

34. Norman Kogan, *Italy and the Allies* (Cambridge MA: Harvard University Press, 1956), 83–87; Gregory Dale Black, "The United States and Italy, 1943–1946: The Drift Toward Containment" (Ph.D. diss., University of Kansas, 1973), 180–84; James Edward Miller, "The Politics of Relief: The Roosevelt Administration and the Reconstruction of Italy, 1943–44," *Prologue* 13, no. 3 (Fall 1981): 193–208.

35. *New York Times*, 28 Oct. 1944; *Il Popolo Italiano*, 8, 19, 23, 29 Oct. 1944; *Ordine Nuovo*, 21 Oct. 1944.

36. *Il Popolo Italiano*, 11, 29 Oct. 1944; *Philadelphia Inquirer*, 19 Oct. 1944.

37. The row votes are from *The Pennsylvania Manual* (1945).

38. *La Libera Parola*, 14 Apr. 1945; *Il Popolo Italiano*, 7 Nov. 1945; letter by Luigi De Pasquale, member of the Advisory Committee of the American-Italian Congress, to Congressman John E. Fogarty, Providence RI, 9 Sept. 1946, John E. Fogarty Papers, Special Folders, box 4, folder 8, Phillips Memorial Library, Providence College, Providence RI.

39. Ernest E. Rossi, "Italian Americans and U.S. Relations with Italy in the Cold War," in *The United States and Italy*, 113–15; Nadia Venturini, "Italian-American Leadership, 1943–1948," *Storia Nordamericana* 2, no. 1 (1985): 50–55; Kogan, *Italy and the Allies*, 132–68.

40. "Public Attitudes Toward Ratification of Italian and Satellite Peace Treaties," 2, Records of the Office of Public Opinion Studies, box 46, folder "Public Opinion on Italy, 1947–49," National Archives II; *Ordine Nuovo*, 27 July, 31 Aug. 1946; 18 May 1947; *Il Popolo Italiano*, 14 Mar. 1947; 2, 9 May 1948; 19 Aug. 1948.

41. U.S. House of Representatives, *Hearings before the Committee of Foreign Affairs Pursuant to H. J. Res. 99*, 51; *Ordine Nuovo*, 24 Aug. 1946; U.S. Senate, 80th Cong., 1st Sess., *Hearings before the Committee on Foreign Relations on Executives F, G, H, and I: Treaties of Peace with Italy, Rumania, Bulgaria, and Hungary* (Washington DC: U.S. Government Printing Office, 1947), 71–74; *Ordine Nuovo*, 21 Aug. 1948; president's appointments, 8 Sept. 1948, Harry S. Truman Papers, Matthew J. Connelly Files, box 3, folder 9, HSTL.

42. Venturini, "Italian-American Leadership," 47–49; minutes of the membership meetings of Local 122, 20 Mar., 16 Apr. 1944, Papers of the Philadelphia Joint Board of the ACWA, box 63; minutes of the executive board meetings of Local 122, 24 Apr. 1944, 9 Apr. 1945, 13 May, 12 Aug. 1946, ibid.

43. Ernest E. Rossi, "NSC 1 and United States Foreign Policy Toward Italy," in *Italian Ethnics*, 160–66; Alexander De Conde, "Foreign Intervention in Domestic Politics: The Italian and American Experience," in *Italia e Stati Uniti dall'indipendenza americana ad oggi*, 118–21; James E. Miller, "Taking Off the Gloves: The United States and the Italian Elections of 1948," *Diplomatic History*

7, no. 1 (Winter 1983): 34–55; E. Timothy Smith, *The United States, Italy, and NATO, 1947–52* (New York: St. Martin's Press, 1991), 31–35.

44. Ernest E. Rossi, "Cold War: Italian Americans and Italy," in *The Italian American Experience*, 121–22; *Ordine Nuovo*, 20, 27 Mar., 3, 10, 24 Apr. 1948; *Il Popolo Italiano*, 23, 26, 30 Mar. 5, 7, 12, 14, 18 Apr. 1948; letter by Carmon D'Agostino to Harry S. Truman, Atlantic City NJ, n.d. [but Mar. 1948], Truman Papers, Official File 233 Misc., folder "Jan.–Aug. 1948."

45. *Philadelphia Inquirer*, 20 Apr. 1948; *Il Popolo Italiano*, 21, 22, 29 Apr., 1, 2 May 1948; *Evening Bulletin*, 27 Apr. 1948.

46. Norman A. Graebner, *The New Isolationism: A Study in Politics and Foreign Policy since 1950* (New York: Roland Press, 1956), 8; Gerson, *The Hyphenate in Recent American Politics*, 146–47; Philip Jenkins, *The Cold War at Home: The Red Scare in Pennsylvania, 1945–1960* (Chapel Hill: University of North Carolina Press, 1999), 142–49, 166–83; Glazer and Moynihan, *Beyond the Melting Pot*, 214–15.

47. *Il Popolo Italiano*, 2 May 1948.

48. "Italian African Colonies," memorandum by Eugene V. Alessandroni et al. to the president, 8 Sept. 1948, Truman Papers, Official File 233 Misc., folder "Sept. 1948–49"; telegram by Samuel B. Regalbuto to Harry S. Truman, Philadelphia, 21 Sept. 1951, ibid., folder "1950–53."

49. Lubell, *The Future of American Politics*, 201–4; Phylis Cancilla Martinelli, "Italian-American Experience," in *America's Ethnic Politics*, ed. Joseph S. Roucek and Bernard Eisenberg (Westport CT: Greenwood Press, 1982), 223; Samuel Lubell, "Who *Really* Elected Truman?," *Saturday Evening Post* (22 Jan. 1949): 17; Jeffries, *Testing the Roosevelt Coalition*, 248; Dahl, *Who Governs?*, 49.

50. The row votes are from *The Pennsylvania Manual* (1949).

51. *New York Times*, 19, 20 Aug. 1948; *Il Popolo Italiano*, 20 Aug., 2, 11 Oct. 1948; *Il Progresso Italo-Americano*, 17 Sept. 1948.

52. Richard M. Freeland, *The Truman Doctrine and the Origin of McCarthyism: Foreign Policy, Domestic Politics, and Internal Security, 1946–1948* (New York: Schocken Books, 1970), 340; *Il Popolo Italiano*, 13 Mar, 4, 6 Oct. 1948; *Il Progresso Italo-Americano*, 4 Aug. 1946.

53. "Recent Press and Other Public Discussion of the Italian Colonies," 20 Sept. 1948, Records of the Office of Public Opinion Studies, box 46, folder "Public Opinion on Italy, 1947–1949"; letter by Ernest L. Biagi to Harry S. Truman, Philadelphia, 9 Mar. 1949, Truman Papers, Official File 233 Misc., folder "Sept. 1948–49"; resolution attached to letter by Eugene V. Alessandroni to Harry S. Truman, Philadelphia, 8 July 1949, ibid.

54. John Bodnar, *Remaking America: Public Memory, Commemoration, and Patriotism in the Twentieth Century* (Princeton: Princeton University Press, 1991), 71–73; memorandum on the president's appointments, 8 Sept. 1948, Truman Papers, President's Secretary's File, box 90, folder "1–12 Sept. 1948"; *Ordine Nuovo*, 11 Sept. 1948.

55. *Observer,* 26 Jan. 1948; *Philadelphia Inquirer,* 25 Apr. 1948; *Evening Bulletin,* 25 Apr. 1948; *Il Popolo Italiano,* 27 Apr. 1948.

56. The row votes are from CBEP, 1948 elections for representatives in Congress; *The Pennsylvania Manual* (1949).

Chapter 6. From Italian Americans to White Ethnics

1. *Italian-American Herald,* 5 Jan., 2 Feb., 2, 9, 23 Mar. 1961; *Il Popolo Italiano,* 14 Oct. 1954; 7, 28 Oct. 1963; 14 Oct. 1965; 10, 17 Feb. 1966; *South Phila American,* 7 July 1967.

2. *Il Popolo Italiano,* 23 Oct. 1963.

3. George Pozzetta, "Italian Americans," in *Gale Encyclopedia of Multicultural America,* ed. Judy Galens, Anna Sheets, and Robin V. Young, 2 vols. (Detroit: Gale Research Inc., 1985), 2:771; *The Festival of Italy: Celebrating the 100th Anniversary of Italian Unification, January 21 to March 26, 1961* (Philadelphia: Commercial Museum, 1961); *New York Times,* 1 June 1967.

4. *Il Popolo Italiano,* 21, 27, 31 May 1953; *Il Progresso Italo-Americano,* 3 June 1953. For Mazzone's anticommunism see his *Communism: The Satanic Scourge* (Philadelphia: Community Press, 1963); Jenkins, *The Cold War at Home,* 167.

5. *Il Popolo Italiano,* 25 May 1953; *Il Progresso Italo-Americano,* 31 May 1953.

6. *Il Popolo Italiano,* 14 June 1953.

7. The row votes are from *The Pennsylvania Manual* (1953).

8. Kogan, *Italy and the Allies,* 82.

9. *Il Popolo Italiano,* 3 November 1952; President's Commission on Immigration and Naturalization, *Whom We Shall Welcome* (1953; rpt. New York: Da Capo Press, 1971), 100, 104; *Chi può emigrare negli Stati Uniti: Le norme della legge McCarran-Walter* (Rome: Italiani nel Mondo, 1953); Divine, *American Immigration Policy,* 164–91; Reed Ueda, *Postwar Immigrant America: A Social History* (Boston: Bedford Books of St. Martin's Press, 1994), 43–44.

10. *Il Popolo Italiano,* 18 May, 28 July, 30 Oct. 1952; *Ordine Nuovo,* 31 May, 26 July, 16, 30 Aug. 1952; "Democratic Platform [1952]," in *History of American Presidential Elections,* 4:3272.

11. *Congress and the Nation, 1945–64: A Review of Government and Politics in the Postwar Years* (Washington DC: Congressional Quarterly Service, 1965), 57a, 61a; *Il Popolo Italiano,* 4 July 1952.

12. Republican National Committee, Research Division and All American Origins Divisions, *Guide Book for Republican Candidates: Re Americans of Italian Origin* (Washington DC, 1952), 6; Edward Martin Papers, Campaign Material, box 3, folder "Campaign Material: 1952," Pennsylvania State Archives.

13. Edward Martin, *Always Be On Time: An Autobiography* (Harrisburg PA: Telegraph Press, 1959), p. 140. The row votes are from CBEP, 1952 election for U.S. Senator; *The Pennsylvania Manual* (1953).

14. *Il Popolo Italiano*, 30 July 1953; *Ordine Nuovo*, 22 Aug., 3 Oct. 1953; Divine, *American Immigration Policy*, 144–45.

15. U.S. Senate, 82d Cong., First Sess., *Third Interim Report of the Special Committee to Investigate Crime in Interstate Commerce Pursuant to S. Res. 202* (Washington DC: U.S. Government Printing Office, 1951); Estes Kefauver, *Crime in America* (Garden City NY: Doubleday, 1951); Michael Woodiwiss, *Organized Crime, USA: Changing Perceptions from Prohibition to the Present Day* (Brighton: British Association for American Studies, 1990), 21–22; Vecoli, "The Search for an Italian American Identity: Continuity and Change," 100. An examination of organized crime in the United States is not among the intents of this study. Nor is an analysis of the American ramifications of the Italian Mafia or an assessment of Italian Americans' participation in criminal syndicates in the United States. For these topics, see *An Inquiry into Organized Crime*, ed. Luciano J. Iorizzo (Staten Island: American Italian Historical Association, n.d.); Joseph L. Albini, *The American Mafia: Genesis of a Legend* (New York: Meredith, 1971); Humbert S. Nelli, *The Business of Crime: Italian and Syndicate Crime in the United States* (New York: Oxford University Press, 1976); Michael Woodiwiss, *Crime, Crusades, and Corruption: Prohibitions in the United States, 1900–1987* (New York: Barnes & Noble, 1988); Umberto Santino and Giovanni La Fiura, *L'impero mafioso: Dall'Italia agli Stati Uniti* (Milan: Franco Angeli, 1990).

16. U.S. Senate, 81st Cong., 2d Sess., *Investigation of Organized Crime in Interstate Commerce: Hearings before the Special Committee to Investigate Crime in Interstate Commerce Pursuant to S. Res. 202*, 16 vols. (Washington DC: U.S. Government Printing Office, 1951), 11:42–43, 54–55, 63–66, 91, 102–5, 150–206, 266–67.

17. Barton J. Bernstein, "Election of 1952," in *History of American Presidential Elections*, 4:3235–37; William H. Moore, *The Kefauver Committee and the Politics of Crime* (Columbia: University of Missouri Press, 1974), 204–5, 235–36; Charles L. Fontenay, *Estes Kefauver: A Biography* (Knoxville: University of Tennessee Press, 1980), 187–207. The row votes are from County Board of Election of Philadelphia, tabulation sheets of the 1952 primary election returns for President, Democratic Party, PCA.

18. Salvatore J. LaGumina, "Case Studies of Ethnicity and Italo-American Politicians," in *The Italian Experience in the United States*, ed. Silvano M. Tomasi and Madeline H. Engel (New York: Center for Migration Studies, 1970), 145; Maria J. Falco, *"Bigotry!" Ethnic, Machine, and Sexual Politics in a Senatorial Election* (Westport CT: Greenwood Press, 1980), 47–52; Sally Stephenson, "Michael Musmanno: A Symbolic Leader" (Ph.D. diss., Carnegie-Mellon University, 1981), 213–19 (to which the percentage of the Italian American vote refers).

19. Rudolph J. Vecoli, "*Contadini* in Chicago: A Critique of *The Uprooted*," *Journal of American History* 51, no. 3 (Dec. 1964): 406, 408, 413; Anthony Sorrentino, *Organizing the Ethnic Community: An Account of the Origin, History,*

and Development of the Joint Civic Committee of Italian Americans (1952–1995) (Staten Island: Center for Migration Studies, 1995), 8–11.

20. Frank Cavaioli, "Italian Americans Slay the Immigration Dragon: The National Origins Quota System," *Italian Americana* 5, no. 1 (Fall–Winter 1979): 71–100; Frank Cavaioli, "Chicago's Italian Americans Rally for Immigration Reform," ibid. 5, no. 2 (Spring–Summer 1980): 142–56; Ueda, *Postwar Immigrant America*, 44–46.

21. Letter by Myron B. Kuropas, special assistant to the president for ethnic affairs, to Americo V. Cortese, Washington DC, 29 Mar. 1976, White House Central Files, Name File, box 3011, folder "Spatuzza, John G.," Gerald R. Ford Library, Ann Arbor MI; "Meeting with Italian-American Leadership," 3 Aug. 1976, Myron B. Kuropas Files, box 4, folder "Italian Ethnic Groups, 1," ibid.

22. *Sons of Italy Times*, 31 July 1978.

23. Mario M. Cuomo, *Forest Hills Diary: The Crisis of Low-Income Housing* (New York: Random House, 1974); Frank Cavaioli, "Returning to Corona's Little Italy," *Italian Americana* 15, no. 1 (Winter 1997): 31–50; Ronald P. Formisano, *Boston Against Busing: Race, Class, and Ethnicity in the 1960s and 1970s* (Chapel Hill: University of North Carolina Press, 1991); Jonathan Rieder, *Canarsie: The Jews and Italians of Brooklyn Against Liberalism* (Cambridge MA: Harvard University Press, 1985); Joseph M. Conforti, "Wasp in the Woodpile Revisited: Italian-American–African-American Conflict," in *Shades of Black and White*, 62–63, 75.

24. Binzen, *Whitetown*; Judith Goode and Jo Ann Schneider, *Reshaping Ethnic and Racial Relations in Philadelphia: Immigrants in a Divided City* (Philadelphia: Temple University Press, 1994). For Puerto Rican immigration to Philadelphia in the postwar years, see Eugene Ericksen et al., *The State of Puerto Rican Philadelphia* (Philadelphia: Temple University Institute for Public Policy Studies, 1985); Carmen Teresa Whalen, "Puerto Rican Migration to Philadelphia, Pennsylvania, 1945–1970: A Historical Perspective on a Migrant Group" (Ph.D. diss., Rutgers University, 1994). See also John H. Fernandez, "Conceptualizing Culture and Ethnicity: Toward an Anthropology of Puerto Rican Philadelphia" (Ph.D. diss., Temple University, 1994).

25. Thomas J. Sugrue, "Crabgrass-Roots Politics: Race, Rights, and the Reaction against Liberalism in the Urban North, 1940–1964," *Journal of American History* 82, no. 2 (Sept. 1995): 551–78; Thomas J. Sugrue, *The Origin of the Urban Crisis: Race and Inequality in Postwar Detroit* (Princeton: Princeton University Press, 1996), 73–81; Arnold H. Hirsch, "Massive Resistance in the Urban North: Trumbull Park, Chicago, 1953–1966," *Journal of American History* 82, no. 2 (Sept. 1995): 522–50; Arnold H. Hirsch, *Making the Second Ghetto: Race and Housing in Chicago, 1940–1960* (New York: Cambridge University Press, 1983). See also the comments on Sugrue's and Hirsch's articles by Gary Gerstle, "Race and the Myth of the Liberal Consensus," *Journal of American History* 82, no. 2 (Sept. 1995): 579–86.

26. Joseph S. Clark Jr. and Dennis J. Clark, "Rally and Relapse, 1946–1968," in *Philadelphia*, 669–71; John F. Bauman, *Public Housing, Race, and Renewal: Urban Planning in Philadelphia, 1920–1974* (Philadelphia: Temple University Press, 1987), 160–64.

27. Juliani, "The Italian Community of Philadelphia," 101; Paolantonio, *Frank Rizzo*, 221–22; Kenneth S. Baer, "Whitman: A Study of Race, Class, and Postwar Public Housing Opposition" (Senior honor thesis, University of Pennsylvania, 1994); *Evening Bulletin*, 19, 27 Apr., 25 May, 7 July, 13 Aug. 1971.

28. *Il Popolo Italiano*, 10 Dec. 1965 (to which the quotation refers); *Philadelphia Inquirer*, 23 May 1969.

29. David K. Shipler, "The White Niggers of Newark," *Harper's Magazine* 245, no. 1467 (Aug. 1972): 78–80; Arvarh E. Strickland, "The School Controversy and the Beginning of the Civil Rights Movement in Chicago," *Historian* 58, no. 4 (Summer 1996): 717–29.

30. Robert L. Freedman, *A Report on Politics in Philadelphia* (Cambridge MA: Joint Center for Urban Studies of the Massachusetts Institute of Technology and Harvard University, 1963), 3:7–8. The row votes are from CBEP, vote on the increase of the debt of the School District of Philadelphia, 1961.

31. Freedman, *A Report on Politics in Philadelphia*, 5:19–20.

32. *Il Popolo Italiano*, 30 Oct. 1963; *Philadelphia Inquirer*, 29 Oct., 7 Nov. 1963. The row votes are from *Annual Reports of the Registration Commission for the City of Philadelphia* (1959, 1963).

33. William J. McKenna, "The Negro Vote in Philadelphia Elections," *Pennsylvania History* 32, no. 4 (Oct. 1965): 414.

34. *Philadelphia Inquirer*, 15, 17, 18, 19, 23, 27, 28, 1 June 1963.

35. Mathias, "From Folklore to Mass Culture," 92, 114, 326; *Violence in the U.S.*, ed. Thomas F. Parker, 2 vols. (New York: Facts on File, 1974), 1:104–11, 179–254; *Il Popolo Italiano*, Sept. 1967.

36. *Philadelphia Daily News*, 29, 30 Aug. 1964; *Sons of Italy Times*, 7 Sept. 1964; 27 Nov. 1967; Lenora Berson, *Case Study of a Riot* (New York: Institute of Human Relations Press, 1966); Lois G. Forer, *No One Will Listen: How Our Legal System Brutalized the Youthful Poor* (New York: John Day, 1970), 269; *Philadelphia Inquirer*, 21 Nov. 1967. For the *Sons of Italy Times*, see Vincent A. Lapomarda, "Press, Italian American," in *The Italian American Experience*, 514.

37. Riggio, "Tales of Little Italy," 102; Conrad Weiler, *Philadelphia: Neighborhood, Authority, and the Urban Crisis* (New York: Praeger, 1974), 88–92; Jon S. Birger, "Race, Reaction, and Reform: The Three Rs of Philadelphia School Politics, 1965–1971," *Pennsylvania Magazine of History and Biography* 120, no. 3 (July 1996): 163–216; letters to Mark Shedd and Richardson Dilworth, Richardson Dilworth Papers, box 43, HSP. For the Shedd Administration, see also Henry S. Resnik, *Turning on the System: War in the Philadelphia Public Schools* (New York: Pantheon Books, 1970).

38. Binzen, *Whitetown*, 296–97; Linda M. Kupferstein, *William A. Barrett: Democratic Representative from Pennsylvania* (Washington DC: Grossman, 1972), 8; *Philadelphia Inquirer*, 19, 20 May 1969; *Sons of Italy Times*, 31 July 1967; 29 Apr. 1968 (to which the first quotation refers); letters by William D. Valente to Richardson Dilworth, Philadelphia, 18 Feb. 1968, Dilworth Papers, box 42, and to Frank C.P. McGinn, Philadelphia, 12 May 1969, ibid., box 46, folder "citizen correspondence" (to which the second quotation refers).

39. *Philadelphia Inquirer*, 21 May 1969; Weiler, *Philadelphia*, 91–92.

40. *Sons of Italy Times*, 15 Apr. 1968; *Philadelphia Inquirer*, 22 May, 5, 6 Nov. 1969; letters by Richardson Dilworth to Thomas M. Foglietta, Philadelphia, 22 Oct. 1969, and by Clifford Brenner, campaign coordinator, to Anthony Cortigene, Philadelphia 26 Sept. 1969, Dilworth Papers, box 45, folder "Endorsements, bond question." The row votes are from CBEP, vote on the proposed loans, 1969.

41. Anthony Lombardo as quoted in A. Harold Datz, "Snatching Defeat from the Jaws of Victory: The 1967 Mayoralty Election in Philadelphia" (A.B. thesis, Temple University, n.d.), xvii.

42. W. Thacher Longstreth with Dan Rottenberg, *Main Line Wasp: The Education of Thacher Longstreth* (New York: Norton, 1990); ADA, press release, 18 July 1971, Americans for Democratic Action Papers, accession 38, box 14, folder 31, TUUA; Hamilton, *Rizzo*, 11; Weed, *The White Ethnic Movement*, 75–79; Peter O. Muller, Kenneth C. Meyer, and Roman A. Cybriwsky, *Metropolitan Philadelphia: A Study of Conflict and Social Cleavages* (Cambridge MA: Ballinger, 1976), 19–20; Paul B. Beers, *Pennsylvania Politics Today and Yesterday: The Tolerable Accommodation* (University Park PA: Pennsylvania State University Press, 1980); Stephanie G. Wolf, "The Bicentennial City, 1968–1982," in *Philadelphia*, 722–23; Mike Madden, "Politics in Mantua and Philadelphia Since World War II," *Penn History Review* 6, no. 1 (Spring 1998): 73–75.

43. Arts Committee for Green, press release, 19 Apr. 1971, Americans for Democratic Action Papers, accession 38, box 14, folder 30; Krist Boardman, "Max Weiner Has a Dream," 28 June 1971, typescript, ibid. The row votes are from the *Annual Report of the Registration Commission for the City of Philadelphia* (1971).

44. Martha Wagner Weinberg, "Boston's Kevin White: A Mayor Who Survives," *Political Science Quarterly* 96, no. 1 (Spring 1981): 89, 91–92; Jon C. Teaford, *The Rough Road to Renaissance: Urban Revitalization in America, 1940–1985* (Baltimore: Johns Hopkins University Press, 1990), 192–99.

45. Longstreth with Rottenberg, *Main Line Wasp*, 253; Birger, "Race, Reaction, and Reform," 169; letter by Mr. and Mrs. Alfred De Panfilis to Paul D'Ortona, President of Philadelphia's City Council, Philadelphia, 13 Oct. 1969, Dilworth Papers, box 50, folder "D'Ortona"; ADA, press release, 28 Sept. 1971, Americans for Democratic Action Papers, accession 38, box 14, folder 34.

46. Bill Biggin, *Rizzo and the Police State* (Philadelphia: Free Press, 1971); Peter C. Buffum and Rita Sagi, "Philadelphia: Politics of Reform and Retreat," in *Crime in City Politics*, ed. Anne Heinz, Herbert Jacob, and Robert L. Lineberry (New York: Longman, 1983), 122–25. For Rizzo's relations with Annenberg, see Gaeton Fonzi, *Annenberg: A Biography of Power* (New York: Weybright and Talley, 1969), 184–86; John Cooney, *The Annenbergs* (New York: Simon and Schuster, 1982), 256; Christopher Ogden, *Legacy: A Biography of Moses and Walter Annenberg* (Boston: Little, Brown, 1999), 388–89. For Rizzo's statement, see *Philadelphia Inquirer*, 18 Nov. 1967. His alleged second quotation is cited in John Lombardi, "Frank Rizzo Without Prejudice: The Reluctant Mellowing of Philly's Attila the Hun," *Esquire* 112, no. 2 (Aug. 1989): 116.

47. Gaeton Fonzi, "The Italians Are Coming! The Italians Are Coming!," *Philadelphia Magazine* 62, no. 12 (Dec. 1971): 98–102, 171–81; Raisa Rebecca Sarah Deber Berlin, "Who Runs?: Congressmen and Realignment Sequences" (Ph.D. diss., MIT, 1977), 141–49; *Politics in America: The 100th Congress*, ed. Alan Ehrenhalt (Washington DC: Congressional Quarterly, 1987), 1281; "The Rizzo Patronage Apparatus," report no. 3, Walter M. Phillips Papers, box 8, folder "Reports on Rizzo, 1975," TUUA.

48. James H. J. Tate with Joseph McLaughlin, "In Praise of Politicians," *Evening Bulletin* (23 Jan. 1973): 18.

49. Neal R. Pierce, *The Megastates of America: People, Politics, and Power in Ten Great States* (New York: Norton, 1972), 269–70; *Philadelphia Inquirer*, 17 May 1967; Richard F. Fenno Jr., *Learning to Legislate: The Senate Education of Arlen Specter* (Washington DC: CQ Press, 1991), 1; Datz, "Snatching Defeat from the Jaws of Victory," x–xi, xvii–xviii.

50. *Sons of Italy Times*, 22, 29 May, 27 Nov. 1967; *South Phila American*, 26 May 1967; *Philadelphia Inquirer*, 20, 21, 27 Nov. 1967.

51. *Philadelphia Daily News*, 27 Jan. 1976; *Philadelphia Inquirer*, 18 Apr., 25 Aug., 1 Oct. 1976; *Evening Bulletin*, 25 Apr. 1976. See also the collection of newspaper clippings in the Papers of the Citizens' Committee to Recall Rizzo, box 1, TUUA.

52. James M. Carlson, "The Impact of Ethnicity on Candidate Image," *Polity* 16, no. 4 (Summer 1984): 667–72; Gary C. Byrne and J. Kristian Pueschel, "But Who Should I Vote for County Coroner?," *Journal of Politics* 36, no. 3 (Aug. 1974): 782–84; Sandra Featherman, "Ethnicity and Ethnic Candidates: Vote Advantages in Local Elections," *Polity* 15, no. 3 (Spring 1983): 406–7, 409–11.

53. *Philadelphia Exclusive*, 28 Oct. 1971.

54. Vito C. Mazzone, "Sermon no. 3," Mazzone Papers; U.S. Bureau of the Census, *1950 Population Census Report: Census Tract Statistics: Philadelphia, Pennsylvania and Adjacent Area* (Washington DC: U.S. Government Printing Office, 1952), 8; *1970 Census of Population: Characteristics of the Population: Pennsylvania*

(Washington, DC: U.S. Government Printing Office, 1973), 356; *1980 Census of Population: Characteristics of the Population: General Social and Economic Characteristics: Pennsylvania* (Washington DC: U.S. Government Printing Office, 1983), 133, 234; *1990 Census of Population: Social and Economic Characteristics: Pennsylvania* (Washington DC: U.S. Government Printing Office, 1993), 362, 621, 669.

55. Binzen, *Whitetown*; Bill Tonelli, "Arrivederci, South Philly," *Philadelphia Magazine* 73, no. 5 (May 1982): 130–43; Hershberg et al., "A Tale of Three Cities," 476–77; transcript of an interview with Walter D'Alessio, executive vice president of Philadelphia's Economic Development Corporation, by Walter M. Phillips, Philadelphia, 7 June 1977, 15–16, Walter M. Phillips Oral History Project Transcripts, box 3, TUUA; Philip Scranton, "Large Firms and Industrial Restructuring: The Philadelphia Region, 1900–1980," *Pennsylvania Magazine of History and Biography* 116, no. 4 (Oct. 1992): 419–65. For Biagi's biographical sketch, see Carnevale, *Americans of Italian Descent in Philadelphia*, 33–34. Figures about membership in the OSIA are from Andreozzi, "The Order Sons of Italy in America," 8, 12; Alfred M. Rotondaro, "Ethnicity at Work," *Altreitalie* 3, no. 6 (Nov. 1991): 120. For the declining appeal of such ethnic organizations as the OSIA among Italian Americans, see also Richard D. Alba, " 'What Then Is the European American?' Some Answers," *Altreitalie* 4, no. 8 (July–Dec. 1992): 95.

56. Richard N. Juliani, "Identity and Ethnicity: The Italian Case," in *The Columbus People*, 56; Frank Cavaioli, "Ethnic Population Patterns on Long Island," in *Ethnicity in Suburbia*, ed. Salvatore J. LaGumina (Garden City NY: Nassau College Press, 1980), 15–25; Salvatore J. LaGumina, *From Steerage to Suburbs: Long Island's Italians* (Staten Island: Center for Migration Studies, 1988); Jerome Krase, "The Spatial Semeiotics of Little Italies and Italian Americans," in *Industry, Technology, Labor*, 103.

57. Juliani, "Una comunità in transizione," 311–12; Gaeton Fonzi, "A Show of Faith," *Philadelphia Magazine* 61, no. 9 (Sept. 1970): 78; Nelli, *From Immigrants to Ethnics*, 175–82; Donna R. Gabaccia, "Peopling 'Little Italy,' " in *The Italians of New York*, 53; memorandum by Myron B. Kuropas to Nellie Yates, 22 Sept. 1976, White House Central Files, Name File, box 1568, folder "Italian A–K," Ford Library.

58. James Reichley, *The Art of Government: Reform and Organization Politics in Philadelphia* (New York: Fund for the Republic, 1959), 79; letter by Ralph Borrelli to Doug, Philadelphia, 27 Jan. 1976, Borrelli Papers, box 1; "List of Addresses for Mediterranean Security," John B. Connally Papers, box 270–73C, folder 1, Lyndon B. Johnson Library, Austin TX. For the purpose of the Citizens Alliance for Mediterranean Freedom, see also Charles McCall Files, box 75, folder 48.76, Ford Library.

59. *Philadelphia Inquirer*, 5 Nov. 1975; Buffum and Sagi, "Philadelphia," 133–34; Paolantonio, *Frank Rizzo*, 188–92; Sandra Featherman, "Italian American Voting in Local Elections: The Philadelphia Case," in *Italian Americans: The*

Search for a Usable Past, 49–51 (to which the percentages of registrations and votes refer); transcript of an interview with Thomas M. Foglietta by Walter M. Phillips, Philadelphia, 24 June 1980, 7, 11–14, Walter M. Phillips Oral History Project Transcripts, box 3, TUUA. Rizzo's quotation about Foglietta is from Southeastern Pennsylvania Chapter of Americans for Democratic Action, *The Sayings of Chairman Frank, or I Never Saw My Mother Naked* (Philadelphia: Southeastern Pennsylvania Chapter of Americans for Democratic Action, 1977), 90.

60. Bauman, *Public Housing, Race, and Renewal*, 202; *Philadelphia Daily News*, 22 Apr. 1975, 22 Nov. 1976; *Philadelphia Inquirer*, 9 Aug. 1978; Wolf, "The Bicentennial City," 723–24; Hizkias Assefa and Paul Wahrhaftig, *The Move Crisis in Philadelphia: Extremist Groups and Conflict Resolution* (Pittsburgh: University of Pittsburgh Press, 1990), 3–94. Scholarly assessments of the Rizzo administration are few and sketchy. See John F. Bauman, "Rizzo, Frank L.," in *Biographical Dictionary of American Mayors, 1820–1980: Big City Mayors*, ed. Melvin G. Holli and Peter d'A. Jones (Westport CT: Greenwood Press, 1981), 306–7; Salvatore J. LaGumina, "The Political Profession: Big City Italian-American Mayors," in *Italian Americans in the Professions*, ed. Remigio U. Pane (Staten Island: American Italian Historical Association, 1983), 97–100; Buffum and Sagi, "Philadelphia," 130–45; Melvin G. Holli, *The American Mayor: The Best and the Worst Big-City Leaders* (University Park PA: Pennsylvania State University Press, 1999), 16, 25. For more detailed but journalistic accounts, see Daughen and Binzen, *The Cop Who Would Be King*, 203–321; Paolantonio, *Frank Rizzo*, 125–243. Hamilton's biography, *Rizzo*, ends with the 1971 election campaign.

61. *Philadelphia Inquirer*, 22, 24 Sept. 1978; *Philadelphia Daily News*, 22 Sept. 1978.

62. The percentages are from Sandra Featherman and William S. Rosenberg, *Jews, Blacks, and Ethnics: The 1978 "Vote White" Campaign in Philadelphia* (New York: American Jewish Committee, 1979), 9, 24–28, 40.

63. *Philadelphia Inquirer*, 29 Mar. 1983, 8 Nov. 1987; *Philadelphia Daily News*, 20 Nov. 1987; Paolantonio, *Frank Rizzo*, 279; W. Wilson Goode with Joann Stevens, *In Goode Faith* (Valley Forge PA: Judson Press, 1992), 276–77. See also Mary Ellen Balchunis, "A Study of the Old and New Campaign Politics Models: A Comparative Analysis of Wilson Goode's 1983 and 1987 Philadelphia Mayoral Campaigns" (Ph.D. diss., Temple University, 1992), esp. 37–47, 122–27, 147–57; Bruce Ransom, "Black Independent Electoral Politics in Philadelphia and the Election of Mayor W. Wilson Goode," in *The New Black Politics: The Search for Political Power*, ed. Michael B. Prenston, Lenneal J. Henderson Jr., and Paul L. Puryear (New York: Longman, 1987), 256–89.

64. Adams et al., *Neighborhoods, Division, and Conflict*, 149; Sandra Featherman, *Philadelphia Elects a Black Mayor: How Jews, Blacks, and Ethnics Vote in the 1980s* (Philadelphia: American Jewish Committee, 1984), 13; Sandra Featherman, *Jews, Blacks and Urban Politics in the 1980s: The Case of Philadelphia*

(Philadelphia: American Jewish Committee, 1988), 3–6 (to which the percentages of the Italian American vote for Rizzo refer); Ransom, "Black Independent Electoral Politics in Philadelphia," 272 (to which the percentages of votes for Lomento refer); *Philadelphia Inquirer*, 14 May 1985; Charles W. Bowser, *Let the Bunker Burn: The Final Battle with MOVE* (Philadelphia: Camino Books, 1989), 1–69; William L. Rosenberg, "Italians, Jews, and Blacks: Ethnic Perspectives of Philadelphia," in *Italian Americans: The Search for a Usable Past*, 38–39.

65. *Sons of Italy Times*, 10 Nov. 1975; 19 Oct. 1987; 9 Oct., 6 Nov. 1978.

66. Sandra Featherman and Allan B. Hill, *Ethnic Voting in the 1991 Philadelphia Mayoral Election* (New York: American Jewish Committee, 1992), 3–4, 8 (to which the percentage of the Italian American vote in 1991 refers); *Sons of Italy Times*, 29 Apr., 13 May 1991; Buzz Bissinger, *A Prayer for the City* (New York: Random House, 1997), 21.

67. Thomas Byrne Edsall and Mary D. Edsall, *Chain Reaction: The Impact of Race, Rights, and Taxes on American Politics* (New York: Norton, 1991), 163–64, 181–84, 225–27; Peter Brown, *Minority Party: Why Democrats Face Defeat in 1992 and Beyond* (Washington DC: Gateway, 1991); Dan T. Carter, *From George Wallace to Newt Gingrich: Race in the Conservative Counterrevolution, 1963–1994* (Baton Rouge: Louisiana State University Press, 1996).

68. Mark R. Levy and Michael S. Kramer, *The Ethnic Factor: How America's Minorities Decide Elections* (New York: Simon and Schuster, 1972), 168–73; Everett Carll Ladd, "On Mandates, Realignments, and the 1984 Presidential Election," *Political Science Quarterly* 100, no. 1 (Spring 1985): 14.

69. The row votes are from the *Annual Report of the Registration Commission for the City of Philadelphia* (1968).

70. *Philadelphia Exclusive*, 27 Oct. 1972; letter by Frank L. Rizzo to Richard M. Nixon, Philadelphia, 9 Aug. 1974, Richard M. Nixon Post-Presidential Papers, Richard M. Nixon Library & Birthplace, Yorba Linda CA (the collection is still uncatalogued); memorandum by Jim Field, 19 Oct. 1976, White House Central Files, Name File, box 2671, folder "Rizzo, Frank," Ford Library.

71. Letters to Richard M. Nixon by T. Richard Butera, Margaret Rose Colarusso, Gustine J. Pelagatti, and Joseph S. Ziccardi, Philadelphia, various dates, Richard M. Nixon Presidential Material Project, President's Personal File, box 161, folder 7, National Archives II. The row votes are from the *Annual Report of the Registration Commission for the City of Philadelphia* (1972).

72. William V. Shannon, "Election of 1984," *History of American Presidential Elections*, 5:301–2; Geraldine Ferraro with Catherine Whitney, *Framing a Life: A Family Memoirs* (New York: Charles Scribner's Sons, 1998), 145–50; *Sons of Italy Times*, 20 Aug. 1984.

73. Frank J. Cavaioli, "The National Italian American Foundation: 1975–1985," in *A. P. Giannini: Banker, Philanthropist, Entrepreneur*, ed. Felice A. Bonadio (Washington DC: National Italian American Foundation, 1985), 124; Geraldine

Ferraro, "Vice-Presidential Acceptance Speech," reprinted in her *Changing History: Women, Power, and Politics* (Wakefield, RI: Moyer Bell, 1993), 4; Geraldine Ferraro with Linda Bird Francke, *Ferraro: My Story* (Toronto: Bantam Books, 1985), 230–35, 315; Ferraro with Whitney, *Framing a Life*, 156–57; *Sons of Italy Times*, 6 Aug. 1984; Mangione and Morreale, *La Storia*, 405.

74. Edsall and Edsall, *Chain Reaction*, 212–13; *The Pennsylvania Manual* (1985), 698 (for the Democratic presidential vote citywide); Featherman, "Italian American Voting in Local Elections," 52–53 (to which the percentage of the Italian American vote in Philadelphia refers); Michael Barone and Grant Ujifusa, *The Almanac of American Politics: 1984* (Washington DC: National Journal, 1983), 1003; Richard T. Smith Jr., "Philadelphia's Deindustrialization: The Impact on Low Wages, African Americans, and Unionization" (Ph.D. diss., Temple University, 1994).

75. *New York Times*, 6 July 1995.

76. *Sons of Italy Times*, 31 May, 14, 28 June 1976; letter by Armand Della Porta to Gerald R. Ford, Philadelphia, 19 May 1976, White House Central Files, Subject File, box 2, folder "General DI 2/CO," Ford Library.

77. Letter by Americo V. Cortese to Gerald R. Ford, Philadelphia, 25 Mar. 1976, Kuropas Files, box 8, folder "Coordinating Committee of National American Italian Organizations"; Bissinger, *A Prayer for the City*, 80, 385.

78. Maddalena Tirabassi, "Interview with Joseph Scelsa," *Altreitalie* 10, no. 17 (Jan.–June 1998): 52–53; Nancy K. Torrieri, "Demography," in *The Italian American Experience*, 501.

79. Juliani, "Italian Organizations in Philadelphia," 114; Joseph Velikonja, "Italian Immigrants in the United States in the Mid-Sixties," *International Migration Review* 1, no. 3 (Summer 1967): 33–34.

80. Scherini, *The Italian-American Community of San Francisco*, 133–37.

81. Juliani, "Italian Organizations in Philadelphia," 113.

82. Campbell and Conley, *The Aurora Club of Rhode Island*, 69.

Chapter 7. Conclusion

1. Victor Greene, *For God and Country: The Rise of Polish and Lithuanian Ethnic Consciousness in America, 1860–1910* (Madison: State Historical Society of Wisconsin, 1975); Nathan Glazer, "Ethnic Groups in America: From National Culture to Ideology," in *Freedom and Control in Modern Society*, ed. Monroe Berger, Theodore Abel, and Charles H. Page (New York: D. Van Nostrand, 1954), 166.

2. Park and Miller, *Old World Traits Transplanted*; Caroline Ware, *Greenwich Village: A Comment on American Civilization in the Postwar Years* (Boston: Houghton Mifflin, 1935); Rudolph J. Vecoli, "An Inter-Ethnic Perspective on

American Immigration History," *Mid-America* 75, no. 2 (Apr.–July 1993): 227; David G. Gutierrez, *Walls and Mirrors: Mexican Americans, Mexican Immigrants, and the Politics of Ethnicity* (Berkeley: University of California Press, 1995); Robert Viscusi, "Il futuro dell'italianità: Il Commonwealth italiano," *Altreitalie* 5, no. 10 (July–Dec. 1993): 26.

3. Zucchi, *Italians in Toronto*; Mormino, *Immigrants on the Hill*, 71–75, 128–30.

4. Elisabetta Vezzosi, *La Chicago di Al Capone* (Florence: Giunti, 1997).

5. Scherini, *The Italian-American Community of San Francisco*, 118.

6. Paul Goldenberg, "Tony Imperiale Stands Vigilant for Law and Order," *New York Times Magazine* (29 Sept. 1968): 30–31, 117–22, 124, 126; Levy and Kramer, *The Ethnic Factor*, 174; Shipler, "The White Niggers of Newark," 77–83; Weed, *The White Ethnic Movement*, 50, 69–72; Kenneth Durr, "When Southern Politics Came North: The Roots of White Working-Class Conservatism in Baltimore, 1940–1964," *Labor History* 37, no. 3 (Summer 1996): 327.

7. William Simon, Samuel Patti, and George Herrmann, "Bloomfield: An Italian Working Class Neighborhood," *Italian Americana* 7, no. 1 (Fall–Winter 1981): 103–15; Mormino, *Immigrants on the Hill*, 240–45; Vecoli, "The Search for an Italian American Identity," 99; Robert P. Lynch, *Federal Hill Case Study: The Story of How People Saved Their Neighborhood* (Warren RI: New England Neighborhood Revitalization Center, 1978); Carmela E. Santoro, *The Italians in Rhode Island: The Age of Exploration to the Present, 1524–1989* (Providence: Rhode Island Heritage Commission, 1990), 8–9.

8. Levy and Kramer, *The Ethnic Factor*, 174–75, 180–83; Salvatore J. LaGumina, *New York at Mid-Century: The Impellitteri Years* (Westport CT: Greenwood Press, 1992), 103–31; Peter Vellon, "Immigrant Son: Mario Procaccino and the Rise of Conservative Politics in Late 1960s New York City," *Italian American Review* 7, no. 1 (Spring–Summer 1999): 117–36.

9. Dino Cinel, "Sicilians in the Deep South: The Ironic Outcome of Isolation," *Studi Emigrazione* 27, no. 97 (Mar. 1990): 55–86; Richard Gambino, *Vendetta: A True Story of the Worst Lynching in America: the Mass Murder of Italian Americans in New Orleans in 1891, the Vicious Motivations Behind It, and the Tragic Repercussions That Linger to This Day* (Garden City NY: Doubleday, 1977), 56–57; George E. Cunningham, "The Italian: A Hindrance to White Solidarity in Louisiana, 1890–1898," *Journal of Negro History* 50, no. 1 (Jan. 1965): 22–36; Giose Rimanelli, "The 1891 New Orleans Lynching: Southern Politics, Mafia, Immigration, and the American Press," in *The 1891 New Orleans Lynching and U.S.–Italian Relations: A Look Back*, ed. Marco Rimanelli and Sheryl Lynn Postman (New York: Peter Lang, 1992), 54–62; Gary R. Mormino and George E. Pozzetta, *The Immigrant World of Ybor City: Italians and Their Latin Neighbors in Tampa, 1885–1985* (Urbana: University of Illinois Press, 1987).

10. Jean Ann Scarpaci, "Immigrants in the New South: Italians in Louisiana's Sugar Parishes, 1880–1910," in *Il movimento migratorio italiano*

dall'unità nazionale ai nostri giorni, 2:197–216; Valentine J. Belfiglio, "Italians in Small Town and Rural Texas," in *Italian Immigrants in Rural and Small Town America,* ed. Rudolph J. Vecoli (Staten Island: American Italian Historical Association, 1987), 34; Dino Cinel, "Italians in the South: The Alabama Case," *Italian Americana* 9, no. 1 (Winter 1990): 7–24; John Santucci, "Early 20th Century Inter-Ethnic Relations: A Case Study in North Carolina," in *Italian Americans in Transition,* ed. Joseph V. Scelsa, Salvatore J. LaGumina, and Lydio Tomasi (Staten Island: American Italian Historical Association, 1990), 127–35; Jerome Krase, "Ironies of Icons: The Slings and Arrows of Outrageous Multiculturalists," in *Italian Americans in a Multicultural Society,* 13–14; Jacobson, *Whiteness of a Different Color,* 56–62; Peter Vellon, "Victims of the Mob: Lynching, the Italian-American Press, and the Racial 'In-betweeness' of Southern Italian Immigrants in the American South, 1891–1927," paper presented at the 32nd annual conference of the American Italian Historical Association, San Francisco CA, 11–13 Nov. 1999.

11. Gordon H. Shufelt, "Strangers in a Middle Land: Italian Immigrants and Race Relations in Baltimore, 1890–1920" (Ph.D. diss., American University, 1998).

12. Ralph Basso, *History of Roseto, Pennsylvania* (Easton PA: Tanzella, 1952), 7–29; Clement Valletta, *A Study of Americanization in Carneta: Italian-American Identity through Three Generations* (New York: Arno Press, 1980), a work in which Roseto is fictitiously dubbed Carneta; Valletta, "The Settlement of Roseto: World View and Promise," in *The Ethnic Experience in Pennsylvania,* 120–43; Carla Bianco, "Emigrazione America / Emigration America," in *Emigrazione / Emigration,* ed. Bianco and Emanuela Agiuli (Bari: Dedalo, 1980), 14–15; Rudolph J. Vecoli, "The Formation of Chicago's 'Little Italies,'" in *Migration Across Time and Nations: Population Mobility in Historical Contexts,* ed. Ira A. Glazier and Luigi De Rosa (New York: Holmes & Meier, 1986), 287–301.

13. Richard N. Juliani, "Social Change and the Ethnic Community: The Italians in Philadelphia," in *Dialettica locale-globale: Continuità e contraddizioni del mondo,* ed. Mario Aldo Toscano (Naples: Ipermedium, 1997), 62–63; Richard N. Juliani, "Community and Identity: Continuity and Change Among Italian Americans in Philadelphia," *Italian American Review* 6, no. 2 (Autumn 1997/Winter 1998): 52–53.

14. Nancy Torrieri, "The Geography of Ethnicity: The Residential Dispersal of Italians in Baltimore," in *Italian Americans in Transition,* 49–64; Dianne Dumanowski, "Boston's Italian North End: Changing Immigrant Still Is 'Home' to Former Residents," *American Preservation* 2, no. 3 (Feb.–Mar. 1979): 42–49; Anthony V. Riccio, *Portrait of an Italian-American Neighborhood: The North End of Boston* (Staten Island: Center for Migration Studies, 1998), 121, 157–63, 167–72; Sergio Campailla, "Little Italy," in *Il sogno italo-americano,* 52; Jerome Krase, "America's Little Italies: Past, Present, and Future," in *Italian Ethnics: Their Languages, Literature, and Life,* ed. Dominick Candeloro et al. (Staten Island:

American Italian Historical Association, 1990), 168–69; Julie P. Curson, *A Guide's Guide to Philadelphia* (Philadelphia: Curson House, 1991), 52, 301–2.

15. Alba, *Italian Americans*, 162.

16. Martinelli, "Italian-American Experience," 226–27; Dominic R. Massaro, "Italian Americans as a Cognizable Racial Group," in *Italian Americans in a Multicultural Society*, 44–55; Juliani, "Identity and Ethnicity," 57; Richard Gambino, "The Crisis of Italian American Identity," in *Beyond the Godfather: Italian American Writers on the Real Italian American Experience*, ed. A. Kenneth Ciongoli and Jay Parini (Hanover: University Press of New England, 1997), 269–88.

17. Hollinger, *Postethnic America*, 166 (to which the first quotation refers); David A. Hollinger, "How Wide Is the Circle of the 'We'? American Intellectuals and the Problem of the Ethnos since World War II," *American Historical Review* 98, no. 2 (Apr. 1993): 317–37.

Bibliography

A. Manuscript Collections

Archivio Centrale dello Stato, Rome, Italy
Papers of the Ministero della Cultura Popolare.
Ministero dell'Interno, Direzione Generale di Pubblica Sicurezza, Casellario Politico Centrale.
Segreteria Particolare del Duce, Carteggio Ordinario, 1922–1943.

Archivio Storico del Ministero degli Affari Esteri, Rome, Italy
Papers of the Ministry of Foreign Affairs.

Balch Institute for Ethnic Studies, Philadelphia PA
Ralph Borrelli Papers.
Leonard Covello Papers.
Vito Mazzone Papers.
Francesco Saracco Papers.
Giambattista Scandella Papers.
Papers of the Società di Mutuo Soccorso fra Castrogiovannesi e Provinciali.
Records of the WPA Historical Survey, Ethnic Survey, 1938–1941, Job. no. 66, "Italians in Pennsylvania."
Nicholas J. A. Tumolo Papers.

Biblioteca di Storia e Letteratura Nordamericana, University of Florence, Florence, Italy

Carlo Tresca, "Autobiography," typescript.

Gerald R. Ford Library, Ann Arbor MI

Myron Kuropas Files.
Charles McCall Files.
White House Central Files.

Historical Society of Pennsylvania, Philadelphia

Richardson Dilworth Papers.
J. Hampton Moore Papers.

Herbert Hoover Presidential Library, West Branch IA

Herbert Hoover Presidential Papers.
James Westbrook Papers.

Immigration History Research Center, University of Minnesota, St. Paul MN

Luigi Cipolla Papers.
Giovanni Di Silvestro Papers.
Papers of the Pennsylvania Grand Lodge of the Order Sons of Italy in America.

Lyndon B. Johnson Library, Austin TX

John B. Connally Papers.

Library of Congress, Washington DC

Calvin Coolidge Papers.

Seedley G. Mudd Library, Princeton University, Princeton NJ

David A. Reed Papers.

National Archives II, College Park MD

Department of State, Record Group 59.
Richard M. Nixon Presidential Material Project.
Records of the Office of Public Opinion Studies.

National Archives, Mid Atlantic Region Branch, Philadelphia
Eastern District of Pennsylvania, Naturalization Records.

Richard M. Nixon Library & Birthplace, Yorba Linda CA
Richard M. Nixon Post-Presidential Papers.

Pennsylvania State Archives, Harrisburg PA
Records of the Department of State.
Edward Martin Papers.

Philadelphia City Archives, Philadelphia
County Board of Elections of Philadelphia, tabulation sheets of the election returns.
Records of the Department of Public Works.
Street Lists of Voters.

Phillips Memorial Library, Providence College, Providence RI
John E. Fogarty Papers.

Franklin D. Roosevelt Library, Hyde Park NY
Adolf A. Berle Papers.
Francis Biddle Papers.
Lorena Hickok Papers.
Papers of the National Committee of the Democratic Party.
Franklin D. Roosevelt Papers.

Temple University Urban Archives, Paley Library, Philadelphia
Americans for Democratic Action Papers.
Papers of the Citizens' Committee to Recall Rizzo.
Papers of the Committee of Seventy.
Papers of the Philadelphia Joint Board of the Amalgamated Clothing Workers of America.
Walter M. Phillips Papers.
U.S. Bureau of the Census, unpublished work sheets for the fifteenth Census of the United States, 1930.

Harry S. Truman Library, Independence MO
Philleo Nash Papers.
Harry S. Truman Papers.

University of Pennsylvania Archives, Philadelphia PA
George W. Pepper Papers.

Washington and Jefferson College, Washington PA
Joseph F. Guffey Papers.

B. Oral Sources

Interviews by the author
Frank C., Philadelphia, 12 Aug. 1989.
Rita R., Philadelphia, 12 Nov. 1989.

Ellis Island Oral History Project
Josephine Reale, interview no. 71 by Nancy Dallett, Haverton PA, 25 Oct. 1985.
Joseph Talese, interview no. 61 by Nancy Dallett, Ocean City NJ, 25 Oct. 1985.

Walter M. Phillips Oral History Project Transcripts, Temple University Archives, Paley Library, Philadelphia
Walter D'Alessio, Philadelphia, 7 June 1977.
Paul D'Ortona, Philadelphia, 17 May 1977.
Thomas M. Foglietta, Philadelphia, 24 June 1980.

C. Newspapers

L'Aurora, 1935–1936.
La Comune, 1912–1915.
Corriere d'America, 1927.
Cronaca Sovversiva, 1915.
Evening Bulletin, 1918, 1920–1924, 1928, 1942, 1944, 1948, 1971, 1973, 1976.
Evening Ledger, 1922.
Giuseppe Garibaldi, 7 July 1907.

Indiana Democrat, 1928.
Italian-American Herald, 1961.
La Libera Parola, 1918–1967.
Il Martello, 1923, 1934.
Il Momento, 1917–1919.
News Bulletin, 1939.
New York Times, 1944, 1948, 1967, 1995.
Observer, 1938, 1940, 1942.
L'Opinione, 1906–1907, 1927–1935.
Ordine Nuovo, 1936–1953.
Philadelphia Daily News, 1928, 1934, 1975–1976, 1978, 1987.
Philadelphia Exclusive, 1971–1972.
Philadelphia Inquirer, 1917–1994.
Philadelphia Record, 1935, 1940, 1942, 1943.
La Plebe, 1907–1908.
Il Popolo, 1905–1906.
Il Popolo Italiano, 1935–1967.
Il Progresso Italo-Americano, 1935–1937, 1941–1942, 1946, 1948, 1953.
Public Ledger, 1918–1933.
La Ragione, 1917.
La Rassegna, 1917.
Sons of Italy Times, 1967–1991.
South Phila American, 1942, 1967.
South Phila American Weekly, 1938.
Southwark Courier, 1943.
La Voce Indipendente, 1938.

D. Government Publications: Volumes

Annual Reports of the Registration Commission for the City of Philadelphia. 46 vols. Philadelphia: Dunlap, 1926–1971.

Congress and the Nation, 1945–1964: A Review of Government and Politics in the Postwar Years. Washington DC: Congressional Quarterly Service, 1965.

Congressional Record. Washington DC: U.S. Government Printing Office, 1927.

Foreign Relations of the United States: Diplomatic Papers, 1935. Washington DC: U.S. Government Printing Office, 1952.

Journal of the Common Council of the City of Philadelphia. 40 vols. Philadelphia, 1880–1919.

Journal of the House of Representatives of the Commonwealth of Pennsylvania. Harrisburg PA: Commonwealth of Pennsylvania, 1939.

Journal of the Selected Council of the City of Philadelphia. 40 vols. Philadelphia, 1880–1919.

Journal of the Senate of the Commonwealth of Pennsylvania. Harrisburg PA: Commonwealth of Pennsylvania, 1939.

Laws of the General Assembly of the Commonwealth of Pennsylvania Passed at the Session of 1939 in the One Hundred and Sixty-Third Year of Independence. Harrisburg PA: Commonwealth of Pennsylvania, 1939.

Manual of the City Council of Philadelphia. Philadelphia: Dunlap, 38 vols. 1920–1957.

Pennsylvania Committee on Public Assistance and Relief. *The Relief Population of Pennsylvania: Report of a Statistical Study of Relief Recipients.* Harrisburg PA: Commonwealth of Pennsylvania, 1936.

The Pennsylvania Manual. 29 vols. Harrisburg PA: Commonwealth of Pennsylvania, 1929–1985.

The Pennsylvania State Manual. 2 vols. Harrisburg PA: Commonwealth of Pennsylvania, 1925–1927.

President's Commission on Immigration and Naturalization. *Whom We Shall Welcome.* 1953. New York: Da Capo Press, 1971.

Smull's Legislative Hand Book and Manual of the State of Pennsylvania. 22 vols. Harrisburg PA: J. L. L. Kuhn, 1881–1923.

U.S. Bureau of the Census. *Tenth Census of the United States: Statistics of Population.* Washington DC: U.S. Government Printing Office, 1882.

———. *Eleventh Census of the United States: Statistics of Population.* Washington DC: U.S. Government Printing Office, 1892.

———. *Twelfth Census of the United States Taken in the Year 1900: Population.* Washington DC: U.S. Government Printing Office, 1902.

———. *Thirteenth Census of the United States Taken in the Year 1910: Population.* Washington DC: U.S. Government Printing Office, 1913.

———. *Fourteenth Census of the United States Taken in the Year 1920: Population.* Washington DC: U.S. Government Printing Office, 1922.

———. *Fifteenth Census of the United States: 1930, Population.* Washington DC: U.S. Government Printing Office, 1932.

———. *16th Census of the United States: Population and Housing, Statistics for Census Tracts, Philadelphia.* Washington DC: U.S. Government Printing Office, 1942.

———. *1950 Population Census Report: Census Tract Statistics: Philadelphia, Pennsylvania, and Adjacent Area.* Washington DC: U.S. Government Printing Office, 1952.

———. *1960 Census of Population: Characteristics of the Population: Pennsylvania.* Washington DC: U.S. Government Printing Office, 1963.

———. *Statistical Abstract of the United States: 1966.* Washington DC: U.S. Government Printing Office, 1966.

———. *1970 Census of Population: Characteristics of the Population: Pennsylvania.* Washington DC: U.S. Government Printing Office, 1973.

———. *1980 Census of Population: Characteristics of the Population: General Social and Economic Characteristics: Pennsylvania.* Washington DC: U.S. Government Printing Office, 1983.

———. *1990 Census of Population: Social and Economic Characteristics: Pennsylvania.* Washington DC: U.S. Government Printing Office, 1993.

U.S. House of Representatives, 74th Cong., 2d Sess. *Hearings before the Committee on Foreign Affairs on H. J. Res. 422 to Maintain the Neutrality of the United States in the Event of War or Threat of War between or among Foreign Nations.* Washington DC: U.S. Government Printing Office, 1936.

———. 79th Cong., 1st Sess. *Hearings before the Committee of Foreign Affairs Pursuant to H. J. Res. 99, a Joint Resolution Requesting the President to Recognize Italy as an Ally and to Extend Lend-Lease Aid.* Washington DC: U.S. Government Printing Office, 1945.

U.S. Senate, 61st Cong., 3d Sess. *Reports of the Immigration Commission.* 41 vols. 1911. New York: Arno Press, 1969.

———. 80th Cong., 1st Sess. *Hearings before the Committee on Foreign Relations on Executives F, G, H, and I: Treaties of Peace with Italy, Rumania, Bulgaria, and Hungary.* Washington DC: U.S. Government Printing Office, 1947.

———. 81st Cong., 2d Sess. *Investigation of Organized Crime in Interstate Commerce: Hearings before the Special Committee to Investigate Crime in Interstate Commerce Pursuant to S. Res. 202,* 16 vols. Washington DC: U.S. Government Printing Office, 1951.

———. 82d Cong., 1st Sess. *Third Interim Report of the Special Committee to Investigate Crime in Interstate Commerce Pursuant to S. Res. 202.* Washington DC: U.S. Government Printing Office, 1951.

U.S. Treasury Department. *Annual Reports and Statements of the Chief of the Bureau of Statistics on the Foreign Commerce and Navigation, Immigration and Tonnage of the United States.* 15 vols. Washington DC: U.S. Government Printing Office, 1880–1894.

E. Government Publications: Articles

Koren, John. "The Padrone System and Padrone Banks." *Bulletin of the Bureau of Labor* no. 9 (Mar. 1897): 113–29.

"Unemployment in Philadelphia, April, 1930." *Monthly Labor Review* 31, no. 1 (July 1930): 35–37.

"Unemployment in Philadelphia, April, 1931." *Monthly Labor Review* 33, no. 1 (July 1931): 66–69.

"Unemployment Survey of Metropolitan Life Insurance Co." *Monthly Labor Review* 32, no. 3 (Mar. 1931): 48–55.

"Unemployment Survey of Philadelphia, 1929." *Monthly Labor Review* 30, no. 2 (Feb. 1930): 17–24.

F. Memoirs

Biddle, Francis. *In Brief Authority*. Garden City NY: Doubleday, 1962.
Grandi, Dino. *Il mio paese: Ricordi autobiografici*. Renzo De Felice, ed. Bologna: Il Mulino, 1985.
Guffey, Joseph F. *Seventy Years on the Red-Fire Wagon: From Tilden to Truman through New Freedom and New Deal*. n.p.: privately printed, 1952.
Martin, Edward. *Always Be On Time: An Autobiography*. Harrisburg PA: Telegraph Press, 1959.
Salvadori, Massimo. *Resistenza ed azione (Ricordi di un liberale)*. Bari: Laterza, 1951.
Salvemini, Gaetano. *Memorie di un fuoruscito*. Gaetano Arfè, ed. Milan: Feltrinelli, 1960.
Stern, David. *Memoirs of a Maverick Publisher*. New York: Simon and Schuster, 1962.

G. Volumes

Adams, Carolyn, et al. *Neighborhoods, Division, and Conflict in a Postindustrial City*. Philadelphia: Temple University Press, 1991.
Aquilano, Baldo. *L'Ordine Figli d'Italia in America*. New York: Società Tipografica Italiana, 1925.
Alba, Richard D. *Italian Americans: Into the Twilight of Ethnicity*. Englewood Cliffs NJ: Prentice Hall, 1985.
———. *Ethnic Identity: The Transformation of White America*. New Haven: Yale University Press, 1990.
Albanese, Catherine L. *A Cobbler's Universe: Religion, Poetry, and Performance in the Life of a South Italian Immigrant*. New York: Continuum, 1997.
Albini, Joseph L. *The American Mafia: Genesis of a Legend*. New York: Meredith, 1971.
Allen, Theodore W. *The Invention of the White Race: Racial Oppression and Social Control*. New York: Verso, 1994.
———. *The Invention of the White Race: The Origin of Racial Oppression in Anglo-America*. New York: Verso, 1997.
Allswang, John M. *A House for All Peoples: Ethnic Politics in Chicago, 1890–1936*. Lexington: University Press of Kentucky, 1971.
American Newspaper Annual and Directory. 3 vols. Philadelphia: N. W. Ayer and Son, 1920, 1930, 1936.

Appiah, Kwame Anthony. *In My Father's House: Africa in the Philosophy of Culture*. New York: Oxford University Press, 1992.

Arpea, Mario. *Alle origini dell'emigrazione abruzzese: La vicenda dell'altipiano delle Rocche*. Milan: Franco Angeli, 1987.

Assefa, Hizkias, and Paul Wahrhaftig. *The Move Crisis in Philadelphia: Extremist Groups and Conflict Resolution*. Pittsburgh: University of Pittsburgh Press, 1990.

Banner-Haley, Charles Peter T. *To Do Good and To Do Well: Middle-Class Blacks and the Depression, Philadelphia, 1929–1941*. New York: Garland, 1993.

Barone, Michael, and Grant Ujifusa. *The Almanac of American Politics: 1984*. Washington DC: National Journal, 1983.

Barton, Joseph J. *Peasants and Strangers: Italians, Rumanians, and Slovaks in an American City, 1890–1950*. Cambridge MA.: Harvard University Press, 1975.

Basso, Ralph. *History of Roseto, Pennsylvania*. Easton PA: Tanzella, 1952.

Bastianini, Giuseppe. *Gli italiani all'estero*. Milan: Mondadori, 1939.

Bauman, John F. *Public Housing, Race, and Renewal: Urban Planning in Philadelphia, 1920–1974*. Philadelphia: Temple University Press, 1987.

———, and Thomas H. Coode. *In the Eye of the Great Depression: New Deal Reporters and the Agony of the American People*. DeKalb IL: Northern Illinois University Press, 1988.

Bayor, Ronald H. *Neighbors in Conflict: The Irish, Germans, Jews, and Italians of New York City, 1929–1941*. Baltimore: Johns Hopkins University Press, 1978.

Beckman, Theodore N., and Herman C. Nolen. *The Chain Store Problem: A Critical Analysis*. New York: McGraw-Hill, 1938.

Beers, Paul B. *Pennsylvania Politics Today and Yesterday: The Tolerable Accommodation*. University Park PA: Pennsylvania State University Press, 1980.

Belliotti, Raymond A. *Seeking Identity: Individualism Versus Community in an Ethnic Context*. Lawrence: University Press of Kansas, 1995.

Bennet, David H. *Demagogues in the Depression: American Radicals and the Union Party, 1932–1936*. New Brunswick NJ: Rutgers University Press, 1969.

Bernardi, Amy. *America Vissuta*. Turin: Bocca, 1911.

Berson, Lenora. *Case Study of a Riot*. New York: Institute of Human Relations Press, 1966.

Biagi, Ernest L. *The Purple Aster: A History of the Sons of Italy in America*. n.p.: Veritas Press, 1961.

———. *The Italians of Philadelphia*. New York: Carlton Press, 1967.

Bianco, Carla. *The Two Rosetos*. Bloomington: Indiana University Press, 1974.

Biggin, Bill. *Rizzo and the Police State*. Philadelphia: Free Press, 1971.

Binchy, Daniel A. *Church and State in Fascist Italy*. London: Oxford University Press, 1970.

Binzen, Peter. *Whitetown, U.S.A*. New York: Random House, 1971.

Bissinger, Buzz. *A Prayer for the City*. New York: Random House, 1997.

Blum, John Morton. *V Was for Victory: Politics and American Culture during World War II*. New York: Harcourt Brace Jovanovich, 1976.

Bodnar, John. *Remaking America: Public Memory, Commemoration, and Patriotism in the Twentieth Century.* Princeton: Princeton University Press, 1991.

Boscia-Mulè, Patricia. *Authentic Ethnicities: The Interaction of Ideology, Gender Power, and Class in the Italian-American Experience.* Westport CT: Greenwood Press, 1999.

Bowser, Charles W. *Let the Bunker Burn: The Final Battle with MOVE.* Philadelphia: Camino Books, 1989.

Briggs, John W. *An Italian Passage: Immigrants to Three American Cities, 1890–1930.* New Haven: Yale University Press, 1978.

Brinkley, Alan. *Voices of Protest: Huey Long, Father Coughlin, and the Great Depression.* New York: Alfred A. Knopf, 1982.

Brizzolara, Andrew, ed. *A Directory of Italian and Italian-American Organizations and Community Services.* Staten Island: Center for Migration Studies, 1976.

Brodkin, Karen. *How Jews Became White Folks and What That Says About Race in America.* New Brunswick NJ: Rutgers University Press, 1998.

Brown, Peter. *Minority Party: Why Democrats Face Defeat in 1992 and Beyond.* Washington DC: Gateway, 1991.

The Bulletin Almanac and Year Book. 2 vols. Philadelphia: Evening Bulletin, 1937–1938.

Burner, David. *The Politics of Provincialism: The Democratic Party in Transition, 1918–1932.* New York: Alfred A. Knopf, 1967.

Campbell, Paul R., and Patrick T. Conley. *The Aurora Club of Rhode Island: A Fifty Year History.* Providence RI: Aurora Civic Association, 1982.

Carnevale, Joseph William. *Americans of Italian Descent in Philadelphia and Vicinity.* Philadelphia: Ferguson, 1954.

Carter, Dan T. *From George Wallace to Newt Gingrich: Race in the Conservative Counterrevolution, 1963–1994.* Baton Rouge: Louisiana State University Press, 1996.

Cassigoli, B. R., and H. Chiariglione. *Libro d'oro degli italiani d'America: Con descrizioni e biografie.* Pueblo, 1904.

Castagna, Biagio. *Bozzetti americani e coloniali: Filadelfia, Stati Uniti d'America.* Salerno: Jovane, 1907.

C. C. A. Baldi Middle School. *Handbook.* Philadelphia: C. C. A. Baldi Middle School, 1986.

Centennial Jubilee: St. Mary Magdalen De Pazzi Parish. Philadelphia: Morgan Printing Co., 1952.

Cerase, Francesco Paolo. *L'emigrazione di ritorno: Innovazione o reazione? L'esperienza dell'emigrazione di ritorno dagli Stati Uniti d'America.* Rome: Facoltà di scienze statistiche demografiche e attuariali dell'Università di Roma, 1971.

Chalmers, David M. *Hooded Americanism: The First Century of the Ku Klux Klan, 1865–1965.* Garden City NY: Doubleday, 1965.

Chi può emigrare negli Stati Uniti: Le norme della legge McCarran-Walter. Rome: Italiani nel Mondo, 1953.

Cinel, Dino. *From Italy to San Francisco: The Immigrant Experience.* Stanford: Stanford University Press, 1982.

———. *The National Integration of Italian Return Migration, 1870–1929.* New York: Cambridge University Press, 1991.

Circolo Maidese in Philadelphia. *Atti ufficiali del banchetto inaugurale, 14 marzo 1934–XII.* Philadelphia, 1934.

Clark, Martin. *Modern Italy, 1871–1982.* London: Longman, 1984.

Cohen, Lizabeth. *Making a New Deal: Industrial Workers in Chicago, 1919–1939.* New York: Cambridge University Press, 1990.

Community Council of Philadelphia. *Neighborhood Relief in Philadelphia: A Study of Sixty Local Relief Agencies Active During the Winter of 1930–1931.* Philadelphia: Community Council of Philadelphia, 1931.

Constitution and By-Laws of the Christopher Columbus Mutual Aid Society. Philadelphia, 1901.

Cooney, John. *The Annenbergs.* New York: Simon and Schuster, 1982.

Corti, Paola. *L'emigrazione.* Rome: Editori Riuniti, 1999.

Covello, Leonard, and Anita E. Giacobbe. *First Book in Italian.* New York: Macmillan, 1938.

Crispino, James A. *The Assimilation of Ethnic Groups: The Italian Case.* Staten Island: Center for Migration Studies, 1979.

Cuomo, Mario M. *Forest Hills Diary: The Crisis of Low-Income Housing.* New York: Random House, 1974.

Curson, Julie P. *A Guide's Guide to Philadelphia.* Philadelphia: Curson House, 1991.

Dahl, Robert A. *Who Governs? Democracy and Power in an American City.* New Haven: Yale University Press, 1961.

Damiani, Claudia. *Mussolini e gli Stati Uniti, 1922–1935.* Bologna: Cappelli, 1980.

Daughen, Joseph R., and Peter Binzen, *The Cop Who Would Be King: Mayor Frank Rizzo.* Boston: Little, Brown, 1977.

De Conde, Alexander. *Half Bitter, Half Sweet: An Excursion into Italian-American History.* New York: Charles Scribner's Sons, 1971.

De Biasi, Agostino. *La battaglia dell'Italia negli Stati Uniti: Articoli e note polemiche.* New York: Il Carroccio, 1927.

De Felice, Renzo. *Storia degli ebrei italiani sotto il fascismo.* 1961. Turin: Einaudi, 1993.

De Marco, William M. *Ethnics and Enclaves: Boston's Italian North End.* Ann Arbor, MI: UMI Research Press, 1980.

Diggins, John P. *Mussolini and Fascism: The View from America.* Princeton: Princeton University Press, 1972.

Di Leonardo, Michela. *The Varieties of Ethnic Experience: Kinship, Class, and Gender among California Italian Americans.* Ithaca: Cornell University Press, 1984.

Discovery: The Columbus Legacy. Harrisburg PA: Pennsylvania Historical and Museum Commission, 1989.

Di Silvestro, Giovanni. *Note e appunti sulle colonie italiane degli Stati Uniti del Nord.* Philadelphia: Stabilimento Tipografico de "La Voce del Popolo," 1908.

Divine, Robert A. *American Immigration Policy, 1924–1952.* New Haven: Yale University Press, 1957.

Dubin, Murray. *South Philadelphia: Mummers, Memories, and the Melrose Diner.* Philadelphia: Temple University Press, 1996.

Edsall, Thomas Byrne, and Mary D. Edsall, *Chain Reaction: The Impact of Race, Rights, and Taxes on American Politics.* New York: Norton, 1991.

Ehrenhalt, Alan, ed. *Politics in America: The 100th Congress.* Washington DC: Congressional Quarterly, 1987.

Erdmans, Mary Patrice. *Opposite Poles: Immigrants and Ethnics in Polish Chicago, 1976–1990.* University Park PA: Pennsylvania State University Press, 1998.

Ericksen, Eugene, et al. *The State of Puerto Rican Philadelphia.* Philadelphia: Temple University Institute for Public Policy Studies, 1985.

Ets, Marie Hall. *Rosa: The Life of an Italian Immigrant.* Minneapolis: University of Minnesota Press, 1970.

Falco, Maria J. *"Bigotry!" Ethnic, Machine, and Sexual Politics in a Senatorial Election.* Westport CT: Greenwood Press, 1980.

Featherman, Sandra. *Philadelphia Elects a Black Mayor: How Jews, Blacks, and Ethnics Vote in the 1980s.* Philadelphia: American Jewish Committee, 1984.

———. *Jews, Blacks, and Urban Politics in the 1980s: The Case of Philadelphia.* Philadelphia: American Jewish Committee, 1988.

———, and Allan B. Hill. *Ethnic Voting in the 1991 Philadelphia Mayoral Election.* New York: American Jewish Committee, 1992.

———, and William S. Rosenberg. *Jews, Blacks, and Ethnics: The 1978 "Vote White" Campaign in Philadelphia.* New York: American Jewish Committee, 1979.

Fenno, Richard F. Jr. *Learning to Legislate: The Senate Education of Arlen Specter.* Washington DC: CQ Press, 1991.

Ferraro, Geraldine, with Linda Bird Francke. *Ferraro: My Story.* Toronto: Bantam Books, 1985.

———, with Catherine Whitney. *Framing a Life: A Family Memoirs.* New York: Charles Scribner's Sons, 1998.

The Festival of Italy: Celebrating the 100th Anniversary of Italian Unification, January 21 to March 26, 1961. Philadelphia: Commercial Museum, 1961.

Feuerlicht, Roberta Strauss. *Justice Crucified: The Story of Sacco and Vanzetti.* New York: McGraw-Hill, 1977.

Foerster, Robert F. *The Italian Emigration of Our Times.* New York: Russell and Russell, 1919.
Fondazione Giovanni Agnelli. *The Italian-Americans: Who They Are, Where They Live, How Many They Are.* Turin: Fondazione Giovanni Agnelli, 1980.
Fontenay, Charles L. *Estes Kefauver: A Biography.* Knoxville: University of Tennessee Press, 1980.
Fonzi, Gaeton. *Annenberg: A Biography of Power.* New York: Weybright and Talley, 1969.
Forer, Lois G. *No One Will Listen: How Our Legal System Brutalized the Youthful Poor.* New York: John Day, 1970.
Formisano, Ronald P. *Boston Against Busing: Race, Class, and Ethnicity in the 1960s and 1970s.* Chapel Hill: University of North Carolina Press, 1991.
Fox, Stephen. *The Unknown Internment: An Oral History of the Relocation of Italian Americans during World War II.* Boston: Twayne, 1990.
Frangini, A. *Italiani in Filadelfia: Strenna nazionale: Cenni biografici.* Philadelphia: Stabilimento Tipografico "L'Opinione," 1907.
Franzina, Emilio. *Gli Italiani al Nuovo Mondo: L'emigrazione italiana in America, 1492–1942.* Milan: Mondadori, 1995.
Freedman, Robert, L. *A Report on Politics in Philadelphia.* Cambridge MA: Joint Center for Urban Studies of the Massachusetts Institute of Technology and Harvard University, 1963.
Freeland, Richard M. *The Truman Doctrine and the Origin of McCarthyism: Foreign Policy, Domestic Politics, and Internal Security, 1946–1948.* New York: Schocken Books, 1970.
Gabaccia, Donna R. *From Sicily to Elizabeth Street: Housing and Social Change among Italian Immigrants, 1880–1930.* Albany: State University of New York Press, 1984.
———. *Militants and Migrants: Rural Sicilians Become American Workers.* New Brunswick NJ: Rutgers University Press, 1988.
Gallagher, Dorothy. *All the Right Enemies: The Life and Murder of Carlo Tresca.* New Brunswick NJ: Rutgers University Press, 1988.
Gallo, Patrick J. *Old Bread, New Wine: A Portrait of the Italian Americans.* Chicago: Nelson-Hall, 1981.
Gambino, Richard. *Blood of My Blood: The Dilemma of the Italian Americans.* 1974. Toronto: Guernica, 1996.
———. *Vendetta: A True Story of the Worst Lynching in America: the Mass Murder of Italian Americans in New Orleans in 1891, the Vicious Motivations Behind It, and the Tragic Repercussions That Linger to This Day.* Garden City NY: Doubleday, 1977.
Gamm, Gerald H. *The Making of New Deal Democrats: Voting Behavior and Realignment in Boston, 1920–1940.* Chicago: University of Chicago Press, 1989.
Gans, Herbert J. *The Urban Villagers: Group and Class in the Life of Italian Americans.* New York: Free Press, 1962.

Gerson, Louis. *The Hyphenate in Recent American Politics and Diplomacy.* Lawrence: University of Kansas Press, 1964.
Gerstle, Gary. *Working-Class Americanism: The Politics of Labor in a Textile City, 1914–1960.* New York: Cambridge University Press, 1989.
Glazer, Nathan, and Daniel Patrick Moynihan. *Beyond the Melting Pot: The Negroes, Puerto Ricans, Jews, Italians, and Irish of New York City.* Cambridge MA: MIT Press, 1963.
Golab, Caroline. *Immigrant Destinations.* Philadelphia: Temple University Press, 1977.
Goode, Judith, and Jo Ann Schneider. *Reshaping Ethnic and Racial Relations in Philadelphia: Immigrants in a Divided City.* Philadelphia: Temple University Press, 1994.
Goode, W. Wilson, with Joann Stevens. *In Goode Faith.* Valley Forge PA: Judson Press, 1992.
Graebner, Norman A. *The New Isolationism: A Study in Politics and Foreign Policy since 1950.* New York: Roland Press, 1956.
Greeley, Andrew M. *Ethnicity in the United States: A Preliminary Reconnaissance.* New York: Wiley, 1974.
Greene, Victor R. *For God and Country: The Rise of Polish and Lithuanian Ethnic Consciousness in America, 1860–1910.* Madison: State Historical Society of Wisconsin, 1975.
———. *American Immigrant Leaders, 1800–1910: Marginality and Identity.* Baltimore: Johns Hopkins University Press, 1987.
Grifo, Richard D., and Anthony F. Noto, *Italian Presence in Pennsylvania.* University Park PA: Pennsylvania Historical Association, 1990.
Hamilton, Fred. *Rizzo.* New York: Viking Press, 1973.
Harris, Chester. *Tiger at the Bar: The Life Story of Charles J. Margiotti.* New York: Vantage Press, 1956.
Higham, John. *Strangers in the Land: Patterns of American Nativism.* New Brunswick NJ: Rutgers University Press, 1955.
Hirsch, Arnold H. *Making the Second Ghetto: Race and Housing in Chicago, 1940–1960.* New York: Cambridge University Press, 1983.
History of the Società di Unione e Fratellanza Italiana. Philadelphia, 1929.
Holli, Melvin G. *The American Mayor: The Best and Worst Big-City Leaders.* University Park PA: Pennsylvania State University Press, 1999.
Hollinger, David A. *Postethnic America: Beyond Multiculturalism.* New York: Basic Books, 1995.
Howells, William Dean. *Italian Journeys.* London: William Heinemann, 1901.
Hutchinson, Edward Prince. *Legislative History of American Immigration Policy, 1798–1965.* Philadelphia: Balch Institute Press, 1981.
Ignatiev, Noel. *How the Irish Became White.* New York: Routledge, 1995.
Iorizzo, Luciano, ed. *An Inquiry into Organized Crime.* Staten Island: American Italian Historical Association, n.d.

Iorizzo, Luciano, and Salvatore Mondello. *The Italian Americans*. 1971. Boston: Twayne, 1980.

Isoleri, Antonio. *"Pati, Non Mori!"*. Philadelphia: Penn Printing House, 1891.

———. *Un ricordo delle feste colombiane celebrate in Philadelphia, Stati Uniti d'America, nell'ottobre del 1892*. Philadelphia: Penn Printing House, 1893.

Jackson, Kenneth T. *The Ku Klux Klan in the City, 1915–1930*. New York: Oxford University Press, 1967.

Jacobson, Matthew Frye. *Whiteness of a Different Color: European Immigrants and the Alchemy of Race*. Cambridge MA: Harvard University Press, 1998.

Jeffries, John W. *Testing the Roosevelt Coalition: Connecticut Society and Politics in the Era of World War II*. Knoxville: University of Tennessee Press, 1979.

Jenkins, Philip. *Hoods and Shirts: The Extreme Right in Pennsylvania, 1925–1950*. Chapel Hill: University of North Carolina Press, 1997.

———. *The Cold War at Home: The Red Scare in Pennsylvania, 1945–1960*. Chapel Hill: University of North Carolina Press, 1999.

Juliani, Richard N. *The Social Organization of Immigration: The Italians in Philadelphia*. New York: Arno Press, 1980.

———. *Building Little Italy: Philadelphia's Italians Before Mass Migration*. University Park PA: Pennsylvania State University Press, 1998.

Kanawada, Leo V. Jr. *Franklin D. Roosevelt Diplomacy and American Catholics, Italians, and Jews*. Ann Arbor: UMI Research Press, 1982.

Kefauver, Estes. *Crime in America*. Garden City NY: Doubleday, 1951.

Klein, Philip S., and Ari Hoogenboom. *A History of Pennsylvania*. New York: McGraw-Hill, 1973.

Kogan, Norman. *Italy and the Allies*. Cambridge MA: Harvard University Press, 1956.

Kupferstein, Linda M. *William A. Barrett: Democratic Representative from Pennsylvania*. Washington DC: Grossman, 1972.

Kurtzman, David H. *Methods of Controlling Votes in Philadelphia*. Philadelphia: University of Pennsylvania Press, 1935.

La Colonia italiana di Filadelfia all'esposizione di Milano. Philadelphia: Officine Tipografiche del Giornale "L'Opinione," 1906.

LaGumina, Salvatore J., ed. *Wop! A Documentary History of Anti-Italian Discrimination in the United States*. San Francisco: Straight Arrow Books, 1973.

———. *From Steerage to Suburbs: Long Island's Italians*. Staten Island: Center for Migration Studies, 1988.

———. *New York at Mid-Century: The Impellitteri Years*. Westport CT: Greenwood Press, 1992.

La Mar, Elden. *The Clothing Workers in Philadelphia: History of Their Struggles for Union and Security*. Philadelphia: Philadelphia Joint Board of the Amalgamated Clothing Workers of America, 1940.

Leonard, Karen Isaksen. *Making Ethnic Choices: California's Punjabi Mexican Americans*. Philadelphia: Temple University Press, 1992.

Levy, Mark L., and Michael S. Kramer. *The Ethnic Factor: How America's Minorities Decide Elections.* New York: Simon and Schuster, 1972.

Lewis, John F. *Christopher Columbus: A Short Oration by John F. Lewis before the United Italian Societies of Philadelphia, October 12, 1892.* Philadelphia: George H. Buchanan, 1892.

Licht, Walter. *Getting Work: Philadelphia, 1840–1950.* Cambridge MA: Harvard University Press, 1992.

Lichtman, Allan J. *Prejudice and the Old Politics: The Presidential Election of 1928.* Chapel Hill: University of North Carolina Press, 1979.

Lipsitz, George. *Rainbow at Midnight: Labor and Culture in the 1940s.* Urbana: University of Illinois Press, 1994.

———. *The Possessive Investment in Whiteness: How White People Profit from Identity Politics.* Philadelphia: Temple University Press, 1998.

Livi Bacci, Massimo. *L'immigrazione e l'assimilazione degli italiani negli Stati Uniti secondo le statistiche demografiche americane.* Milan: Giuffrè, 1961.

Longstreth, W. Thacher, with Dan Rottenberg. *Main Line Wasp: The Education of Thacher Longstreth.* New York: Norton, 1990.

Lopez, Ian F. Harney. *White by Law: The Legal Construction of Race.* New York: New York University Press, 1998.

Loucks, Emerson Hunsberger. *The Ku Klux Klan in Pennsylvania: A Study in Nativism.* Harrisburg PA: Telegraph Press, 1936.

Lubell, Samuel. *The Future of American Politics.* 1952. New York: Harper Colophon Books, 1965.

Lynch, Robert P. *Federal Hill Case Study: The Story of How People Saved Their Neighborhood.* Warren RI: New England Neighborhood Revitalization Center, 1978.

Lyons, Paul. *Philadelphia Communists, 1936–1956.* Philadelphia: Temple University Press, 1982.

McCaffery, Peter. *When Bosses Ruled Philadelphia: The Emergence of the Republican Machine, 1867–1933.* University Park PA: Pennsylvania State University Press, 1993.

McKay, Janet S. *Pennsylvania Children in New Jersey Cranberry Farms.* Philadelphia: Public Education and Child Labor Association of Pennsylvania, 1923.

Mangione, Jerre, and Ben Morreale. *La Storia: Five Centuries of the Italian American Experience.* New York: Harper-Collins, 1992.

Margariti, Antonio. *America! America!.* Casalvelino Scalo: Galzerano, 1980.

Meier, August, and Elliott Rudwick. *Black Detroit and the Rise of UAM.* New York: Oxford University Press, 1979.

Mazzone, Vito C. *Communism: The Satanic Scourge.* Philadelphia: Community Press, 1963.

———. *The Oldest Italian Church in the U.S.A.: Saint Magdalen de Pazzi, Philadelphia, Pa.* Philadelphia: Farr-Welt, 1983.

Migone, Gian Giacomo. *Gli Stati Uniti e il Fascismo: Alle origini dell'egemonia americana in Italia.* Milan: Feltrinelli, 1980.
Militello, Pietro. *Italians in America.* Philadelphia: Franklin, 1973.
Moore, William H. *The Kefauver Committee and the Politics of Crime.* Columbia: University of Missouri Press, 1974.
Morello, Celeste A. *Beyond History: The Times and Peoples of St. Paul's Roman Catholic Church, 1843 to 1993.* Philadelphia: Jeffries & Manz, 1992.
Mormino, Gary Ross. *Immigrants on the Hill: Italian Americans in St. Louis, 1882–1982.* Urbana: University of Illinois Press, 1986.
———, and George E. Pozzetta. *The Immigrant World of Ybor City: Italians and Their Latin Neighbors in Tampa, 1885–1985.* Urbana: University of Illinois Press, 1987.
Muller, Peter O., Kenneth C. Meyer, and Roman A. Cybriwsky. *Metropolitan Philadelphia: A Study of Conflict and Social Cleavages.* Cambridge MA: Ballinger, 1976.
Murray, Robert K. *Red Scare: A Study in National Hysteria, 1919–1920.* Minneapolis: University of Minnesota Press, 1955.
Natali, Alfred M. *St. Mary Magdalen de Pazzi: First Italian Parish in the U.S.A.* Philadelphia, 1991.
Nelli, Humbert S. *Italians in Chicago, 1880–1930: A Study in Ethnic Mobility.* New York: Oxford University Press, 1970.
———. *The Business of Crime: Italian and Syndicate Crime in the United States.* New York: Oxford University Press, 1976.
———. *From Immigrants to Ethnics: The Italian Americans.* New York: Oxford University Press, 1983.
Novak, Michael. *The Rise of Unmeltable Ethnics: Politics and Culture in the Seventies.* New York: Macmillan, 1972.
———. *Unmeltable Ethnics: Politics and Culture in American Life.* New Brunswick NJ: Transaction Publishers, 1996.
Noyes, Dorothy. *Uses of Tradition: Arts of Italian Americans in Philadelphia.* Philadelphia: Samuel S. Fleisher Museum, 1989.
Ogden, Christopher. *Legacy: A Biography of Moses and Walter Annenberg.* Boston: Little, Brown, 1999.
Open House: St. Rita's Parish. Philadelphia, 1972.
Order Sons of Italy in America. *By-Laws of the Grand Lodge of Pennsylvania.* Philadelphia: Model Printing House, 1936.
O'Rourke, Lawrence. *Geno: The Life and Mission of Geno Baroni.* New York: Paulist Press, 1991.
Palmer, Gladys L. *Recent Trends in Employment and Unemployment in Philadelphia.* Philadelphia: Philadelphia Labor Market Studies, 1937.
———, and Ada M. Stoflet. *The Labor Force of the Philadelphia Radio Industry.* Philadelphia: Philadelphia Labor Market Studies, 1938.

Paolantonio, S. A. *Frank Rizzo: The Last Big Man in Big City America*. Philadelphia: Camino, 1993.
Park, Robert A., and Herbert A. Miller. *Old World Traits Transplanted*. Chicago: University of Chicago Press, 1921.
Parker, Thomas F., ed. *Violence in the U.S.*. New York: Facts on File, 1974.
Parrish, Michael E. *Anxious Decades: America in Prosperity and Depression, 1920–1941*. New York: Norton, 1992.
Philadelphia Chamber of Commerce. *Americanization in Philadelphia: A City-Wide Plan of Co-Ordinated Agencies under the Direction of the Americanization Committee*. Philadelphia: Edwin E. Bach, 1923.
Pierce, Neal R. *The Megastates of America: People, Politics, and Power in Ten Great States*. New York: Norton, 1972.
Pisani, Lawrence F. *The Italian in America: A Social Study and History*. New York: Exposition Press, 1957.
Polenberg, Richard. *One Nation Divisible: Class, Race, and Ethnicity in the United States Since 1938*. New York: Viking Press, 1980.
Polk's (Boyd's) Philadelphia (Pennsylvania) City Directories. 3 vols. Philadelphia: R. L. Polk & Co., 1927, 1930, 1935–1936.
Potter, Gary W., and Philip Jenkins. *The City and the Syndicate: Organizing Crime in Philadelphia*. Lexington MA: Ginn Press, 1985.
Preston, William Jr. *Aliens and Dissenters: Federal Suppression of Radicals, 1903–1933*. 1963. Urbana: University of Illinois Press, 1994.
Presbyterian Church of St. Andrew and St. Philip. *Commemorating Seventy-Five Years Work and Worship*. Philadelphia, 1980.
Putnam, Robert D. *Making Democracy Work: Civic Traditions in Modern Italy*. Princeton: Princeton University Press, 1993.
Relazione del Primo e Secondo Congresso degli Italiani degli Stati Uniti. Philadelphia: Nardello Press, 1913.
Renshaw, Patrick. *Il sindacalismo rivoluzionario negli Stati Uniti*. 1967. Bari: Laterza, 1970.
Renzulli, Michele. *L'Italia e il Fascismo negli Stati Uniti d'America*. Rome: Poliglotta, 1938.
Republican National Committee, Research Division and All American Origins Divisions. *Guide Book for Republican Candidates: Re Americans of Italian Origin*. Washington DC, 1952.
Resnik, Henry S. *Turning on the System: War in the Philadelphia Public Schools*. New York: Pantheon Books, 1970.
Riccio, Anthony V. *Portrait of an Italian-American Neighborhood: The North End of Boston*. Staten Island: Center for Migration Studies, 1998.
Richards, David A. J. *Italian American: The Racialization of an Ethnic Identity*. New York: New York University Press, 1999.
Rieder, Jonathan. *Canarsie: The Jews and Italians of Brooklyn Against Liberalism*. Cambridge MA: Harvard University Press, 1985.

Roediger, David R. *The Wages of Whiteness: Race and the American Working Class*. New York: Verso, 1991.

———. *Toward the Abolition of Whiteness: Essays on Race, Politics, and Working Class History*. New York: Verso, 1994.

Rolle, Andrew. *The Italian Americans: Troubled Roots*. Norman: University of Oklahoma Press, 1980.

Romano, Ruggiero. *Paese Italia: Venti secoli di identità*. Rome: Donzelli, 1994.

Roosens, Eugeen E. *Creating Ethnicity: The Process of Ethnogenesis*. Newbury Park CA: Sage, 1989.

Roosevelt, Franklin D. *The Public Papers and Addresses of Franklin D. Roosevelt*. Samuel I. Rosenman, ed. 13 vols. New York: Macmillan, 1938–1950.

———. *F.D.R.: His Personal Letters, 1928–1945*. Elliott Roosevelt, ed. 3 vols. New York: Duell, Sloane and Pearce, 1950.

Rose, Philip. *The Italians in America*. New York: Doran, 1922.

St. Rita's Parish. *Golden Jubilee Souvenir*. Philadelphia, 1957.

Salter, John T. *The People's Choice: Philadelphia's William Vare*. New York: Exposition Press, 1971.

Salvemini, Gaetano. *Italian Fascist Activities in the United States*. Philip V. Cannistraro, ed. New York: Center for Migration Studies, 1977.

Sammartino, Peter, and Tommaso Russo. *Il primo libro*. New York: Harper, 1936.

Sanchez, George J. *Becoming Mexican American: Ethnicity and Identity in Chicano Los Angeles, 1900–1945*. New York: Oxford University Press, 1993.

Santino, Umberto, and Giovanni La Fiura. *L'impero mafioso: Dall'Italia agli Stati Uniti*. Milan: Franco Angeli, 1990.

Santoro, Carmela E. *The Italians in Rhode Island: The Age of Exploration to the Present, 1524–1989*. Providence: Rhode Island Heritage Commission, 1990.

Sarfatti, Michele. *Mussolini contro gli ebrei: Cronaca dell'elaborazione delle leggi del 1938*. Turin: Zamorani, 1994.

Scartezzini, Riccardo, Roberto Guidi, and Anna Maria Zaccaria. *Tra due mondi: L'avventura americana tra i migranti italiani di fine secolo: Un approccio analitico*. Milan: Franco Angeli, 1994.

Scherini, Rose Doris. *The Italian-American Community of San Francisco: A Descriptive Study*. New York: Arno Press, 1980.

Schiavo, Giovanni E. *The Italians in America before the Civil War*. New York: Vigo Press, 1934.

———. *Italian-American History*. New York: Vigo Press, 1947.

———. *Four Centuries of Italian-American History*. New York: Vigo Press, 1952.

Schlesinger, Arthur M. Jr., and Fred L. Israel, eds. *History of American Presidential Elections, 1789–1984*. 5 vols. New York: Chelsea, 1971–1986.

Schultz, April R. *Ethnicity on Parade: Inventing the Norwegian American through Celebration*. Amherst MA: University of Massachusetts Press, 1994.

Scranton, Philip. *Proprietary Capitalism: The Textile Manufacture at Philadelphia*. Philadelphia: Temple University Press, 1983.

———. *Endless Novelty: Speciality Production and American Industrialization, 1865–1925*. Princeton: Princeton University Press, 1997.

———, and Walter Licht. *Work Sights: Industrial Philadelphia, 1890–1950*. Philadelphia: Temple University Press, 1986.

Sforza, Carlo. *The Real Italians: A Study in European Psychology*. New York: Columbia University Press, 1942.

Silcox, Harry C. *Philadelphia Politics from the Bottom Up: The Life of Irishman William McMullen*. Philadelphia: Balch Institute Press, 1989.

Smith, E. Timothy. *The United States,Italy, and NATO, 1947–52*. New York: St. Martin's Press, 1991.

Smith, Judith E. *Family Connections: A History of Italian and Jewish Immigrant Lives in Providence, Rhode Island, 1900–1940*. Albany: State University of New York Press, 1985.

Smulyan, Susan. *Selling the Radio: The Commercialization of American Broadcasting*. Washington DC: Smithsonian Institution Press, 1994.

Sollors, Werner. *Beyond Ethnicity: Consent and Descent in American Culture*. New York: Oxford University Press, 1986.

———, ed. *The Invention of Ethnicity*. New York: Oxford University Press, 1989.

Sori, Ercole. *L'emigrazione italiana dall'Unità alla seconda guerra mondiale*. Bologna: Il Mulino, 1979.

Sorrentino, Anthony. *Organizing the Ethnic Community: An Account of the Origin, History, and Development of the Joint Civic Committee of Italian Americans (1952–1995)*. Staten Island: Center for Migration Studies, 1995.

Southeastern Pennsylvania Chapter of Americans for Democratic Action. *The Sayings of Chairman Frank, or I Never Saw My Mother Naked*. Philadelphia: Southeastern Pennsylvania Chapter of Americans for Democratic Action, 1977.

Stack, John F. Jr. *International Conflict in an American City: Boston's Irish, Italians, and Jews, 1935–1944*. Westport CT: Greenwood Press, 1979.

Steinberg, Stephen. *The Ethnic Myth: Race, Ethnicity, and Class in America*. New York: Atheneum, 1981.

Stevens, Sylvester K. *Pennsylvania: The Heritage of a Commonwealth*. West Palm Beach FL: American Historical Company, 1968.

Strafile, Alfonso. *"Memorandum" coloniale ossia sintesi storica di osservazioni e fatti che diano un'idea generale della vita coloniale degli Italiani nel Nord America con monografia illustrativa della colonia di Philadelphia*. Philadelphia: "Mastro Paolo" Printing House, 1910.

Sturino, Franc. *Forging the Chain: Italian Migration to North America*. Toronto: Multicultural History Society of Ontario, 1990.

Sugrue, Thomas J. *The Origin of the Urban Crisis: Race and Inequality in Postwar Detroit*. Princeton: Princeton University Press, 1996.

Taormina, Felicita, and Irina Smith. *To the Market, To the Market: Philadelphia's Italian Market*. Philadelphia: privately printed, 1979.

Teaford, Jon C. *The Rough Road to Renaissance: Urban Revitalization in America, 1940–1985*. Baltimore: Johns Hopkins University Press, 1990.
Thompson, Fred. *The I.W.W.: Its First Fifty Years, 1905–1955*. Chicago: Industrial Workers of the World, 1955.
Tull, Charles J. *Father Coughlin and the New Deal*. Syracuse: Syracuse University Press, 1965.
Ueda, Reed. *Postwar Immigrant America: A Social History*. Boston: Bedford Books of St. Martin's Press, 1994.
Unemployment Committee of the National Federation of Settlements. *Case Studies of Unemployment*. Marion Elderton, ed. Philadelphia: University of Pennsylvania Press, 1931.
Valletta, Clement. *A Study of Americanization in Carneta: Italian-American Identity through Three Generations*. New York: Arno Press, 1980.
Van Valkenburg, Carol Bulger. *An Alien Place: The Fort Missoula, Montana, Detention Camp, 1941–1944*. Missoula MT: Pictorial Histories, 1995.
Varacalli, Joseph A. et al., eds. *The Saints in the Lives of Italian Americans*. Stony Brook NY: Forum Italicum, 1999.
Venturini, Nadia. *Neri e Italiani ad Harlem: Gli anni Trenta e la guerra d'Etiopia*. Rome: Edizioni Lavoro, 1990.
Verdicchio, Pasquale. *Bound by Distance: Rethinking Nationalism through the Italian Diaspora*. Madison, NJ: Fairleigh Dickinson University Press, 1997.
Vezzosi, Elisabetta. *Il socialismo indifferente: Immigrati italiani e Socialist Party negli Stati Uniti del primo Novecento*. Rome: Edizioni Lavoro, 1991.
———. *La Chicago di Al Capone*. Florence: Giunti, 1997.
Villari, Luigi. *Gli Stati Uniti e l'emigrazione italiana*. Milan: Treves, 1912.
Ware, Caroline. *Greenwich Village: A Comment on American Civilization in the Postwar Years*. Boston: Houghton Mifflin, 1935.
Warner, Sam Bass Jr. *The Private City: Philadelphia in Three Periods of Its Growth*. Philadelphia: University of Pennsylvania Press, 1968.
Waters, Mary C. *Ethnic Options: Choosing Identities in America*. Berkeley: University of California Press, 1990.
Weed, Perry L. *The White Ethnic Movement and Ethnic Politics*. New York: Praeger, 1973.
Weiler, Conrad. *Philadelphia: Neighborhood, Authority, and the Urban Crisis*. New York: Praeger, 1974.
Wirt, Frederick. *Power in the City: Decision Making in San Francisco*. Berkeley: University of California Press, 1974.
White, Theodore. *America in Search of Itself: The Making of the President, 1956–1980*. New York: Harper and Row, 1982.
Whyte, William Foote. *Street Corner Society: The Social Structure of an Italian Slum*. 1943. Chicago: University of Chicago Press, 1955.
Woodiwiss, Michael. *Crime, Crusades, and Corruption: Prohibitions in the United States, 1900–1987*. New York: Barnes & Noble, 1988.

———. *Organized Crime, U.S.A: Changing Perceptions from Prohibition to the Present Day*. Brighton: British Association for American Studies, 1990.
Yans-McLaughlin, Virginia. *Family and Community: Italian Immigrants in Buffalo, 1880–1930*. Ithaca: Cornell University Press, 1971.
Zieger, Robert H. *Republicans and Labor, 1919–1929*. Lexington: University of Kentucky Press, 1969.
———. *The CIO, 1935–1955*. Chapel Hill: University of North Carolina Press, 1995.
Zucchi, John E. *Italians in Toronto: Development of a National Identity, 1875–1935*. Kingston and Montreal: McGill-Queen's University, 1988.

H. Articles

Alba, Richard D. " 'What Then Is the European American?' Some Answers," *Altreitalie* 4, no. 8 (July–Dec. 1992): 93–99.
———. "Identity and Ethnicity among Italians and Other Americans of European Ancestry." In *The Columbus People: Perspectives in Italian Immigration to the Americas and Australia*, ed. Lydio F. Tomasi, Piero Gastaldo, and Thomas Row. Staten Island: Center for Migration Studies, 1994, 21–44.
———. "Italian Americans: A Century of Ethnic Change." In *Origins and Destinies: Immigration, Race, and Ethnicity in America*, ed. Silvia Pedraza and Ruben G. Rumbaut. Belmont CA: Wadsworth, 1996, 172–81.
Aldrovandi, L. "Note sull'emigrazione italiana in Pennsylvania," *Bollettino dell'Emigrazione* no. 3 (1911): 3–51.
Andreozzi, John. "The Order Sons of Italy in America: Historical Summary." In *Guide to the Records of the Order Sons of Italy in America*, ed. John Andreozzi. St. Paul: Immigration History Research Center, 1989, 7–14.
Anthes, Louis C. " 'The Search for the Order': The Order Sons of Italy in America and the Politics of Ethnicity." In *Industry, Technology, Labor, and the Italian-American Communities*, ed. Mario Aste et al. Staten Island: American Italian Historical Association, 1997, 5–32.
Arcangeli, Bianca. "Le colonie italiane di Philadelphia," *Annali della Facoltà di Lettere e Filosofia dell'Università di Napoli* 16 (1973–74): 217–54.
"Arena Factory Addition Will Raise Output," *Norristown Times Herald* (13 Sept. 1937): 29.
Asard, Eric. "Father Coughlin and Populist Insurgency against the New Deal," *Storia Nordamericana* 6, no. 1–2 (1989): 91–107.
Aversa, Alfred Jr. "Italian Neo-Ethnicity: The Search for Self-Identity," *Journal of Ethnic Studies* 6, no. 2 (Summer 1978): 49–56.
"Avventure degli italiani in America," *L'Eco del Rhode Island* (6 Nov. 1915): 1.
Barbaro, Fred. "Ethnic Affirmation, Affirmative Action, and the Italian American," *Italian Americana* 1, no. 1 (Autumn 1974): 41–58.
Bardaglio, Peter W. "Italian Immigrants and the Catholic Church in Providence, 1890–1930," *Rhode Island History* 34, no. 1 (Feb. 1975): 46–57.

Baroni, Geno. "Ethnicity and Public Policy." In *Pieces of a Dream: The Ethnic Worker's Crisis with America*, ed. Michael Wenk, Silvano M. Tomasi, and Geno Baroni. Staten Island: Center for Migration Studies, 1972, 1–11.

Barrett, James R. "Americanization from the Bottom Up: Immigration and the Remaking of the Working Class in the United States, 1880–1930," *Journal of American History* 79, no. 3 (Dec. 1992): 996–1020.

———, and David Roediger. "Inbetween Peoples: Race, Nationality, and the 'New Immigrant' Working Class," *Journal of American Ethnic History* 16, no. 3 (Spring 1997): 3–44.

Barth, Fredrick. "Introduction." In *Ethnic Groups and Boundaries: The Social Organization of Cultural Differences*, ed. Fredrick Barth. Boston: Little, Brown, 1969, 9–38.

Bauman, John F. "Public Housing in the Depression: Slum Reform in Philadelphia Neighborhoods in the 1930s." In *The Divided Metropolis: Social and Spatial Dimension of Philadelphia, 1800–1975*, ed. William W. Cutler III and Howard Gillette Jr. Westport CT: Greenwood Press, 1980, 227–48.

———. "Rizzo, Frank L." In *Biographical Dictionary of American Mayors, 1820–1980: Big City Mayors*, ed. Melvin G. Holli and Peter d'A. Jones. Westport CT: Greenwood Press, 1981, 306–7

Bean, Philip A. "Fascism and Italian-American Identity: A Case Study: Utica New York," *Journal of Ethnic Studies* 17, no. 1 (Summer 1989): 101–19.

Belfiglio, Valentine J. "Italian Culture in Eighteenth-Century Philadelphia," *Italian Quarterly* 23, no. 87 (Winter 1982): 75–83.

———. "Italians in Small Town and Rural Texas." In *Italian Immigrants in Rural and Small Town America*, ed. Rudolph J. Vecoli. Staten Island: American Italian Historical Association, 1987, 31–49.

Bentivegna, Joseph J. "Trends in Italian American Heritage," *Il Caffè* 10, no. 1 (April 1990): 23–27.

Bernstein, Barton J. "Election of 1952." In *History of American Presidential Elections, 1789–1984*, ed. Arthur M. Schlesinger Jr. and Fred L. Israel. 5 vols. New York: Chelsea, 1971–1986, 4:3215–66.

Bianco, Carla. "La politica culturale degli Stati Uniti," *Studi Emigrazione* 12, no. 37 (Mar. 1975): 97–108.

———. "Emigrazione America / Emigration America." In *Emigrazione / Emigration*, ed. Carla Bianco and Emanuela Agiuli. Bari: Dedalo, 1980, 11–39.

Birger, Jon S. "Race, Reaction, and Reform: The Three Rs of Philadelphia School Politics, 1965–1971," *Pennsylvania Magazine of History and Biography* 120, no. 3 (July 1996): 163–216.

Brunetta, Gian Piero. "Il sogno a stelle e strisce di Mussolini." In *L'estetica della politica*, ed. Maurizio Vaudagna. Rome and Bari: Laterza, 1989, 173–86.

Buffum, Peter C., and Rita Sagi. "Philadelphia: Politics of Reform and Retreat." In *Crime in City Politics*, ed. Anne Heinz, Herbert Jacob, and Robert L. Lineberry. New York: Longman, 1983, 97–147.

Burt, Nathaniel, and Wallace E. Davies. "The Iron Age." In *Philadelphia: A 300-Year History*, ed. Russell F. Weigley. New York: Norton, 1982, 471–523.

Byrne, Gary C., and J. Kristian Pueschel. "But Who Should I Vote for County Coroner?" *Journal of Politics* 36, no. 3 (Aug. 1974): 778–84.
Cafarelli, Annette Wheeler. "The Making of Tradition." In *Shades of Black and White: Conflict and Collaboration between Two Communities*, ed. Dan Ashyk, Fred Gardaphe, and Anthony Julian Tamburri. Staten Island,: American Italian Historical Association, 1999, 28–44.
Campailla, Sergio. "Little Italy." In *Il sogno italo-americano: Realtà e immaginario dell'emigrazione negli Stati Uniti*, ed. Sebastiano Martelli. Naples: CUEN, 1998, 49–64.
Cannistraro, Philip V. "Fascism and Italian Americans in Detroit, 1933–1935," *International Migration Review* 9, no. 1 (Spring 1975): 29–40.
———. "Gli Italo-Americani di fronte all'ingresso dell'Italia nella Seconda Guerra Mondiale," *Storia Contemporanea* 7, no. 4 (Dec. 1976): 855–64.
———. "Fascism and Italian Americans." In *Perspectives in Italian Immigration and Ethnicity*, ed. Silvano M. Tomasi. New York: Center for Migration Studies, 1977, 51–66.
———. "Per una storia dei Fasci negli Stati Uniti (1921–1929)," *Storia Contemporanea* 25, no. 6 (Dec. 1995): 1061–1144.
———. "Mussolini, Sacco-Vanzetti, and the Anarchists: The Transatlantic Context," *Journal of Modern History* 68, no. 1 (Mar. 1996): 31–62.
———, and Theodore P. Kovaleff. "Father Coughlin and Mussolini: Impossible Allies," *Journal of Church and State* 13, no. 3 (Autumn 1971): 427–43.
———, and Gianfausto Rosoli. "Fascist Emigration Policy in the 1920s: An Interpretative Framework," *International Migration Review* 13, no. 4 (Winter 1979): 673–92.
Carlson, James M. "The Impact of Ethnicity on Candidate Image," *Polity* 16, no. 4 (Summer 1984): 667–72.
Cartosio, Bruno. "Sicilian Radicals in Two Worlds." In *In the Shadow of the Statue of Liberty: Immigrants, Workers, and Citizens in the American Republic, 1880–1920*, ed. Marianne Debouzy. Saint-Denis: Presses Universitaires de Vincennes, 1988, 117–28.
Cavaioli, Frank. "Italian Americans Slay the Immigration Dragon: The National Origins Quota System," *Italian Americana* 5, no. 1 (Fall–Winter 1979): 71–100.
———. "Chicago's Italian Americans Rally for Immigration Reform," *Italian Americana* 5, no. 2 (Spring–Summer 1980): 142–56.
———. "Ethnic Population Patterns on Long Island." In *Ethnicity in Suburbia*, ed. Salvatore J. LaGumina. Garden City NY: Nassau College Press, 1980, 15–25.
———. "The National Italian American Foundation: 1975–1985." In *A. P. Giannini: Banker, Philanthropist, Entrepreneur*, ed. Felice A. Bonadio. Washington DC: National Italian American Foundation, 1985, 119–25.

———. "A Sociodemographic Analysis of Italian Americans and the Twilight of Ethnicity." In *Italian Ethnics: Their Languages, Literatures, and Lives*, ed. Dominic Candeloro, Fred L. Gardaphe, and Paolo A. Giordano. Staten Island: American Italian Historical Association, 1990, 191–99.

———. "Returning to Corona's Little Italy," *Italian Americana* 15, no. 1 (Winter 1997): 31–50.

———. "Geno Baroni: Italian-American Civil Rights Priest." In *Shades of Black and White: Conflict and Collaboration between Two Communities*, ed. Dan Ashyk, Fred Gardaphe, and Anthony Julian Tamburri. Staten Island: American Italian Historical Association, 1999, 45–54.

Cinel, Dino. "Sicilians in the Deep South: The Ironic Outcome of Isolation," *Studi Emigrazione* 27, no. 97 (Mar. 1990): 55–86.

———. "Italians in the South: The Alabama Case," *Italian Americana* 9, no. 1 (Winter 1990): 7–24.

Clark, Joseph S. Jr., and Dennis J. Clark, "Rally and Relapse, 1946–1968." In *Philadelphia: A 300-Year History*, ed. Russell F. Weigley. New York: Norton, 1982, 649–703.

Cohen, Anthony. "Culture as Identity: An Anthropologist's View," *New Literary History* 24, no. 2 (Winter 1993): 195–209.

Cohen, Rina, and Gerald Gold. "Constructing Ethnicity: Myth of Return and Modes of Exclusion among Israelis in Toronto," *International Migration* 35, no. 3 (1997): 373–92.

Conforti, Joseph M. "Wasp in the Woodpile Revisited: Italian-American–African-American Conflict." In *Shades of Black and White: Conflict and Collaboration Between Two Communities*, ed. Dan Ashyk, Fred Gardaphe, and Anthony Julian Tamburri. Staten Island: American Italian Historical Association, 1999, 62–77.

Conzen, Kathleen N., et al., "The Invention of Ethnicity: A Perspective from the U.S.A.," *Journal of American Ethnic History* 12, no. 1 (Fall 1992): 3–41.

Cunningham, George E. "The Italian: A Hindrance to White Solidarity in Louisiana, 1890–1898," *Journal of Negro History* 50, no. 1 (Jan. 1965): 22–36.

Dadà, Adriana. "Contributo metodologico per una storia dell'emigrazione e dell'antifascismo italiani negli Stati Uniti," *Annali dell'Istituto di Storia dell'Università di Firenze* 1 (1979): 197–218.

D'Agostino, Peter R. "The Scalabrini Fathers, the Italian Emigrant Church, and Ethnic Nationalism in America," *Religion and American Culture* 7, no. 1 (Winter 1997): 121–59.

———. "The Triad of Roman Authority: Fascism, the Vatican, and Italian Religious Clergy in the Italian Emigrant Church," *Journal of American Ethnic History* 17, no. 3 (Spring 1998): 3–37.

D'Amelio, Dan A. "A Season of Panic: The Internments of World War II," *Italian Americana* 17, no. 2 (Summer 1999): 147–62.

Daniels, Roger. "L'internamento di 'Alien Enemies' negli Stati Uniti durante la seconda guerra mondiale," *Acoma* 4, no. 11 (Summer-Autumn 1997): 39-49.
De Ciampis, Mario. "Storia del movimento socialista rivoluzionario italiano," *La Parola del Popolo* 50, no. 37 (Dec. 1958-Jan. 1959): 136-63.
De Clementi, Andreina. "La sfida dell'insularità: Generazioni e differenze etniche tra gli emigranti italiani negli Stati Uniti." *Memoria e ricerca* 4, no. 8 (Dec. 1996): 99-113.
De Conde, Alexander. "Foreign Intervention in Domestic Politics: The Italian and American Experience." In *Italia e Stati Uniti dall'indipendenza americana ad oggi (1776-1976): Atti del I congresso internazionale di storia americana.* Genoa: Tilgher, 1978, 113-21.
De Felice, Renzo. "Alcuni temi per la storia dell'emigrazione italiana," *Affari Sociali Internazionali* 1, no. 3 (Sept. 1973): 3-10.
DeLeo, Nicholas V. "A Look at the Early Years of Philadelphia's Little Italy," *Pennsylvania Folklife* 45, no. 1 (Autumn 1995): 31-36.
De Schweinitz, Karl. "Philadelphia Takes Heart," *Survey* (15 May 1931): 217-19.
Di Bartolomeo, Albert. "A South Philly Tradition Went Up with Palumbo's," *Philadelphia Inquirer* (1 July 1994): A15.
Dickinson, Joan Younger. "Aspects of Italian Immigration to Philadelphia," *Pennsylvania Magazine of History and Biography* 90, no. 4 (Oct. 1966): 445-65.
Di Comite, Luigi, and Ira A. Glazier. "Socio-Demographic Characteristics of Italian Emigration to the United States from Ship Passenger Lists: 1880-1914," *Ethnic Forum* 4, no. 1-2 (Spring 1984): 78-90.
Dinwiddle, Emily Wayland. "Some Aspects of Italian Housing and Social Conditions in Philadelphia," *Charities* 12, no. 5 (May 1904): 490-94.
Di Stasi, Lawrence. "How World War II Iced Italian American Culture." In *Multi America: Essays on Cultural Wars and Cultural Peace*, ed. Ishmael Reed. New York: Viking, 1997, 169-78.
Downs, Jere. "Procession Carries on Sicilian Traditions," *Philadelphia Inquirer* (25 Aug. 1994), section C: 2.
Duff, John B. "The Italians." In *The Immigrants' Influence on Wilson's Peace Policies*, ed. Joseph P. O'Grady. Lexington: University of Kentucky Press, 1967, 111-39.
Dumanowski, Dianne. "Boston's Italian North End: Changing Immigrant Still Is 'Home' to Former Residents," *American Preservation* 2, no. 3 (Feb.-Mar. 1979): 42-49.
Durr, Kenneth. "When Southern Politics Came North: The Roots of White Working-Class Conservatism in Baltimore, 1940-1964," *Labor History* 37, no. 3 (Summer 1996): 309-31.
"Elenco delle società italiane esistenti negli Stati Uniti alla fine del 1910," *Bollettino dell'Emigrazione* no. 4 (1912): 497-530.

Fabiano, Domenico. "La Lega Italiana per la Tutela degli Interessi Nazionali e le origini dei Fasci italiani all'estero (1920–1923)," *Storia Contemporanea* 16, no. 2 (Apr. 1985): 203–50.

Featherman, Sandra. "Ethnicity and Ethnic Candidates: Vote Advantages in Local Elections," *Polity* 15, no. 3 (Spring 1983): 397–415.

———. "Italian American Voting in Local Elections: The Philadelphia Case." In *Italian Americans: The Search for a Usable Past*, ed. Richard N. Juliani and Philip V. Cannistraro. Staten Island: American Italian Historical Association, 1989, 43–54.

Fenton, Edwin. "Italians in the Labor Movement," *Pennsylvania History* 26, no. 2 (Apr. 1959): 133–48,

Ferraro, Geraldine. "Vice-Presidential Acceptance Speech." In Geraldine Ferraro, *Changing History: Women, Power, and Politics*. Wakefield RI: Moyer Bell, 1993, 3–10.

Ferro, Gaetano, and Adele Maiello. "Un secolo e mezzo di flussi migratori." In Università degli Studi di Genova, *L'emigrazione nelle Americhe dalla provincia di Genova: Questioni generali e introduttive*. Bologna: Patron, 1990, 75–177.

Ficken, Robert E. "Political Leadership in Wartime: Franklin D. Roosevelt and the Elections of 1942," *Mid-America* 57, no. 1 (Jan. 1975): 20–37.

Fields, Barbara Jeanne. "Slavery, Race, and Ideology in the United States of America," *New Left Review* no. 181 (May–June 1990): 95–118.

Filippelli, Roland L. "Philadelphia Transit Strike of 1944." In *Labor Conflict in the United States: An Encyclopedia*, ed. Roland L. Filippelli. New York: Garland, 1990, 419–21.

Finkelstein, Monte S. "The Johnson Act, Mussolini, and Fascist Emigration Policy: 1921–1930," *Journal of American Ethnic History* 8, no. 1 (Fall 1988): 38–55.

Fones-Wolf, Elizabeth. "Industrial Unionism and Labor Movement Culture in Depression-Era Philadelphia," *Pennsylvania Magazine of History and Biography* 109, no. 1 (Jan. 1985): 3–26.

Fonzi, Gaeton J. "Philadelphia's Italians: A Bubbly Minestrone," *Philadelphia Magazine* 52, no. 1 (Jan. 1961): 24–28, 66–69.

———. "A Show of Faith." *Philadelphia Magazine* 61, no. 9 (Sept. 1970): 78–82, 186–89.

———. "The Italians Are Coming! The Italians Are Coming!," *Philadelphia Magazine* 62, no. 12 (Dec. 1971): 98–102, 171–81.

"The Foreign Language Press," *Fortune* 22, no. 5 (Nov. 1940): 90–93, 102–4.

Fraser, Steve. "Dress Rehearsal for the New Deal: Shop-Floor Insurgents, Political Elites, and Industrial Democracy in the Amalgamated Clothing Workers." In *Working-Class America: Essays on Labor, Community, and American Society*, ed. Michael H. Frish and Daniel J. Walkowitz. Urbana: University of Illinois Press, 1983, 212–55.

———. "*Landslayt* and *Paesani*: Ethnic Conflict and Cooperation in the Amalgamated Clothing Workers of America." In *Struggle a Hard Battle: Essays on Working-Class Immigrants*, ed. Dirk Hoerder. DeKalb: Northern Illinois University Press, 1986, 280–303.
Frezza Bicocchi, Daria. "Propaganda fascista e comunità italiane in U.S.A: La Casa Italiana della Columbia University," *Studi Storici* 11, no. 4 (Oct. 1970): 661–97.
Friedman, Murray, and Carolyn Beck. "An Ambivalent Alliance: Blacks and Jews in Philadelphia, 1940 to 1985." In *Philadelphia Jewish Life, 1940–1985*. ed. Murray Friedman. Ardmore PA: Seth Press, 1986, 143–65.
Fuchs, Lawrence H. "Election of 1928." In *History of American Presidential Elections, 1789–1984*, ed. Arthur M. Schlesinger Jr. and Fred L. Israel. 5 vols. New York: Chelsea, 1971–1986, 3:2585–2609.
———. " 'The Invention of Ethnicity': The Amen Corner," *Journal of American Ethnic History* 12, no. 1 (Fall 1992): 53–58.
Gabaccia, Donna. "Italian History and Gli Italiani nel Mondo, Part I," *Journal of Modern Italian Studies* 2, no. 1 (Spring 1997): 45–66.
———. "The 'Yellow Peril' and the 'Chinese of Europe': Global Perspectives on Race and Labor, 1815–1930." In *Migration, Migration History, History: Old Paradigms and New Perspectives*, ed. Jan Lucassen and Leo Lucassen. New York: Peter Lang, 1997, 177–96.
———. "Peopling 'Little Italy'." In *The Italians of New York: Four Centuries of Struggle and Achievement*, ed. Philip V. Cannistraro. New York: New York Historical Society, 1999, 45–54.
Gambino, Richard. "Are Italian Americans in 'the Twilight' of Ethnicity, or a New Dawn'?" In *Industry, Technology, Labor, and the Italian-American Communities*, ed. Mario Aste et al. Staten Island: American Italian Historical Association, 1997, 161–74.
———. "The Crisis of Italian American Identity." In *Beyond the Godfather: Italian American Writers on the Real Italian American Experience*, ed. A. Kenneth Ciongoli and Jay Parini. Hanover: University Press of New England, 1997, 269–88.
Gans, Herbert J. "Symbolic Ethnicity: the Future of Ethnic Groups and Cultures in America." In Herbert J. Gans et al., *On the Making of Americans: Essays in Honor of David Riesman*. Philadelphia: University of Pennsylvania Press, 1979, 193–220.
Gardaphe, Fred. "Presidential Address." In *Shades of Black and White: Conflict and Collaboration Between Two Communities*, ed. Dan Ashyk, Fred Gardaphe, and Anthony Julian Tamburri. Staten Island: American Italian Historical Association, 1999, vii–xii.
Garroni, Maria Susanna. "Italian Parishes in a Burgeoning City: Buffalo, 1880–1920," *Studi Emigrazione* 28, no. 103 (Sept. 1991): 351–67.

Gerstle, Gary. "Working-Class Racism: Broaden the Focus," *International Labor and Working Class History* 44, no. 2 (Fall 1993): 33–40.

———. "The Protean Character of American Liberalism," *American Historical Review* 99, no. 4 (Oct. 1994): 1043–73.

———. "Race and the Myth of the Liberal Consensus," *Journal of American History* 82, no. 2 (Sept. 1995): 579–86.

Gertrude, M. Agnes. "Italian Immigration into Philadelphia: I," *Records of the American Catholic Society of Philadelphia* 58, no. 2 (June 1947): 133–44.

———. "Italian Immigration into Philadelphia: II," *Records of the American Catholic Historical Society of Philadelphia* 58, no. 3 (Sept. 1947): 189–208.

Gibelli, Antonio. "La risorsa America." In *Storia d'Italia: Le regioni dall'Unità a oggi: La Liguria*, ed. Antonio Gibelli and Paride Rugafiori. Turin: Einaudi, 1994, 583–650.

Gilkey, George R. "The United States and Italy: Migration and Repatriation," *Journal of Developing Areas* 2, no. 1 (Oct. 1967): 23–36.

Ginzburg Migliorino, Ellen. "Il proletariato italiano di Filadelfia all'inizio del secolo," *Studi Emigrazione* 13, no. 41 (Mar. 1976): 23–39.

———. "La comunità italo-americana nel clima conservatore di Filadelfia agli inizi del Novecento." In *Italia e Stati Uniti dall'indipendenza americana ad oggi (1776–1976): Atti del I congresso internazionale di storia americana*. Genoa: Tilgher, 1978, 315–21.

———. "Immigrati italiani nelle scuole di Filadelfia (Pennsylvania)." In *Il movimento migratorio italiano dall'unità nazionale ai giorni nostri*, ed. Franca Assante. 2 vols. Geneva: Droz, 1978, 2:165–80.

———. "Jewish Emigration from Trieste to the United States after 1938, with Special Reference to New York, Philadelphia, and Wilmington," *Studi Emigrazione* 28, no. 103 (Sept. 1991): 369–77.

Glazer, Nathan. "Ethnic Groups in America: From National Culture to Ideology." In *Freedom and Control in Modern Society*, ed. Monroe Berger, Theodore Abel, and Charles H. Page. New York: D. Van Nostrand, 1954, 158–73.

Glazier, Ira A. "Ships and Passengers in Emigration from Italy to the U.S., 1880–1900." In *Le genti del mare Mediterraneo*, ed. Rosalba Ragosta. 2 vols. Naples: Pironti, 1981, 2:1092–1125.

———. "Introduction." In *Italians to America: Lists of Passengers Arriving at U.S. Ports, 1880–1899*, ed. Ira A. Glazier and P. William Filby. Wilmington DE: Scholarly Resources Inc., 1992, ix–xix.

———, and Robert Kleiner. "Analisi comparata degli emigranti dall'Europa meridionale e orientale attraverso le liste passeggeri delle navi statunitensi," *Altreitalie* 4, no. 7 (Jan.–June 1992): 115–25.

Gleason, Philip. "Americans All: World War II and the Shaping of American Identity," *Review of Politics* 43, no. 4 (Oct. 1981): 483–518.

Gobel, Thomas. "Becoming American: Ethnic Workers and the Rise of the CIO," *Labor History* 29, no. 1 (Spring 1988): 173–98.
Golab, Caroline. "The Immigrant and the City: Poles, Italians, and Jews in Philadelphia, 1870–1920." In *The Peoples of Philadelphia: A History of Ethnic Groups and Lower Class Life, 1790–1940*, ed. Allen D. Davis and Mark H. Haller. Philadelphia: Temple University Press, 1973, 203–30.
Goldenberg, Paul. "Tony Imperiale Stands Vigilant for Law and Order," *New York Times Magazine* (29 Sept. 1968): 30–31, 117–22, 124, 126.
Grandi, Dino. "Ai Figli d'Italia: Discorso agli italo-americani in Filadelfia." In Dino Grandi, *La politica estera dell'Italia dal 1929 al 1932*, ed. Paolo Nello. 2 vols. Rome: Bonacci, 1985, 2:569–76.
Grandinetti, Emilio. "Amalgamated Clothing Workers of America: Il contributo degli italiani al sindacato dell'abbigliamento maschile," *La Parola del Popolo* 50, no. 37 (Dec. 1958–Jan. 1959): 165–78.
Greenberg, Irwin F. "Philadelphia Democrats Get a New Deal: The Election of 1933," *Pennsylvania Magazine of History and Biography* 97, no. 2 (Apr. 1973): 210–32.
Greenberg, Stephanie W. "Neighborhood Change, Racial Transition, and Work Location: A Case Study of an Industrial City, Philadelphia 1880–1930," *Journal of Urban History* 7, no. 3 (May 1981): 267–314.
Haller, Mark H. "Recurring Themes." In *The Peoples of Philadelphia: A History of Ethnic Groups and Lower Class Life, 1790–1940*, ed. Allen D. Davis and Haller. Philadelphia: Temple University Press, 1973, 277–89.
"Hate Strike, Philadelphia," *Monthly Summary of Events and Trends in Race Relations* 2, no. 1–2 (Aug.–Sept. 1944): 6–7.
Hershberg, Theodore, et al. "A Tale of Three Cities: Blacks, Immigrants, and Opportunity in Philadelphia, 1850–1880, 1930, 1970." In *Philadelphia: Work, Space, Family, and Group Experience in the Nineteenth Century: Essays Toward an Interdisciplinary History of the City*, ed. Theodore Hershberg. New York: Oxford University Press, 1981, 461–91.
Higham, John. "Introduction: The Forms of Ethnic Leadership." In *Ethnic Leadership in America*, ed. John Higham. Baltimore: Johns Hopkins University Press, 1978, 1–18.
Hirsch, Arnold H. "Massive Resistance in the Urban North: Trumbull Park, Chicago, 1953–1966," *Journal of American History* 82, no. 2 (Sept. 1995): 522–50.
Hollinger, David A. "How Wide Is the Circle of the 'We'? American Intellectuals and the Problem of the Ethnos since World War II," *American Historical Review* 98, no. 2 (Apr. 1993): 317–37.
Jensen, Richard. "The Cities Reelect Roosevelt: Ethnicity, Religion, and Class in 1940," *Ethnicity* 8, no. 2 (June 1981): 189–95.
Juliani, Richard N. "The Origin and Development of the Italian Community in Philadelphia." In *The Ethnic Experience in Pennsylvania*, ed. John E. Bodnar. Lewisburg PA: Bucknell University Press, 1973, 233–62.

———. "Italians and Other Americans: The Parish, the Union, and the Settlement House." In *Perspectives in Italian Immigration and Ethnicity*, ed. Silvano M. Tomasi. New York: Center for Migration Studies, 1977, 179–83.

———. "The Italian Community of Philadelphia." In *Little Italies in North America*, ed. Robert F. Harney and J. Vincenza Scarpaci. Toronto: Multicultural Society of Ontario, 1981, 85–104.

———. "The Interaction of Irish and Italians: From Conflict to Integration." In *Italians and Irish in America*, ed. Francis X. Femminella. Staten Island: American Italian Historical Association, 1985, 27–34.

———. "The Parish as an Urban Institution: Italian Catholics in Philadelphia," *Records of the American Catholic Historical Society of Philadelphia* 96 (1986): 49–65.

———. "The Position of Italian Americans in Contemporary Society." In *The Melting Pot and Beyond: Italian Americans in the Year 2000*, ed. Jerome Krase and William Egelman. Staten Island: American Italian Historical Association, 1987, 61–71.

———. "Immigrants in Philadelphia: The World of 1886." In *Italian Americans: The Search for a Usable Past*, ed. Richard N. Juliani and Philip V. Cannistraro. Staten Island: American Italian Historical Association, 1989, 4–15.

———. "Identity and Ethnicity: The Italian Case." In *The Columbus People: Perspectives in Italian Immigration to the Americas and Australia*, ed. Lydio F. Tomasi, Piero Gataldo, and Thomas Row. Staten Island: Center for Migration Studies, 1994, 54–57.

———. "Italian Organizations in Philadelphia." In *Invisible Philadelphia: Community through Voluntary Organizations*, ed. Jean Barth Toll and Mildred S. Gillam. Philadelphia: Atwater Kent Museum, 1995, 109–14.

———. "Images, Interactions, and Institutions: The Emergence of an Italian Community in Philadelphia." In *Origins and Transitions: Towards a Plural Citizenship*, ed. Mario Aldo Toscano. Naples: Ipermedium, 1996, 185–206.

———. "Social Change and the Ethnic Community: The Italians in Philadelphia." In *Dialettica locale-globale: Continuità e contraddizioni del mondo*, ed. Mario Aldo Toscano. Naples: Ipermedium, 1997, 53–73.

———. "Community and Identity: Continuity and Change Among Italian Americans in Philadelphia," *Italian American Review* 6, no. 2 (Autumn 1997/Winter 1998): 45–58.

———. "Philadelphia." In *The Italian American Experience: An Encyclopedia*, ed. Salvatore J. LaGumina et al. New York: Garland, 2000, 461–63.

———. "Una comunità in transizione: Il caso italiano a Filadelfia." In *Atti del Convegno "Le società in transizione: italiani e italo-americani negli anni Ottanta,"* Balch Institute, Philadelphia, 11–12 ottobre 1985. Rome: Ministero degli Affari Esteri, n.d., 305–13.

Kazal, Russell A. "Revisiting Assimilation: The Rise, Fall, and Reappraisal of a Concept in American Ethnic History," *American Historical Review* 100, no. 2 (Apr. 1995): 437–71.

Keller, Richard C. "Pennsylvania's Little New Deal." In *The New Deal: The State and Local Levels,* ed. John Braeman, Robert H. Bremner, and David Brody. 2 vols. Columbus: Ohio State University Press, 1975, 2:45–76.
Kelly, Mary F., and Tracy X. Karner. "Reclaiming and Inventing Ethnic Identity: Lithuanians and Finns at the Turn of the Twentieth Century," *Ethnic Forum* 14, no. 2 (Summer 1994): 5–21.
Keyes, Charles F. "The Dialectics of Ethnic Change." In *Ethnic Change,* ed. Charles F. Keyes. Seattle: University of Washington Press, 1981, 4–30.
Kibria, Nazli. "The Construction of 'Asian American': Reflections on Intermarriage and Ethnic Identity among Second-Generation Chinese and Korean Americans," *Ethnic and Racial Studies* 20, no. 3 (July 1997): 523–44.
Klaczynska, Barbara. "Why Women Work: A Comparison of Various Groups—Philadelphia, 1910–1930," *Labor History* 17, no. 1 (Winter 1976): 73–87.
Krase, Jerome. "America's Little Italies: Past, Present, and Future." In *Italian Ethnics: Their Languages, Literature, and Life,* ed. Dominick Candeloro et al. Staten Island: American Italian Historical Association, 1990, 167–84.
———. "Ironies of Icons: The Slings and Arrows of Outrageous Multiculturalists." In *Italian Americans in a Multicultural Society,* ed. Krase and Judith N. DeSena. New York: Forum Italicum, 1994, 1–18.
———. "The Spatial Semeiotics of Little Italies and Italian Americans." In *Industry, Technology, Labor and the Italian-American Communities,* ed. Mario Aste et al. Staten Island: American Italian Historical Association, 1997, 98–127.
Kyvig, David E. "Raskob, Roosevelt, and Repeal," *Historian* 37, no. 3 (May 1975): 469–87.
Ladd, Everett Carll. "On Mandates, Realignments, and the 1984 Presidential Election," *Political Science Quarterly* 100, no. 1 (Spring 1985): 1–25.
"Lay Off the Italians," *Collier's* (3 Aug. 1940): 54.
LaGumina, Salvatore J. "Case Studies of Ethnicity and Italo-American Politicians." In *The Italian Experience in the United States,* ed. Silvano M. Tomasi and Madeline H. Engel. New York: Center for Migration Studies, 1970, 17–33.
———. "The Political Profession: Big City Italian-American Mayors." In *Italian Americans in the Professions,* ed. Remigio U. Pane. Staten Island: American Italian Historical Association, 1983, 77–110.
Lapomarda, Vincent A. "Press, Italian American." In *The Italian American Experience: An Encyclopedia,* ed. Salvatore J. LaGumina et al. New York: Garland, 2000, 509–18.
Lesser, Jeffrey. "(Re) Creating Ethnicity: Middle Eastern Immigration to Brazil," *Americas* 53, no. 1 (July 1996): 45–65.
Licht, Walter. "Studying Work: Personnel Policies in Philadelphia Firms, 1850–1950." In *Masters to Managers: Historical and Comparative Perspectives on American Employers,* ed. Sanford M. Jacoby. New York: Columbia University Press, 1991, 43–73.

Lograsso, Angeline H. "Piero Maroncelli in Philadelphia," *Romanic Review* 24, no. 4 (Oct.–Dec. 1933): 323–29.

Lombardi, John. "Frank Rizzo Without Prejudice: The Reluctant Mellowing of Philly's Attila the Hun," *Esquire* 112, no. 2 (Aug. 1989): 114–17.

Lombardi, Vincent M. "Italian-American Workers and the Response to Fascism." In *Pane e Lavoro: The Italian-American Working Class*, ed. George E. Pozzetta. Toronto: Multicultural Society of Ontario, 1980, 141–57.

Lubell, Samuel. "Who *Really* Elected Truman?," *Saturday Evening Post* (22 Jan. 1949): 15–17, 54–58, 61, 64.

McClymer, John F. "The Americanization Movement and the Education of the Foreign-Born Adult, 1914–1925." In *American Education and the European Immigrant, 1840–1940*, ed. Bernard J. Weiss. Urbana: University of Illinois Press, 1982, 96–116.

MacDonald, John S., and Leatrice D. MacDonald. "Urbanization, Ethnic Groups, and Social Segmentation," *Social Research* 29, no. 4 (Winter 1962): 433–48.

———. "Migration, Ethnic Neighborhood Formation, and Social Networks," *Milbank Memorial Fund Quarterly* 42, no. 1 (Jan. 1964): 82–97.

McGirr, Lisa. "Black and White Longshoremen in the IWW: A History of the Philadelphia Marine Transport Workers Industrial Union Local 8," *Labor History* 36, no. 3 (Summer 1995): 377–402.

McKenna, William J. "The Negro Vote in Philadelphia Elections," *Pennsylvania History* 32, no. 4 (Oct. 1965): 406–15.

Madden, Mike. "Politics in Mantua and Philadelphia Since World War II," *Penn History Review* 6, no. 1 (Spring 1998): 65–83.

Maiello, Adele. "L'emigrazione dal chiavarese: Sue origini e caratteristiche," *Annali della Facoltà di Scienze Politiche dell'Università degli Studi di Genova*, 11–13 (1983–1986), 3 vols., 2:155–83.

Mangano, Antonio. "The Associated Life of the Italians in New York City" [1904]. In *The Italian in America: The Progressive View*, ed. Lydio F. Tomasi. Staten Island: Center for Migration Studies. 1978, 153–63.

Marraro, Howard R. "Italo-Americans in Pennsylvania in the Eighteenth Century," *Pennsylvania History* 7, no. 3 (July 1940): 159–66.

Martellone, Anna Maria. "Italian Immigrant Settlement and Repatriation." In *The United States and Italy: The First Two Hundred Years*, ed. Humbert S. Nelli. Staten Island: American Italian Historical Association, 1977, 147–53.

———. "Introduzione." In *La "questione" dell'immigrazione negli Stati Uniti*, ed. Anna Maria Martellone. Bologna: Il Mulino, 1980, 7–81.

———. "Italian Mass Emigration to the United States, 1876–1930: A Historical Survey," *Perspectives in American History* 1 (1984): 379–423.

———. "Prefazione." In Elisabetta Vezzosi, *Il socialismo indifferente: Immigrati italiani e Socialist Party negli Stati Uniti del primo Novecento*. Rome: Edizioni Lavoro, 1991, ix–xvii.

———. "Italo-American Ethnic Identity: A Plea against the Deconstruction of Ethnicity and in Favor of Political History," *Altreitalie* 3, no. 6 (Nov. 1991): 106–13.

———. "Italian Immigrants, Party Machines, Ethnic Brokers in City Politics, from the 1880s to the 1930s." In *The European Emigrant Experience in the U.S.A.*, ed. Walter Hölbling and Reinhold Wagnleitner. Tübingen: Gunter Narr Verlag, 1992, 171–87.

———. "Tra memoria del passato e speranza del nuovo: L'identità italiana negli Stati Uniti," *Memoria e ricerca* 4, no. 8 (December 1996): 57–75.

Martinelli, Phylis Cancilla. "Italian-American Experience." In *America's Ethnic Politics*, ed. Joseph S. Roucek and Bernard Eisenberg. Westport CT: Greenwood Press, 1982, 217–31.

———, and Leonard Gordon. "Italian Americans: Images Across Half a Century," *Ethnic and Racial Studies* 11, no. 3 (July 1988): 319–31.

Massaro, Dominic R. "Italian Americans as a Cognizable Racial Group." In *Italian Americans in a Multicultural Society*, ed. Jerome Krase and Judith N. DeSena. New York: Forum Italicum, 1994, 44–55.

Medina, Laurie Kroshus. "Defining Difference, Forging Unity: The Co-Construction of Race, Ethnicity and Nation in Belize," *Ethnic and Racial Studies* 20, no. 4 (Oct. 1997): 757–80.

Meyer, Gerald. "Italian Harlem: Portrait of a Community." In *The Italians of New York: Four Centuries of Struggle and Achievement*, ed. Philip V. Cannistraro. New York: New York Historical Society, 1999, 57–67.

Miller, James Edward. "The Politics of Relief: The Roosevelt Administration and the Reconstruction of Italy, 1943–44," *Prologue* 13, no. 3 (Fall 1981): 193–208.

———. "Taking Off the Gloves: The United States and the Italian Elections of 1948," *Diplomatic History* 7, no. 1 (Winter 1983): 34–55.

Molinari, Augusta. "I giornali delle comunità anarchiche italo-americane," *Movimento operaio e socialista* 4, no. 1–2 (Jan.–June 1981): 117–30.

Monti, Daniel J. Jr. "Some Sort of Americans: The Working and Reworking of Italian-American Ethnicity in the United States." In *Italian Americans in a Multicultural Society*, ed. Jerome Krase and Judith N. DeSena. New York: Forum Italicum, 1994, 19–32.

Moretti, Enrico. "Social Networks and Migrations: Italy, 1876–1913," *International Migration Review* 33, no. 127 (Fall 1999): 640–57.

Morgan, Alfred L. "The Significance of Pennsylvania's 1938 Gubernatorial Election," *Pennsylvania Magazine of History and Biography* 102, no. 2 (Apr. 1978): 184–211.

Nazzaro, Pellegrino. "Il manifesto dell'Alleanza Anti-Fascista del Nord America," *Affari Sociali Internazionali* 2, no. 1–2 (June 1974): 171–85.

Nelli, Humbert S. "Italians." In *Harvard Encyclopedia of American Ethnic Groups*, ed. Stephan Thernstrom. Cambridge MA: Belknap Press of Harvard University Press, 1980, 545–60.

Nelson, Bruce. "Class, Race and Democracy in the CIO: The 'New' Labor History Meets the 'Wages of Whiteness,'" *International Review of Social History* 41, no. 3 (Dec. 1996): 351–74.

Ngai, Mae M. "The Architecture of Race in American Immigration Law: A Reexamination of the Immigration Act of 1924," *Journal of American History* 86, no. 1 (June 1999): 67–92.

Nolan, Hugh J. "Cardinal Dougherty: An Appreciation," *Records of the American Catholic Historical Society of Philadelphia* 62, no. 3 (Sept. 1951): 135–41.

Noyes, Dorothy. "From the *Paese* to the *Patria*: An Italian American Pilgrimage to Rome in 1929." In *Studies in Italian American Folklore*, ed. Luisa Del Giudice. Logan: Utah State University Press, 1993, 127–52.

O'Brien, Jay. "Towards a Reconstruction of Ethnicity: Capitalist Expansion and Cultural Dynamics in Sudan." In *Golden Ages, Dark Ages: Imagining the Past in Anthropology and History*, ed. Jay O'Brien and William Roseberry. Berkeley: University of California Press, 1991, 126–38.

Ogburn, William F., and Nell Snow Talbot, "A Measurement of the Factors in the Presidential Elections of 1928," *Social Forces* 8, no. 2 (Dec. 1929): 175–83.

Orsi, Robert. "The Religious Boundaries of an Inbetween People: Street *Feste* and the Problem of the Dark-Skinned Other in Italian Harlem, 1920–1990," *American Quarterly* 44, no. 3 (Sept. 1992): 313–47.

Parsons, Talcott. "Some Theoretical Considerations on the Nature and Trends of Change of Ethnicity." In *Ethnicity: Theory and Experience*, ed. Nathan Glazer and Daniel Patrick Moynihan. Cambridge MA: Harvard University Press, 1975, 53–83.

Pellegrino, Joanne. "An Effective School of Patriotism." In *Studies in Italian American Social History: Essays in Honor of Leonard Covello*, ed. Francesco Cordasco. Totowa NJ: Rowan and Littlefield, 1975, 84–104.

Pileggi, Nicholas. "Risorgimento: The Red, White, and Greening of New York." In *America and the New Ethnicity*, ed. David R. Colburn and George E. Pozzetta. Port Washington NY: Kennikat, 1979, 118–32.

Pozzetta, George. "Italian Americans." In *Gale Encyclopedia of Multicultural America*, ed. Judy Galens, Anna Sheets, and Robin V. Young. 2 vols. Detroit: Gale Research Inc., 1985, 2:765–82.

———, and Gary R. Mormino. "The Politics of Christopher Columbus and World War II," *Altreitalie* 10, no. 17 (Jan.–June 1998): 6–15.

Pugliese, Stanislao G. "The Culture of Nostalgia: Fascism in the Memory of Italian Americans," *Italian American Review* 5, no. 2 (Autumn–Winter 1996–97): 15–26.

Ransom, Bruce. "Black Independent Electoral Politics in Philadelphia and the Election of Mayor W. Wilson Goode." In *The New Black Politics: The Search for Political Power*, ed. Michael B. Prenston, Lenneal J. Henderson Jr., and Paul L. Puryear. New York: Longman, 1987, 256–89.

Reinhold, Frances L. "Anna Brancato: State Representative." In *The American Politician*, ed. John T. Salter. Chapel Hill: University of North Carolina Press, 1938, 348–58.

Riggio, Jim. "Tales of Little Italy," *Philadelphia Magazine* 62, no. 3 (Mar. 1971): 72–83, 96–105.

Rimanelli, Giose. "The 1891 New Orleans Lynching: Southern Politics, Mafia, Immigration, and the American Press." In *The 1891 New Orleans Lynching and U.S.-Italian Relations: A Look Back*, ed. Marco Rimanelli and Sheryl Lynn Postman. New York: Peter Lang, 1992, 53–105.

Roche, John Patrick. "Suburban Ethnicity: Ethnic Attitude and Behavior among Italian Americans in Two Suburban Communities," *Social Science Quarterly* 63, no. 1 (Mar. 1982): 145–53.

Rosenberg, William L. "Italians, Jews, and Blacks: Ethnic Perspectives of Philadelphia." In *Italian Americans: The Search for a Usable Past*, ed. Richard N. Juliani and Philip V. Cannistraro. Staten Island: American Italian Historical Association, 1989, 32–42.

Rosoli, Gianfausto. "Santa Sede e propaganda fascista all'estero tra i figli degli emigranti italiani," *Storia Contemporanea* 17, no. 4 (Apr. 1986): 293–318.

———. "From 'Promised Land' to 'Bitter Land': Italian Migrants and the Transformation of a Myth." In *Distant Magnets: Expectations and Realities in the Immigrant Experience, 1840–1930*, ed. Dirk Hoerder and Horst Roessner. New York: Holmes & Meier, 1993, 222–40.

Rossi, Ernest E. "Italian Americans and U.S. Relations with Italy in the Cold War." In *The United States and Italy: The First Two Hundred Years*, ed. Humbert S. Nelli. Staten Island: American Italian Historical Association, 1977, 108–29.

———. "NSC 1 and United States Foreign Policy Toward Italy." In *Italian Ethnics: Their Languages, Literatures, and Lives*, ed. Dominic Candeloro, Fred L. Gardaphe, and Paolo A. Giordano. Staten Island: American Italian Historical Association, 1990, 147–68.

———. "Cold War: Italian Americans and Italy." In *The Italian American Experience: An Encyclopedia*, ed. Salvatore J. LaGumina et al. New York: Garland, 2000, 120–23.

Rotondaro, Alfred M. "Ethnicity at Work," *Altreitalie* 3, no. 6 (Nov. 1991): 119–23.

Ruggieri, Nicholas. "Italian Provincial Groups Give Way to Nationalism," *Providence Evening Bulletin* (16 Mar. 1936): 15.

Russo, Pietro. "La stampa periodica italo-americana." In Rudolph J. Vecoli et al. *Gli italiani negli Stati Uniti: L'emigrazione e l'opera degli italiani negli Stati Uniti d'America*. Florence: Istituto di Studi Americani, 1972, 493–546.

Salituro, Joseph. "The Italians in Kenosha, Wisconsin." In *Italian Americans and Their Public and Private Life*, ed. Frank J. Cavaioli, Angela Danzi, and Salvatore J. LaGumina. Staten Island: Italian American Historical Association, 1993, 54–64.

———. "Italian American and Nationalism: A Case of Mixed Loyalties." In *To See the Past More Clearly: The Enrichment of the Italian Heritage, 1890–1990*, ed. Harral E. Landry,. Austin TX: Nortex Press, 1994, 256–67.

Salter, John T. "Letters from Men in Action," *National Municipal Review* 26, no. 9 (Sept. 1937): 417–24, 456.

Salvetti, Patrizia. "La comunità italiana di S. Francisco tra italianità e americanizzazione negli anni '30 e '40," *Studi Emigrazione* 19, no. 65 (Mar. 1982): 3–39.

Santucci, John. "Early 20th Century Inter-Ethnic Relations: A Case Study in North Carolina." In *Italian Americans in Transition*, ed. Joseph V. Scelsa, Salvatore J. LaGumina, and Lydio Tomasi. Staten Island: American Italian Historical Association, 1990, 127–35.

Saudino, Domenico. "Il Fascismo alla conquista dell'Ordine Figli d'Italia," *La Parola del Popolo* 50, no. 37 (Dec. 1958–Jan. 1959): 247–56.

Savereno, Joan. "The Italians of Reading: Forging an Identity in the 1920s," *Historical Review of Berks County* 56, no. 3 (Fall 1991): 172–97.

———. " 'Domani Ci [sic] Zappa': Italian Immigration and Ethnicity in Pennsylvania," *Pennsylvania Folklife* 45, no. 1 (Autumn 1995): 2–22.

Scarpaci, Jean Ann. "Immigrants in the New South: Italians in Louisiana's Sugar Parishes, 1880–1910." In *Il movimento migratorio italiano dall'unità nazionale ai nostri giorni*, ed. Franca Assante. 2 vols. Geneva: Droz, 1978, 2:197–216.

Scherini, Rose D. "Executive Order 9066 and Italian Americans: The San Francisco Story," *California History* 70, no. 4 (Winter 1991–1992): 367–77, 422–24.

Scott, William R. "Black Nationalism and the Italo-Ethiopian Conflict, 1935–1936," *Journal of Negro History* 63, no. 2 (April 1978): 118–34.

Scranton, Philip. "Large Firms and Industrial Restructuring: The Philadelphia Region, 1900–1980," *Pennsylvania Magazine of History and Biography* 116, no. 4 (Oct. 1992): 419–65.

———. "The Transition from Custom to Ready-to-Wear Clothing in Philadelphia, 1890–1930," *Textile History*, 25, no. 2 (Autumn 1994): 243–73.

Shannon, William V. "Election of 1984." In *History of American Presidential Elections, 1789–1984*, ed. Arthur M. Schlesinger Jr. and Fred L. Israel. 5 vols. New York: Chelsea, 1971–1986, 5:273–308.

Shenton, James P. "Fascism and Father Coughlin," *Wisconsin Magazine of History* 44, no. 1 (Autumn 1960): 6–11.

Shipler, David K. "The White Niggers of Newark," *Harper's Magazine* 245, no. 1467 (Aug. 1972): 77–83.

Shover, John L. "Ethnicity and Religion in Philadelphia Politics, 1924–1940," *American Quarterly* 25, no. 5 (Dec. 1973): 499–515.

Simon, William, Samuel Patti, and George Herrmann. "Bloomfield: An Italian Working Class Neighborhood," *Italian Americana* 7, no. 1 (Fall–Winter 1981): 103–15.

Spencer, Thomas T. " 'Labor is with Roosevelt': The Pennsylvania Labor's Non-Partisan League and the Election of 1936," *Pennsylvania History* 46, no. 1 (Jan. 1979): 3–16.

Spikard, Paul R. "Mapping Race: Multiracial People and Racial Category Construction in the United States and Britain," *Immigrants & Minorities* 15, no. 2 (July 1996): 107–19.

Steele, Richard W. " 'No Racials': Discrimination Against Ethnics in American Defense Industry, 1940–42," *Labor History* 32, no. 2 (Winter 1991): 66–90

Strickland, Arvarh. "The School Controversy and the Beginning of the Civil Rights Movement in Chicago," *Historian* 58, no. 4 (Summer 1996): 717–29.

Sugrue, Thomas J. "Crabgrass-Roots Politics: Race, Rights, and the Reaction against Liberalism in the Urban North, 1940–1964," *Journal of American History* 82, no. 2 (Sept. 1995): 551–78.

Sutherland, John F. "Housing the Poor in the City of Homes: Philadelphia at the Turn of the Century." In *The Peoples of Philadelphia: A History of Ethnic Groups and Lower Class Life, 1790–1940*, ed. Allen D. Davis and Mark H. Haller. Philadelphia: Temple University Press, 1973, 175–201.

Tasca, Annamaria. "Italians." In *The Immigrant Labor Press in North America, 1840s–1970s: An Annotated Bibliography*, ed. Dirk Hoerder. 3 vols. Westport CT: Greenwood Press, 1987, 3:13–150.

Tate, James H. J., with Joseph McLaughlin. "In Praise of Politicians," *Evening Bulletin* (23 Jan. 1973): 18.

Tinkcom, Margaret B. "Depression and War, 1919–1946." In *Philadelphia: A 300-Year History*, ed. Russell F. Weigley. New York: Norton, 1982, 601–48.

Tirabassi, Maddalena. "Interview with Joseph Scelsa," *Altreitalie* 10, no. 17 (Jan.–June 1998): 52–55.

Tomasi, Silvano M. "Militantism and Italian-American Unity." In *Power and Class: The Italian American Experience Today*, ed. Francis X. Femminella. Staten Island: American Italian Historical Association, 1973, 20–27.

Tonelli, Bill. "Arrivederci, South Philly," *Philadelphia Magazine* 73, no. 5 (May 1982): 130–43.

Topp, Michael Miller. "The Italian-American Left: Transnationalism and the Quest for Unity." In *The Immigrant Left in the United States*, ed. Paul Buhle and Dan Georgakas. Albany: State University of New York Press, 1996, 119–47

———. "The Transnationalism of the Italian-American Left: The Lawrence Strike of 1912 and the Italian Chamber of Labor of New York City," *Journal of American Ethnic History* 17, no. 1 (Fall 1997): 39–63.

Torrieri, Nancy. "The Geography of Ethnicity: The Residential Dispersal of Italians in Baltimore." In *Italian Americans in Transition*, ed. Joseph V. Scelsa, Salvatore J. LaGumina, and Lydio Tomasi. Staten Island: American Italian Historical Association, 1990, 49–64.

———. "Demography." In *The Italian American Experience: An Encyclopedia*, ed. Salvatore J. LaGumina et al. New York: Garland, 2000, 500–3.

Tricarico, Donald. "Contemporary Italian American Ethnicity: Into the Mainstream." In *Italian Americans: The Search for a Usable Past*, ed. Richard N. Juliani and Philip V. Cannistraro. Staten Island: American Italian Historical Association, 1989, 258–81.

Unti, Aurora. "The Italians in Philadelphia," In International Institute, *Foreign Born in Philadelphia*. Philadelphia: International Institute, 1930, 1–9.

Valletta, Clement. "The Settlement of Roseto: World View and Promise." In *The Ethnic Experience in Pennsylvania*, ed. John E. Bodnar. Lewisburg PA: Bucknell University Press, 1973, 120–43.

Varbero, Richard A. "Philadelphia's South Italians in the 1920s." In *The Peoples of Philadelphia: A History of Ethnic Groups and Lower Class Life, 1790–1940*, ed. Allen D. Davis and Mark H. Haller. Philadelphia: Temple University Press, 1973, 255–75.

———. "Philadelphia's South Italians and the Irish Church: A History of Cultural Conflict." In *The Religious Experience of Italian Americans*, ed. Silvano M. Tomasi. Staten Island: American Italian Historical Association, 1975, 31–52.

———. "The Politics of Ethnicity: Philadelphia's Italians in the 1920's." In *Studies in Italian American Social History: Essays in Honor of Leonard Covello*, ed. Francesco Cordasco. Totowa NJ: Rowan and Littlefield, 1975, 164–81.

———. "Workers in City and County: The South Italian Experience in Philadelphia, 1900–1950." In *Italian Americans: The Search for a Usable Past*, ed. Richard N. Juliani and Philip V. Cannistraro. Staten Island: American Italian Historical Association, 1989, 16–32.

Vecoli, Rudolph J. "*Contadini* in Chicago: A Critique of *The Uprooted*," *Journal of American History* 51, no. 3 (Dec. 1964): 404–17.

———. "Prelates and Peasants: Italian Immigrants and the Catholic Church," *Journal of Social History* 2, no. 3 (Spring 1969): 217–68.

———. "Ethnicity: A Neglected Dimension of American History." In *The State of American History*, ed. Herbert Jacob Bass. New York: Quadrangle Books, 1970, 70–88.

———. "Born Italian: Color Me Red, White, and Green," *Soundings* 61, no. 1 (Spring 1973): 117–23.

———. "Italian-American Workers, 1880–1920: Padrone Slaves or Primitive Rebels?" In *Perspectives in Italian Immigration and Ethnicity*, ed. Silvano M. Tomasi. New York: Center for Migration Studies, 1977, 25–49.

———. "The Italian Immigrants in the United States Labor Movement from 1880 to 1929." In Fondazione Giacomo Brodolini, *Gli italiani fuori d'Italia: Gli emigrati italiani nei movimenti operai dei paesi d'adozione (1880–1940)*, ed. Bruno Bezza. Milan: Franco Angeli, 1983, 257–306.

———. "The Search for an Italian American Identity: Continuity and Change." In *Italian Americans: New Perspectives in Italian Immigration and Ethnicity*, ed. Lydio F. Tomasi. New York: Center for Migration Studies, 1985, 88–112.

———. "The Formation of Chicago's 'Little Italies.'" In *Migration Across Time and Nations: Population Mobility in Historical Contexts*, ed. Ira A. Glazier and Luigi De Rosa. New York: Holmes & Meier, 1986, 287–301.

———. "An Inter-Ethnic Perspective on American Immigration History," *Mid-America* 75, no. 2 (Apr.–July 1993): 223–35.

———. "Italian Immigrants and Working-Class Movements in the United States: A Personal Reflection on Class and Ethnicity," *Journal of the Canadian Historical Association* 4 (1993): 293–305.

———. "Are Italian Americans Just White Folks?" *Italian Americana*, 13, no. 2 (Summer 1995): 149–61.

———. "Ethnicity and Immigration." In *Encyclopedia of the United States in the Twentieth Century*, ed. Stanley I. Kutler. 4 vols. New York: Charles Scribner's Sons, 1996, 1:161–93.

———. "From Pennsylvania Dutch to California Ethnic: The Odyssey of David Hollinger," *Reviews in American History* 24, no. 3 (Sept. 1996): 519–23.

———. "The Italian Immigrant Press and the Construction of Social Reality, 1850–1920." In *Print Culture in a Diverse America*, ed. James P. Danky and Wayne A. Wiegand. Urbana: University of Illinois Press, 1998, 17–33.

Velikonja, Joseph. "Italian Immigrants in the United States in the Mid-Sixties," *International Migration Review* 1, no. 3 (Summer 1967): 25–37.

———. "The Periodical Press and Italian Communities." In *The Family and Community Life of Italian Americans*, ed. Richard N. Juliani. Staten Island: American Italian Historical Association, 1983, 47–60.

Vellon, Peter. "Immigrant Son: Mario Procaccino and the Rise of Conservative Politics in Late 1960s New York City," *Italian American Review* 7, no. 1 (Spring–Summer 1999): 117–36.

Ventresco, Fiorello B. "Italian Americans and the Ethiopian Crisis," *Italian Americana* 6, no. 1 (Fall–Winter 1980): 4–25.

Venturini, Nadia. "Le comunità italiane negli Stati Uniti tra storia sociale e storia politica," *Rivista di storia contemporanea* 13, no. 2 (Apr. 1984): 189–218.

———. "Prominenti at War: The Order Sons of Italy in America," *Rivista di Studi Anglo-Americani* 3, no. 4–5 (1984–1985): 441–70.

———. "Italian-American Leadership, 1943–1948," *Storia Nordamericana* 2, no. 1 (1985): 35–62.

Villari, Luigi. "L'emigrazione italiana nel distretto consolare di Filadelfia," *Bollettino dell'emigrazione* no. 16 (1908): 1860–79.

Viscusi, Robert. "Il futuro dell'italianità: Il Commonwealth italiano," *Altreitalie* 5, no. 10 (July–Dec. 1993): 25–32.

———. "Viaggio Continuo: Resisting Identity." In *Il sogno italo-americano: Realtà e immaginario dell'emigrazione negli Stati Uniti*, ed. Sebastiano Martelli. Naples: CUEN, 1998, 377–90.

Ware, Caroline F. "Cultural Groups in the United States." In *The Cultural Approach to History*, ed. Caroline F. Ware. New York: Columbia University Press, 1940, 62–73.

Warner, Sam Bass Jr. "If All the World Were Philadelphia: A Scaffolding for Urban History, 1774–1930," *American Historical Review* 74, no. 1 (Oct. 1968): 26–43.

Warren, Jonathan W., and France Winddance Twine. "White Americans, the New Minority? Non-Blacks and the Ever-Expanding Boundaries of Whiteness," *Journal of Black Studies* 28, no. 2 (Nov. 1997): 200–18.

Weiss, Richard. "Ethnicity and Reform: Minorities and the Ambience of the Depression Years," *Journal of American History* 66, no. 3 (Dec. 1979): 566–85.

Whiteman, Maxwell. "Out of the Sweatshop." In *Jewish Life in Philadelphia, 1830–1940*, ed. Murray Friedman. Philadelphia: Institute for the Study of Human Issues, 1983, 64–79.

Weinberg, Martha Wagner. "Boston's Kevin White: A Mayor Who Survives," *Political Science Quarterly* 96, no. 1 (Spring 1981): 87–106.

Williams, Brakette F. "A Class Act: Anthropology and the Race to Nation Across Ethnic Terrain," *Annual Review of Anthropology* 18 (1989): 401–44.

Wilson, Diane Vecchio. "Assimilation and Ethnic Consolidation of Italians in Cortland, New York: 1892–1930." In *The Family and Community Life of Italian Americans*, ed. Richard N. Juliani. Staten Island: American Italian Historical Association, 1983, 183–91.

Winkler, Allan M. "The Philadelphia Transit Strike of 1944," *Journal of American History* 59, no. 1 (June 1972): 73–89.

Wolf, Stephanie G. "The Bicentennial City, 1968–1982." In *Philadelphia: A 300-Year History*, ed. Russell F. Weigley. New York: Norton, 1982, 704–34.

Yancey, William L., Eugene P. Ericksen, and Richard N. Juliani. "Emergent Ethnicity: A Review and Reformulation," *American Sociological Review* 41, no. 3 (June 1976): 391–403.

I. Dissertations and Other Unpublished Secondary Sources

Baer, Kenneth S. "Whitman: A Study of Race, Class, and Postwar Public Housing Opposition." Senior honor thesis, University of Pennsylvania, 1994.

Balchunis, Mary Ellen. "A Study of the Old and New Campaign Politics Models: A Comparative Analysis of Wilson Goode's 1983 and 1987 Philadelphia Mayoral Campaigns." Ph.D. diss., Temple University, 1992.

Bauman, John F. "The City, the Depression, and Relief: The Philadelphia Experience, 1929–1939." Ph.D. diss., Rutgers University, 1969.

Berlin, Raisa Rebecca Sarah Deber. "Who Runs? Congressmen and Realignment Sequences." Ph.D. diss., MIT, 1977.

Black, Gregory Dale. "The United States and Italy, 1943–1946: The Drift Toward Containment." Ph.D. diss., University of Kansas, 1973.

Datz, A. Harold. "Snatching Defeat from the Jaws of Victory: The 1967 Mayoralty Election in Philadelphia." A.B. thesis, Temple University, n.d.

Dauria, Susan Renee. "Deindustrialization and the Construction of History and Ethnic Identity: A Case in Upstate New York." Ph.D. diss., State University of New York at Albany, 1994.

Dickinson, Torry. "Redivided Lives: The Formation of the Working Class in Philadelphia, 1870–1945." Ph.D. diss., State University of New York at Binghamton, 1983.

Fernandez, John H. "Conceptualizing Culture and Ethnicity: Toward an Anthropology of Puerto Rican Philadelphia." Ph.D. diss., Temple University, 1994.

Goodman, Madeline Jane. "The Evolution of Ethnicity: Fascism and Anti-Fascism in the Italian-American Community." Ph.D. diss., Carnegie Mellon University, 1993.

Greenberg, Irwin F. "The Philadelphia Democratic Party, 1911–1934." Ph.D. diss., Temple University, 1972.

Grove, Stephen Brian. "The Decline of the Republican Machine in Philadelphia, 1936–52." Ph.D. diss., University of Pennsylvania, 1976.

Harris, Howell John. "The Deluge: The New Deal and the Open Shop Era." Paper presented at the "New Deal Conference," Sidney Sussex College, Cambridge, England, 21–23 Sept. 1993.

Hartigan, John McDonald Jr. "Cultural Construction of Whiteness: Racial and Class Formation in Detroit." Ph.D. diss., University of California, Santa Cruz, 1995.

Henwood, James J. H. "Politics and Unemployment Relief, Pennsylvania, 1931–1939." Ph.D. diss., University of Pennsylvania, 1975.

Ianni, Francis Anthony. "The Acculturation of the Italo-Americans in Norristown, Pennsylvania: 1900 to 1950." Ph.D. diss., Pennsylvania State College, 1952.

Jarrell, Donald Winfield. "A History of Collective Bargaining at the Camden-Area Plants of the Radio Corporation of America with Special Attention to Bargaining Power." Ph.D. diss., University of Pennsylvania, 1967.

Juliani, Richard N. "The Social Development of Italian-American Communities." Paper presented at the 28th annual conference of the American Italian Historical Association, Lowell MA, 9–12 Nov. 1995.

Lee, Jae-Hyup. "Identity and Social Dynamics in Ethnic Community: Comparative Study on Boundary Making among Asian Americans in Philadelphia." Ph.D. diss., University of Pennsylvania, 1994.

Maiale, Hugo. "The Italian Vote in Philadelphia between 1928 and 1946." Ph.D. diss., University of Pennsylvania, 1950.

Makarewicz, Joseph T. "The Impact of World War I on Pennsylvania Politics with Emphasis on the Election of 1920." Ph.D. diss., University of Pittsburgh, 1972.

Mathias, Elizabeth Lay. "From Folklore to Mass Culture: Dynamics of Acculturation in the Games of Italian-American Men." Ph.D. diss., University of Pennsylvania, 1974.

Nishime, LeiLani Linda. "Creating Race: Genre and Cultural Construction of Asian-American Identity." Ph.D. diss., University of Michigan, 1997.

Passero, Rosara Lucy. "Ethnicity in the Men's Ready-Made Clothing Industry, 1880–1950: The Italian Experience in Philadelphia." Ph.D. diss., University of Pennsylvania, 1978.

Rizzo, Maria. "L'emigrazione italiana negli Stati Uniti d'America dal 1880 alla prima guerra mondiale: I problemi dell'adattamento in un case study: Gli italiani a Philadelphia." Ph.D. diss., University of Naples, 1985–1986.

Savereno, Joan Lynn. "Private Lives, Public Identities: The Italians of Reading and Berks County, Pennsylvania, 1890–1940." Ph.D. diss., University of Pennsylvania, 1996.

Shufelt, Gordon H. "Strangers in a Middle Land: Italian Immigrants and Race Relations in Baltimore, 1890–1920." Ph.D. diss., American University, 1998.

Smith, Richard T. Jr. "Philadelphia's Deindustrialization: The Impact on Low Wages, African Americans, and Unionization." Ph.D. diss., Temple University, 1994.

Stephenson, Sally. "Michael Musmanno: A Symbolic Leader." Ph.D. diss., Carnegie-Mellon University, 1981.

Varbero, Richard A. "Urbanization and Acculturation: Philadelphia's South Italians, 1918–1932." Ph.D. diss., Temple University, 1975.

Vellon, Peter. "Victims of the Mob: Lynching, the Italian-American Press, and the Racial 'In-betweeness' of Southern Italian Immigrants in the American South, 1891–1927." Paper presented at the 32nd annual conference of the American Italian Historical Association, San Francisco CA, 11–13 Nov. 1999.

Whalen, Carmen Teresa. "Puerto Rican Migration to Philadelphia, Pennsylvania, 1945–1970: A Historical Perspective on a Migrant Group." Ph.D. diss., Rutgers University, 1994.

Index

Abate, Erasmo, 44
A. B. Kirschbaum Co., 58, 76
Addonizio, Hugh J., 153
African Americans, 5–6, 9–12, 40, 45, 66, 73–74, 104, 125–36, 139–40, 142, 144–46, 150–57
Alba, Richard D., 156–57
Alessandroni, Eugene V., 53, 64, 80–81, 86–88, 96, 98, 100–101, 110–11, 113, 115–16, 121
Alessandroni, John, 72
Alien Registration Act (1940), 99
Altieri, James, 116
Amalgamated Clothing Workers of America (ACWA), 40, 71, 77, 102, 110, 132–33
American Committee Against Racial Discrimination, 49
American Committee on Italian Migration, 125
American Federation of Labor (AFL), 73
Americans for Democratic Action (ADA), 133–34, 137
American-Italian Congress, 109
American Jewish Committee, 125
American Stores Co., 82
Amodei, Charles, 48
Amodei, Joseph, 66
Andreani, Paolo, 17
Angelucci family, 28
Annenberg, Walter, 135
Anticommunism, 111–16, 120–21, 140, 150
Anti-Fascist Alliance of North America, 85–86
Antisemitism, 85–86
Arts Committee for Green, 133
Ascoli, Max, 97
Asian Americans, 5, 156
Associazione Lucchesi nel Mondo (Italians in the World Association), 148
Associazione Nazionale Abruzzese, 147
Assunta House, 40
Atwater Kent, 22
Aurora Club, 52, 148
Aurora, L', 29
Avena, John, 47
Aversa, Alfred, 12

Badoglio, Pietro, 103
Baldassarre, G., 44
Baldi, Charles C. A., Jr., 64–65, 80
Baldi, Charles C. A., Sr., 18–19, 33–37, 60, 65, 80, 83
Banca Calabrese, 28

Banca Commerciale Italiana & Trust Co., 59
Banca dell'Aquila, 28
Banca d'Italia & Trust Co., 59
Banca di Napoli, 28, 59
Banca di Torino, 28
Banca M. Bernardini, 59
Barbaro, Fred, 12
Baroni, Geno, 10
Barrett, William, 116, 122
Bartilucci, Joseph, 91
Batacchi, Joseph, 17
Belliotti, Raymond A., 11
Benedetto, Warren N., 124
Bernardy, Amy, 25
Bettain Brothers Co., 76
Bianco, Carla, 7
Biblioteca Circolante del Littorio (Lictor Lending Library), 92
Biagi, Ernest L., 97, 115, 137–38
Biddle, Francis, 106
Blum, Jon, 134
B'nai B'rith, 136; San Francisco chapter of, 152
Bocchini, Filippo, 42, 79, 88
Bodnar, John, 115
Bonnelly, Adrian, 70, 99
Borrelli, Ralph (Ralffaele), 83, 90, 99, 102, 140
Bowser, Charles W., 137, 141
Brancato, Anna M., 65–66, 78
Briggs, John W., 7, 32
British Americans, 45
Bruni, Luigi, 44
Bruno, Giuseppe, 42
Byrnes, James F., 109–10

Calvello, Antonio, 81
Candilora, Mary, 128
Cannon, Joseph G., 35
Capone, Al, 152
Capponi, Ottaviano, 37
Carducci, Giosuè, 36
Carletti, Herman E., 107
Carter, Jimmy, 145
Casablanca Conference, 103
Caserta, Mike, 123

Cassettari, Rosa, 24
Castiglioni Luigi, 17
Castille, Roland, 144
Catania, Biagio, 65–66, 78
Catholic Standard and Times, 40
Cavagnaro, Bartolomeo Alfredo, 31
Cavagnaro, Paul, 31, 64
Celebrezze, Antony, 120
Censi, Ludovico, 87, 96
Centro Educativo (Educational Center) Arnaldo Mussolini, 92
Ceracchi, Giuseppe, 17
Christian Democratic Party, 111–13, 120, 140
Christopher Columbus Mutual Aid Society, 31
Churchill, Winston, 103, 107
Church of Santa Maria, 94
Cianfalone, Giuseppe, 52
Ciarrocchi, Monsignor Joseph, 94
CIO, 57, 60, 71
Cimino, Joseph J., 70
Cingolo, Ralph, 138
Circolo Francisco Ferrer, 42
Circolo Italiano, 34, 37
Circolo Maidese, 52
Citizens Alliance for Mediterranean Freedom, 140
City Charter referendum (1978), 141–42
Civilian Conservation Corps, 61
Clark, Joseph S., Jr, 124, 137
Clinton, William Jefferson, 147
Clothing Workers' strikes (1919–1922), 76
Cohen, J. H., 22
Collier's, 99
Colonna, Principe Ascanio, 103
Columbia Republican League, 80
Columbus Day, 35, 36, 91–92, 102
Columbus Forum, 132
Comitato Amici dell'Italia (Friends of Italy Committee), 87, 94
Comitato Italiano per la Difesa degli Immigrati (Italian Committee for the Defense of Immigrants), 100
Comitato pro Sacco-Vanzetti, 49

Communist Party (Italy), 111, 113, 120–21, 140, 150
Communist Party (United States), 97
Comune, La, 42, 44
Connally, John B., 140
Conte Luna Products Inc., 83
Coolidge, Calvin, 80
Corona di Ferro, 32
Coraggio della gioventù mussoliniana, Il (The Bravery of Mussolini's Youth), 91
Corsi, Edward, 108
Cortese, Americo V., 107, 125
Cortigene, Anthony, 132–33
Cosa Nostra, 119
Costantini, Costantino, 41
Coughling, Father, Charles E., 89
Crusco, J. Louis, 123
Cuccetta, Jayne, 128
Cuneo, Frank, 18, 31
Cuneo Frederick, 64
Cunningham, George E., 154
Cuomo, Mario, 145

D'Alonzo, Andrea, 28
D'Annunzio, Gabriele, 43
D'Auria, Vincenzo, 111
Da Grossa, John, 72, 79
Davis, James J., 45, 47, 72
De Bernardo, Henry, 137
De Biasi, Agostino, 84
De Gasperi, Alcide, 111, 121
Della Porta, Armand, 132, 147
Del Raso, Joseph V., 147
Del Russo, Giuseppe, 84
De Luca, Philip, 110
Democratic Party, 43, 57, 60–73, 78, 80–81, 95–96, 102–103, 107, 114, 116, 133, 140, 144–46, 150
De Nero, John, 64, 67, 116–17
De Nobili Cigarettes, 81
De Pinedo, Francesco, 86
De Vito, Joseph, 67
Dewey, Thomas E., 108–109, 114–15, 117
Diaz, Armando, 43–44
Di Bartolomeo, Albert, 2

Di Bernardino Firm, 26
Di Bernardino, Frank, 26, 28
Di Bernardino, Henry, 54
Di Febo, Annibale, 96
Diggins, John P., 97, 110
Di Lauro, Thomas, 98
Di Lemmo, Nicholas, 65
Dillingham Immigration Commission, 11, 19
Dillworth, Richardson, 129, 131
Di Silvestro, Anthony, 67–69, 72, 77–78, 81, 83, 99
Di Silvestro, Arpino Giuseppe, 19, 33–34, 36–37, 42, 67, 80
Di Silvestro, Giovanni, 19, 33, 34, 36–37, 42, 46, 48–50, 79, 80, 85, 88, 97
Di Stasi, Lawrence, 97
D'Ortona, Paul, 100, 106
Dougherty, Cardinal Dennis, 54–55, 93, 111
Dougherty, Harry V., 66
Duff, James F., 115
Durante, Jimmy, 1
Downes, Jack, 137

Earle George H., 61, 69–70
Eighteenth Amendment, 32, 62
Eisenhower, Dwight D., 120–21, 123
EIAR, 91
Elections: 1916, 43; 1920, 43; 1926, 61; 1928, 61; 1930, 61; 1932, 61; 1933, 67; 1934, 61, 69, 88; 1936, 61, 68, 74, 88, 95–96; 1938, 71–72, 74; 1940, 72, 95, 96; 1942, 103; 1944, 103, 108; 1948, 114, 117; 1952, 121–24; 1956, 123; 1959, 129; 1968, 144–45; 1971, 133; 1972, 145; 1975, 141; 1983, 143; 1984, 146; 1987, 143; 1991, 144
Electrical Workers Local 98, 130
Eliot Bill, 98
Ellis, Furey, 109, 111
Emergency Quota Act (1921), 44–45, 63
Enemy aliens: Italian immigrants as, 98, 106

Ente Opere Assistenziali, 96
Epton, Bernard, 142
Erdmans, Mary Patrice, 5
Ethnicity: as a pentagon, 4–5; as social construction, 3–4, 151–52; as whiteness, 5–10; Italian American scholarship on, 6–13

Farrakhan, Louis, 142
Fascism, 8, 73–74, 79, 83–94, 96–97, 103, 149–50
Federation of Community Councils and Neighborhood Associations, 128
Federation of Italian World War Veterans, 87, 96
Ferraro, Geraldine, 145–46
Fields, Barbara Jeanne, 6
First Congress of Italians (1911), 50
First Italian Presbyterian Church, 29
Foglietta, Thomas M., 132, 140–41
Ford, Gerald R., 125
Forer, Louis G., 130
Fornara, Henry, 130
Fortune, 98
Fragale, Paul, 85
Free Italy American Labor Council, 110
Fuchs, Lawrence H., 10

Gabaccia, Donna R., 27
Gallagher, James, 116
Gambino, Richard, 11, 157
Gans, Herbert J., 8
Garibaldi, Giuseppe, 36
Gatt, Father Simplicio, 54
Gayda, Virginio, 96
Gazzetta Italiana, La, 32, 33
General Electric, 81
Genna brothers, 152
German Americans, 45, 53, 76, 82, 136
Gersle, Gary, 67
Gertrude, M. Agnes, 27
Giannini, Ferruccio A., 64
Gibson, Kenneth A., 153
Gillepsie, Thomas F., 137

Giornale d'Italia, 6
Girard, Vincent, 66, 72
Girone, Joseph, 119
Giuseppe Garibaldi, 36
Giuliani, Reginaldo, 94
Glazer, Nathan, 9, 112, 151
Gleason, Philp 97
Goglia, Michael, 70
Golab, Caroline, 49
Goldman, William, 136
Goode, Wilson W., 142–44
Gore, Albert, 147
Graduate Club, 52
Granaham, William T., 122
Grandi, Dino, 79, 86, 90
Great Atlantic & Pacific Tea Co., 82
Green, William Jr., 133
Gualdo, Giovanni, 17
Guasco, Father Bruno, 94
Guffey, Joseph F., 70, 103
Gutierrez, David G., 152

Hagan, William A., 67
Haller, Mark H., 48
Hallmark, 125
Haluska, John J., 71
Harding, Warren, 43
Hart-Celler Act (1965), 125
Henry, Edward W., 66
Hickok, Lorena, 69
Hicks, Louise Day, 134
Hiss case, 115
Hollinger, David A.,157
Home Owners' Loan Corporation, 61
Hoover, Edgard J., 100
Hoover, Herbert, 60, 61, 63, 65
Hopkins, Henry, 69
Hoskins, Harold B., 99
Howells, William Dean, 24
Humphrey, H. Hubert, 145
Hyde Park Declaration, 107

Iannucci, James, 108
Immigration restriction, 35, 44–45, 49, 63–64, 121–23
Impellitteri, Vicent R., 154

Indiana Democrat, 62
Inverso, Pat, 105
Independent Democratic Campaign Committee (IDCC), 66–67
Industrial Workers of the World, 44, 76
Intesa Libertaria, 86
Irish Americans, 40–41, 51, 53, 66, 74, 126–27, 131, 142, 148, 150
Isoleri, Father Antonio, 29, 55
Italian-American Anti-Defamation League, 119, 120
Italian-American Citizen's Alliance, 70
Italian American Congressional Delegation, 12
Italian Americans: and the Catholic Church, 29–30, 40–41, 54–55, 93–94; and ethnic stereotypes, 39–41, 47–48, 68, 119–20, 125, 146; and natural calamities in Italy, 36–37, 147; and organized crime, 12, 47–48, 68, 119, 123–24, 146, 142; and politics, 43, 53–54, 60–72, 77–79, 88–89, 95–96, 103,107–8,114–17,121–23, 124, 129, 133–38, 140–46, 150, 152–54 (*see also* elections); as birds of passage, 49–50; conflicts with African Americans, 9–10, 11–12, 73–74, 125–35, 144–45, 150–55; conflicts with Irish, 40–41, 51; conflicts with Jewish Americans, 51, 73–74, 150; ethnic broadcasting, 82–83, 90–91; ethnic consumption, 28, 81–83, 155; ethnic organizations, 31–32, 50–53, 59, 80–81, 147–48 (*see also* single organizations); ethnic press, 32–34; 80–81; 86–130 (*see also* single newspapers); labor militancy, 74–77; occupations in Philadelphia, 20–22; origin of immigrants to Philadelphia, 22–23; political refugees in Philadelphia, 23; regional antagonism of, 30–32; settlements in Philadelphia, 17–18, 26–27; suburbanization of, 139, 155; unemployment of, 58 (*see also* Little Italies);
Italian Evangelical Church, 29
Italian Federation of Philadelphia, 37
Italian Socialist Federation of North America, 75
Italian Welfare Council, 124
Italian Workingmen's Progressive Institute, 85
Italo-American Bicentennial Celebration, 147
Italo-American Republican League of Pennsylvania, 107
Italo-Ehiopian War, 10, 73–74, 87–89, 94, 150
Italo-Turkish War, 42
Italy: and the Fiume controversy, 42–43; elections in: 1948, 111–12, 1953, 120–21, 1976, 140; in World War I, 39; in World War II, 100, 103, 105, 107; natural calamities in, 36–37, 147; 1919 concordat, 93; postwar settlement, 108–11, 113–14
Iverso, Donato, 83

Jablonky Alexander, 128
Jackson, Reverend Jesse, 142
Jenkins, Philip, 112
Jewish Americans, 45, 51, 73–74, 76, 82, 125–26, 136, 142, 150
Joint Civic Committee of Italian Americans, 125
John B. Stetson Hat Company, 59
Johnson-Reed Act (1924), 44–45, 63–64
Jones, Charles Alvin, 70, 71
Journeymen Tailor's International Union, 76
Juliani, Richard N., 14–15, 148, 157

Katz, Samuel, 144
Kefauver Committee, 123–24
Kefauver, Estes, 123–24
Kelly, John B., 66–68, 70
Kennedy, Thomas, 70–71

King, Martin Luther, Jr., 10
Krase, Jerome, 156
Ku Klux Klan, 11, 45–46

La Cavera, Father Salvatore, 94
La Guardia, Fiorello H., 154
Lagomarsino, Agostino, 18, 31
Land, Emory S., 99
Lanzetti, Ignatius, 47, 152
Lanzetti, Leo, 47, 152
Lanzetti, Lucien, 47, 152
Lanzetti, Pius, 47, 152
Lanzetti, Teo, 47, 152
Lanzetti, Willie, 47, 152
Lateran Treaties (1929), 93
Latta, James, 17
Lawrence, David, 70
League of Nations, 87–88
Lega Italiana per la Difesa degli Interessi Nazionali (Italian League for the Safeguard of National Interests), 85
Lemke, William, 88
Libera Parola, La, 34, 43, 46, 54, 67, 73–74, 80, 81, 86–87, 89, 92, 102
Liberatore, Silvio, 34
Lindsay, John, 134, 153–54
Literacy Test (1917), 35, 50
Little Italies: Ardmore, 139; Baltimore, 156; Boston, 24, 156; Canarsie, 126; Cleveland, 25; Corona, 126; Cortland, 25; Long Island, 139; New York City, 24–25; Norristown, 25; Roseto, 155; Philadelphia, 17–18, 27; Providence, 24; Toronto, 24; gentrification of, 155–56
Lodge, Henry Cabot, 46
Lombardi, Robert, 19, 64
Lomenro, Frank, 143
Longstreth, W. Thacher, 133
Lopez, Ian F. Harney, 6
Lutheran Men, 136

Madonna House, 40
Mafia, 12, 48, 119, 123–24, 154
Maglio, Il, 86

Mahoney, George P., 152
Makransky, 51
Malan, Teofilo D., 29
Manerba, Carlo, 101
Manfredi, Louis A., 72
Mangano, Antonio, 25
Mangione, Jerre, 120, 133
Mangione, Joseph, 105
Margariti, Antonio, 49
Marchi, John, 134, 153–54
Margiotti, Charles J., 69–72
Marine Corps Supply Center, 139
Marinelli, Joseph, 67–68, 70, 72, 78
Marine Transport Workers' strike (1913), 76
Marino, Donald C., 119
Maroncelli, Piero, 23
Marshall Plan, 114
Martello, Il, 88
Martin, Edward, 122–23
Martinelli, Don, 30
Marutani, William, 137
Mascagni Restaurant, 28
Massimiano, Anthony, 22
Matteotti, Giacomo, 86
Mazzone, Father Vito C., 55, 94, 120, 138
Mastro Paolo, 28, 42
McCarran, Pat, 122
McCarran-Walter Act (1952), 121–23
McCloskey, Edward, 71
McDetmott, James T., 129
McMenamin, James, 104
Melchiorre, Charles, 65–66, 78, 100, 106
Melocchi, Raffaele, 28
Menicucci, Umberto, 84
Meranze, Joseph B., 130
Middishade, 51
Miller, Herbert A., 151
Miller, William, 120
Minnick, Thomas J., 66
Miserendino, Charles, 22
Mexican Americans, 10, 151, 154
Momento, Il, 41, 44
Mondale, Walter, 145
Moore, J. Hampton, 44, 53, 91

Mormino, Gary Ross, 32
Moroni, Father Marcellino, 30
Morriconi, Albert, 76
MOVE, 141, 143
Moynihan, Daniel Patrick, 9, 112
Multicon Corporation, 141
Municipal Service Building controversy, 129–30
Musmanno, Michael A., 124
Mussolini, Benito, 8, 48, 73–74, 79, 84–91, 97, 103

Nardi, Emanuel V. H., 36
Nardi, Lorenzo L., 14–15, 31, 36
National Association for the Advancement of Colored People, 129, 136
National Italian American Foundation, 12, 145
National Industrial Recovery Act (NIRA) (1933), 21, 76
National Italian American Women's Organization, 12
Nativism, 11, 45–49, 98–101, 106
Navy Engineering Group, 139
Nelli, Humbert S., 7, 12, 155
Neumann, Bishop John N., 29
Neutrality Acts, 114
New Deal, 61–62, 64, 67
New York Times, 120, 146
Nixon, Richard M., 122, 144–45
Nocella, Sam, 76
Norris, J Austin, 73
Novak, Michael, 9–10

O' Donnell, John, 65–67
Observer, 96
Office of War Information, 99, 101
Opinione, L', 33–36, 42, 45, 51, 68, 80, 84, 86, 88, 90
Opinione-Il Progresso Italo-Americano, L', 80
Opinione Italiana, L', 80
Order of Brotherly Love, 108
Order Sons of Italy in America (OSIA), 31, 39, 46, 50, 53, 80, 84–85, 91, 100, 112, 115, 119, 125, 130, 138; Commission for Social Justice of, 12; Italo Balbo Lodge, 97; Pennsylvania Grand Lodge of, 34, 39, 80–81, 88, 102, 115, 132; San Francisco Anti-Defamation Commission of, 152
Ordine Nuovo, 81, 86, 100, 101, 106, 108, 111, 116, 122, 130
Orsi, Robert, 9
Osservatore, L', 99
Our Lady of Good Counsel, 29, 54, 93
Our Lady of Pompei, 30

Palladino, John, 22
Palermo, Angelo, 76
Palermo, Frank "Blinky", 123
Palumbo, Angelo, 112
Palumbo, Francesco, 1
Palumbo, Frank, 86, 123
Palumbo's, 1–2, 32, 86, 156
Panetta, Angelo M., 48, 66
Paris Peace Conference: 1919, 43; 1946, 109
Park, Robert E., 151
Pellegrino, Charles, 65
Pellico, Silvio, 23
Pennsylvania House Committee on Education, 132
Pennsylvania Railroad Company, 20
Pepper, George W., 64
Perri, Joseph M., 48, 64
Philadelphia and Reading Railroad Company, 20, 58
Philadelphia Board of Public Education, 128–32
Philadelphia Building Trades Council, 130
Philadelphia Chamber of Commerce, 44
Philadelphia Commission on Human Relations, 128, 130
Philadelphia Congress of Racial Equality, 129
Philadelphia Daily News, 48, 68
Philadelphia Democratic City Committee, 65, 67

Philadelphia Evening Bulletin, 45, 46, 47, 48, 112, 127
Philadelphia Evening Ledger, 47
Philadelphia Exclusive, 138
Philadelphia Housing Authority, 127
Philadelphia Inquirer, 2, 48, 105, 135–36
Philadelphia Public Ledger, 41, 48
Philadelphia Rapid Transit Employees Union (PRTEU), 104
Philadelphia Record, 48, 63, 73, 104, 106
Philadelphia Transportation Company (PTC), 104–105
Philco Corporation, 22, 77
Pileggi, Nicholas, 12
Pinchot, Cornelia Bryce, 105, 108
Pinchot, Gifford, 54
Pincus, 51
Pittman, Key, 88
Pittman-McReynolds Bill, 87–89
Pius XII, 112
Plebe, La, 75
Poccardi, Gaetano, 42
Polenberg, Richard, 4 , 157
Polish American Affairs Council, 125
Polish Americans, 5, 51, 82, 125, 127–28, 131, 142, 153
Pope, Generoso, 80, 91
Popolo, Il, 33, 36
Popolo, Italiano, Il, 80, 86–87, 89, 96, 100–101, 105, 107, 111, 113, 115, 120–22, 130
Porreca, Norman, 81
Porreca's, 80
Potter, William, 42
Procaccino, Mario, 134, 153–54
Progresso Italo-Americano, Il , 80, 89, 114–15, 120
Proletario, Il, 75
Prudente, Amato, 83
Presbyterian Church of Saint Andrew and Saint Paul, 29
Puerto Ricans, 10, 126, 153

Radio and Metal Workers Industrial Union, 76

Radio Corporation of America (RCA), 22, 58, 81
Ragione, La, 34
Ranieri, Nicholas, 22
Ranseley, Harry C., 68
Rassegna, La, 34
Rea, Gene, 102
Reagan, Ronald, 145
Reale, Josephine, 26
Red Scare, 44
Reed, David A., 63
Refugee Relief Act (1953), 123
Regalbuto, Samuel B., 114
Rendell, Edward G., 144
Renzulli, Michele, 50
Republican Party, 43, 60–72, 78–80, 96, 103, 107–108, 115–17, 122, 136, 142–44
Revolutionary Action Movement, 134
Riccinti, Leonora, 137
Richards, David A. J., 13
Rizzo, Frank, 130, 133–38, 140–45, 147, 153
Rolandi Ricci, Vittorio, 46
Roma Cafe, 32
Romanowki, William, 128
Roosevelt, Franklin D., 58, 60–62, 66, 68, 78, 95, 98–99, 102–108, 114
Roosevelt, Theodore, 35
Ross, F. Cair, 103
Rossi, Joseph A., 70
Rosso, Augusto, 101
Ross, William, 136
Russian Americans, 127–28

Sacco, Nicola, 44, 49, 84
Sacks, Leon, 72–74, 77, 102
St. Ambrose, 30, 94
St. Augustine's Church, 10
St. Mary Magdalen de Pazzi, 17, 29, 55, 155
St. Michael of the Saints, 30
St. Paul, 41
St. Rita, 93
Salandra, Antonio, 39
Salituro, Joseph, 92
Salvadori, Massimo, 90

Salvemini, Gaetano, 90
San Giorgio Macaroni, 83
Sansa, Louis P., 81
Saracco, Francesco, 53
Sassi, Damiano, 103, 106
Saturday Evening Post, 101
Scandella, Giambattista, 17
School Administration Building incident, 130–31
School referendum: 1961, 128–29; 1969, 131–33
Schnader, William, 69
Schuylkill Valley Railroad, 19
Scott, Amos, 54
Scott, Hugh, 115, 133
Sebastian, Robert L., 130, 136
Second Italian Presbyterian Church, 29
Sedita, Frank A., 134
Sega, Giacomo, 23
Shedd, Mark R., 131, 134
Signal Corps Supply Center, 139
Silvagni, F., 34
Simonni Oil, 83
Sinatra, Frank, 1
Sircana, Leone, 92
Slomiski, Alfreda, 134
Smith, Alfred, 61–63, 65, 78
Smith, Thomas B., 42
Società Beniamino Gigli fra' Marchegiani, 37
Società di Mutuo Soccorso e Beneficienza Unione Calabrese, 53
Società di Mutuo Soccorso fra Castrogiovannesi e Provinciali, 32
Società di Mutuo Soccorso Maria Santissima delle Grazie di Acquavilla-Cilento, 36
Società di Mutuo Soccorso Roma e Provincia, 37
Società di Mutuo Soccorso Santa Barbara, 36
Società di Unione e Fratellanza Italiana, 17, 31
Società Fraterna Cosenza, 32
Società Italiana Unione Abruzzese, 31, 43, 51, 53–54

Società Sulmonse, 32
Società Unite, 53
Sole Mio Cigars, 81
Sons of Italy Bank, 59
Sons of Italy Times, 130, 136, 143–46
Sorgi's, 81
South Philadephia Bussinessmen's Associaton, 138
Spatola, Michael A., 68, 70
Specter, Arlen, 136
Spiziri, Frank S., 23
Steinberg, Stephen, 8
Stenving, Charles, 134
Stettinius, Edward R., Jr., 107
Stevenson, Adlai, 121, 123
Stimson, Henry L., 107
Stonemasons' strikes (1933–1936), 76–77
Suvich, Fulvio, 89

Tailors' strike (1909), 76
Talese, Joseph, 28
Tate, James H. J., 129, 130, 135–36
Transport Workers Union (TWU), 104
Tresca, Carlo, 75–76
Truman, Harry S., 110, 114–15, 121–22, 148
Tumolillo, Joseph, 66

Unione Abruzzese. *See* Società Italiana Unione Abruzzese
Union Party, 88
United Hatters, Cap, and Millinery Workers International, 59
United Italian Societies of Philadelphia, 36
United Nations Relief and Rehabilitation Administration (UNRRA), 107
United Nations Security Council, 147
U.S. Department of Housing and Urban Development, 127

Valachi, Joseph, 119
Valeo, Antonio, 52

Valinote, Joseph, 83
Vanzetti, Bartolomeo, 44, 49, 80
Vare Bros. Construction Co., 60
Vare, William S., 60–61, 63–67, 80
Vecoli, Rudolph J., 11, 42, 75, 151, 155, 157
Verdi, Giuseppe, 36
Vesuvio, Il, 32
Victor Emmanuel III, 88, 103
Vignola, Joseph, 1
Villari, Luigi, 41, 47
Viscusi, Robert, 12, 151
Voce della Colonia, La, 33
Voce del Popolo, La, 33–34, 42
Voce Indipendente, La, 86
Volstead Act, 152

Wallace, George C., 144, 152
Walter, Francis, 122
War Labor Dispute Smith-Connally Act, 105
Watergate investigation, 145
Washington, Harold, 142
WDES, 83
Welfare capitalism, 58–59
White, Kevin, 1934
White, Theodore H., 9
Whiteman Park controversy, 127–28, 141

Whiteness, 5–6; among Italians Americans, 7–10
Whyte, William Foote, 25
Wible, Bill, 137
Willkie, Wendell L., 72
Wilson, S. Davis, 85
Wilson, Woodrow, 43, 114
Wineshop Criscuolo, 28
World War I, 39, 41–44; and recognition for Italian-Americans, 41–42
World War II, 95–108; allegiance of Italian Americans in, 100–102; and aids to Italy, 107–108; and end of the Depression, 98; and ethnic bigotry, 98–101, 105; Italy's entry into, 95–96; Italy's surrender, 103–104; response of Italian Americans to, 96–97, 102–103, 106
Works Progress Administration (WPA), 26, 61, 62
WPEN, 82, 99
WRAX, 82, 83, 90
WTEL, 102

Yannessa, Thomas D., 28

Zaccaro, John, 146
Zerqueni, Marcello, 92

Made in the USA
Monee, IL
13 July 2020